Australian
Democracy
in Crisis

PENING of PARLIAMENT
"...My Government's resolve is strengthened by the peoples' conviction that the basic direction of the Government policies, reflects their aspirations and interests..."
AYE
AYE
Advertising
Media
Government
Opposition
Foreign Monopolies
Boards
Finance Cos
Land
Liberal Country Party
Market Forces
Law
Speaker
G.G.
Banks
Public Service
Security
A.L.P.
Universities
Third World
Marxist-Trotsky-Maoist
Prices
Unions
Royal Commissions
Churches
Women
KEY
Ketty

I dedicate this work to my parents, Maria and Charalambos.

Australian Democracy in Crisis

a radical approach to Australian Politics

Andrew C Theophanous

Melbourne
Oxford University Press
Oxford Wellington New York

Oxford University Press

OXFORD LONDON GLASGOW
NEW YORK TORONTO MELBOURNE WELLINGTON
NAIROBI DAR ES SALAAM CAPE TOWN
KUALA LUMPUR SINGAPORE HONG KONG TOKYO
DELHI BOMBAY CALCUTTA MADRAS KARACHI

Cover and text design by Guy Mirabella

First published 1980

NATIONAL LIBRARY OF AUSTRALIA CATALOGUING
IN PUBLICATION DATA

Theophanous, Andrew.
  Australian democracy in crisis.

  Index
  ISBN 0 19 554278 9
  ISBN 0 19 554200 2 Paperback

1. Australia – Politics and government.
I. Title.
320 9'94

Typeset by Pearl Island Filmsetters (HK) Ltd.
Printed in Hong Kong by Brighter Printing Press Ltd.
Published by Oxford University Press, 7 Bowen Crescent, Melbourne

Foreword

'We must show our people it's not a choice now between
the capitalist society, a corrupt, decadent and disappearing
society with all its moral infamy, it is not a choice between
that and the so-called communist societies, which so far,
and I say so far underlined, have been characterised by what
I call spiritual popery, conformism and greyness of spirit.
We've got to show our people that there is a third and
exciting possibility to which Australians can contribute.
We've got to release the creative forces of our day to help
them to build that.'

> Manning Clark,
> addressing Citizens for Democracy,
> 1976

Contents

Preface

This book has a dual purpose. Firstly, it is intended as a general introduction to Australian politics and society from a radical perspective. To achieve this, I have provided the reader with a mix of theoretical and empirical material and have attempted to show how the theory is directly relevant to the understanding of Australian events and situations.

Secondly, the book introduces new material in presenting and developing the theory of crisis. This is then applied to illuminate the current crisis in economy and social life, and the political crises of the recent past. The aim is to give the reader a deeper theoretical understanding of the fundamental problems facing Australia at present.

The book can be read in a variety of ways. Those readers preferring to skip the theoretical sections until last, can proceed by reading the sections on Australia in each chapter first or by beginning with Part III.

I should like to thank several people for their support and assistance. First my friend Boris Frankel for his constructive and helpful criticisms. I should also like to thank Alistair Davidson, Eric LeBretton, Ron Anderson, Hugh Emy and Warwick Du Ve. The members of the Melbourne Radical Social Theory and Philosophy Group have helped with their criticisms. I am grateful to Sarah Brenan of Oxford University Press who was meticulous in her editing demands, Kay Smith who assisted with the index and Mrs Whiter who typed the manuscript. Finally I wish to thank my wife Petra without whose support I could not have completed the work in the time taken.

A. C. Theophanous
October 1979

Prologue:
Introduction to Crisis Theory

Australian society has been hit by a deep and fundamental crisis. This fact is being increasingly recognized by a variety of social and political commentators.[1] Some believe the causes of crisis to be entirely economic, deriving from the character of Australian manufacturing industry. Thus Peter Robinson writes, in *The Crisis in Australian Capitalism*:

> If we fail to evolve a coherent manufacturing strategy we will find ourselves racked by periodic economic crises, given to internal bickering and doomed to a steadily declining standard of living.
>
> At worst, the strains which such a scenario suggests will lead to the kind of schisms in Australian society that Professor Manning Clark foresees in his direst moods. Questions such as who controls Australia's natural wealth, who profits from it and who disposes of it will divide Australians, embitter their society and leave them vulnerable to external pressures.[2]

Here Robinson alludes to, but does not spell out, the fact that massive unemployment and economic stagnation give rise to a set of social problems, which themselves constitute a socio-cultural crisis. Keith Windschuttle in his recent book, *Unemployment*, asserts that

The crisis has fallen most heavily on youth who have become the most disadvantaged, disillusioned and abused generation this century. The incidence of drug-taking, alcoholism and other forms of escapist behaviour among young people has, as a result, risen abruptly.

Unemployment among adult heads of families, particularly migrant families, has increased sharply as the recession has deepened. The slump has been a major contributor to the accelerating breakdown of the family and the falling birth rate. It is a main source of domestic violence.

Unemployment is an important cause of crime.[3]

The economic crisis of the 1970s, with its problems of inflation, unemployment, stagnation and a general decline in living standards, is indeed a deep and abiding factor, due to the structure of the Australian economy. However, in addition to the economic crisis, I shall argue that there is an independent crisis in the socio-cultural system, which threatens the social integration of Australian society. Many people are no longer provided with a meaningful identity or role in society and this creates an uneasy sense of purposelessness in their lives. Using the insights of certain major social theorists, I argue that this breakdown of social identity is a consequence of the twentieth-century development of Western culture. What is more important, from the perspective of political analysis, is that these deep social and economic crises are now interlocked and create severe pressures on the democratic state, often forcing it to respond in contradictory ways. This leads to a series of political upheavals which may affect the legitimacy of the state itself.

My general claim here is that we cannot understand the paradoxical events and actions in Australian society and politics unless we include a radical analysis of the crisis in the systems of society. But this requires a comprehensive and interdisciplinary overview of Australian society. Thus this book includes an analysis of

(i) the nature of, and dynamic forces within, the state, the economy, and the socio-cultural system;

(ii) the pressures each system places on the other and the consequent interaction between them;

(iii) the internal and external causes of crisis within each system. By crisis, I mean the continuing failure of the system to adequately perform the major functions which those who hold power in the system and/or the majority or near-majority of the people ascribe to it. Thus our economic system which has as its ascribed goals growth, full employment and stable prices is clearly in crisis during times of stagflation and unemployment.

In considering the inter-relations between these three systems of society, and the causes of crisis within them, I draw on the work of Jurgen Habermas, a modern West German philosopher and social theorist.[4] Habermas' view of these interactions can be represented by means of the following schema:

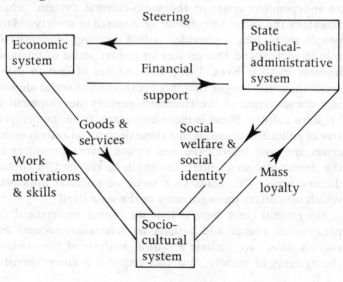

Each system receives inputs from, and gives an output to, the others. This theory treats the political-administrative system as one totality—the state. In Australia, however, the matter is complicated because of the existence of the federal structure, whereby the functions and powers of the state are divided between the national parliament, government, public service and judiciary, and the powers of the governments and public services in the separate Australian States. In this book, when the abstract term 'the state' is used in relation to Australia, it refers to the national government and public service, since state power is being increasingly centralized in these bodies.

According to Habermas' theory, the state receives its financial support from the economic system and is required to steer that system—in other words, to manage the economy. The capacity of the state to do this, however, is limited, firstly by the character of the capitalist economy itself, secondly by the democratic basis of the state and thirdly by the demands coming from the socio-cultural system. In order to understand these limits to state power and the problems which the state faces in times of crisis, we need to examine each of the systems of Australian society from a theoretical and empirical perspective and to analyse the crises which arise within them. This I have attempted in Part I of the book.

As will become evident, I hold that political science, like all other sciences, must concern itself not simply with the description of these events, but with the explanation of them. This requires a penetration beyond the myriad of often conflicting and contradictory phenomena to the real causes and relations which underlie them. Yet in the realm of Australian politics the appearance has too often been accepted for the reality. We have in schools, colleges, universities and the media focused too much on the formal principles of operations of institutions, or on the personalities involved. Only if we examine the dynamics of society and the central issue of locating where power *really* lies in society can the pivotal role of the state be properly understood.

Even where the question of the location and distribution of power in Australia has been taken up, the mainstream theories have been too readily accepted. Thus most of the Australian people believe that power lies ultimately with the people, who express their will through the elected represent-atives in parliament (the democratic theory). Alternatively, in most politics courses, it is claimed that power resides in a plurality of interest groups who pressurize the government; it then determines policy on the basis of a balanced considera-tion of, and response to, the interests of these groups. (This is the pluralist theory.)

The democratic theory is discussed in Chapter 1 as a worthy ideal; however, it is shown clearly that because of constitutional barriers and social inequalities it is not achieved in the political practice of Australia. The pluralist theory, on the other hand, obscures rather than illuminates the *real* sources of power in Australia and the real determinants of the direction of Australian life.

In contrast to the above two theories, there is, of course, the orthodox Marxist view that real power lies with the capitalist class—the owners and controllers of the means of production, distribution and exchange. On this view, the democratic state is invariably the pawn of the capitalist class. This theory will also be discussed in some detail, in Chapter 2, and will be shown to have considerable plausibility. Yet I am also critical of it, for two reasons. Firstly, power no longer resides *only* in the hands of the owners of the means of production but also in the hands of managers, politicians, bureaucrats, ideology-makers and others, most of whom nevertheless form a *ruling class*. I thus put forward an amended model of this ruling class in Australia. Secondly, the modern state, because of the increase in its functions and formal power, is often subject to contradictory pressures and may sometimes act independently of, and even in opposition to, the interests of the ruling class. On this theory of power, the ruling class is more extensive than merely the owners of capital and it does not *automatically* control the state, although the struggle for the state is strongly biased in its favour.

This view of power focuses on the difficult relationship between the Australian political system, when it is supposedly pursuing democratic ideals, and the wider capitalist economy and socio-cultural system in which the political system is embedded. The basic proposition here is that there is a tension between the democratic ideals which ostensibly underlie the state and the goals and purposes of the Australian ruling class. Australian social and cultural life is deeply divided by the values of democracy on the one hand, and economic and social inequality on the other.

The structure of the book is in line with this approach. Thus in Chapter 1 the democratic ideal is outlined, and the Australian Constitution and the formal distribution of state power are both analysed in relation to the requirements of democracy.

In Chapter 2, the general character of the capitalist economy is outlined, with reference to the views of Marx on human needs, alienation and exploitation. Then I explore class divisions and the inequalities of wealth and income in Australia, before developing the amended model of the Australian ruling class mentioned above.

In Chapter 3, several theories of economic crisis are examined and an analysis of the current crisis in Australian economy is given. I draw on Habermas' theory which links *economic crisis*—the failure of the system to provide the goods and services required by the people—and *rationality* or *state-political crisis*—due to the failure of the state to provide adequate steering of the economy. Habermas believes that, because people in Western society have come to see the state as the power which is responsible for steering the economy, economic management is a key demand of public opinion. Failure to manage or steer the economy can lead to a substantial reduction in support for the government, or for the state as a whole. Habermas and others believe that this failure is likely in capitalist democracies because of the divisive structure of the capitalist economy itself. The consequent contradictory pressures on the state will be examined in Chapter 3C.

Even if the state were capable of reconciling these pressures, there would still be conflict with its other functions. For the state must, to some degree at least, respond to demands from the socio-cultural system of society. This latter system is discussed theoretically and in the Australian context in Chapter 4. Its major function is to secure the social integration of society without threatening the identity of individuals. It seeks to reproduce individuals who, on the one hand, have an identity of their own and, on the other, are able to fit the roles and obey the rules required of them by the economic and political systems, and by social structures such as the family.

It is argued in Chapter 4 that modern Western culture, with its emphasis on materialism and with the demise of religion, is failing to secure the social integration of individuals into society. This creates a crisis within the socio-cultural system which manifests itself, according to Habermas, in *motivation crisis*; it arises because either the economic rewards of labour are insufficient to persuade a sizeable section of the people to participate fully in their roles within the productive process, or because people see the system as illegitimate and lacking rationality. They are therefore no longer motivated to perform their working roles within it. The result may be increasing demands by the forces of labour on the economy, reinforced by strikes and work bans, or it may be that people turn to alternative life-styles and against the dominant work ethic, or it may be both.

Combinations of the above three kinds of crisis—economic, state-political and motivation crises—may, according to the theory, give rise to a *legitimation crisis*. This is the failure of the state to retain the support of the people for its power. This may occur because the state cannot, or refuses to, provide the welfare services which give people a meaningful place in the system, or because of the *perceived* failure of the state to live up to its legitimating ideology (the principles of democracy). Both situations may occur when, in seeking to accommodate economic crises by active intervention, the state is forced to cut back dramatically on social and welfare services and/or to redistribute resources in favour of the ruling class. Yet in so doing it comes into conflict with those egalitarian ideals from which it receives its legitimacy. Economic crisis may therefore lead to a state-political crisis and this in turn to a legitimation crisis.

Thus the problem of the legitimacy of the systems of society is a central one in politics and is taken up in Part II of the book. In Chapter 5, I explore the techniques and ideologies whereby the dominance of the ruling class—which normally holds both economic and political power—is sustained in Australia. In this context, I analyse both conservatism and liberalism, and their incorporation into the Liberal Party philosophy. The role of the media in legitimizing the systems of society is also explored.

In contrast to this, in Chapter 6, I develop the theory of legitimation crisis and refer to some short-term responses to this and to the economic crisis. I also consider the problem of the ambiguous responses to crisis made by the ALP, because of its conflicting ideologies, and by the Australian unions, because of their conflicting functions.

In Part III of the book, I consider recent Australian political and social events from the perspective of crisis theory, believing that this illuminates certain events which hitherto have appeared obscure. In particular, the conflict within the ruling class prior to 1972, the undermining of state legitimacy during the Vietnam war and the transformation of the Labor Party are all discussed as causal factors leading to the change of government. Yet, almost immediately after its election, Labor was under attack from the economic and political sectors of the ruling class. Moreover, in addition to a local withdrawal of investment the government was hit by a severe recession in the international capitalist economy. It is shown that in attempting to respond to these economic ills, the Labor Party behaved in a contradictory manner, partly because of the ideological divisions within it. Economic crisis thus became a state-political crisis, in which the Labor government suffered a dramatic loss of support. This was the signal for the Liberal opposition, and the ruling class generally, to mobilize against the Whitlam government. The method employed to achieve this, however (the dismissal of the elected government by the Governor-General) severely undermined the democratic principles on which legitimacy in Australia is based, causing a legitimation crisis. In Chapter 9, it will be explained how this crisis was accommodated, resulting in a resounding victory for the conservative forces. Nevertheless, under the ultra-conservative policies of Mr Fraser, the economic crisis has deepened, with further dramatic increases in unemployment and continuing stagnation. Moreover, as expected from the theory, a state-political crisis has arisen for the Liberals, as they fail to steer the economy back to recovery. These events are explained in relation to the Fraser government's increasingly desperate actions in the face of crisis.

I conclude with some projections into the future as to the possible long-term consequences of the current crisis, including some likely state-political upheavals and further legitimation crises. There is also a sketch of some radical solutions to the current crisis.

I
Democracy, Capitalism and the Australian Crisis

1
The Democratic State and Political Power

The key element linking the various aspects of crisis in society is the political crisis of the state. In order to explain this kind of crisis, we must first look at the character of the Australian political system and the extent to which it meets the requirements of democracy. But what do we mean by 'democratic' and to what extent is Australia a democracy? This raises difficult and highly controversial issues, particularly since the dismissal of the Whitlam government in 1975 by the Governor-General, an act which is seen by many as the negation of the very principles of democracy. Indeed the Labor Party's campaign in that year was based on the slogan 'Return Democracy'. Yet this led many people to question whether the Australian Constitution and the Australian state had ever been democratic.[1] Thus at a meeting in the Sydney Town Hall organized by Citizens for Democracy and attended by 4500 people, the following resolutions were passed:

> The present monarchic constitution is being used as a threat to democracy. It should be replaced by a democratic constitution. To this purpose there should be a broad national debate followed by a people's convention to draft a new constitution for submission to the Australian people.[2]

Another resolution passed was:

> Now that representative democracy is becoming even
> more limited, it is essential to Australian political
> freedom that Australians be ready to engage in extra-
> parliamentary activity.[3]

Here are two quite different strategies for democracy.
Yet both are consistent with a general concept of 'democracy'.
How can this be? To answer this, we must turn to the
examination of the democratic ideal.

A THE DEMOCRATIC IDEAL: ROUSSEAU

As is often noted, the term 'democracy' comes from the
Greek *demos* and *kratos*, meaning the people's rule. In its
most general sense it is interpreted as those forms of government in which the will of the people is expressed in making
the laws and ensuring that they are executed. Abraham
Lincoln expressed it in the well-known slogan: 'Government
by the people, of the people, for the people'.[4] Yet when we
seek to define democracy more precisely, we immediately
come up against a plurality of alternative systems calling
themselves democratic.

Perhaps we can approach the matter by considering the
basic values and principles which historically have been
accepted as characteristic of democracy: moral egalitarianism
and self-determination.[5]

Moral equality of persons

The ideal of democracy is based on the principle of equality
of persons and equality of rights; that is, that all people in
the society have an equal right to determine how the society
should be run and what goals, if any, the society should have.
What is the justification for this principle of equality? Why
should human beings, who are blatantly unequal in most
physical and psychological respects, be treated equally and
have the same rights in society?[6] The principle of the

4

equality of persons is based on the principle of the respect for persons as ends in themselves, that is, on the notion that persons are of intrinsic value in the universe. This is the ethic of *humanitarianism* which asserts that human suffering, destruction of human life, degradation of another's dignity and maltreatment of others are all morally evil and ought to be eradicated in society.

There are many different philosophical and religious expressions of this ethic. For example, it is in certain Christian doctrines such as: do unto others as you would have them do unto you; love your neighbour as you do yourself; all men are equal in the eyes of God, etc. Or, if we turn to philosophy, we find Kant and Rousseau arguing that all persons have an intrinsic moral worth.[7] This same principle of equal moral worth underlies the utilitarian theory that we should aim for the greatest happiness for the greatest number of persons.

Most modern democratic societies accept in the abstract the principle of equality of moral worth of persons. Yet there are great differences as to the actual distribution of rights and privileges in societies which proclaim this belief in equality. Indeed this difference between proclaimed principles and social practice is one of the root causes of crisis in modern society.

Self-determination

Democracy is opposed to those forms of government, such as aristocracy and autocracy, in which the citizen does not determine his own destiny. Democracy, therefore, attempts to maximize self-determination. To let others determine goals for you, without your participation, is tantamount to becoming a slave. Jean-Jacques Rousseau, the eighteenth-century French philosopher who became a major champion of democracy, in his *Social Contract*, rejects the notion of one person determining the social goals of another and thereby ruling over him—for this leads to tyranny and oppression. An anti-democrat could answer this argument by claiming that the strong ruler is necessary to ensure the unity of society (particularly law and order). To this Rousseau replies:

> It will be said that a despot gives his subjects the assurance of civil tranquility. Very well, but what does it profit them, if those wars against other powers which result from a despot's ambition, if his insatiable greed, and the oppressive demands of his administration, cause more desolation than civil strife could cause . . . There is peace in dungeons but is that enough to make dungeons desirable?[8]

For Rousseau, it is only when all the persons who are members of a society or a social group make a collective determination of their will, that we have genuine democracy. On this criterion, a society is more democratic the more the people participate collectively to determine the goals and purposes of the society.

Rousseau argued passionately for the institution of a democratic society which embodied the two major principles of equality and self-determination. Yet he also recognized that such a society would be difficult to achieve. For in most societies, it is not the will of the people which is paramount, but only the will of minority groups. Hence Rousseau called the society of his time an 'artificial civilization'. Such societies were based on two factors. Firstly, the establishment of private property: 'the first man who having enclosed a piece of ground, bethought himself of saying *this is mine*, and found people simple enough to believe him was the real founder of civil society'.[9] This development brought with it untold evils, for society divided into conflicting groups or classes. 'Usurpations by the rich, robbery by the poor, and the unbridled passions of both, suppressed the cries of natural compassion and the still feeble voice of justice.'[10] This situation was, in itself, inherently unstable. For human beings were transformed so that they lost their natural sympathy with others, and egoistically pursued material gain. This necessitated the second factor—the establishment of government and law to control the conflicts over property and its accumulated evils. But this coercive government merely led to a state of slavery. 'All ran headlong to their chains in the hope of securing their liberty; for they had just wit enough to perceive the advantage of political institutions, without sufficient experience to enable them to foresee the dangers.'[11] Societal unity was achieved by this method, but at a very great price. Rousseau would probably claim that the above remarks apply to most modern societies as well.

For Rousseau, the central problem of human society is

> to find a form of association which will defend the person and goods of each member with the collective force of all, and under which each individual, while uniting himself with the others, obeys no one but himself, and remains as free as before.[12]

His *Social Contract* is a brave attempt to determine an answer to this problem. We must consider it further, for even though there are weaknesses in this work, it sets down some of the essential principles of democracy.

Rousseau proposes a contract whereby we invest power in ourselves, that is, in the people as a whole, considered as a collective entity. 'Each one of us puts into the community his person and all his powers *under the supreme direction of the general will*; and as a body, we incorporate every member as an indivisible part of the whole.'[13] By the formation of a society based on the general will, each person becomes both ruler and ruled, both the law-giver and the subject of laws. This is the inner meaning of self-determination. Rousseau tells us that this collective body has 'its common identity, its life, its will'. It has a passive and an active aspect, and each individual belongs to it, under each aspect. Therefore, each individual as subject agrees to obey himself as

7

law-giver or citizen. In so doing, he agrees to obey the sovereign and at the same time to participate in the formation of the sovereign will. When all persons do this, we have a democratic state.

Rousseau makes it clear that not *any* determination by the majority of people is, *ipso facto*, the general will. Here he makes a further stipulation, which is a third major characteristic of democracy.

Equality of rights and equality in the execution of the laws
According to Rousseau,

> the social pact establishes equality amongst the
> citizens in that they all pledge themselves under the
> same conditions and must all enjoy the same rights.
> Hence by the nature of the compact, every act of the
> sovereignty, that is, every authentic act of the general
> will, binds or favours all the people equally, so that
> the sovereign recognizes only the whole body of the
> nation and *makes no differentiation between any of the
> members who compose it*.[14]

What this means is that the general will cannot rule only in favour of one particular man or one particular group: 'the sovereign has never any right to impose greater burdens on one subject than on another'.[15]

By its very definition, the general will seeks to pursue 'the greatest good of all', and this, 'which ought to be the goal of every system of law ... comes down to two main objects, *freedom* and *equality*: freedom because any individual dependence means that much strength withdrawn from the body of the state, and equality because freedom cannot survive without it'.[16] Rousseau leaves it up to the people as a whole to determine the degrees of freedom and equality for their society. To do otherwise would be to undermine self-determination and would be dictating policies for the people.

8

Rousseau was so afraid of the tendency for leaders to usurp the people's rights to self-determination that he insisted that only the people assembled as a whole can be the law-makers. He rejected rule by representatives, for the general will 'cannot be represented by anyone but itself'. Even when an executive body is formed to administer or to interpret the law it must be continuously answerable to the people.

> The moment the people is lawfully assembled as a sovereign body all jurisdiction of the government ceases; the executive power is suspended, and the person of the humblest citizen is as sacred and inviolable as that of the highest magistrate, for in the presence of the represented there is no longer any representation.[17]

Rousseau's ideal of the best society is often rejected today on the grounds that it is impractical. For it is argued that in the modern world, with its huge cities and large industrial complexes, the people cannot all assemble in the one place to debate the laws. Furthermore, there are so many laws involved that each person could not possibly have the time to determine all of them.[18] It may have been possible in ancient Athens where the population was small and the citizens had leisure time to consider the problems of society, but it is totally impracticable today. Direct democracy of the kind advocated by Rousseau is generally rejected in favour of other, *indirect* forms of democracy.

However, rejecting direct self-determination and substituting indirect forms leads to a problem: how far can a system of government move away from the direct participation of the people and still claim to be pursuing the democratic ideal? It is because this question is open to a variety of answers that we find serious disagreement as to what a 'real' democracy is. Indeed in the modern world, we have an absurd situation where nearly every state claims to be a democracy.[19] This devaluing of the democratic ideal has meant that the ruling group within a state can promptly attach the democratic label to that state and thereby legitimize its rule. For it is always possible for any state to claim that it is expressing 'the will of the people'.

There are two major forms of society which adopt the label 'democratic' in the modern world:

(a) *Representative democracy* The theory here is that since the will of the people cannot be directly determined, the people should elect a group of individuals whose task it will be to represent the people's will. The people therefore entrust their power to a group of individuals who then determine the laws of society. This is the form of indirect democracy adopted in Australia.

Notice that, in this form of society, a minority rules over the majority. It is thus clearly distinct from the democratic ideal of self-determination. This point is made even by one of the strongest defenders of representative democracy, Giovanni Sartori, who says:

> All our democracies are indirect; that is, they are representative democracies in which we are governed by delegates, not by ourselves . . . the democracy of antiquity was undoubtedly the closest possible approximation to a literal democracy in which governors and governed worked side by side and dealt with each other face to face. Even though we may question the degree of intensity of self-government in the *polis* nonetheless the fact remains that the difference between direct and indirect democracy is radical.[20]

Yet we are entitled to ask of such a representative democracy, to what extent is the people's will expressed in the determinations by the representatives? and to what extent are the democratic goals of equality and freedom achieved within it? These questions will be taken up in the next section. There is, however, a prima facie case for scepticism:

for most such representative democracies are societies in which there are radical inequalities in wealth, status and power (see Chapter 2C).

(b) *'People's democracy'*   This is the form of democracy proclaimed in the communist countries—although some other countries also have it. The theory behind this is that democracy and genuine freedom are only possible if the goods, services and privileges of a society are distributed equally. Here the focus is not so much on the procedures of representing the people's will, but rather on implementing the common goals which the people are presumed to want. It is rule, not by the people, but 'in the interests of the people'.[21]

This is not to say that a considerable number of policies determined under such a system are not egalitarian and in the people's interests. The problem, however, is that because such policies are not referred back to the people, it is *never* possible to establish that they are indeed in the people's interest, as they perceive it.

There are, therefore, weaknesses in both of these major types of society which label themselves democratic.[22] In both cases, the participation of the people is small, as is the extent of direct self-determination. The democratic ideal is *not* achieved in either case.

In contrast to both of these, I shall speak of a possible kind of society in which the democratic ideal is taken much more seriously and implemented much more extensively.

(c) *Participatory democracy*   I use this term to stand for a political system wherein

the major policy decisions of society are made directly by the people, where the people actually discuss and vote on major policies and priorities;

all minor decisions are made after discussion, consultation and participation of the members of the groups affected. Thus, for example, the decision as to how to run a factory should be made by the workers working within it;

all decisions are implemented by organizations which serve

the people and all positions in such an administration are open to scrutiny by the people, with power to recall those who usurp such positions.

We return now to the question whether such a participatory democracy can be achieved.[23] The New Left in America has argued that society should be divided into small regions and everyone should take part in the government of their own region, as in ancient Greece.[24] However, in today's modern world, where decisions are made for whole nations or groups of nations involving millions of people, division into regions with each region making different decisions would not be practical and could lead to chaos.

The alternative is to aim for the maximum democratization at each level of society. Thus, important goals of national policy should be decided by the people of the whole nation. This would require frequent referenda and discussion of proposals. These are not, however, impracticable given the development of modern telecommunications. Indeed it is possible to televise debates on major referendum proposals. People would also be involved in decision-making by smaller groups in society. Thus they would be able to determine policies of their own local community, and of the organizations for which they work. (This latter concept of self-management by workers I shall discuss again in Chapter 6D.)

It is clear that for such a system to work, people would have to be encouraged and educated to take part in the basic decisions which affect their lives. This requires that the people be presented with a variety of points of view and that arguments for and against any issue be aired. Such a system would substantially reduce the division between governors and governed inherent in a purely representational democracy. The differences between the participatory and representational forms are clearly identified by Sartori:

> In direct democracy there is continuous participation
> of the people in the direct *exercise* of power, whereas
> indirect democracy amounts to a system of *limitation*

12

and *control* of power. In our democracies there are those who govern and those who are governed; there is the State, on one side, and the citizens on the other; there are those who deal with politics professionally and those who forget about it, except at rare intervals —whereas all of those distinctions have very little meaning in ancient democracies.[25]

Consider now a further objection to a more participatory democracy: the people are insufficiently informed and too apathetic to wish to participate in every major decision. They *prefer* to leave the governing to others.[26] Yet this argument can just as easily be used to attack representational democracy. In fact, it raises a central dilemma for representational theory: if the people are apathetic and do not wish to make determinations on the major questions affecting them and their society, then how is it that the members of parliament can represent the will of the people? Either the people have a will to express, in which case they can express it directly or the people have no such will (when they are too apathetic), in which case it is meaningless to say of the members of parliament that they are representing the will of the people.

Indeed, because of important considerations like these, certain American scholars such as Schumpeter and C. Wright Mills have argued, for different reasons, that Western democracy has very little to do with representation.[27] This, among other difficulties with democratic theory, has led several thinkers—both conservative and radical—to argue that the democratic ideal is not meant to be pursued seriously. The ideals of equality, of self-government, of the participation of the people in the determination of their communal goals are thus seen by many as a chimera.

This impression is reinforced when one considers the contradiction between the values which underlie the democratic ideal on the one hand, and on the other hand those values prevalent within a capitalist economic system that co-exists with the representative state system, as in Australia.

Some claim that because these two contradictory systems of values co-exist, we can conclude that the democratic ideal is not taken seriously. It is merely a useful tool of the ruling groups. Yet while such groups may not take the democratic ideal seriously, this is not true of the majority of the people. If anything, the demands coming from the people are for more democracy, more participation and consultation. Indeed, it is because the people take the idea of democracy seriously, that the Western state has been able to entrench itself as *legitimate*.[28] This legitimacy of course relies on inculcating the view that the democratic ideal is indeed manifested, at least to a considerable degree, in modern representative states, such as Australia. We must now consider this claim more critically.

B REPRESENTATION BY PARTIES

According to the theory of representation, there is an individual or group of individuals whose determinations stand for, and reflect, the will of the people. But what is meant by the will of the people here? It could mean the majority will of the nation as a whole, or it could mean the majority of the constituents, the constituency being that section of the electorate which a given member of parliament represents; alternatively, the people's will could refer to the general will, that is, the majority will when it is acting in accordance with the common good of the whole people.[1]

As we have seen, several democratic theorists do not believe in the existence of the majority will.[2] Yet, even if we concede that it exists, there is a central dilemma which the representative faces: how can she/he correctly interpret and represent the wills of so many people in her/his constituency? Before she/he can represent the wills of the majority, she/he must determine what the majority want on a given policy issue. For example, if the representative is faced with the policy choice between an increase in education spending or in defence spending, how is she/he to determine what the majority in the electorate favours, if indeed there is a majority in favour of either? And what if the majority wants several incompatible things, such as increased spending on defence and/or education, together with reduced taxation?

Is there a way out of this dilemma? One could argue that the development of the party system of representation is an attempt to overcome some of these problems. For democracy by means of competition between parties involves a different manner of representation. In this situation there are elected parliamentarians, each of whom in the first instance does not directly represent the people but rather a party with a specific platform or programme, and this party is then said to represent the majority in his electorate. The significant feature of this theory of party representation is that people do not vote for their representative directly, but indirectly; he is a representative of a particular party with a platform.

This version of party government is similar to that practised in most Western democracies. Parliament consists of representatives of particular parties. This parliament is the legislature, and the party or parties which are in the majority have control of it. There are two kinds of relationship between the legislature and the government or the executive. In the British tradition, the executive is chosen by the majority party so that the executive springs from the majority in parliament. In the American system the executive (the President) is elected independently of the legislature. Therefore it is possible in the American system to have a President from one party and a legislature controlled by another party. For example, a Democratic President can co-exist with a Republican legislature, or vice versa.[3]

In Australia, the party system operates in a different way again. There are two houses of elected members, the most important of which is the House of Representatives, which is elected on the basis of particular constituencies. In fact even the Senate, which was originally intended to give representation to each State, has now come to be elected on the basis of party platforms. Thus when people vote for the Senate they do *not* do so on the basis of the best individual to represent Victoria, or Tasmania, as was originally intended; rather they vote for Labor, Liberal or one of the minor parties. The government thus springs from the House of Representatives and some members of the Senate. In Australia, this executive is in the form of a cabinet chosen from the party or parties which have the majority in the House of Representatives.[4] At least, this was the convention until November 1975, when it was temporarily suspended.

Let us now consider the idea that the party system helps to overcome some of the problems of representation. The argument is that if the majority of the people have chosen a person as a representative of a party, they have *ipso facto* approved the policies of that party. This supposedly solves the dilemma. For while the representative could not possibly know what the people in the constituency want on every policy in advance, by offering them his platform and securing a majority vote from them, he can now determine in general what the people want; in voting for him, they have voted for his party platform.

This theory of party representation, with its justification of representing the will of the majority, is the classical theory to which politicians appeal in order to justify their actions, particularly the actions of the government. Governments in power often claim that 'our party was elected with the following policy, and hence we are carrying out the will of the people in implementing that policy'. Since the policy was part of their party platform which the people voted for, those who reject it are accused of being undemocratic. This was the argument used by Prime Minister Whitlam, for example, when the Senate refused to pass certain legislation in Labor's platform.[5] The same approach was used in 1977 by the Liberal government in attacking the unions for refusing to mine uranium. I think it can be said in general that such arguments are used by politicans of all parties when it suits them, and discarded when it does not.

This ties up with the fact that a party's policy is not always carried out after it has been elected into power. Thus a policy might be delayed temporarily or, quite often, permanently. An example is Labor's policy for the socialization of industry, which has been in the party platform even before the formation of the Australian federation and has continued to be the first objective of their programme. Yet very rarely has it ever been acted on, or even contemplated, by a Labor government.[6] Alternatively, the policy might be contradicted —the government might actually change course. There are usually two methods that politicians use to justify this: they argue that the policy has to be changed because circumstances are now different from what they were when the government was first elected; they claim that the present policy is not really a change in policy at all (consider Mr Fraser's statement in 1975 that Medibank would be retained: by 1978 it had obviously been emasculated, yet some of his ministers still claimed to have retained Medibank!).

The second dilemma of representational democracy therefore is this: between elections, there is no way to ensure that a party must indeed act in accordance with its platform. Under the present system of government, there is nothing to guarantee that a party will not shelve its policies, or act contrary to its policy in various ways as the situation dictates. How can such a system be justifiably called democratic, if the party can simply proceed to ignore large sections of its platform whenever it is convenient?

But do the people actually vote for the party platform? Do they actually vote for all the policies which are ascribed to the party? There are several arguments which suggest this is not the case.

One of these arguments—that the people do not vote for a party's platform in full—is in fact the third dilemma of representational democracy. The claim here is that the formation of political parties with fixed platforms makes it difficult for the people's will to be effectively expressed. For the people could favour some policies of one party, some of the other, and some of neither. Hence, whichever party they vote for, they are likely to get certain policies which they are opposed to. For example, suppose I am opposed to government handouts to business and to the encroachment by the Federal government on the States. During the 1970s, if I voted Liberal and my vote was in accordance with the majority, I would get a policy of non-encroachment by the Federal government; but I would also be supporting assistance to business. If I voted Labor, I would be voting for less government support of business but greater encroachment on the States.[7] In situations like this, the voter is faced with having to accept policies he does not like, whichever party he votes for.

The existence of this dilemma has been used to justify opposition to government policies. Thus opponents of uranium mining refused to recognize the result of the 1977 election as evidence that Australians want to mine uranium. They argued that people voted Liberal for all kinds of reasons and not necessarily because of their policy on uranium. This is an argument which has substantial credence if one considers, in addition, the system of preferential voting. A large proportion of Liberal seats were won by preference; they received close to 50 per cent of the preferences from Don Chipp's Australian Democrats Party, which is opposed to uranium mining.[8]

It seems therefore absurd to assume that when a majority votes for party X rather than party Y, they in fact agree with every policy in the platform of that particular party. Against this, some people have come up with the argument that it is a matter of priorities when the voter is making his choice. For example, consider a person who in 1969 was in favour both of an end to the Vietnam war and of greater controls on the unions. To achieve the first goal, he would have needed to vote Labor and for the second, Liberal. So what should he do? It is argued by those who claim that party government is representative, that whichever way he votes will represent the way in which he has ordered his priorities here. Thus if he votes Labor, it shows that he places higher value on ending the war than he does on controlling the unions. However, if this is the case, then he is merely accepting what he cannot change, rather than actually having his will represented. If this happens for the majority of the people, it is difficult to see how a party government can actually represent the people's will.

This raises a further, and very serious danger, with the system of representation by parties: *the absence of an effective choice* in the platforms of the competing parties. Many Americans complain, for example, that the Democratic Party and the Republican Party do not really offer a wide enough choice. Thus when voting for a Democrat or a Republican, most of the time they have to vote for the person rather than for the party platform, since the platforms are not really very different. The same objection is increasingly being raised against the Australian parties. In the 1977 election, the party platforms of the Labor and Liberal parties moved together in order to capture the so-called middle ground.[9]

Many democratic theorists consider this development of a convergence between the major parties as both inevitable and right. Thus Henry Mayo, in his *Introduction to Democratic Theory* says:

> It is not surprising that the two parties which make up the 'ins' and 'outs' should come to resemble each other markedly. Each, in striving for electoral support, tries to antagonize as few voters as possible and to win the support of as many as possible, and hence is driven to become moderate.[10]

He applauds this development because 'When they do so, the parties become "informally representative" of the total public, and this party "representativeness" serves tolerably as a substitute for cross-sectional representation in legislatures'.[11] On this view, then, the more the opposition party comes closer to the governing party, the more certain it is that the general consensus opinion of the majority will be represented.

This is one of the most bogus arguments in democratic theory. Its purpose is to justify not more, but less, real choice and hence less real democracy. Consider some arguments against it. Firstly Mayo, like many modern Western theorists, rejects the view that the members of parliament can or should 'enact the wishes or "will" of the electorate as revealed in the voting'.[12] Yet, as we saw above, he applauds the creation of broad parties with vague platforms that do not differ substantially from each other on the grounds that they are informally representative of the total public. He is here either flatly contradicting himself or else what these broad parties represent is *not* the wishes of the majority of the people at all. Indeed what often happens, according to C. Wright Mills,[13] is that both major parties represent a prevailing ethos—the same basic set of values and view of society. For Mills, this prevailing ethos means the apparent choice is *not* a very real choice: for whichever party wins power, they tend to emerge from the same *ruling elite* with the same basic ideology (although there may be some differences in policy).[14]

Secondly, a common objection to Soviet-style democracy is the argument that, if there is only one party, then there is no real choice at all. Mayo, for example, terms Soviet elections 'a race with one horse'.[15] This is true, notwithstanding the fact that the people are offered a choice between different individual members of the Communist Party, for all candidates represent the same basic point of view. However if this objection has force, then it applies equally well to those Western representative states in which the differences between the major parties are minimal. If the people are only offered a choice between person A and person B, where A and B represent the same ideology and policies, what difference does it make whether A and B *formally* belong to the same party or not? In either case, the choice available to the people is severely restricted.

This requirement, that political parties should represent substantially different alternatives if there is to be genuine choice, has been obscured by those who define democracy simply in terms of an institutional arrangement for the choosing of rulers. This view was popularized by Schumpeter who, having rejected the concept of representing the people's will, defines the democratic method as 'that institutional arrangement for arriving at political decisions in which individuals acquire the power to decide by means of a competitive struggle for the people's vote'.[16] He specifically rejects requirements that the wishes of the people be represented and has no requirement that substantially different viewpoints be put. Yet the above definition is consistent with a struggle in which the people are offered merely a choice between individuals (whether of the same or separate parties) whose policies are very similar. This, however, is a negation of the very argument which we saw earlier allows us to treat representative government as democratic. When the platforms of the major parties become so similar, there is a danger that the people's will may not be accurately expressed, for there are clearly major alternative policies which are not offered to the populace in the election.

To this it may be replied that others with more radical alternatives are at liberty to form minor parties and canvass for the people's vote. This however does not take into account the problem of how parties are financed and to what extent they have access to advertising and the media to present their point of view.[17] This becomes a serious problem in a society where the major parties have a vested interest in sustaining the general structures of the society. When these parties dominate the political arena, they are unlikely to offer the voters much choice. The result is likely to be a serious disenchantment on the part of many people with the political process and a cynicism regarding its claims to be democratic.

Thus I would argue that for a representative state to properly call itself democratic, it must open up its processes to greater participation and scrutiny by the people. It must seek to consult the people on important policies. Furthermore, where the government is determined on the basis of competition between parties, these parties should represent substantially different political philosophies and different visions of the kind of society which they would like to work towards. If this criterion is not satisfied, the choice can become one between 'Tweedledum and Tweedledee'.[18] To prevent this happening, the financing of political parties should become a public responsibility and minor parties should be given generous funds to present their point of view.

With the above analysis of democracy in mind, we must now inquire to what extent does the Australian situation meet the requirements of democracy, and to what extent does it frustrate those requirements? To answer this, we must look, in the first instance, at the Australian Constitution and its relation to democracy.

C THE AUSTRALIAN CONSTITUTION AND DEMOCRACY

In discussing the relationship between the Constitution and democracy, we must constantly keep in mind that the fundamental issue here is—*what is the source of legitimacy in the state*? It is often asserted that it is the constitution which gives legitimacy, yet this is a serious error. As Professor Hugh Emy recognizes,

> The constitution is not the only or even the chief source of legitimacy in the state. There always remains the constituent power which in fact legitimizes the constitution, namely the will of the community.[1]

In other words, it is the mantle of democracy which confers legitimacy on the Australian state. Even a good constitutional document is only a *means* for ensuring that a state and the bodies of the state follow rules and procedures designed to enhance and entrench democracy. A good constitution therefore serves mainly to specify in more concrete terms a generally accepted basis for legitimacy: in Australia, this basis is said to be the democratic ideal itself.[2]

Assuming for the moment that it is the democratic character of the Australian state which confers legitimacy on it, then one thing is clear. It is not the written constitution, if that document is understood literally, which makes the Australian state democratic. As L. F. Crisp pointed out long before the 1975 crisis, the democratic aspects of the Australian state are based on conventions.

> The essential nature of the Commonwealth's working system of executive government comes then, not from the words of the Constitution but rather from a whole set of the constitutional conventions of responsible governments . . . By these conventions the Governor-General commissions the leader of the majority in the House of Representatives—or the leader of one or two or more parties which between them command a majority of seats and have undertaken to work together upon an agreed programme—to provide and lead a ministry.[3]

This point—that the democratic features of the constitution are based on convention—had not been emphasized prior to 1975, because no one expected that the conventions would be questioned. However, conventions are open to interpretation, and such interpretations do not necessarily refer back to the principles of democracy. Furthermore, it is *not* clear in Australia, as it is in the United Kingdom, that such constitutional conventions will be considered binding by all persons in the struggle for power.

The fact that conventions are not always interpreted by reference to democratic principles has created a serious area of *ambiguity* as regards the extent to which the Australian state is democratic. Thus Allan Patience has argued that Australia's Constitution pays scant attention to the principles of parliamentary democracy. He says: 'Rather than liberal constitutional principles, it has been the politics of a narrow pragmatism and parochialism, tempered by an obsequious deference to outmoded colonial authority, that has guided constitution making in this country'.[4]

We can examine the extent of democratization in the Australian Constitution by considering each of the basic principles of parliamentary democracy and asking: to what extent are these guaranteed by the Australian Constitution?

Representation in parliament

According to the first section of the Constitution, 'The legislative power of the Commonwealth shall be vested in a Federal Parliament, which shall consist of the Queen, a Senate and a House of Representatives'.[5] Legislative power is therefore not exclusively in the House of Representatives, which is the sole democratic body of the above three. Section 24 asserts that this House 'shall be composed of members directly chosen by the people of the Commonwealth'. The House of Representatives, however, is not vested with the full powers which apply in other democratic parliaments, such as the House of Commons.

A central problem here is that the Senate—the Upper House supposedly representing the interests of the separate States, but in fact elected on party lines—can and often does frustrate the will of the Representatives. The Senate can reject or amend key draft legislation based on the platform on which the majority party in the House of Representatives has been elected.[6] It can therefore, under section 57, completely wreck the legislative programme of the democratically elected majority.

To this it may be replied: surely the Senate is also an elected body and represents the will of the people? This is a bogus argument. For the Senate is elected on the basis of *equal* numbers of Senators per State. Thus Tasmania, with a population of less than half a million, has as many Senators as New South Wales, which has more than 4.5 million people. A vote in Tasmania has therefore more than nine times the value of a vote in New South Wales. What is extraordinary here is that such a body, established not on democratic principles, but on archaic colonial jealousies which existed at the time of Federation,[7] should have the power to completely frustrate the majority government. Furthermore, under normal circumstances, only half the Senate faces the people at the general election—yet the people's will as expressed at that election can be frustrated.

The most awesome and most controversial power of the Senate is its 'capacity' to reject the budget proposals of the House of Representatives. Writing on this matter, Sir Robert Menzies stated the problem for democracy clearly:

> This [the rejection of the budget], of course, would create an impossible situation and would make popular government unworkable . . . It would be a falsification of democracy if, on any matter of government policy approved by the House of Representatives, possibly by a large majority, the Senate representing the States and not the people, could reverse the decision.[8]

Unfortunately, Sir Robert did not stick to this view when the Liberals blocked supply in 1974 and 1975, using their numbers in the Senate.

The tremendous powers assumed by the Senate derive from the colonial origins of the Constitution. Yet even the generally conservative founding fathers of the Constitution were divided about the granting of so much power to a non-democratic chamber. Hall and Iremonger, in their book *The Makers and the Breakers*, give details of the conflicts that occurred. Victorian Premier Munro declared of the intention to give the Senate power to amend financial legislation: 'Such a monstrous proposition as that was never before submitted to a free people'.[9] As a consequence, the Senate's power was cut back so that it could *not* amend budget legislation.

Did this, however, still allow the Senate the right to reject the whole budget? Most authorities believe that it can. However, Sir Richard Eggleston, a constitutional lawyer of considerable standing, has argued that the Senate has no such power.[10] Whatever the merit of his argument, it is now established as constitutionally valid, through the actions of the conservative parties in 1974 and 1975, that the Senate can threaten and deny supply. (For a full discussion of these events, see Chapter 8D.)

Notwithstanding the disagreements over the Senate's power with respect to the budget, what is clear is that the Senate can block all other forms of legislation, including critical features of the government's programme. The result has been of serious consequence for representative democracy. In 1897 Edmund Barton warned

> I hold rather strongly that if we are to have two Houses, and intend to act upon the principles of responsible government, and conserve those principles, we ought not to put in the hands of one House the ability to utterly destroy the financial policy of the Government.[11]

A second problem surrounding the question of democratic representation in the parliament concerns the powers of the Governor-General with respect to the legislative capacities of the two Houses. Consider these remarkable powers:

> *Section 58.* When a proposed law passed by both Houses of the Parliament is presented to the Governor-General for the Queen's assent, he shall declare, according to his discretion, but subject to this Constitution, that he assents in the Queen's name, or *that he withholds assent, or that he reserves the law for the Queen's pleasure.* (my italics)
> The Governor-General may return to the House in which it originated any proposed law so presented to him, and may transmit therewith any amendments which he may recommend, and the Houses may deal with the recommendation.

The powers given to the Governor-General under these provisions are enormous and do not derive from any democratic requirement. Whatever democratic features exist thus arise from a faith or a *trust* that the Queen's representative shall act in accordance with the *conventions* of democracy. It is on this trust, and not on the constitutional document itself, that the legitimacy of the state as democratic is based.[12] Yet how powerful are these conventional understandings? What is to prevent a Governor-General acting in an undemocratic fashion here and frustrating the majority's will by refusing to sign important draft legislation and thereby make it law?

The difficulty with the reliance on conventions is dramatically highlighted when conventions are broken. Consider this power:

> *Section 5.* The Governor-General may appoint such times for holding the sessions of the Parliament as he thinks fit, and may also from time to time, by Proclamation or otherwise, prorogue the Parliament, and may in like manner dissolve the House of Representatives.

On this power, the Governor-General may dissolve a popularly elected parliament whenever he chooses to do so. Of course, even at the time of the drafting of this document, it was understood that the convention would be that the Governor-General would only prorogue parliament on the *advice* of the Prime Minister.[13] Because this was a convention, however, it was claimed by Sir John Kerr and others that it could be broken without shaking the foundations of democracy. This was not the view of most of the founding fathers. Barton stated the generally accepted view:

> every prerogative which the Queen retains is retained in trust for the people, and it does not matter whether she is told in the Statute that she is to exercise that prerogative by the advice of the Executive Council or

not, if she is given the power in the Statute she can only exercise that power of prerogative *by and on the advice of Ministers*.[14] (my italics)

The matter, however, does not rest there. For a literal reading of the Constitution can support an alternative view, put by R. J. Ellicott, the shadow Attorney-General who played a key role in the 1975 crisis.[15] At a 1976 seminar, he said:

> It is apparent from a reading of the Constitution that some powers are given to the Governor-General in Council and others simply to the Governor-General. It is, I think, significant, that the powers of dissolution conferred by Ss. 5 and 57 are given to the Governor-General . . . My own view is that these powers exist and under our Constitution as presently framed are necessary to deal with extreme cases. They are there to protect the people . . .[16]

How these undemocratic powers are supposed to protect the people is not, however, made clear. The 1975 case will be discussed in detail in Chapter 8.

One vote one value

This major principle of democracy is the one which embodies the value of *equality*. I have already shown that this principle does not apply in the Australian parliament as a whole, for the Senate has wide powers and yet is *not* elected on the basis of the equal value of people's votes. What of the House of Representatives itself? Surely here at least the people's voice is fairly expressed? Not necessarily. For there is no constitutional requirement to prevent an electoral gerrymander, to ensure that the number of voters in each electorate is roughly equal. Colin Howard in his book *Australia's Constitution* points to 'the absence of any constitutional provision to ensure that each person's vote is of approximately equal value'.[17] He concludes:

What is clear is that in the opinion of the present high court the constitution comes nowhere near implying that votes shall be equal in value. Only if the situation approached a denial of the basic system which the constitution contemplates would the court see any ground for invalidating a gerrymandered voting system.[18]

In practice, this means that a government could introduce an electoral redistribution which was so designed as to ensure that their opponents would not win power, even if they won the majority of the people's votes. Indeed, such gerrymandered voting systems have existed at both a Federal and a State level. They are still severe in Queensland.[19] The danger to democracy of gerrymandered electorates is serious, and yet it does not appear to generate much passion in Australian politics.

Democratic government and executive power

The disparity between the written constitutional arrangements and conventional practice in Australia becomes clearly evident when we ask: who is legitimately endowed to exercise executive power in Australia? If one looks at the constitutional document, one finds no section that requires that the party or group which has the parliamentary majority shall form the government. Instead section 61 vests executive power in the Governor-General and section 62 defines this further:

> There shall be a Federal Executive Council to advise the Governor-General in the government of the Commonwealth, and the members of the Council shall be chosen and summoned by the Governor-General and sworn as Executive Councillors, and *shall hold office during his pleasure.* (my italics)

Why is it that this document leaves it up to the 'pleasure' of the Governor-General to appoint whoever he wishes (provided that they are, or become within three months, members of parliament) to be the executive government of the nation? This is particularly puzzling since, until November 1975, it had always been the constitutional convention that the party or parties with the majority vote in the House of Representatives (the people's chamber) would form the government and would be the government while they retained the confidence of that House.

On a literal reading, the other sections of Chapter 2 of the Constitution seem to vest the Governor-General with other enormous powers. Yet this is discordant with actual political practice in Australia, at least until 1975. Colin Howard puts the matter thus:

> We live our lives and vote at elections in the belief
> that the person who chooses and leads the government
> is the prime minister, who in turn is easily identified as
> the leader of the party which won most seats in
> parliament at the election . . . The notion that the
> Governor-General can create or dispose of departments
> in the public service as he thinks fit, or appoint or
> dismiss cabinet ministers at his discretion, does not
> seem to square with the events which actually happen.
> This glaring discrepancy between Chapter 2 of the
> constitution and the real structure of government is
> one of several serious and fundamental problems
> which the constitution creates for this country.[20]

Since 1975, when the Governor-General overthrew some of the above constitutional conventions, several commentators have tried to show that his act was wrong by referring back to the intentions and expressed views of the framers of the Constitution. I have already quoted Barton on the limits to the royal prerogative. Consider another example of the thinking of the founding fathers on the importance of democratic representation, this time from Alfred Deakin:

the ambition of the democracy of this country is an ambition to shape its laws, to guide its destinies, to widen its opportunities, to make life in this country better worth living than it has been hitherto. For this purpose the position of a representative in any of these colonies is infinitely superior to that of governor-general . . . If he (the governor-general) becomes a personage in the political life of the country, his office must be elective. We cannot afford to have in our constitution any man exercising authority, unless he derives it from the people of Australia.[21]

Thus, some of the founding fathers, such as Deakin, Reid and Carruthers, wanted it specifically stated that, when the term Governor-General was used, this would *always* be taken to refer to the Governor-General acting on the advice of ministers representing the majority in parliament.[22] Barton felt that it was unnecessary to do this, even though he firmly believed that the Governor-General's powers were purely ceremonial. Hall and Iremonger conclude that 'the ambiguities regarding the Governor-General arose because men like Barton had no cause for scepticism about the developing maturity of Australian parliamentary democracy. At least there was no cause until 1975'.[23]

Those who argue in favour of a narrow literal inter-pretation and ignore the democratic principles on which the Constitution bases its claims to legitimacy, are thereby charting a dangerous course. For the Constitution consists not only of the legal document, but also of the conventions and understandings which make the state 'democratic' and which are the real bases of legitimacy. To quote Emy again,

The terms of the written constitution can not exhaust the values and purposes we customarily attribute to the idea of constitutional government. A constitution can not be fully evaluated without reference to a series of related practices and rules. It is doubtful if the constitution or a positive legal system *can be*

adequately understood without referring to the primary
rules of obligation which assist us to grasp the meaning
of social and political life.[24] (my italics)

However, appeals to the founding fathers, the principles
of democracy or the traditions of constitutional practice
presuppose that the major actors in the struggle for state
power will be basically rational and reasonably decent. It
presupposes that the democratic basis of legitimacy is widely
understood and respected by the community. It presupposes
that an alternative basis for legitimacy could *not* be imposed
by powerful forces determined to destroy a government
acting contrary to their interests. All these preconditions for
legitimacy do not apply in Australia. (See Chapter 6A.)

The point here is that legitimacy can, within certain limits,
be redefined by those who have the power to impose their
view of legitimacy. In Australia, the monopolized media,
although some expressed disagreement with Sir John Kerr's
dismissal of the PM and the appointment of a caretaker
government in 1975, did not attack it as unconstitutional
and demand the restoration of democratic order. Would they
have behaved in this way had it been socialist forces seizing
power, rather than conservative ones? I believe not—they
would have accused the Governor-General of organizing a
coup, by subverting the Constitution.

The failure to resolve the 1975 crisis in favour of the
principles of democratic practice and responsible government
gave power to the conservative forces in the short term. In
the long term, however, it may have ensured that an authoritarian response to the current economic crisis will be easier
to impose. For it gave legitimacy to such authoritarian and
anti-democratic interpretations of the Governor-General's
powers. This will be explained in detail in Chapters 8 and 9.

The legitimation of this action was not, however, inevitable. It could have been and—given that it was clearly
contrary to the principles of democracy—should have been
resisted. One reason given by Prime Minister Whitlam for
his reluctance to challenge the legitimacy of Kerr's action in

dismissing his majority government was the fear that Kerr would attempt to use the armed forces to impose his ruling.[25] For under section 68, 'The command in chief of the naval and military forces of the Commonwealth is vested in the Governor-General as the Queen's representative'. Yet, again, this power was never intended to be exercised without the advice of ministers having the confidence of the House of Representatives. So Kerr would have been compounding one constitutional breach with another if he had used the armed forces.

Significantly, Kerr has exclaimed that he *never* considered the idea of using the armed services, for he was convinced that Whitlam would not dare challenge the dismissal.[26] This was not just a personal judgement on Whitlam; Kerr was also aware that powerful forces in the community—in economy, the media and the conservative parties—would propagate the view that his action was legitimate and lawful. Only full-scale resistance would have undermined that strategy and it was not readily forthcoming from the labour movement.

Allan Patience, in the essay mentioned earlier, concludes:

> Constitutionally, the Australian state is underwritten
> by a document whose main clauses are increasingly
> being reinterpreted in the light of the needs of
> contemporary capitalism to continue to serve those
> interests for whom the Australian constitution was
> originally devised. The labour movement has never had
> a say in shaping Australian constitutionalism.[27]

This observation raises several questions. Why did the conservative parties go as far as to overthrow tradition and negate the very principles which the founding fathers had accepted and established? Why did the modern labour movement fail to fight for even a liberal democratic constitution? These questions must wait until later in the book after we have surveyed the character of Australian society, within which these ambiguous constitutional provisions of the Australian state are embodied.

I begin with an analysis of the formal organization of political power in Australia, in order to determine whether this illuminates or obscures the real basis of power in our society.

D THE FORMAL ORGANIZATION OF POWER IN AUSTRALIA

After reading the Constitution and casually looking at the Australian political system, the observer may conclude that political power is diffused and distributed amongst a variety of individual and group interests. This model of power is propounded in many textbooks on Australian politics which focus on the dynamics of parliament, cabinet, the public service, the judiciary, etc.[1] These formal organizations and functions are extensively discussed in the standard literature on Australian politics, and my analysis here will be brief. I shall argue that the formal separation of powers disguises the fact that serious conflicts over fundamental goals and values are the exception, rather than the rule, in Australian politics.

The first factor which is usually emphasized is the distribution of power between the three levels of government—Federal, State and local. Indeed the separation of powers between the first two is included in the provisions of the Constitution. Thus the original justification of the Senate, with its huge powers, was to protect the interests of the six States as separate centres of power—a function it has rarely performed.

Concentration of power at the national level

Within the national state, there is a further separation of formal powers. This can be illustrated thus:

Governor-General

Legislative	*Executive*
HOUSE OF	CABINET OF
REPRESENTATIVES	MINISTERS
SENATE	FEDERAL PUBLIC SERVICE

The House of Representatives consists of members elected from constituencies of supposedly roughly equal populations. It is the most democratic chamber, since election to it most closely resembles the principle of one vote, one value. The Senate, however, has equal numbers of Senators from each State (at the moment, ten from each State and two from the Australian Capital Territory and the Northern Territory). Although these two Houses have the formal power of enacting legislation, it is clear that state power does *not* reside with members of parliament, either in the Senate or the Representatives (at least on normal occasions).[2] This is due to the way in which the party system has developed in Western democracy. Spurred on by the party whip, every representative is bound to support his own party's policies. Since policy is usually decided by the cabinet (or even the inner cabinet), the representative is reduced to a mere pawn. He may be able to express what he feels on the legislation (even this is rare) but he cannot—without severe risk to his career—vote against the party line.[3]

The cabinet or executive is chosen from the majority party or parties in the House of Representatives (unless the Governor-General intervenes, as in 1975, to appoint a minority caretaker government). This cabinet may include ministers drawn from the Senate, although it is an unwritten convention that the majority of ministers should come from the House of Representatives. When the Liberal and National Country parties govern, the cabinet is chosen by the Prime Minister. When Labor governs, the cabinet is elected from the caucus of all the Labor MPs.[4] Thus power is concentrated in the executive, and usually in the group of senior ministers known as the 'inner cabinet'. If a Liberal leader appoints his own men to this inner group, he may be able to centralize power even more firmly into his own hands, as has been the case with Mr Fraser.

It has been claimed by some that even the cabinet does not, in reality, fashion policy and hold real power. For ministers often decide on the basis of advice given to them by top public servants. Theoretically, the role of the public servant is firstly, to implement the decisions of the parliament in the most efficient and unbiased manner and secondly, to advise government properly by putting before it different sets of policy proposals and explaining the possible consequences of each proposal. A good public servant should provide the minister with all the major choices available; if in an area several proposals are possible, they should all be put to the minister.[5] In fact, however, it is possible for the bureaucracy to deliberately frustrate the implementation of the government's policy or to sabotage that policy; and in their capacity as advisers, public servants will often not even mention some proposals, while others will be denigrated. Thus the minister will often be offered only one option or course of action—for example, the Treasurer may be told there is no other option but to impose a credit squeeze.[6] Weber, the great social theorist, insisted that public service bureaucracies should not determine policy (the ends or goals of society) but only the most rational *means* of implementing them.[7] However, this distinction between means and ends has broken down, for if a minister is advised that a policy cannot be implemented, he will have no option (if he believes the advice) but to revise the policy.

Top public servants can thus advise and act against courses of action because of their own ideological biases and commitments. People who object to the development of the modern state because of increasing bureaucracy thus have a point; the problem is not just size, but the fact that it is organized as a hierarchical structure. Weber believed that the development of such hierarchical structures in the modern state was inevitable, and that this was the most rational and efficient form of organization.[8] Yet he also cautioned against such concentration of power, having foreseen the problems discussed above.

Thus at the same time as parliamentary and executive power has been taken over by senior ministers, civil service administrative and advisory powers have been concentrated in the hands of top public servants. But which of these groups holds real state power? The question, often asked, is a misleading one; it suggests that the interests of senior ministers and top public servants are often antagonistic. This, however, is far from being the case. For, as I shall argue in the next chapter, both these groups generally belong to the ruling class, and act in the interests of that class. Conservative governments have little trouble with top public servants—although they may have difficulty with the rank and file bureaucrats.[9] In contrast, a reforming government (such as the Whitlam Labor government) may find that it is given conservative advice or its policies are frustrated by top public servants committed to preserving the interests of the ruling class.[10]

Any long-term solution to this concentration of power among top public servants must involve the introduction of more participatory democracy and less hierarchical organization in the running of government departments. This would make them more difficult to manipulate and more responsive to the people's needs. It would also, I believe, make them more efficient in implementing humane policies.

Failing such reform and while the hierarchical concentration of power exists, I believe we should adopt the US practice. There, it is recognized that the political values of the top public servants affect their advice and enthusiasm in implementing policy. When a new President is elected, they all resign and the President appoints new men whom he entrusts to carry out his policies. The Australian practice should be changed, for it is unrealistic to suppose that these top bureaucrats will serve equally any master, irrespective of ideological differences. However, as I have said, this only becomes a source of conflict on the rare occasions when a reformist or radical government is elected, when the conservatives need a further means to use in sabotaging and frustrating change.[11]

I conclude, then, that though in theory state power is

dispersed, in actual practice it is centralized in the cabinet and the top of the public service.

The myth of pluralism

While this view of the concentration of state power is widely accepted, there is much disagreement on the question, in whose interests do these power centres act? The most common view is the pluralist theory of power, which asserts that this concentrated state power is exercised in the interest of a diversity of pressure or interest groups, with the government acting to give a balanced response to these different groups. On this model, as outlined by several political scientists such as Robert Dahl, people express their will and individuality, not in direct participation in state power (except at elections), but indirectly in the many social groups to which they belong and from which they gain a sense of identity, a sense of having a meaningful role to play in society.[12] These groups then share power in society, either by acting independently of the state or by having their interests represented in the exercise of state power. As Robert Presthus puts it:

> Many of these organizations are 'extraofficial'. They
> have neither legal nor constitutional status but instead
> exercise their influence on government informally.
> Using many paths of access, they apply pressure in an
> attempt to shape proposed action to their own design.
> Obviously, no group succeeds in achieving its
> preferences all the time, nor are all groups equally
> concerned with all issues. Instead, each bargains and
> marshals its resources to do battle on those issues that
> impinge upon its interests.[13]

From this view, one could conclude that power is dispersed in a variety of groups throughout society. Yet if this supposedly empirical theory of society were true, then it would surely result in much more conflict over general goals than actually exists. The policies of the state would also generally be *ad hoc* and moving in a multitude of directions at once. For in balancing the requirements of the different pressure groups the state, on this model, generally acts as a passive entity, responding to the group demands placed upon it. Its room for manoeuvre is severely limited, no matter which party is in power. The balance of forces cannot be changed.

In reply to this point, pluralists usually insist on two further conditions for 'democracy'. Firstly, while there may be conflict between groups, there cannot be—as Hugh Emy puts it—'high levels of partisanship and/or a great intensity of conflict'; pluralist politics 'implicitly excludes ideological politics, for the system cannot survive cultural consensual agreement over the goals and procedural norms of a society'.[14] Thus, in effect, groups may place demands on the state, provided that they do not seek any radical transformation of structures in society. However, this raises a question: is the pluralist theory of power a description of what really happens, or is it primarily a justification for the existing social, economic and political structures of society?

As a descriptive theory, there are serious problems with it. Firstly, as Emy himself points out, it is not clear whether the state is to be conceived in the role of a referee or of a policeman in balancing the claims of conflicting groups.

> Should the government merely 'referee' the group struggle, ratify group decisions in legal form, and broadly ensure that conditions of equal political opportunity (and organization) apply? . . . Or should government controls and decisions have a final and decisive significance in policing the group struggle, and in determining the acceptable limits to policy outcomes? If so, the government does have a public role and a responsibility which we can define and assess independently of the group forces.[15]

The latter perspective, which Emy suggests most pluralists prefer, tells us very little about the real location of power, for no one denies that governments sometimes respond to the demands of particular pressure groups. If the role of the government is an active, rather than a passive, one, then we are entitled to ask: on what values and ideology does the government base its decisions *and* in whose interests are these decisions made?

Secondly, there are qualitative and quantitative differences in the resources and power of different groups, even those pressurizing on the same issue. The Uranium Producers Forum has enormous economic strength and media power, yet the Movement Against Uranium Mining has one advantage: it can mobilize large numbers of Australians to demonstrate in its cause.[16] To suggest that the government, in responding on the uranium issue, is merely referee between the two groups seems mistaken. But even if it were, how is this balancing exercise supposed to take place, for the forms of pressure exercised by the two groups are entirely different. UPF has money and media support; MAUM has the democratic weapon of turning voters against the government. These two pressures may be responded to differently by different governments, depending on their ideology and on pragmatic considerations (such as an imminent election). This will be explained further below.

A third problem with pluralism is that it assumes a multiplicity of conflicting and contradictory interest groups in society. But this view is open to serious challenge. It can be argued that many of these 'different' groups may be pursuing interlocked aims. My view is that the major groups in society are divisible into *progressive groups*, favouring equality in social, political and economic life, assistance to the needy, and the protection of the environment—in other words, pressuring the state to live up to the democratic and egalitarian principles outlined in sections A and B of this chapter; and *reactionary groups*, favouring inequality, social and economic privilege, industrial growth at the expense of the environment and workers' conditions, emphasizing voluntary or self-help rather than state resistance to the needy.[17]

40

I shall argue in the next chapter that the most powerful groups in the second set constitute part of a ruling class, which dominates (but does not totally determine) the actions of the state in Australia. I shall provide there an account of the general nature of this class and of the extent of its power. On the other hand, the power of the above progressive groups, which spring from outside the ruling class, is severely circumscribed, for they do not have much economic strength and their access to the media is limited. They are not insignificant: they have the weapons of the vote and the strike with which to pressurize governments and bureaucracies. It is only when progressive groups are transformed into popular movements with mass support, or when they organize workers to strike, that conservative (and even some Labor) governments will consider them seriously.

If I am right, the pluralist picture of balanced power groups pressurizing the state in all directions is mistaken. Rather, we have two major blocs, with the economic and ideological power in the hands of the reactionary forces.

Pluralism, then, not only fails to give an accurate portrayal of what is really happening, it also provides an ideological smokescreen, which hides the real determinants of decisions by government and the state as a whole.

Federalism

At this juncture, it might be argued that the federal division of power, with the six State governments, allows for much less domination by the ruling class than would otherwise be the case. After all, it is common for some States to be governed by an alternative party to that which holds Federal power. Does this not mean that conflicts will arise and that the actions of conservative central governments will be resisted by Labor State governments and vice versa? There is something in this, which counts against those who claim that the ruling class has total control of all aspects of people's lives (the view that there is a complete *hegemony*: see Chapter

5A). As I shall argue in the Epilogue, the existence of the different governments can make it more difficult for the ruling class to abolish democratic forms and impose a blatantly authoritarian regime. This does not provide guarantees against more subtle techniques to undermine democratic processes, however.

Nevertheless, it still remains the case that the federal system does generally protect the interests of the ruling class. As Professor Groenewegen explains:

> Stronger States and a weaker central government generally allow greater opportunities for private interests to get their own way in general economic development, particularly in minerals. The more power is divided and imperfectly co-ordinated, the more such sectional interests can play off State governments against Federal governments and vice versa. Thus a strengthening of the traditional concept of federalism improves the bargaining strength and power of private industry and reduces the strength of government.[18]

The point here is that the powerful economic interests of the ruling class may align themselves to frustrate the economic policies of a reformist (not to mention a radical) central government. This partly stems from the fact that the usual areas of proposed reforms—education, transport, public utilities, health services—come under powers which the Constitution gives to the States. These areas are also, as Jean Holmes notes, those which have become policy priorities for electors. She claims that these services 'have all come in for severe criticism from Australia's state-centred urban populations over the past decade, while federally supplied services like communications have developed in technological luxury'.[19] Indeed, massive tied grants to the States in these areas (that had been neglected for many years) were a major feature of Labor's win in 1972 (see Chapter 7). Conservative

State governments did not generally oppose these initiatives. It was a different story, however, when ruling class economic interests were threatened, as in resources policy. Here conservative State governments challenged Labor in the High Court, attacked it electorally and refused to pass important enabling legislation. What would they have done if a radical government had been in power?

On the other hand, if a conservative central government is being frustrated by a reformist State government, ruling class forces will align themselves with the central government to badger it into cooperation.[20] This can be done by using the substantial economic powers of the central government against the State. Since any new services are dependent on Federal financial outlays, a State reformist programme would be severely limited by a conservative central programme. If the State government attempts more radical changes, such as nationalization, these can often be frustrated by those business interests moving to another State (as some allege occurred with South Australia under Dunstan).[21]

The division of powers which gives the central government the power to tax and make grants, while the State governments have most of the powers to spend, has resulted in conflicting and unco-ordinated services being provided to the Australian people.[22] It has also resulted in an extraordinary and highly inefficient duplication of bureaucratic functions—decisions have to be made and implemented by two public services, for most State functions. This means that more money and effort is spent on administration, and less on the actual programmes themselves. It does not mean that reforms cannot be carried out because of the federal system: perseverance and the use of Federal financial powers may force improvements in education, health and welfare services. The division of powers, however, certainly ensures that fundamental changes to the social and economic systems will have little hope of success. Groenewegen sums up the situation thus: 'the 1970s have revealed the inherent flexibility of the federal system, a lesson to be absorbed by both the reformer and the conservative. The resilience of this institution as a whole carries little hope for those interested in more serious structural change'.[23]

The armed forces and police

These two sectors of the state are supposed to serve the 'national interest' and to be responsible to the democratically elected government. Yet, as Playford remarks, most members of the armed forces and most policemen are extremely conservative politically. Many see their role not in terms of democratic principles, but in opposition to radical people who seek to change the economic, political and social systems. This became evident in Australia when the activities of the special branches were exposed in South Australia and New South Wales. It was found in South Australia that the elected government had been misled about the files, which included reports on members of the governing Labor Party itself. What is more serious is that when Premier Dunstan sacked his Chief Commissioner of Police over this issue, many people questioned his right to do so. Not only were the police above the law in this matter, many felt that they were not answerable to the elected government.[24]

The development of these attitudes by Australian police forces was not, however, inevitable. The processes of recruitment and the education of officers as to their responsibility towards protecting people's democratic rights have been extremely poor; junior police have virtually been indoctrinated into these attitudes by the police hierarchy.[25] It is for this reason that Australian police forces generally find it difficult to work with even moderate Labor governments. Thus the Chief Commissioner in New South Wales resigned in June 1979 because of conflicts with the Wran government.

During the Vietnam war, many police were involved in direct attacks on demonstrators which went beyond any requirements for keeping the peace.[26] Fortunately, in several States at least, an increasing awareness has developed that police should use restraint in confrontations with students and workers. However, as the economic and social crises deepen, civil unrest will increase. People will increasingly take to the streets to express their anger. Will the police continue with the more restrained approach or will they revert to the confrontation tactics used in most States until 1972?

More controversial than the State police forces and the special branches is the Australian Security Intelligence Organization. In 1979, the Fraser government introduced legislation which had the net effect of ensuring that many previously illegal ASIO activities would become legal. These included powers which severely invaded people's privacy, such as bugging and house-breaking. More seriously, legislation provided that ASIO could carry out these activities against anyone suspected of 'subversion'. This was vaguely defined so as to, in theory, include anyone with radical, Marxist or socialist views.[27] It is a measure of the ideological weakness of the Labor Party under Hayden that they did not oppose these provisions *in toto*.

With respect to the ideological views of the armed forces, some debate arose, following the dismissal of the Whitlam government in 1975, as to whether the armed forces would indeed be neutral in a crisis. Whitlam himself believed that, in any conflict, they would be loyal to the Governor-General rather than the elected Prime Minister.[28] But it is more likely that ideological conservatism (particularly of top officers) rather than institutional loyalties would have inclined them to act against the Labor government. Nevertheless, it is not clear that all top soldiers would have followed orders in such an eventuality; a serious division might have developed within the armed forces themselves.[29]

The judicial system

It might be argued that while the ruling class dominates most political and economic processes, there is still an avenue of independent action, namely, the courts. In the United States, with the First Amendment and its liberal interpretation in the courts, it can plausibly be argued that the judicial system provides an alternative centre of power, which can be used, to some degree, to protect the people against total domination by the ruling class.[30]

Unfortunately, however, even these limited protections are not available in Australian law. Here there is a *positivist* or narrow formal interpretation of the law, without reference to any more fundamental principles of justice.[31] As Playford points out, this becomes important in the exercise of discretion.

> Judges are not the mere exponents of the law as they find it: there is plenty of room for judicial discretion in the application of the law and for judicial creativity in making law, particularly at the Federal level where under the Constitution the High Court marks out the limits of parliament's discretion. In interpreting and making law, judges are deeply affected by their view of the world. Of course, they frequently see themselves as guided exclusively by values which transcend class interests, but these are usually a cloak for their conservative bias.[32]

The conservative world view of judges often means that they make decisions in favour of the interests of the ruling class, while at the same time pretending to some concern with justice. Yet rarely is the principle of equality linked by them to justice. This is most evident in the magistrate's courts where conviction statistics correlate closely with class background and economic situation. Up to 80 per cent of the prison population of Australia is from the manual working class.[33] This factor is due not only to the bias of judges, but also to that of the police and political leaders. Indeed, the almost total failure to pursue and prosecute white-collar criminals stands out as an obvious example of the dominance of the ruling class, to the point of putting themselves above the law.[34]

46

Does all this mean that the public service, the police, the judiciary and the government (the state as a whole) never acts on behalf of the people, but only in the interests of the powerful? Some Marxists believe that this is so. My view, however, is that while the top bureaucrats and ministers may be strongly motivated to act in the interests of the ruling class, there are limits as to how far they can go. These limits are dictated by, firstly, the need for laws to appear democratic and universal, that is, as if they apply equally to all. For the legitimacy of the state would be thrown into question if they did not (see Chapter 6A). Secondly, since the public service is required by its charter to serve the people and to implement laws without fear or favour, bias and favouritism cannot go too far—otherwise, lower-ranking officers are likely to rebel and expose their superiors. Furthermore, many lower-ranking public servants, including some police, take their democratic duties seriously, and this can impede action in favour of ruling class interests. Thus the Fraser Liberal—National Country Party government has been frustrated in its attempts to cut back on the numbers of people receiving unemployment benefits, even though it has tightened the criteria and extended supervision over its staff. If a person has a right to the dole, it is not easy to take it away from him without severely undermining democratic ideology.

Knowledge of the formal distribution of power in Australia, separated from any concept of the struggle between classes or of the general tensions within the modern state, does not illuminate us sufficiently as to where the real power lies and what the real determinants of social life are. To analyse this, we need to look at the economic and social systems, and the relation of the state's functions to them.

2
Capitalist Economy and Classes

Let us assume that the democratic ideal, discussed in the last chapter, is manifested to some degree in the Australian political system. Does this mean that Australian society is dominated by the ethic of equality which underlies democracy? Clearly it is not; for there is another more dominant aspect of Australian society which seems to be in contradiction with the values of equality. I refer here to the capitalist economy and the way in which this economy dominates virtually all aspects of social life in Australia.

A   THEORY OF CAPITALISM

The study of economy is very important, not merely because of its relation to the state, but also because its character infuses the social fabric of our lives in a manifold way. Where persons work; what job they do; how happy they are in their occupations; whether the rewards of their labour are sufficient to keep them motivated; whether they can purchase some or all of the things they desire by the wages they receive for their labour—all these and many other questions of economy penetrate our everyday lives, as well as the political world.

Australia, like all Western countries, has a capitalist economy. Now I shall argue that, in both theory and practice, the values and ideals inherent in a capitalist economy are

48

those of inequality in the distribution of wealth, income, power and status. Further, I shall defend the view that capitalist economy has its own internal dynamic which exploits the labour of the vast majority of people in the society, for the benefit of the minority who are rich and powerful. The evidence for this will be provided in Section C.

The fundamental principle which underlies capitalist economy is the *accumulation of private property or wealth* to a virtually unlimited degree.[1] How does this accumulation process lead to the development of the capitalist economy? With the historical development of technology, there arose the need for communal production, that is, people had to work co-operatively in groups. The Industrial Revolution thus raises a problem for all societies: how is communal production to be organized? There are logically two basic possibilities here: .

(i) to pool the resources of the society to develop productive machinery which is communally owned, controlled and worked by the society as a whole;

(ii) to allow individuals who have accumulated more property than others, to invest that property in machinery and other means of production, so as to own and control such production processes, and to buy the labour of others so as to initiate communal production. Of course, if individuals are to be enticed to invest their capital in this way, they shall only do so if they are rewarded in the form of profit. For historical reasons, only (ii) was a real possibility at the dawn of the Industrial Revolution.[2] The major reason for this was that in Britain and Europe there existed a wealthy, aristocratic class and very poor peasant farmers. The latter had few or no resources of their own which could be pooled into publicly owned means of production.

The capitalist economy thus sprang up with the development of modern technology and communal production. Its nature can be explained by the schema on page 50.

The process can be thought of as follows.[3] Firstly, we have individuals or groups of individuals (capitalists) who, having

Schema of capitalist production

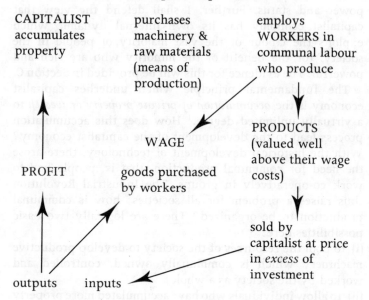

CAPITALIST accumulates property

purchases machinery & raw materials (means of production)

employs WORKERS in communal labour who produce

WAGE

goods purchased by workers

PRODUCTS (valued well above their wage costs)

PROFIT

sold by capitalist at price in *excess* of investment

outputs   inputs

MARKET

accumulated large amounts of property, convert it into capital and use it to purchase machinery and raw materials. In addition, the capitalist employs workers in a communal production process; their labour gives rise to a series of products. The capitalist or his representatives then take over these products and places them in the market, at a price intended to ensure that as many products as possible are actually sold, and that a *profit* is made (the price must exceed the amount invested in materials and wages). This generation of profit is the dynamism of the system: it is the original reason for the capitalist investing his money. In this system, people are not motivated to invest, unless they believe that they can reap substantial profit from their investment.

Why does this situation result in a struggle between the workers and the employers, between labour and capital?

After all, in return for his labour, the worker receives a wage, which he can use to purchase goods in the market at the prices determined by the capitalist. The reason is because of the enormous power which the capitalist has over the worker. What, in theory at least, does the capitalist control? He has power over what shall be produced, the conditions and mode of production, the wages to be paid to workers, the minimum price at which the products will be sold, who shall be employed, when and for what reasons. In addition, together with other capitalists, he controls the total goods available to workers as a whole, on which they can spend their wages.

Thus, in theory at least, this economic system results in the capitalists becoming richer and more powerful and the worker becoming poorer and less able to control his or her economic destiny. In actual fact, it does result in huge inequalities of wealth, power and status, although it is not as disastrous as some theorists forecast. The total impoverishment of the workers has, I believe, been prevented by the force of unionism—the workers uniting to enforce demands for better wages and conditions (this will be discussed below).

There are several arguments often voiced in support of the capitalist economy. The first is to associate capitalism with freedom. This is done continuously in the Australian media, where the economy is always referred to as 'a free enterprise system'. Indeed, Encel documents that spokesmen for big business go out of their way to stress this description of capitalism. For example, he quotes the Director-General of the Institute of Directors:

> There is an inbuilt resistance to free enterprise by those who have not the enterprise to be free . . . Thousands of otherwise intelligent people are convinced that the free enterprise system is some sort of gigantic racket perpetuated by those who have a vested interest in its survival . . . If directors

themselves cannot see the point of speaking up for
themselves, and the system by which they survive,
we might as well join the chorus singing *The Red
Flag*.[4]

The thesis here is that there is a kind of freedom in that the
capitalist can choose where he wishes to invest his money—
which goods and services to provide. However, although
some choice is available to the individual capitalist, it is in
fact the profit potentiality of particular enterprises which
fundamentally influences which goods and services are
provided. Moreover, for the vast majority of the society who
do not own capital, this 'freedom' is a meaningless one.

The second justification is the notion of claim to efficiency,
guaranteed by competition. The argument here is that
capitalists compete with each other with respect to the prices
of goods and the efficiency of their production. Thus,
prices will be determined not by the capitalist himself, but
by the competitive forces of the market.

Let us consider this market mechanism more closely. The
theory is that there is a large group of consumers who have
natural desires for goods and services of various kinds.
(I refer to these as 'natural' because we shall later speak of
created desires and values for the system.) The individual
consumers, having their own desires, create a demand for
goods which will satisfy them. The claim is that those capitalists who produce the goods which people desire, will be in
a much better position than those who produce goods for
which there is a low demand. Further, if there is a great
demand and a short supply of a certain commodity, then
those capitalists who produce it will be in a position to increase their prices. However, those people who produce
goods for which there is less demand will decrease their
prices commensurate with this lower demand. Thus the
demand determines what ultimately shall be produced. For
the capitalists will shift their resources towards the production of those goods for which there is the greatest demand.

This means that initially when demand increases, prices will increase, but as more capitalists compete to satisfy the new demand, the prices will stabilize and might even be reduced.[5] Hence the capitalist system provides the goods and services which people require, at the best price for them.

The above characterization is, however, extremely superficial. For, suppose we ask: what actions will capitalists carry out as competition between them becomes more intense? Each will attempt, on the above analysis, to reduce his prices and gain a greater share of the market than his competitors. How can he do this and still maintain a profit, if his competitors also reduce prices? He can only do so by cutting the wages of his own workers (or by cutting his profit margin per item, while producing more goods). However, if each capitalist reduced wages, the whole working population would suffer an overall wage reduction. This would mean that they could not afford to buy most of the products of individual capitalist enterprises, even at the slightly reduced prices. In this case, there would be two consequences: the workers would become poorer and poorer, and the capitalists would become a smaller group, for they would drive out their competitors by forcing them to make losses.[6] Although the latter trend towards more monopoly has occurred to an amazing degree, the former trend towards impoverishment of the working class was halted by the formation of workers' unions and the use of collective bargaining against employers, using the threat of strikes. At first, these moves towards greater unionization were strongly resisted by employers (consider the bitter workers' struggles in Australia during the 1890s).[7] As union pressure became stronger, capitalists accepted increases in the wages of workers—provided they were regulated—for these could be offset by increases in prices, and would allow the average worker to consume more goods, thus allowing for increases in production and the restoration of profit levels. This reversed the trend towards complete poverty for the workers, and gave at least some of them relative prosperity.

In order for this to be achieved, however, it was necessary for the state to interfere to reverse certain trends in the capitalist economy.[8] The policy of state intervention was given a huge boost with the popularization of the theories of John Maynard Keynes, whose work has been the basis of the resurrection of the capitalist economies which occurred after World War II.[9] Whereas traditional economists had argued that the capitalist system tends towards full employment of workers, Keynes argued that the system could reach equilibrium even at a level of high unemployment. According to Keynes, the level of employment depends on *effective demand* which is the sum of expenditure on consumer goods and on capital investment. Yet these two factors are controlled by different groups of people. Thus consumers, most of whom are workers, determine for subjective reasons what proportion of their income is to be saved and what is to be spent on goods. On the other hand, it is capitalists who determine what proportion of their capital should be invested and what proportion shall be held in money form. (Keynes calls this their 'liquidity preference'.) This decision depends firstly on the rate of interest which money will fetch and secondly on the rate of profit generated from the capital invested.

Keynes points out that, as consumers save more, capitalists are more reluctant to increase investment. Hence effective demand falls, prices are reduced and economic activity becomes sluggish: thus workers are sacked. The cause of all this is reduced investment, and under-consumption.[10] Keynes maintained that the state could intervene directly into economy to control the rate of interest, undertake investment itself through such things as public works expenditure and regulate the general level of investment in various industries through special subsidies, investment allowances, etc. The state can also intervene to raise the purchasing power of those groups in the community who are likely to spend their incomes, through increasing public sector salaries and social security payments. Keynes believed that these actions would increase investment and consumption and would overcome any stagnation in the economy.

This strategy of Keynes has been credited with the general economic boom in the West after 1948.[11] Yet this boom has not resulted in a better distribution of wealth. Thus a small percentage (4 per cent) of shareholders own the vast majority of the shares in the top companies of Australia, as is shown by Wheelwright.[12] The consequence of this is a vast difference between rich and poor, with the minority owning an enormous amount of wealth (see Section C).

This crucial fact is often obscured by the myth that Australia is an egalitarian society, in which the gap between the rich and poor is much less than other countries. This pernicious myth persists to this day, notwithstanding the enormous evidence against it. In 1970, Professor Encel concluded this survey of income and wealth in Australia with the observation

> It should be noted, however, that the distribution of income appears to have remained largely unchanged during this century, and that the share of national income received by the working class, in particular, has remained virtually the same, whereas in Britain and Western Europe, the share of the working class in national income has risen appreciably . . . There is, moreover, considerable evidence of real poverty in Australia, affecting at least 10 per cent of the population, which is rarely taken into account even by those people who favour a more even distribution of income.[13]

This problem of poverty has received some attention in recent times through the efforts of Professor Henderson and the national poverty inquiry which he conducted. His conclusions were dramatic.

> Our overall measure of poverty, in terms of adult income units, shows that on an annual income basis,

10.2 per cent were 'very poor' (below 100 per cent of the poverty line) and 7.7 per cent were 'rather poor' (between 100 percent and 120 per cent of the poverty line).[14]

Inequality and poverty would not, in themselves, have resulted in severe problems for the political and legitimation systems. However, during the 1970s a serious economic crisis has hit Western societies. The Keynesian dream became a nightmare. The capitalist economies are once again plagued with seemingly insurmountable problems. The causes for these appear to be the fundamental features of capitalism which Marx identified in his critiques. We must turn to examine these now.

B ALIENATED LABOUR AND CLASSES: MARX

Marx's analysis of capitalism is primarily concerned with the impact of this system on human beings, considered individually and collectively. To understand this, we must consider briefly Marx's concept of man, particularly as propounded in his early works.[1]

There are two general tendencies in theories of human nature: the first is the tendency to see man as primarily or exclusively a biological being, a kind of sophisticated animal. The other, opposite, tendency sees man as primarily a mind, a consciousness, a creature of thought; here reason is man's crowning achievement and other things are secondary and unimportant. This dichotomy was, to a considerable degree, rejected by Marx. He wants to accept that man is an animal, a being within nature, 'a sensuous being'. At the same time, man is more than an animal, insofar as he transcends nature and is capable of fashioning it in accordance with his own ideas.[2] Man is capable of both concrete and abstract thought, yet he remains a sentient being tied to nature. Because of this, man is capable of something which he would hardly possess if he were pure mind viz., the capacity to *suffer*. The philosopher Hegel saw this suffering as a necessary evil which we go through in the achievement of the full self-consciousness of the spirit. For Marx, suffering is *not* merely a consequence of the human condition, but caused mostly by the structure of society.

How then does suffering arise? Man is not only capable of reason; he is also capable of understanding the limitation of his own actions. Thus human beings are capable of seeing their plans, even the best laid ones, frustrated. Each recognizes that many possibilities which he/she can conceive of are not available as concrete choices in his/her life. What is the point of a choice in one's mind that one cannot carry out because of an existing social, political or economic arrangement?

This fact of human suffering leads Marx to ask: what are the causes of human suffering, particularly within the capitalist system? Now it is quite clearly a consequence of man's being in nature that he has needs which he did not himself determine. Indeed Marx wants to maintain that man has *universal* needs, that is needs which arise in virtue of his being the sort of entity which he is. For Marx there is a a dialectical relation between nature and man. Persons need to transform nature to achieve the fulfilment of their needs. For human needs are not such that they can be fulfilled by simply thinking or by doing nothing whatsoever. Thus persons must externalize themselves in the world. The distinctive characteristic of human beings, therefore, is that process whereby their ideas become objective, concrete things in the world. This process is that of human labour, work.

What does Marx mean by human labour in this context? He means not simply the creation of a physical product, not simply taking a piece of material nature and moulding it into something else. He also means any human activity which is creative—he means productive human action, whether writing a book, painting a picture, producing a table, or teaching mathematics. Whether work is physical or mental, there is always something which results from that work, namely, a product. Most such products are a mixture of some feature of nature with human creative force.[3]

In the above natural situation, each person recognizes his needs and this leads him to labour to create products which he requires to satisfy these needs. This is the case, whether the need is the aesthetic desire to be surrounded by beautiful things, or the simple physiological need for food. Yet this natural situation does not exist under capitalism. This is because human beings do not exist as isolated individuals. They do not exist in a state of nature, that is a state of separation from each other, as conceived by previous political writers.[4] They exist in groups and societies, and with increasing technology, we have the inevitable development of *communal labour*. People must work co-operatively in groups to produce the required goods.

In a capitalist economy, the accumulation of private property merges with the means for organizing communal production. Accumulated wealth is used to buy the means of production and thereby purchase and control the labour of others. The root foundation of capitalism is, therefore, the right to indefinite accumulation of private property. Even if there were an initial situation in which each person had the same proportion of nature (e.g., in the form of land), because some people work harder, or are more creative or more fortunate than others, they would accumulate more than others. Even in an agricultural society, the person who produces very little must turn to he who has accumulated in excess of his needs. In order to survive, the former is forced to sell his labour or his land to the latter. Finally the gap between them will became greater and the worker will be left in total dependence on the owner of land or the other means of production.

Hence the right to indefinite accumulation of property transforms an initial equal situation into an unequal one. Of course, this could be rectified to some degree if, when the two people died, their sons reverted to the initial equal situation. However, because the right to *inheritance* is fundamental to capitalism,[5] the accumulation by the rich is carried further and further.

In his analysis Marx points out that inequality is based on an important fact about nature, viz., the *scarcity* of land, raw materials and later on in capitalism, of the means of production. Because of this scarcity, the accumulation of private property by some leaves others with no means of production and no share in such means. They must therefore work, not for themselves, but for others. Thus the labour of workers is no longer used to produce goods determined by their needs, but rather goods which go towards the production of profit. The owners of the means of production, the capitalists, who have the power to determine what shall be produced in that society are concerned only with those products which will make the largest profit for them. Thus there is no necessary correlation between the products of a capitalist society and the fulfilment of human needs.[6]

If men are coerced into working by withdrawal of the means for satisfying even the most basic physical needs, then their labour will become akin to that of animals. 'The animal produces in a one-sided way what man produces universally ... Man produces *free of physical need* and only genuinely so in freedom from such need.'[7] Yet man has basic *human* needs independent of sheer physical survival. The most important of these is the need for creative labour: 'Man reproduced the whole of nature, man is free when he confronts his product ... Man also creates according to the laws of beauty'.[8]

Indeed art and craft are, for Marx, the models of human labour. Self-realizing labour is that in which man controls that which he creates, and puts all his basic characteristics into it, including his reason and his emotion. Thus human labour should be a creative endeavour, like art. Human beings have a need to appreciate the product of their own labour, something which they cannot do in the capitalist process.

Capitalism has another serious problem. It is not only

necessary to produce the goods, but to sell them as well. This requires that the workers as a whole consume the goods which are produced primarily for profit. However people normally do not buy goods which they do not want. Hence it is often necessary to create artificial wants and desires in people for products which they previously did not want, particularly since the economic system tends to over-produce. This is done by means of huge advertising campaigns. Thus a person may be persuaded to drink worthless and unhealthy soft drinks because these are associated with a sexy image, whereas being a reader of philosophy books (for example) is not.

Marx claimed that increasingly products become meaningless to man and do not satisfy his basic needs. Yet he becomes obsessed with the possession of more and more such worthless things. A materialist culture thus springs up in the society. Money becomes the means for determining the value of everything, including human beings.[9] (New problems arise from the materialist culture, as we shall see in Chapters 4 and 6.)

For Marx, there are four dimensions of *alienation* under capitalism:

(i) The alienation of the worker from his labour, since he does not control the character of the work he is engaged in, or the general organization of labour within the workplace;

(ii) The worker's alienation from his product. He does not identify himself in any way with the product, feels separated from it and does not feel responsible for it, in the way that a creative artist or an author feels responsible for his painting or book. In the latter case, the product is seen as a reflection of the creator's potentialities. But nobody holds the worker at General Motors responsible for the final condition of the car—and for what goes wrong with it. The worker feels degraded and alienated in the production line process; his labour is mechanistic, boring and exhausting;

(iii) The worker's alienation from other persons. The worker is forced into relations with other people which are not based on their value as persons, but rather on their value as an object or a commodity. Their value lies in their material usefulness for the creation of profit or in the extent of their possession of property. A person's value in popular culture relates to the possession of certain symbolically significant goods, e.g., sports car, swimming pool, colour TV.

(iv) Alienation from himself or his species being. Under capitalism we all come to feel inadequate and insecure within ourselves. We are not, if I may use a Christian term, at peace with ourselves. This disharmony within the human psyche is due, for Marx, not to any intrinsic characteristic, as Freud would have it, but rather to the social system under which we live.[10]

This alienation from one's self implies the notion of a real self—which is simply the sum of the person's potentialities. Marx makes the distinction between human nature in itself and human nature under particular kinds of society. Thus there is what I really want to do, what I really want to be, and then there is what I am, what I become under capitalism. In contrast to what a person is as a set of potentialities, his lived existence is determined by the process of the artificial creation of wants. Thus we find ourselves pursuing goals, values, purposes, etc. which were not there inherently. After a while, however, one can no longer distinguish. A person becomes mostly this 'unreal' self. Further, we come to see him entirely in terms of the roles given to him by the system.

Yet Marx is optimistic. For society never completely destroys the real self of a person. It might be submerged, frustrated (sometimes to the point of rebellious explosion), yet it is not destroyed as a potentiality. It is still there. This contrasts with the view that socialization totally determines human nature and that man is a plastic being who can be completely moulded to suit the requirements of society.

Marx holds that the productive relations between people are the basis for the division of society into classes. There are those who own and control the means of production—the capitalist class—and the vast majority who are dependent on them—the working class (called the proletariat by Marx). This definition of class is a dynamic, not a structural one, for Marx sees history in terms of the conflict of classes. The classes in a capitalist society, having contradictory aims, are involved in a struggle with each other, the proletariat wanting alleviation of their alienation, the bourgeoisie working for greater profits. As capitalism develops, people tend to fall into one class or the other, and the division between the classes becomes accentuated. However, while the struggle of a society for an end to alienation can be represented structurally in terms of the conflict between the two classes, this should not blind us to conflicts and divisions within classes.[11]

In order to understand the character of class conflict, we must turn to Marx's account of the dynamics of the capitalist system as given in *Capital*, his later major work. The basic problem of *Capital* is to determine the real character of the exploitation within capitalist society which gives rise to alienation. To come to grips with the dynamics of capitalist economy, Marx introduces three concepts of value: use value, 'real' value and exchange value.

The *use value* of a product or commodity derives from the fact that an individual or group has a *subjective* desire or want for it. Thus a table has a certain use value in a particular culture because it is desired for a particular purpose. Marx makes it clear that not all such wants are the same as basic human needs: 'the nature of such wants, whether they spring from the stomach or from fancy, makes no difference'.[12] Clearly, economics based on attempts to quantify such a subjective thing as the use values of commodities will be very difficult to achieve (although pro-capitalist economists are constantly trying).[13]

The '*real*' value of a product or commodity lies, according to Marx in the quantity of *labour power* which goes into its production. Marx recognizes that he must give more precision to this notion of labour power. He says:

Some people might think that if the value of a commodity is determined by the quantity of labour spent on it, the more idle and unskilful the labourer, the more valuable would his commodity be, because more time would be required in its production. The labour, however, that forms the substance of value, is homogeneous human labour, expenditure of one uniform labour-power. The total labour-power of society, which is embodied in the sum total of the values of all commodities produced by that society, counts here as one homogeneous mass of human labour-power, composed though it be of innumerable individual units. Each of these units is the same as any other, so far as it has the character of the average labour-power of society, and takes effect as such; that is, so far as it requires for producing a commodity, no more time than is needed on an average, no more than is socially necessary. The labour-time socially necessary is that required to produce an article under the normal conditions of production, and with the average degree of skill and intensity prevalent at the time.[14]

Thus in order to determine what the 'real' value of an article is, as distinct from its use value, we must determine the average labour power which would be required in that particular society, given its technological level, to produce that type of good. Marx calls this the *socially necessary labour power* for the production of that commodity.

The *exchange value* of a commodity does not depend on its use value, for this is not constant but differs from person to person. Rather the exchange value, according to Marx, depends on its 'real' value, that is, on the quantity of labour time socially necessary for its production. Thus when two goods involve, in their whole process of production (including the production of the machinery used to produce them), roughly equal quantities of human labour, it can then be said that they will achieve a roughly equal exchange value. These exchange values are represented within the system of money which is, in the first instance, an efficient intermediary for achieving exchange of goods.[15]

While I agree with Marx that the labour cost involved in the production of goods is a major determinant of the exchange value, reflected in the price, I do not believe that it is the sole determinant. For clearly an increase in demand would, at least temporarily, increase the price which the product fetches on the market. Marx was aware of this. However, he argued that because of competition between capitalists, the price would stabilize around the labour values involved in all the stages of its production. However, Marx also foresaw the increasing tendency of the capitalist system towards *monopoly*, in which the nature of competition is transformed. When this occurs, it is possible for dominant companies to fix prices far above the real values of commodities (a point of great importance in understanding the modern crisis of capitalism: see Chapter 3A).

Using the three concepts above, Marx derives what he considers to be the real dynamics of capitalism. This economic system, as we have seen, relies on the generation of *profit*. It is not the raw materials or the machines (for these are of fixed value at a given time, their value is determined by their exchange value in the market place), rather, it is the labour of the workers who use them, which is responsible for the increase in value and the generation of profit.

How does this come about?[16] According to Marx, the capitalist buys the labour power of the worker(s). In purchasing this labour power (which for his purposes is just another commodity like the machines he must buy), the capitalist must pay at the exchange value of labour. This exchange value of labour power of the worker is, in accordance with the above principles, determined by the socially necessary labour time required to reproduce the worker and his family, at an acceptable minimum standard of living. By minimum level here, Marx does not mean the level required in order to survive physically, that is, mere subsistence level. He means the minimum level which is the socially acceptable standard of living in the culture. Marx is aware that the reproduction of a culture—and one needs this minimum level in order to reproduce one's culture—can only be a continuing process at the level at which the average person is accustomed. It would, for example, be absurd to claim that Australian culture was being reproduced, if everybody were suddenly reduced in material welfare to a level equivalent to that of, say, Bangladesh.

In order to reproduce his own life and that of his family, the worker will strive to receive a wage which will allow him to purchase goods and services (such as education) at the minimum level. Marx therefore claims that the wages of workers will tend to stabilize around this norm: the minimum acceptable level for the reproduction of life. However the worker's labour power generates exchange value far in excess of that required to reproduce his own life. It is this excess which Marx calls the surplus value. Thus:

$$\text{Surplus value} = \begin{array}{c}\text{Exchange value} \\ \text{of products} \\ \text{of worker's} \\ \text{labour} \\ \text{(less material} \\ \text{costs)}\end{array} \quad \text{less} \quad \begin{array}{c}\text{Exchange value} \\ \text{of worker's} \\ \text{labour power} \\ \text{(reflected in wages)}\end{array}$$

For example, to workers in a particular factory, the minimum level of reproduction of life (reflected in wages) might require two and half hours of the labour power of each person per day. Yet the average person in this culture works eight hours per day. So, the question arises: what happens to the labour power (five and a half hours) above the minimum necessary for the reproduction of the worker at the existent level of culture? This excess labour power creates surplus value, which contributes to the profit of the capitalist

We can now clearly see the source of class conflict. The capitalist seeks to increase the proportion of the working day used to generate surplus value and to decrease the proportion which goes to pay the worker for the reproduction of his life. It follows that if the capitalist process is entirely unchecked, the worker would be reduced in his standard of living to a pauper who barely manages to survive. Marx, at times, believed that this tendency would become dominant and that the working class would be reduced to absolute poverty.[17] The fact that they have not done so does not mean that exploitation has been eradicated. On the contrary, it may increase even when wages increase, or remain fixed.

There are several ways this can be done. One is by increasing the *intensity* of work or labour. This is done by a variety of means, such as increasing pressure on workers to work harder through threats of dismissal and more intense supervision by foremen. Again, the employer may introduce conveyer belts and production lines, whose speed may be increased, thus forcing workers to increase output. Another way is to increase productivity through the introduction of more sophisticated technology. With such improved means of production, the output per worker may dramatically increase while wages remain relatively fixed or increase slightly.

The fundamental feature of capitalism pointed to by Marx thus remains essentially valid. The workers toil for part of the day and are paid a wage, whose value allows for the reproduction of life at a certain standard of living. The remainder of their working day goes into the production of a surplus of value, which is embodied in the products of labour and when exchanged, generates a profit for the capitalist. The greater the proportion of labour time spent in generating surplus value, the greater the profit, and the less the proportion of labour time which goes directly to increase the standard of living of the worker.

Marx does not merely condemn the fact that the worker is unpaid for this surplus labour. He also condemns the uses of this surplus labour time within a capitalist economy. Here, workers are required to invest their excess labour power in the production of commodities, which are chosen not because they satisfy human needs, but rather for their exchange value, that is, their capacity to generate profit. In a capitalist economy, the profit motive, not human needs or the utility of commodities, determines what shall be produced.[18]

Already implicit in the above distinctions is Marx's concept of socialism. A socialist society is one in which culture would also be reproduced at the minimum acceptable level for everyone. However, in addition to this, excess labour time would be directed towards the production of goods and services which would satisfy people's real needs, and which have a high use value, as distinct from exchange value.

What if it is objected that workers' wages, in advanced capitalism, give them more money than is required for the minimum level of reproduction of culture to be achieved? Marx would make two observations here. Firstly, he would point to the fact that for a large number of people in the society their total income is in fact insufficient to reproduce life, even at this minimum acceptable standard, as for example, the significant percentage of the Australian people (approximately 20 per cent) below or at the poverty line, that is, they do not have enough income to reproduce even at the minimum acceptable level.[19] But Marx would also point out that a large number of people are just above that poverty line, that is, their income is just sufficient to reproduce culture at this minimum standard of living, while their contribution in terms of labour power is far in excess of this.

What of the others whose wage levels allow them income in excess of what is required for the minimum standard of living? Marx argues that, even though these people receive a money income in excess of the minimum standard of living, this does not mean that their real human needs are being satisfied. For workers generally do not *control* the uses to which surplus labour power is to be put—it is controlled by the profit motive. Hence even if a person receives more in money income for his labour, he still does not control the use of his labour power, nor does he have any guarantee that his money income will provide greater satisfaction. For he can only use it to purchase goods which are produced primarily for the generation of profit and not goods and services which satisfy his real needs. He may thus accumulate many material goods, yet receive less meaning from them. (This is one source of the current social crisis: see Chapter 4.)

The struggle between labour and capital manifests itself in three ways. Firstly, there is the demand for higher and higher wages, a demand which the working class still pursues through its unions and the use of the strike. Secondly, there is the struggle for better conditions of employment, also demanded through unions. Thirdly, there are demands for control of the productive process itself—with respect to both *what* is produced and *how* it is produced. This demand for more workers' control of the means of production, and of the priorities of production, has not generally been pursued by unions, yet it strikes at the heart of the capitalist system.[20]

Thus, for Marx, socialism is not simply a matter of the redistribution of the goods produced in society, using surplus labour power. It is re-orientation of the labour power towards the production of those goods and services, which the people have collectively determined as being most useful and most conducive to the satisfaction of their needs. All this ties up with the theory of alienation as developed in the early works. For Marx, workers' ownership of the means of production is not sufficient unless it involves *control* of what is produced and hence of the uses to which their labour power is put. This requires their democratic participation in the determination of the general needs of society (a factor lacking in Soviet communist systems).[21]

Marx believed that in advanced industrial societies like our own, and for the first time in human history, man is able to feed, clothe and provide the basic material needs of every person. Furthermore, the excess labour power that remains after the production of basic material goods and services, can be used to provide services which satisfy other human needs, such as the intellectual and the artistic. This can only be achieved, however, when the class struggle reaches the point where the workers seize the means of production and regain control of the uses to which their labour power is put. This situation, Marx believed, would only arise after a struggle in which the proletariat were victorious.

Yet Marx did not suppose that an intense level of class struggle would arise spontaneously, simply because of the alienated condition of the working class. He foresaw obstacles, the most important of which was the *false consciousness* of the working class. Marx makes an important distinction. between the class-in-itself and the class-for-itself.[22] The proletariat, by virtue of its alienation from the productive process, constitutes a separate class. This is the class-in-itself. Yet it only becomes a class-for-itself when, through specific forms of class struggle (such as strikes), its members gain a consciousness of themselves as belonging to the same class, and as having the potential to free their labour power from the bondage of capitalism.

This change from a false to a true consciousness is not an automatic occurrence. On the contrary, even though alienation itself often sharpens their perception of their position, the system acts to perpetuate their false consciousness.[23] The reproduction of the capitalist system thus depends, not only on the material rewards given to workers, but on the reproduction of those cultural forms which give the workers a motivation to continue working within the system and a feeling of a meaningful social identity. I shall return to these matters in Chapters 4 and 5.

In conclusion, the above general features of Marx's analysis of capitalism seem to me sound (except for the relation between exchange value and labour). However his analysis was incomplete in several places. In particular, he did not pay sufficient attention to his own thesis that capitalism would become less competitive and more monopolistic.

Furthermore, his analysis of the state and of its active role in intervening to alleviate crises in capitalism has proved to be inadequate. These points will become clearer when we consider Marx's and other theories of economic crisis. I shall argue that the ultimate deep-seated cause of crisis is the exploitative character of the capitalist economy, and the consequent inequalities, injustices and struggles which Marx documented. But first we need to show how these features apply in the Australian context.

C CLASS AND INEQUALITY IN AUSTRALIA

In Australia, nearly all sociologists and political scientists examining the problem of inequality of wealth, status and power use the term 'class'. There are, however, three different conceptions of class.[1] A class refers to that totality of people who

(i) *subjectively* see themselves as falling within such a group;

(ii) are *objectively* determined as falling within the group because of their positions within the hierarchies of income, accumulated wealth (often correlated with income, but different from it), occupation, etc. and

(iii) are objectively determined as falling within the group, because of their function within society, conceived as a dynamic system (e.g., their relation to the means of production, as in Marx's theory).

Subjective class

There are two ways by which sociologists survey the class situation subjectively. They might ask people questions like 'do you consider that you belong to a class, and which class is it?' When they ask the question in this way, they tend to get a substantial number of people who are reticent about identifying themselves with any class at all, because they feel that social classes no longer exist.[2] However, these same people, when offered a list of class descriptions, will put themselves in a particular position within it, and this is the second way in which one might make a class evaluation. With the first method, when Australians identify themselves as members of a class, they overwhelmingly identify themselves as members of the middle class, by distinguishing an upper class and a working or lower class and identifying themselves as intermediate, between them. But of more interest to us are the replies of people when the second approach is used.

I list here the results of two surveys which used the second method to determine class—referred to by Encel in his *Equality and Authority*.[3] First there was the Australian Gallup Poll survey of 1961, which came out with the following results:

5.5% ⎫		Upper middle
44% ⎬	61.5%	Middle
12% ⎭		Lower middle
38.5%		Working

Another survey in 1969 gave the distribution below.

1%	Upper
47%	Middle (divided into three groups)
47%	Working (divided into three groups)
5%	Refused to identify

It appears from this survey that Australians identified themselves in roughly equal proportions as belonging either to the middle class, or to the working class.

From the above, it seems that results will vary depending on which list of classes we offer people in our surveys. What would we discover if we had a totally adequate method of determining how people categorize themselves in terms of class? This question is not discussed in depth. Often, explanations are given linking the subjective representation of one's class and the way one votes. Thus it can be shown that blue-collar workers who classify themselves as middle class tend to vote Liberal.[4] While this is interesting, it does not go very far towards explaining *why* people subjectively represent themselves as being in the middle class rather than the working class.

Subjective questionnaires on class rarely attempt to analyse people's conception of class conflict. From a radical perspective, this is an important matter. Persons may identify themselves as 'working class', but may see no conflict of interest between this and the middle or upper classes. Others who do so may be contrasting the working class with 'the capitalist class' or 'the ruling class'—that is, the conflict between labour and capital may be a key feature in their subjective representation. It is only when we have this additional information that we can determine whether a person's subjective representation constitutes *false consciousness* of his class situation.

Structural definitions of class

Here the major determinant is position on measurable objective hierarchies such as income, wealth, occupation, etc. However the choice of which hierarchy to consider or emphasize makes a great difference to the result. In Australia, the most common hierarchies surveyed are personal income, occupational status, and the white collar—blue collar division.[5]

Occupational status can be used because of the increasing specialization and the division of labour within a modern capitalist economy.[6] This specialization extends not only to types of jobs, such as teacher and unskilled labourer, but also within the process of production. Thus in a factory producing motor cars, each person is assigned a specific job, such as putting on the right tyres, or putting a specific part into an engine. The rationalization for this extreme division of labour is that it is very efficient, and efficiency is of major importance to the capitalist economy.

Sociologists, then, produce an occupational status hierarchy —based on the ranking of different occupations in community surveys. The result of this ranking process is surprisingly similar every time. Let me cite one that is listed in

Encel's book.[7] The top occupations are ranked thus: 1 doctor; 2 university professor; 3 solicitor; 4 architect; 5 professional engineer; 6 director of large enterprise; 8 dentist; 9 veterinary surgeon; 10 clergyman; 11 university lecturer; 12 school principal. At the bottom of the list are occupations such as truck driver, railway shunter, porter, night watchman, waitress, packer, barman, cane cutter, seasonal labourer, wharf labourer, charwoman and road sweeper. There are, of course, greater changes from survey to survey with respect to middle-range jobs. Thus we find certain occupations which by income and educational standard one would expect to rank highly, but which are held in low esteem—a significant example here being politicians. On the other hand, in a culture heavily dominated by sport, we find jockeys, footballers, etc., highly ranked.

Because of the subjectivity involved in an occupational status hierarchy of this kind, some sociologists fit occupations to classes on the basis of educational standards required to gain such occupations. This gives a supposedly objective occupational hierarchy, as distinct from one based on people's subjective rankings. Another common 'objective' occupational characterization of class simply classes white-collar and professional workers as middle class and manual workers as working class, ignoring such distinctions as whether they are self-employed (in small business) or working for a wage.[8]

Yet the hierarchy which is most important for a structural view of class is that of the *distribution of wealth*. It is very difficult to compile data on this, although some have attempted to do so. One recent study by Phil Raskell produced the dramatic result shown in Table 1 on p. 74.[9]

Raskell sums up his results in this way:

> This data reveals that 1 per cent of the adult
> population owns 22 per cent of personal wealth; the
> 'top' 5 per cent, 46 per cent; and the 'top' 10 per cent,
> almost 60 per cent of the wealth of Australians. Half of
> all Australians own less than 8 per cent of Australian

wealth. The top 5 per cent own more than the bottom 90 per cent put together.[10]

Table 1	Distribution of wealth

	Cumulative proportion of individuals (%)	Cumulative proportion of wealth (%)
least wealthy	1	0.005
	5	0.077
	10	0.270
	20	1.036
	30	2.569
	40	4.860
	50	7.935
	60	12.330
	70	18.695
	80	27.816
	85	33.947
	90	41.500
	95	54.500
	99	78.000
most wealthy	100	100.000

Concentration co-efficient 0.7017
Mean wealth* $10 957
*Defined to include sums insured under life policies and superannuation equities.

These data are consistent with the earlier (1972) findings of Groenewegen, who concluded that 'about 11 per cent of the population owns nearly 40 per cent of the wealth while at the other end more than 15 per cent of the population owns less than 5 per cent of the wealth'.[11]

Using Raskell's figures, we can provide *one* possible structural account of class, based on wealth. This would be as follows:

	Percentage of population	Percentage of wealth
Upper class	10	58.50
Middle class	40	33.57
Lower class	40	7.66
Under class	10	0.27

Thus the upper class (defined as the top 10 per cent) owns more than the other classes of society put together. For each $100 of wealth in the society, $58.50 is owned by the top 10 per cent, while only 27 cents is owned by the bottom 10 per cent. This totally iniquitous situation completely explodes the myth of Australia as an egalitarian society.

What of the relation between 'objective' structural accounts of class and subjective estimates?[12] Why do some persons who, on the 'objective' criteria, are in the working class (manual workers) represent themselves as being middle class? The answer is, I believe, that many people have expectations of improving their situation. Putting people into hierarchical structures inculcates the desire for promotion—the notion of moving up the hierarchy. Not all people expect to achieve good results in this way, but those with the greatest expectations of upward social mobility tend to identify themselves with the middle class.

David Kemp has recently expounded the view that people are decreasingly identifying themselves on the basis of their 'objective' class situation.[13] In fact, he argues that increasingly more working class people place themselves in the middle class, or if they refuse to classify themselves, have values and attitudes which are traditionally considered to belong to the middle class. He identifies two sets of values and attitudes: (i) individualism—each person trying to promote his own interests (see above)—and the need for stable order and authority in society;

(ii) egalitarianism and the need to change society to provide for the needs of those who are disadvantaged.[14] Kemp then uses the occupational division of white-collar and professional versus manual workers to define the middle and working class 'objectively'. He argues that we would normally expect the middle class (so defined) to hold the first set of values and attitudes and the working class (manual workers) to hold the second. Not surprisingly, after surveying a cross-section of people, he found that the objective class situation *based on occupation* was no longer relevant in determining people's values and attitudes. Yet he claims it is the latter which determine voting patterns. Hence many manual workers (whom he classifies as working class) tend to vote for the Liberal Party, because they hold the first set of attitudes.[15]

Kemp's results would not have been surprising to Marx; indeed, they are to be expected in a society where the media are dominated by middle-class values and attitudes, and where vestiges of working-class consciousness are repressed. Indeed, values such as egalitarianism and sympathy for the underdog would disappear completely if it were not for three factors: the development of alternative critical attitudes in some parts of the education system; the lingering role of *some* religious perspectives on the world; popular working-class struggles which reinforce these values.

Dynamic conception of class

A basic flaw in all structural accounts of class is that they are, at best, symptoms of the deeper, dynamic class division of society. This dynamic concept of class is based on the conflict or dynamic interaction between classes; it is based on the *power* relationship. Here there is a powerful or ruling class and a powerless oppressed class, and a struggle between them.

The most important dynamic definition of class is that of Marx. Here classes are defined in relation to people's position within the productive process.[16] The conflict is between the owners and controllers of capital, who seek to maximize their profitability by extracting the maximum surplus value from workers, and the working class, who seek to maximize the rewards for labour and to control the productive process in the interests of human needs (see Chapter 2B). According to Marx, this conflict between the capitalist class and the working class is the major power struggle in society. The struggle for state power is of secondary importance, for the state is always controlled by the capitalist class.[17]

In contrast to this, C. Wright Mills maintained that there exists, in modern capitalist societies, a ruling or *power elite*.[18] This group can be treated as a ruling 'class' in that they functionally operate to monopolize power in their own hands. Mills believed that the interlocking groups forming this elite hold political, economic, military, ideological and bureaucratic power. He demonstrated that, in the USA, the members of this elite come from similar social and educational backgrounds; they often interact with each other socially and they share the same overall value system and world view or, as he calls it, the same 'ethos'.

Mills' theory presented a challenge to both the pluralist and the classical views of democracy. He claimed that, in America where such an elite rules, all you do in an election (normally) is to change the membership of the elite, so that the same elite competes for power in government and runs the economic, bureaucratic and other sectors.[19]

Mills' view differs from that of Marx in that power is not primarily or exclusively located in the capitalists. Power is diffused in its forms: there is political, military, bureaucratic and ideological, as well as economic power. Nevertheless it is retained in the hands of the one elite, with the same basic ethos. On the other hand, for Marx, power is primarily in the hands of the capitalists, who form an independent class in society.

I agree with Marx that the division between the interests of labour and those of capital is still the major source of power conflict in Western society. However, I believe this conflict has now changed so as to include the struggle for the control of the state itself. Thus whereas Marx conceived of the early state as a mere superstructure (which always supports the capitalist class),[20] this is not so in late capitalism. Because of the struggles by workers to reform the state and make it more democratic, the state is—in theory at least— not *necessarily* always controlled by any particular class. Recognizing this, the capitalists have, since the time of universal suffrage (democratic elections), developed an alliance with those groups in political parties, the law and the public service which share their attitudes towards private accumulation of wealth, profit and the exploitation of workers. Indeed, where such groups as these did not exist, capitalists financed and encouraged their formation and continued to finance their activities. As these groups affiliated with the capitalists, and as the role of the state in sustaining profits became more critical, their actions directed against workers forged them into one class.

D   THE RULING CLASS: AN ALTERNATIVE TO THE ORTHODOX MARXIST MODEL

It has been a constant criticism of Marx that he underestimated the extent to which state or political power may gain a relative autonomy from the owners and controllers of the means of production. It is here that some of Weber's conceptions become important. For Weber, there were three basic determinants of *real* power: the economic divisions between the propertyless and the propertied (class); the sentiments of a community with respect to the worth of individuals and groups (status); the authority given to political leaders within the bureaucratic state sector (party).[1] For Weber, it was possible for groups with high status, but little economic power, to gain and hold the political leadership of a society. The state was the central focus of power in the society; bureaucracies in the state were the most powerful people because they were underpinned by the monopoly over the legitimate use of physical force (coercion).[2] Thus it was a contingent matter as to whether the economic bourgeoisie controlled the state and hence became rulers.

For Weber, the principal problem in the area of domination was the development of bureaucracy itself, a development which he saw as rational and virtually inevitable in both the state and the private organization of economy. Principles of hierarchical organization and increased division of labour in both private and state sectors would come to dominate advanced Western society (as indeed they have). In this situation, the fundamental form of exploitation is the domination by bureaucratic processes. This domination is co-ordinated by the state, with its legitimized power (supposedly based on principles of democracy).

However, the central flaw in Weber's analysis is that he places insufficient weighting on the non-bureaucratic elements involved in the domination relations within the capitalist economy. Even though major capitalist firms have now become bureaucratic organizations, the power still resides in the hands of owners and their delegated managers, and is exercised in order to maximize profits and to minimize the gains of labour. The basic division set out by Marx has been virtually swept aside in Weber's preoccupation with bureaucracy. Clearly both elements need to be taken into account.

In contrast to both Marx and C. Wright Mills, I now present a third view: the ruling class is tied to the interests of capital, nevertheless it is not limited to the owners of the means of production, distribution and exchange. In late capitalist society, those who act to sustain the exploitation of workers and the alienation of people from their real needs are not merely the capitalists, but also managers, politicians, bureaucrats, academics, etc. These people, while they may have independent sources and forms of power, nevertheless exercise that power in the interests of capital.[3]

I thus concede to the pluralist that there has been a formal separation of power into a variety of forms and institutions.

In my view, the main ones here are: political, economic, bureaucratic, legal-judicial, military, educational (including academic) and media power.[4] The important point here, however, is that in each of these areas there are rules, roles and usually hierarchical structures, which establish a relationship of *domination*, and which concentrate power in few hands.

Thus political power is concentrated in the Cabinet and bureaucratic power in the top public servants (see Chapter 1D). Ideological power is increasingly in the hands of media monopolies (see Chapter 5D) and top academics, many of whom rationalize the domination of the ruling class.

There has also been increasing concentration of economic power in Australia, following the trend in the Western world (see Chapter 3A). In a survey of the 1967–68 statistics, Wheelwright discloses that of 77 630 companies, the top 333 accounted for 42 per cent of taxable income; of the 900 largest companies, 296 accounted for roughly four-fifths of the total assets.[5] More recent figures, based on the Bureau of Statistics study of 13 February 1976, reveal the following pattern in Australian manufacturing industry, see p. 81 (reproduced from the pamphlet *Australia Uprooted*).[6]

Two points should be noted from the figures. Firstly, many of the smaller companies are so small and employ so few workers that they are virtually ignored and considered irrelevant by the major firms. Indeed the very small capitalists (employing up to five workers) play a much smaller role in the class struggle on behalf of the ruling class than certain political, professional and public service figures—who may nevertheless own no means of production themselves.

Secondly, many of the biggest and most powerful companies are merely branches of multi-national companies and are owned (and controlled) not by Australians, but by foreigners. Under these circumstances, Australians are recruited to manage and supervise these enterprises and, in fact, to act as substitute capitalists (often these people are given a small measure of ownership, so that their motivation

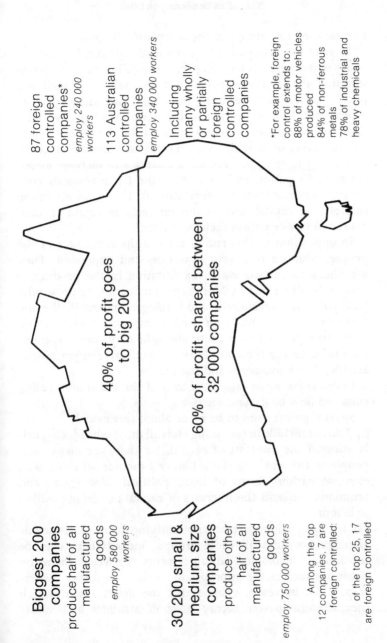

87 foreign controlled companies* *employ 240 000 workers*

113 Australian controlled companies *employ 340 000 workers*

Including many wholly or partially foreign controlled companies

*For example, foreign control extends to: 88% of motor vehicles produced 84% of non-ferrous metals 78% of industrial and heavy chemicals

40% of profit goes to big 200

60% of profit shared between 32 000 companies

Biggest 200 companies

produce half of all manufactured goods

employ 580 000 workers

30 200 small & medium size companies

produce other half of all manufactured goods

employ 750 000 workers

Among the top 12 companies, 7 are foreign controlled:

of the top 25, 17 are foreign controlled

(Source: Bureau of Statistics, Study 13/2/76, ref. no. 12.35 Figures Compiled.)
Reproduced with permission from the Amalgamated Metal Workers' and Shipwrights' Union

to raise the profitability of the company will increase).

Most of the groups holding economic, political and other forms of power in society are part of the ruling class. Notwithstanding the divisions between them, which Connell has noted may be quite serious,[7] they have two unifying characteristics: their opposition to the demands of the working class for greater services and rewards for their labour, and for workers' ownership and control of enterprises (anti-socialism); their opposition to all attempts to increase democratic participation and to reverse the trend towards concentrated power (anti-democratization). They thus act in the interests of capital and in the interests of retaining concentrated power within their own class.

In opposition to this ruling class is the remainder of the people, who are relatively powerless and oppressed. They are alienated in two ways: exploitation in the productive process (as described by Marx) and domination by those who hold political, bureaucratic and ideological power. Following tradition, I term this oppressed group the *working* class. Their only power lies in unity and solidarity: their weapons are the strike and the vote. Their only effective organizations are the mass movements and the unions.

Given these observations, a map of the Australian ruling class can now be drawn, see p. 83.

Several points need to be made about this model:

(i) I do not include in the ruling class all those who ideologically support the interests of capital, for there are many such people in the working class. Rather I include all those who exercise various forms of legal, political, ideological, and economic *power* in the interests of capital and in opposition to labour;

(ii) I do not suppose that any unifying form of conscious ideology pervades all these groups; indeed there may be substantial ideological disagreements between them on questions such as the appropriate level of Australian ownership. I do, however, assume that the directions in which they exercise power betray a set of attitudes and values

The ruling class

Australian operatives of multi-national firms	Large Australian capitalist firms (owners & managers)	Smaller capitalists (but not self-employed businessmen)
Political representatives acting for capital—Liberal, NCP parties, right-wing Labor Party representatives	Top public servants making decisions in the interests of capital	Academics advising and disseminating ideas on behalf of capital
Lawyers and judges acting for capital and against labour	Military and espionage forces acting for capital	Major media propagandizing for capital

in opposition to the interests of the working class;
(iii) I do not assume that all the actions of the different groups in the ruling class are directed to the domination of the working class, only that this latter is the major factor.

The central unifying principle of the ruling class is that they act in the interests of capital. Their goal is to ensure the conditions for the *reproduction of capital* and for the *maximization of profit* and capital accumulation. (On maximizing capital, see Chapter 3.) Ensuring the reproduction of capital is difficult, especially in the context of a 'democratic' representational system. Here it is necessary to reproduce a culture and ideological forms which sustain and support the existing structure. Thus it is necessary to have: media propaganda which extols the virtues of individual initiative and 'free' enterprise, while attacking collectively determined goals by workers (especially unions seeking wage increases); educational and intellectual elites which seek to reinforce a non-questioning attitude to existing authority structures and myths about the supposedly existing equality of opportunity; legal-judicial arrangements and judgements which reinforce existing economic and bureaucratic arrangements, protect and legitimize the rights of those who hold power, and punish those who fail to respect those rights.

I do not agree with the orthodox Marxist view that the state as a whole, and all its powerful centres, is *inevitably* controlled by the ruling class. The state has a formal autonomy from the interests of capital, even though it is *generally* controlled by those who favour these interests. The possibility of a reform or radical government cannot be *a priori* excluded, even though it is unlikely. But the very fact that the non-political sectors of the ruling class need to mobilize to prevent working-class gains itself illustrates the relative autonomy of the state sector. Furthermore, those few people who hold power but do not exercise it in the interests of capital seem to me to fall in an intermediate category between the oppressed (or working) class and the ruling class. They are a new phenomenon which has arisen in advanced capitalism, and then have an important role to play in bringing about change.

A complete account of the Australian ruling class using the above model is not yet available, and requires further research.

Two issues need to be treated at this stage. Firstly, do the ruling class groups constitute interlocking elites which are in constant consultation with each other, or are they disparate groups which act in the same general direction because of the general structure of the social and economic relations of society? There is a divergence of viewpoints on this matter, with empirical material being used to bolster both perspectives.[8] Thus Encel concludes his analysis claiming that, in Australia, there is only 'a loose collection of elite groups linked together by what may be called a governing consensus. It is this consensus which maintains the existing structure of class, status and power and the settled policies of the country on which this structure depends'.[9] However, it is not just consensus which brings about this result, but action guided by attitudes and interests. Yet Encel refuses to call this governing collection a 'ruling class'.

On the other hand, R. A. Wild believes that there is considerable interaction between the various elites, to the point that they can control recruitment to their ranks. 'The country is characterized by a governing class, because there is a relatively closed pattern of recruitment to elite positions and there are complex rational-legal restrictions on the power of elite groups'.[10] It is not clear, however, to what degree such restrictions are based on social interaction within and between the elite groups of the ruling class.

Wild believes that 'Australia does not have a ruling class because of the level of autonomy between the political and economic sectors and the pervasiveness and strength of bureaucratization'.[11] This is, I believe, a mistaken argument. Although the state as a body is independent from capitalists, it does not follow that many important elites who compete for power are dynamically independent of capitalist forces. Indeed, Wild seems to concede that powerful political and bureaucratic groups act in the interests of capital.[12]

Another view of the relationship between the dominant elites of the ruling class is given by R. W. Connell in *Ruling Class, Ruling Culture*. He argues that there emerges in the ruling class a group of business leaders on the one hand and political leaders on the other. Both act in the interests of capital, but the liaison between them may at times break down.[13] Yet, paradoxically, Connell suggests that public servants are 'the most powerful men in the country' even though they do not belong to the ruling class since civil servants are often only small property owners.[14] This does not seem a sufficient reason for excluding them, for after all there are political leaders of his ruling class (some members of the Liberal Party) who also do not own capital. Both top bureaucrats and political leaders may nevertheless belong to this class, by virtue of the way they exercise power.

This brings us to the second issue: how does the dynamic class analysis I have given relate to inequalities in income and wealth? If we refer to the structural definition of class in terms of wealth given earlier, we would expect that the over-whelming majority of the top 10 per cent in wealth ownership (structurally 'upper' class) would belong to the ruling class, as dynamically defined. However, we would expect to find many members of the ruling class who are not personally extremely rich (even though they act to support wealthy capitalist interests). Most of these would nevertheless own considerable personal property and fall in the top part of the 'middle' class (structurally defined).

On the other hand, most of the members of the 'middle' class (defined in terms of personal wealth) share objective interests with those who belong to the 'lower' class (who own only 7 per cent of wealth) in that together they belong dynamically to the working class and struggle to increase its economic share and its control.[15]

Armed with these understandings of the vast inequalities in wealth and the basis for them in the struggle between the ruling class and the working class, we can now turn to consider the causes of economic crisis.

3
Economic and Political Crises

A THEORIES OF ECONOMIC CRISIS

There are a variety of theories on the causes of economic crisis within capitalism. Most of these theories, whether they agree with him or not, draw on the elements of capitalist crisis as outlined by Marx. I shall begin with an outline of Marx's theory of crisis and, after some criticisms, develop what I conceive to be the causes of the modern economic crisis in the West.

Marx on capitalist crisis

The characteristic feature of capitalist production is that each capitalist unit, in seeking to maximize its profits, acts in competition with other producers, yet independently of their goals and purposes. His decisions are determined by his own estimates as to his ability to sell his products at prices which will realize a sufficient profit for him. Yet while capitalist production seems totally chaotic and anarchic in character, there is one set of laws which operate to impose some order on this chaos. As Engels says: 'These laws are manifested in the sole form of social relationship which continues to exist, in exchange, and enforce themselves on the individual producers as laws of competition'.[1]

We have seen, in Chapter 2B, that the capitalist generates surplus value from the workers' labour, but this value is not realized as capital plus profit until the produced commodities are sold at profitable prices. Thus while production is the source of surplus value, it is only in the process of exchange that this extra value becomes realized profit for the capitalist. In other words, the capitalist must reconvert the produced commodities into money capital.

However there is no necessity, within capitalism, that he shall be able to sell his commodities at the price he requires. The level of effective demand, that is, demand by those who have the will and purchasing power to buy, may not reach the same level as the total output of that kind of commodity by competing firms. Indeed, Marx argued that, in certain periods of capitalism, there is a relative over-production of commodities which exceeds the demand for them.[2] This situation arises especially when a new technology develops to replace obsolete forms. The company or individual that first employs this new mode will seize the advantage over its competitors and seek to produce as many goods as possible, using the new productive means. It thus stands to make handsome profits. Its rivals, in order to survive, will also need to introduce the new technology and will seek to win back their share of the market. The result is that goods will be over-produced, beyond the level of demand at the old prices.

Since the new technology will generally require less human labour to produce the same goods, the 'real' value (in Marx's terms) of the products will be reduced.[3] Because of the competition between capitalists, the price under the new technology will thus tend to be reduced also. Hence there will be a *fall* in the rate of profit, for the capitalist cannot now sell his goods at the previous prices. Furthermore, because of the over-production, he may be forced to sell his goods at prices below their real value, in order to realize his capital. This may cause a loss, and bankrupt the weaker firms.

The major causes of crisis, for Marx, are therefore the tendencies towards over-production and the reduction in the rate of profit. Why do these lead to crisis? Marx believed that, when faced with an actual or possible reduction in profits, many capitalists cut back new investment, reduce production and hence sack workers. The reduction in the rate of profit thus results in increased unemployment and decreased investment by those firms that have survived. The total number of commodities produced is therefore reduced. This is the stage of *depression* or stagnation.

Marx, however, did not believe that this situation would result in the breakdown of the capitalist system. True, it is a difficult time in human, social terms for both workers and capitalists. Many capitalists will go bankrupt or will be bought out by more powerful ones; most workers will be forced to accept reductions in real wages and increases in exploitation.[4] Marx believed that such crises can have the effect of strengthening capitalism in the short term, for they increase the concentration of capital in fewer hands. They force companies to introduce new forms of technology which reduce the labour component in production and lower costs.

Once production has been reduced by cutbacks in investment and by forcing the weaker competitors out of business, the survivors begin to gradually increase production as demand increases. The cautious new investment leads to the employment of some of those unemployed during the depression, with the consequent increase in consumer spending. This increased consumption creates greater confidence in capitalists who continue to invest. Competition increases; new technologies are introduced. Yet this boom period again results in over-production of commodities in excess of demand and sows of seed of the next depression.

Hence Marx predicted a cycle of booms and depressions for the capitalist economy—based on over-production and on the tendency for the rate of profit to fall. This thesis that the economy moves in cycles has now been accepted by many pro-capitalist economists.[5] The tendencies on which it is based—over-production and reduction in profit rates— are of great importance in the modern crisis.

Yet Marx foresaw a cataclysmic crisis which would involve the final doom of the capitalist economy. This crisis would arise as a consequence of two factors:

(a) *The tendency for the organic composition of capital to rise*
In calculating the cost of production of goods, we must take into account the cost of the machinery and raw materials (in Marx's terms, 'constant capital') and the cost of labour power ('variable capital'). Marx correctly argued that, with increased technology and more sophisticated machinery, the role of constant capital in production would increase, and the role of variable capital would decrease. In other words, the amount of labour power required for each item produced would decrease. This Marx called an increase in the organic composition of capital.[6]

When this occurs, the proportion of the costs in the production of each item which are fixed (machinery and raw materials) increases, and the proportion on which a profit relies (the surplus value extracted from the workers' labour) decreases. This means that, in a competitive capitalist situation, the profit margin per item produced tends to decrease. There are three major possible responses to this situation:

(i) the company can attempt to sustain (or increase) its overall profit and offset the reduction of the profit per item by substantially increasing the number of goods produced. Indeed this is one of the factors leading to the over-production which, as we have seen, is a major factor in capitalist depressions;

(ii) companies may attempt to reduce the wages of workers and hence extract more surplus value per item, even though the proportion of labour power involved in the production of that item is diminished. This response is only likely to succeed, however, if unionism of workers is weak and ineffectual. I shall discuss this tendency below;

(iii) companies may substantially reduce prices temporarily, and carry the consequent reduction in profit. Their competitors will be unable to compete, and will either be bankrupted or taken over in mergers.

The consequence of this, as Marx recognized, is for small companies to be swallowed up by larger ones and for economic power to become more concentrated—that is, the trend towards monopoly capitalism. Marx was aware that this trend would increase as the rate of profit fell, and thereby create huge operations. However he did not foresee that this development would change the structure of capitalism to such an extent that it would dramatically change the relationship between the exchange value of products and their labour (real) value.[7]

We might agree with Marx that, if a large number of companies produce a particular product, then the competitive situation creates a price which approximates the real value of the commodity. However, if only one company produces a particular product, then it can control the price. Similarly, if two or three companies produce a particular product, then the danger of monopoly arises from the potential for these few companies to engage in a conspiracy; they could raise or fix prices in a way which was not possible under the original market theory where each capitalist was competing against every other. Thus, while Marx may have been correct in postulating that the rate of profit would tend to fall in competitive capitalism, he does not appear to have recognized that the trend towards monopoly would create a new situation in which the capitalist becomes more powerful and is now able to determine *unilaterally* what the consumer shall pay for the product.[8] In this case, products may be priced above their real value in terms of the labour power involved in their production.

At this stage, it may be asked: is there not a tendency for monopoly capitalism to revert to the competitive phase? For surely, as other people who have accumulated money recognize that large profits are to be made in a particular area of production, they will seek to establish enterprises in competition with existing ones. While this occasionally happens, it is not common. For the established monopoly company has enormous powers to squash any potential competitor—particularly a small one. It can use these in a variety of ways: by temporarily reducing prices, forcing the would-be competitor into bankruptcy, since the latter cannot sustain the losses which the more powerful competitors can; by preventing the competitor's products from reaching consumers by monopolizing distribution outlets and blackmailing retailers who deal with the alternative produce; by using political and legal channels to stifle the competitor. This last brings in the role of the state in sustaining monopolies and outlawing competitors.

Yet some capitalist governments may seek to increase competition and break up monopolies.[9] The power of the state to do this, however, has been seriously eroded by a further development within monopoly capitalism: the formation of mutli-national corporations. Thus not only is there a movement towards monopoly but at present, in the Western world, major companies have bases in different countries of the world which results in an increase in their power. Their position *vis-à-vis* any one state is strengthened because, if a state places undue restrictions upon them, then they simply threaten to withdraw from that country (for example, Ford's continuous threat to withdraw from England during the 1970s). Since World War II, monopoly production and ownership by multi-national concerns have increased dramatically.[10]

The capacity of multi-nationals and other big corporations to determine prices above the real value of goods is one of the fundamental causes of modern inflation (see below). It does not follow, however, that the tendency for the rate of profit to fall has been reduced; on the contrary, it continues to intensify as more sophisticated machinery decreases the contribution of living labour involved in the production process. At this stage, the question arises: why couldn't monopoly and multi-national companies simply use their power to put a stop to this tendency? Why not act to slow down the technological revolution, the continuous replacement of people's labour by machines?

There are several factors involved here. Firstly, competition between companies still remains, even if prices are not reduced. A company which introduces new machinery may record a short-term increase in profitability, thereby forcing its competitor to do the same. Secondly, the replacement of people by machines reduces the unpredictability involved in the increasing wage demands and the industrial actions taken in support of them. Often a company will introduce very expensive machinery merely to reduce reliance on 'volatile' workers.

These pressures might normally have led to a breakdown of the capitalist process if it had not been for the increasing capacity to set prices at levels higher than real value. There is, however, a further factor: much of the cost of introducing the sophisticated machinery has been taken up by the state, through subsidies, depreciation and investment allowances. Thus the rate of profit has been artificially boosted by more state intervention (see below).

(b) *The tendency for the relative price of labour to fall*   This was the second major factor in Marx's theory of the collapse of capitalism. A distinction (first put forward by the economist Ricardo) must be made here between money wages and real wages. As Chris Starrs has pointed out, both Ricardo and Marx define real wages in terms of real value (the amount of labour contained in the commodities) which the worker can purchase with his wage.[11] Thus Marx says:

> The value of wages has to be reckoned not according
> to the quantity of the means of subsistence received by
> the workers, but according to the quantity of labour
> which these means of subsistence cost (in fact the
> proportion of the working day which he appropriates
> for himself), that is according to the *relative share* of
> the total product, or rather of the total value of this
> product, which the worker receives. It is possible that,
> reckoned in terms of use values (quantity of
> commodities or money), his wages rise as productivity

increases and yet the value of the wages may fall and vice-versa.[12]

In order to come to grips with this issue, we thus need to distinguish three concepts:

(i) the formal money value of wages. An increase need not result in any increase in the total goods the worker can buy, for the price of those goods may have risen through inflation;

(ii) the real money value of wages. This increases when the worker can purchase more commodities of use value than he could previously. Such increases may result in an increased standard of living for workers. Yet this may occur without any reduction in the rate of exploitation of workers;

(iii) the real value of wages, that is, the real value (in terms of labour time encapsulated in them) of the commodities which the wage can buy. Only an increase here would reduce exploitation.

Marx believed that the tendency for the real value of wages to decrease was inherent in capitalism. But even if this occurs, it is not inconsistent with an increase of the real money value of wages. While Marx sometimes recognizes this (as in the above quotation), in other places he argues that capitalism will lead to the impoverishment of the working class, to the point when they will, in desperation, seize economic power.[13] This would only occur, however, if a decrease in real money wages were to become prevalent.

What, in fact, has been the history of modern capitalism with respect to the value of wages? I divide this into four phases.

Phase I In early capitalism, the pressure was towards a reduction in the real value of wages and a reduction in the money value of wages. This resulted in the continuous impoverishment of the working class and in bitter struggles between unions and employers.[14] However, it was recognized by capitalist governments that reductions in real money wages aggravate the problem of over-production and under-consumption. Under the aegis of people like Keynes, the state intervened to increase real money incomes to the poorest workers and to improve working conditions. In so doing, it increased effective demand, since these poorer people tend to spend all of their income (see Chapter 2A).

Phase II The development of the welfare state has directly and indirectly contributed to the increase in real money wages. Thus with the development of a large bureaucracy or public service (which involves the employment of large numbers of people outside capitalist activity), the state could force up wages in the private sector by increasing wages to its own employees. Public-sector wage increases result in general increases, otherwise the threat of a movement of the most talented people from the private sector to the public sector becomes a painful reality for company managers. Thus as soon as the state begins to become a large employer of labour, a change occurs in the economic situation, a change in the character of the struggle between workers and capitalists. Whereas previously workers had directly gained increases in wages and conditions from struggles with private enterprise, they could now focus many of their struggles with the state as employers and, if they won concessions from the state, these could filter through to private companies. In fact that was the strategy which was used by many unions throughout the Western world especially in Australia in the 1960s. The state can also increase the real money value of wages indirectly, by taxing capitalists and those with high incomes in order to provide social services (such as health and education) which previously the workers paid for through their salaries.[15]

Phase III Following World War II, capitalists found it difficult to reduce real money wages.[16] A crisis was prevented, however, by the boom in consumer spending and the increase in effective demand. Keynesian policies were beginning to work. Capitalists were confident in investing in new technology and increasing productivity. Real money wages thus kept their levels, and even increased—notwithstanding an increase in the rate of exploitation.[17]

However, the increased standard of living accompanying the increase in consumer spending led to a massive rise in the material *expectations* of the working class. These expectations were contained, to some degree, by intensifying the division of the working class. Thus, criteria such as skill, education and managerial ability became the basis for increasing the differential wages of workers and forcing a division into 'middle' and 'lower' classes (see Chapter 2C). This trend was accentuated, in several Western countries, by the introduction of guest or migrant labourers prepared to take on dirty and low-paid jobs. In Australia, the introduction of migrant labour initially allowed for the increased material expectations of the 'middle class' to be met, without these material demands being generalized to all. (Many migrants came from poorer countries and were happy to receive wages which provided them with a higher standard of living; they did not recognize until later that, in relative terms, they were being used to bolster the material rewards of the 'middle class'.)

Another development in this phase was a further dramatic increase in the role of the state. Since, during the boom, both capitalists and workers were increasing their income (although not equally), the state was able to introduce further programmes and to expand its services. Indeed many leaders acted on the false assumption that the economic boom could last indefinitely, and that they could continue without altering the general character of the economy.[18]

Phase IV The attempts to divide the working class so as to contain the material expectations of the lower sector failed. As manual workers perceived that their neighbours who were engaged in white-collar occupations were living better and accumulating more personal property, their demands increased and they became more militant.[19] Furthermore, because of the level of social security achieved during the boom, workers were no longer motivated to perform their duties efficiently unless visible increases in material rewards were forthcoming. The working class as a whole was thus demanding an increasing share of generated wealth and, with industrial action, was achieving increases in real money wages. A reserve pool of unemployed workers (which had been a characteristic feature of capitalist economy used to frighten union leaders and workers) virtually disappeared with the boom years of full employment.[20] The working class also won substantial concessions with the increase in state services referred to above. The distribution of GNP between wages and profits began to be altered in the late 1960s, a process accelerated by promises made to the people by political parties eager to win the heart of the average voter by appealing to his pocket.

These increases in wages, combined with increasing technology, gave rise to a reduction in surplus value. Had capitalism still been in a competitive, rather than a monopoly stage, there is no question that this situation would have resulted in a depression of the classical kind as described by Marx. The fact of monopoly, however, prevented this from happening. The monopoly companies, seeing their profits reduced, and not wishing direct confrontations with workers, took the simple expedient of increasing prices. This situation gave rise to the following spiral:

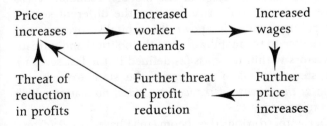

This is a simple representation of the spiral of *price-wage inflation*. Yet what is inflation? From the above remarks, it is clear—as Bruce McFarlane has noted[21]—that inflation is a *repressed* capitalist crisis. It is due to the attempt by capitalists to avoid direct confrontation with workers, by fixing prices and hence exchange values way above the (decreased) real value of goods. In the absence of competition monopoly capitalists could sustain prices at these levels. This means that there could be a decrease in the number of commodities produced, and yet an increase in prices—neither factor is governed by the market, but rather by the decisions of monopoly firms.[22] Thus there can be a decrease in growth in the economy (stagnation) and yet an increase in prices, followed by wage increases (inflation). These two phenomena, which according to Keynesian theory should not co-exist, are the major symptoms of the modern economic crisis.

While each capitalist acts from self-interest to increase the prices of his goods and sustain profit levels, the general result for the whole society is very serious. Workers' real money incomes are threatened, and tension mounts as they seek to attain catch-up awards. For capitalists, the capital generated from sales dramatically loses its value: new machinery and raw materials become much more expensive to buy. The value of money itself is seriously threatened. Fear grips both workers and capitalists under these conditions. Everyone turns to the state to steer the economy out of crisis and this general pressure on the state can be, as we shall see in Chapter 3C, the source of political crisis.

The hyper-inflation stage of the modern economic crisis produces increased solidarity amongst the different sectors of the ruling class. The powerful capitalist owners and managers turn to the mobilization of the political and bureaucratic sectors within the class (as defined in the last section). Drastic steps are taken to commit the state to reducing inflation *at the expense of the working class*, no matter which party is in power.

Furthermore, during the boom in Phase III, Western states had extensively increased state services in areas which indirectly benefited workers, such as health, education, pensions, etc. Once the crisis hit, governments were forced to act to protect profits and capital, while reducing inflation. At this stage, most Western governments seized on the theory, proposed by the conservative economist Milton Friedman,[23] that deficit spending by the state and rapid growth in the money supply were the major causes of inflation, and hence of the current crisis. This led to a rash of actions by Western governments to cut spending on welfare and other pro-worker programmes, while doing everything to protect and promote profit rates. The result has been a reduction of many services to the people and hence a decrease in the standard of the reproduction of life.

There are serious problems with this approach however. Firstly, the state cannot cut back social welfare and services beyond a certain level without seriously damaging the social and cultural fabric of society (see Chapters 4A and 6A on this). Secondly, these measures cannot in themselves resolve the economic crisis as a whole, even if they may make *some* impact on inflation—for they do not eradicate the causes of crisis.[24]

Many members of the ruling class believe that the above actions should be combined with state intervention to achieve a *massive* redistribution of economic resources in favour of capital. The strategy here may take a variety of forms, such as:

(i) Massive subsidies and allowances to companies from state revenue, thereby boosting capital's profits. This action is highly inflationary unless it is accompanied by cuts in the state's budget in the areas of welfare and general services.

(ii) Intervention by the state in pay disputes, so as to reduce real wages. This may take the form of using state power to directly attack workers and support capitalists in confrontations. The most dramatic example of this was the attempt by the British Labour government to reduce wages by fixing ceilings below the level of inflation in 1975–78.

The militancy of workers in rejecting cuts surprised even those union leaders who connived with the Callaghan government in this.

(iii) Increases in taxation and other state charges on workers, thereby effectively reducing the capitalist's burdens and moving them on to the shoulders of workers. Again, this can only work in periods when the government of the state is secure in its power. At election times, or in an unstable political atmosphere, the government would be unlikely to pursue such a blatantly unpopular course.

(iv) Cutting back state employment at a time when employment in the private sector is low or decreasing, thereby creating high levels of unemployment. The hope here is that, notwithstanding the cost in human and social terms, the working class will be disciplined and become 'responsible'.[25]

Attempts to introduce these measures in Australia and many Western countries have been strongly resisted. For it is difficult to impose a massive reduction in the living standards of the working class. The gains in goods and services made by this majority have been entrenched in their culture and non-economic social relations (see Chapter 4A). Furthermore, these have been reinforced by a political culture which claims to be 'democratic' and 'responsive' to the peoples' wishes.[26] Capitalism, in seeking to legitimize its exploitative behavior, has created human beings whose values and social identities place increasing material demands on both the economy based on profit and the state based on democratic forms. Under these circumstances, there are limits to any attempt by capital to increase exploitation by reducing real money wages. Hence I believe that the current economic crisis is, unlike earlier forms, deep and abiding.

The abiding character of the current economic crisis can be seen by the failure of the measures redistributing massive amounts of state moneys to boost the profits of capital. The reduction in real wages, plus the fear of unemployment, has had the consequence of a dramatic drop in consumer confidence together with an increase in bank savings. Hence, although profits have risen or been artificially boosted in most Western countries, the re-investment of capital in those countries has not been forthcoming because of the low demand. Thus unemployment has increased to the highest levels since the 1930s depression and the economic crisis shows no signs of abating.

I turn now to consider the specific character and dimensions of this crisis in Australia today.

B   THE CURRENT CRISIS IN AUSTRALIAN ECONOMY

In Australia in 1979, the official unemployment figure has risen to half a million people and other estimates put the figure much higher. Inflation, which was very high in 1975–76, abated at first under the tough policies of the Fraser government but then surged forward again in 1979. The economy continues to be stagnant, with much manufacturing potential severely under-utilized. While many companies have reported record profits, there seems to be little investment in areas which will create large increases in employment.[1]

The human dimensions of the tragedy of unemployment have become a focus of increasing concern. Robert Hawke, President of the ACTU explained this in an *Age* interview (February 1979):

> being unemployed carries a failure syndrome. This is most undesirable and can be very damaging socially. There is evidence from social workers, for instance, of increasing resort to crime and the use of hard drugs among young people. This reflects a sense of hopelessness. So it's not just an economic problem.[2]

Yet the unemployed are not the only ones suffering from the crisis. Most workers have had to accept cuts in real money wages over the last three years. At the same time, there have been drastic cuts in health, education and welfare services, thus reducing the value of the social wage to people generally.[3]

In order to understand how the crisis has developed, we must first consider two other matters: the different sectors of the Australian economy and the tensions between them; and aspects of Australia's economic development during the long boom (1946–1970) prior to crisis.

The structure of the Australian economy

As I indicated in the map of the ruling class (Chapter 2C), capitalist enterprises in Australia can be divided into the multi-national corporations, the large Australian companies such as BHP and CSR, and many small companies and businesses. This division gives us a vertical dimension in the analysis of the Australian economy, with the first two monopoly groups exercising enormous power compared to the small competitive enterprises which are constantly struggling for survival. Yet there is tension between the first two groups as well, a tension which places pressure on the government to introduce guidelines for Australian ownership of companies on the one hand and to relax that pressure on the other (see later in this section).

However, the Australian economy is also divided into what I shall call horizontal sectors, each concerned with separate areas of enterprise and having its own dynamism. I shall divide these into four major groupings: rural, manufacturing, banking and finance, and mining. Each of these sectors may place different pressures on the state, by demanding policies favouring their profit-making interests.

(a) *Rural industries* Up to the mid 1950s Australia's economy was heavily reliant on exports of rural products, particularly wool, wheat, canned fruits and meat. However by the early 1970s, rural exports had dropped dramatically, accounting for less than 50 per cent of the total.[4] This change was the result of highly protectionist policies on agricultural products by nations which had previously welcomed Australian imports: the problem became severe with Britain's entry into the EEC.[5]

(b) *Australian manufacturing* Production here was geared to local demand, which increased considerably during the period of the boom. However, these industries developed and survived only because of heavy protection from foreign competition through tariff barriers and quotas on foreign imports.[6] The result was that much Australian manufacturing capital could determine the quality and prices of goods without fear of being undercut by foreign products. Australian manufacturers thus became increasingly inefficient in their techniques of production and out of step with the more vigorous standards achieved in Europe, the US and Japan. This meant that, as tariffs were relaxed because of international pressures, many Australian firms found that they could not compete. The situation has become so serious that Peter Robinson, once editor of the *Financial Review*, believed it to be the main cause of 'The Crisis in Australian Capitalism'.[7]

(c) *Banking and finance* Banks, insurance companies and building societies developed into, and have remained, a monopoly clique, because of the actions of government. No licence for a new trading bank has been issued for forty years. The banks have achieved co-operative arrangements of such a high order that their campaigns promoting 'the virtues of competition between banks' are clearly dishonest. Insurance companies are also highly protected and integrated into the activities of the state by arrangements requiring these companies to invest large amounts of their income in government bonds.[8] Reflecting on these arrangements, Robinson concluded that the Treasury 'is an arch-proponent of protectionism and cartelism in the massive financial sector of the economy. It protects Australian banks from serious outside competition and colludes with them in imposing its own form of financial management of the economy'.[9]

Nevertheless, under these conditions the banks, insurance companies and other financial institutions reap enormous profits, which are generally not redistributed to the Australian people. Furthermore, the investments which this financial sector makes in other sectors of the Australian economy can be of enormous importance in the overall performance of the economic system as a whole.

(d) *The mining and raw materials industry*[10]   The situation in this sector is aptly summed up by the political economists, Brezniak and Collins:

> It was the mineral industry which, with an extra-ordinary growth rate from the mid-1960's, replaced much of the decline in rural exports. The output of this industry increased from \$A492 million in 1964 to \$A1867 in 1972, and the export of mineral products grew from less than \$230 million to \$A1450 million . . . Much of the expansion of this industry was through the operations of subsidiaries of multi-nationals, and towards the end of the boom years, the inflow of foreign capital into mining completely swamped capital inflows into other industries. In the five years from 1967 to 1972 alone, more than \$1000 million of direct investment poured into the mining sector, which was over twice the investment in manufacturing. And by 1972, this sector was 60 per cent foreign controlled.[11]

Thus, in an analysis of the Australian economy, we need to take into account the tensions of the different vertical and horizontal sectors. It is difficult to list all Australian companies on the basis of these sectors, because of the continuous changes in ownership which take place (shifts from locally-owned to foreign-owned are occurring constantly) and also because, as some companies own large shares of others, the chain of ownership is not easily traced.[12]

As these different sectors of capital develop, they place conflicting demands on the government. These conflicts seriously impair the unity of the ruling class. Indeed Connell claims that 'there is really no lobby that reflects the interests of businessmen in general. To get to the level of the collective interests of businessmen, one has to penetrate to a very basic institutional level: to the level of the institution of private property itself. At no other level is there unanimity in business: not even on an issue such as conceding wage demands to the unions'.[13] I would not go as far as this, for clearly there is unity in the ruling class on their goals: they all seek to maximize profits. As I have already argued, monopoly sectors can concede wage demands since they can pass these on in increased prices and while this is a lot more difficult for the small businessman facing competition, all firms seek to increase surplus value through greater exploitation. Thus while tactics against the working class may differ, the general thrust is similar because of the very structure of capitalist relations of productions.

Nevertheless, as Connell has documented, severe tensions may arise within the different sectors of the ruling class, making it even more difficult for the state to act in a united way to overcome crisis.[14] There are three major conflicts that need to be noted here. Firstly, there is the conflict between Australian big business and the multi-nationals. This conflict between monopolies results in divisions within both the Liberal and Labor parties (see Chapters 7C and 8) as to laws governing Australian ownership and control. Secondly, the manufacturing sector, favouring high protectionism, conflicts with the mining and rural sectors which want to bring tariff barriers down, thus increasing the trade-off between Australian agricultural goods and foreign manufactures. This conflict will be discussed below.

The third conflict is between small businesses and the monopolies. Although the political representatives of the ruling class are constantly making noises about the importance of small private enterprise and about the need to break up monopolies, this is rarely backed up by action. Geoffrey Walker, in his book *Australian Monopoly Law* summed up the situation to 1967 thus:

Australia is an interesting case study of the effects of unrestrained monopoly, for until recently it was one

of the few industrial countries in the world where a
laissez-faire policy towards monopolies and restrictive
trade practices had survived . . . the country has never
seen sustained effort at protecting the economy from
powerful combines, or ensuring equality of business
opportunity.[15]

Since then the Trade Practices Act has been introduced to
prevent such manoeuvres as price fixing. Its effect on the
degree of monopolization has been negligible. It has, however,
generated considerable debate within the Liberal Party (see
Chapter 5C). Compared with the other two conflicts, this third
one has been muted. Yet the fact that the interests of monopolies have dominated the political process has itself determined the direction of the crisis.

The post-war economic boom

From 1945 to 1970 Australia's economy experienced a sustained boom with increases in investment and in productivity. Real GDP grew at an average of 4.5 per cent per
annum.[16] While profits increased handsomely, workers
gained increases in real money wages, and a rise in standards
of living. Furthermore, there were considerable increases in
the state sector—in welfare and educational services and in
social security.

What were the factors involved in this boom? Firstly,
there was the increasing integration of the Australian economy
in the world capitalist system, which itself was undergoing
considerable change. The major aspect of this was the emergence of the United States as the leader and organizer of the
capitalist world after the destruction of Europe during World
War II. Through the World Bank, the International Monetary
Fund and other such agreements, the US was able to establish
the dollar as the basis of the international monetary system.
It was able to impose an order in the capitalist world by
regulating not only the monetary system, but the general
process of world trade. The capitalist economies boomed,
led by remarkable Japan which achieved an average increase

in GDP of 10.4 per cent per annum over the boom period.[17] Real growth was accompanied by a marked increase in world trade.

All this was achieved with extraordinarily low levels of unemployment, together with high levels of government spending on social and welfare services. Furthermore, inflation was low and prices relatively stable. As Bob Catley notes, this boom period 'has now assumed such golden proportions that even sectors of the labour movement regard its recreation as their final objective'.[18]

Yet the United States did not sustain this international order for nothing. US corporations began to penetrate the economies of the other capitalist countries and thus began a remarkable concentration of economic power.[19] American capital poured into the other growing capitalist countries, particularly into Japan and Germany. This situation resulted in a strengthening of the overall power of the multi-nationals and contributed to the high degree of monopoly in Western economies, noted in Chapter 2D.

Australia was also locked into this new international set-up. Both its exports and imports increased substantially. Imports from Japan rose from 1 per cent in 1952 to 17 per cent in 1972, while exports to Japan rose from 10 per cent of the Australian total to 31 per cent.[20] Foreign investment in Australia from the United States dramatically increased, while investment from British multi-nationals remained at a high level.[21] By 1970, this foreign capital was playing a major role in ownership and control of companies in Australia. At the seminar, 'Big Business in Australia', held by the Australian Institute of Political Science, Harold Bell showed that 'of the 12 companies with profitability over $10m there were 5 locally owned, 6 foreign owned or controlled, and 1 with significant overseas participation. Taking the 40 companies with profits in excess of $5m, there were 23 local, 15 foreign owned or controlled, and 2 with significant foreign participation'.[22]

The growth in world trade and the injection of foreign investment were significant causes of the post-war boom.

However, there were also important internal factors. There was the fact that World War II had transformed Australia's economy, giving it a stronger industrial base and making the nation more self-reliant in several major areas of production. After the war, demand for goods and services—which had been scarce—ensured that industrial production and new investment continued. However, while workers had been prepared to make sacrifices during the war, this was no longer so in the late 1940s and struggles by the union movement achieved important gains such as the forty-hour week.[23]

Once the economy was on a growth path, workers could sustain their standards of living and participate in the consumer boom. This was made possible because certain manufacturers took advantage of high tariff protection and produced a whole variety of consumer goods—particularly household items and motor cars. During such periods of full employment and growth, workers' power is at a maximum: yet worker militancy was low in the 1950s and early 1960s. Indeed the number of working days lost on strikes dropped dramatically to an average of 0.47 days per year.[24] This reduction in militancy meant that few gains were made by labour relative to capital. Furthermore, the relative distribution of incomes remained almost unchanged throughout the boom.[25] Thus profits were very healthy.

Several factors have been identified as responsible for the passivity of the working class during this boom period. Firstly, there was the ideological impact of the Cold War and anti-communist propaganda. Secondly, there was the degrading exploitation of the three million migrants who came to Australia, most of whom were employed in the dirty jobs. This factor is considered by some to have been the most crucial. John Collins, in his detailed analysis, demonstrated that by 1966 between 40 and 50 per cent of jobs in different manufacturing sectors were in migrant hands and concluded:

Immigration is important to Australian capitalism not only in providing workers to be exploited. It is also important because of its effects on wage levels within Australia. Full employment adds greatly to the bargaining power of the class vis-a-vis the employers and leads to increased money wages (so-called 'wage inflation'). An inflow of immigrant labour can offset this, especially if the migrants have no tradition of trade union organisation or are generally ignored by the Australian trade unions . . . immigration tends to lower both the level of wages and the rate at which wages increase.[26]

This factor was also responsible for the reorientation of native-born Australians into offices and away from manual labour. It was thus the basis of the stereotype of the 'middle-class' Australian and it was not 'proper' for such people to strike.

Although there was little trouble from workers during this period, there were serious conflicts between the different sectors of capital. The rural sector wanted tariffs reduced and more open trade. For manufacturing this would have been disastrous. John McEwen, Country Party leader and a shrewd conservative, hit upon a compromise: the tariffs could remain high, provided that the state subsidized the rural sector.[27] This would make up for the latter's real and imagined losses. It was an excellent idea; often it meant that the state would guarantee to buy a certain quantity of agricultural products, no matter what price it could get for them on local and overseas markets. Farmers, large and small, felt more secure. Meanwhile, manufacturers continued to build up uncompetitive industries behind tariff walls. The alliance worked out by McEwen lasted until the late 1960s when the rural sector began to link its interests to the spectacularly developing mining sector—both being opposed to the enormous protection given to manufacturing.

This conflict between the different horizontal sectors of capital was accompanied by another: between the multi-national sector and Australian capital. This conflict became serious, particularly after the spectacular collapse of the boom on mining shares on the Australian stock exchange. The conflict not only divided the political leaders of the ruling class (see Chapter 7C), it divided capitalists and managers as well. As Connell explains:

> Thus while some business men were hostile to foreign capital because of competition, others because of direct threats to their control of their own companies, and others were agitated about the question for electoral reasons, there were large sections of Australian business which had a definite interest in the maintenance of the flow of investment. There was a structural tension within the class of owners and its most active section, the managers and directors of companies.[28]

The other significant feature of the boom was the increasing role of the Federal and State governments in providing the infrastructure, such as roads, railways and power supplies, for the new industries. The large numbers of migrant workers needed housing, suburban roads, water, sewerage as well as educational, health and welfare services. Catley sums up the boom period so:

> It would be difficult to exaggerate the extent to which contemporary Australia was transformed, and in some senses created by this boom. The population almost doubled, the state capital cities more than doubled in size; new industries were created and new modes of transport—particularly road and air—became dominant; the education system was reconstructed; the capital became a city with a new industry, government; city centres were rebuilt with monuments to finance capital; levels of consumption leapt; and a new medium, television, rose to ascendency in the creation and recreation of ideology.[29]

Australian inflation—international and local factors

The United States' domination of the capitalist economies began to wane as other nations, notably Germany and Japan, achieved levels of growth much higher than that of America. An imbalance of trade was sustained by huge deficits in the budget of the US. The enormous cost of the Vietnam war was also borne by printing more US dollars to pay for it. At the same time, other nations were engaged in deficit spending. The result was an enormous growth in the world's money supply. The value of money was supposed to be kept constant by fixed exchange rates with the US dollar, which in turn was fixed to gold. When, however, individuals and nations began to demand gold, the US realized it would lose its valuable reserves. It created an international monetary crisis in 1971 by breaking the link between the dollar and gold.[30]

There were two immediate consequences: first, a sharp increase in demand for durable goods and property among investors—which created inflation throughout the world; second, a large increase in money available as capital for investment. Thus large amounts of money poured into Australia during 1970–72. As Brezniak and Collins report:

> Foreign investment in 1970–71 was $1399 million; more than double the $675 million that entered Australia in 1969–70, and stayed high at $1306 million in 1971–72. Much of this was speculative capital—the so-called 'hot money' that flowed into Australia in anticipation of currency realignments in the wake of breaking of the ties of the US dollar to gold in August 1971. A significant amount of this money found its way into the skyscraper and mining shares boom of the early 1970's . . . These factors were instrumental in the large increase in the domestic money supply, which had shot up from 6.8 per cent in the year 1970–71 to 10.5 per cent in 1971–72 and 25.7 per cent in 1972–73.[31]

In addition to the international factor, the economy was faced with increased demands for more wages arising from a new level in union militancy. The materialist expectations of the people had been raised considerably during the 1960s. As industrial action was seen to achieve results, more groups engaged in it. The level of union membership and activity increased (see Chapter 6D). Because the demand for labour was still high, the workers were able to achieve, through strikes and arbitration, significant increases in real money wages. This had a dual consequence. Small competitive enterprises were squeezed in their profitability; many were bankrupted.[32] Larger monopolies (particularly the multi-nationals which could draw on reserves until matters improved) simply passed on increases in prices. The price-wage spiral (see Chapter 3A) hit with a vengeance in Australia.

To these two inflation pressures was added a third. McMahon, Prime Minister in 1972, panicked in the face of the impending election defeat for his government and reversed his strategy of keeping a tight rein on government spending (see Chapter 7C). He introduced a budget with a deficit of $215 million. He did not win the election—but he fuelled inflation further.

Economic crisis intensified
By the time the Whitlam government took office in December 1972, the consequences of the increased investment—namely greater economic growth and decreasing unemployment—were beginning to show. However, in response to the Labor government's election and its proposed policies, foreign investment dropped off sharply in 1972–73. The situation was made more complex by the fact that since inflation was still running at 6 per cent, the Whitlam ministry introduced a 25 per cent across-the-board tariff cut to stabilize prices.[33] This was premised on the view that inflation was due primarily to high demand and not to price fixing by monopoly companies. It proved to be false. The investment of 1971 and 1972 became a crisis of over-produc-

tion. There were large increases in stocks of all kinds of goods, which could not quickly be sold at profitable prices. To counter this, companies cut back production and released their accumulated stocks at a slower rate, but at higher prices. In Australia, they could do this because of the high degree of monopoly and collaboration of major industrial firms. The result was, of course, decreased growth and increases in both unemployment and inflation.[34] From the middle of 1974 to December 1975, unemployment in Australia more than doubled and inflation hit 17 per cent.

While these phenomena were universal in the capitalist world, in Australia the crisis was deeper and more complex. For, firstly, Australia's manufacturing industry—long protected at completely uncompetitive levels by world standards —came under severe stress with the tariff cuts.· Local business had to squeeze its profits severely in order to compete. Secondly, the militancy of the working class was continuing and intensifying under Labor. Indeed, 1974 saw the highest level of industrial unrest and strikes since before the Great Depression. This pressure for wage increases was supported by several senior Labor ministers.[35] Yet they had no plan to change the structure of economy to accommodate the change in the relative strengths of labour and capital.

The results were predictable. Inflation eroded profits. Fear of unemployment led more people to save and this, in turn, led to a further decrease in demand. Profitability itself was hit both through cutbacks in the value of profit and through the increased costs of wages. It was also hit by the need to compete with overseas goods. A large number of companies, which earlier in the Labor government's reign had recorded high profits, suffered losses. There was a dramatic rise in business bankruptcies.[36]

A struggle ensued within the Labor government itself, between those who insisted on wage reductions and cutbacks in government services, and those who resisted this, seeing it correctly as an attack on the working-class gains which had been made. The first group won (see Chapter 8 for details) and under Hayden instituted a tough budget—cutting back many major areas of welfare, reducing wages and subsidizing capital in areas such as the car industry. Thus, in just one budget, a large redistribution back to capital was achieved.

This gesture to capital did not help the Labor government. It was routed after a massive ruling-class campaign against it. Unfortunately for Australian workers, the party's leaders had no plan to achieve a transformation of the capitalist economy and to introduce strategies to protect jobs and workers' standards of living. In the end, it not only secured its own demise; it also gave Malcolm Fraser the elements of the strategy to use in support of capital, a strategy which he implemented more ruthlessly.

The Fraser strategy will be discussed in detail in Chapter 9. For the moment, we should note the following elements in it:
(i) substantial subsidies and allowances to all companies to stimulate new investment, particularly for export markets;
(ii) substantial reductions in all areas of state services—education, health, welfare funds for Aborigines, urban development;
(iii) pressure on the Arbitration Commission, on employers and on public service boards for reductions in real wages;
(iv) direct support for the mining and rural sectors of capital, as against the manufacturing sector. Here Fraser has attempted to expand export industries while moving carefully on the restructuring of Australian manufacturing.

In this latter exercise he had generated further tension within the ruling class. Many capitalists want some form of expansionary policy, based on increases in consumer demand. Since Fraser has put a damper on wages, such an increase in domestic demand seems unlikely, unless stimulated by the state itself. Yet Fraser has not been prepared to carry out this step.

The result of Fraser's policies is that profits for major monopoly companies have soared, while many small businesses have been bankrupted. The increased profits have not, however, shown up in increased investment for the purposes of growth. For demand is still low. Even if it increases, it is more profitable and safer to raise prices than to fall for the trap of over-production. Consequently, employment within both the state sector and the private sector has been cut back.

After three years of Fraser rule, there seems to be no light at the end of the tunnel for the working class: the prospects facing them seem very gloomy—more unemployment, more insecurity, more reductions in real wages and greater pressure from the bosses.[37] For sectors of the ruling class, the increase in profits (due mostly to state subsidies and handouts) must be seen as satisfactory under the circumstances. However, for the future of the Australian economy as a whole, the signs are alarming. For Fraser is relying on the hope that there will be new investment which will create new jobs and contribute to economic growth. Yet unemployment is not expected to change for the better by such wishful thinking. As Robinson puts the matter:

> In September 1978 the Minister for Employment and Industrial Relations, Tony Street, formally confirmed the extent and complexity of Australia's unemployment crisis—and by implication, admitted the inadequacy, even the irrelevance of the government's policies for economic recovery. The strategy for economic recovery enunciated in the tough 1978–79 budget lay in tatters, since it was based on the presumption that recovery, renewed economic growth, a gradual restructuring of industry and an expansion of employment opportunities would all flow from a victory over inflation.[38]

The Fraser government has failed to realize that huge new export markets are unlikely to open up for Australia; that most of the investment of profits is in labour-replacing machinery, and will not create jobs, but will often destroy them; and that many companies, Australian and multi-national, are seeking to invest overseas in Third World countries, in which labour is cheaper and more heavily exploited. These points are also made by Robinson.[39] However, he does not recognize that these things are symptoms of the deeper crisis in capitalism to which we have referred in Chapter 3A, in particular the development of a materialist culture.

We have thus reached the stage described in the last section: under-production, price fixing by monopolies, rationalization of the work force through automation and new pressures on workers (rapidly increasing organic composition of capital) plus low demand, heavy unemployment and unfulfilled materialist expectations from the working class. The economic crisis continues.

C POLITICAL CRISIS IN THE STATE

In the Prologue, I indicated that the causes of crisis in the state arise from the diverse demands which are made on it and the contradictory responses which it may give to such demands. These contradictory responses are due to the fact that the modern state is not a monolithic entity; it consists of several components or sectors.[1] The components of the modern state are often said to be the government, the parliament, the public service and the judicial system. I have discussed some of the features of these formal structures in Australia in Chapter 1D.

However, in my analysis, I would like to concentrate on four *functions* of the state. It is important to distinguish these different types of activity if we are to appreciate the contradictory pressures within the modern state. There is also a central administrative sector which attempts to co-ordinate the other sectors through, for example, the allocation of state moneys. The sectors are schematically represented on p. 117.[2]

Considering each of these sectors in turn, we have first the so-called productive sector of the state, 'productive' in

Sectors of the modern state

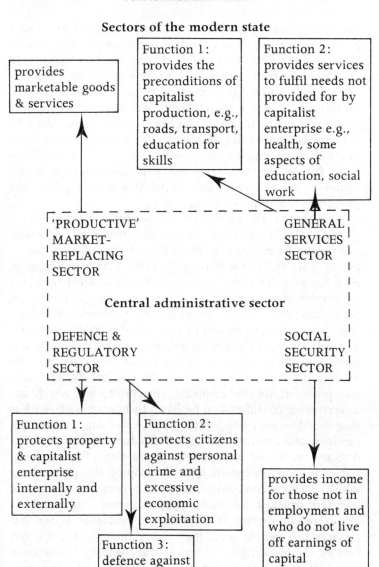

the sense used by market economists, that is, it provides a service which people pay for directly; examples are Telecom Australia and the Gas and Fuel Corporation of Victoria. In this way the state can be said to be engaged in a market-replacing function.[3] It is market-replacing because there is no inherent reason why telephone services or the supply of gas should not be in the hands of private enterprise. Here the state provides a service, people pay for it on the basis of how much they use, and it is supposedly run at sufficient profit to fund future capital works and expenses—though if, for example, the Gas and Fuel Corporation makes a loss, the government is required to make it up.

Next there is the *general services* sector of the state which provides a wide variety of things—all of which are important, yet people do not pay for them directly (within the market place), only indirectly (through taxation). Thus while users may pay a small fee, the main costs of such services are borne by general state revenue. The services sector performs two main functions: one, it provides the preconditions or infrastructure for production in a capitalist economy (thus, for example, it builds roads, maintains transport services and provides education in skills and technology essential to modern production); two, it provides services to *fulfil needs* not provided for by capitalist enterprise, but which are nevertheless considered to be basic to human welfare (thus this function provides health, social work and counselling services, and controls that aspect of education which is not directly orientated towards the production of work skills, but is instead concerned with developing the person as a whole).[4] This second function of the general services sector is often attacked for being 'unproductive'. Although its critics recognize that it is producing valuable goods and services that people need, they resent the fact that it is not part of the market mechanism of the economy in the same way that the services which are paid for directly. It is not, therefore, centrally guided by the profit motive.[5]

Of course, there is no economic reason why something

which is part of the general service available to all could not become a service which people have to pay for directly. Thus, in some countries education and health services are a privilege, not a right. Each individual pays for them from his own pocket; they are not subsidized through general taxation. In these cases, the service is not generally available to poorer people. In Australia, while the state provides education and health services for all, the quality of service varies dramatically and does depend on the capacity to pay. This results in a *de facto* disadvantage for poorer people, particularly in education.

The third sector carries out the regulatory functions of the state, the enforcement of laws by means of courts, police forces, traffic officers, prison officials, regulatory agencies, etc. There are various aspects to this. This sector of the state makes and enforces law which protect the foundations of economy, viz., the accumulation of private property and the dynamics of capitalist enterprise. These laws range from those governing property relations (such as the very important right to inheritance) to laws concerning industrial disputes.[6] It is also concerned with the laws and regulations which protect citizens against personal crime (such as murder and rape) and, to some degree, against excessive economic exploitation (such as laws controlling industrial production under unsafe and unhealthy conditions).[7] Finally, it is responsible for defence against external aggressors. This is the prime responsibility of the army, navy and air force of the state. A central issue that arises from a radical perspective is: will a time arise when the defence forces are employed against their own people, to put down rebellions and demonstrations? (See Chapter 9A.)

The functions of this sector are extremely important for the continued integration of a modern Western society. People must be regulated to conform to laws which respect the general structure of economy, particularly the right to accumulate wealth. Similarly, because of the tremendous social problems created by such societies, tough laws are instituted to prevent personal injury to others. Only the laws and regulations governing economic exploitation are controversial: these are often attacked as barriers to economic growth and competitiveness. In general, however, they serve the economic system since they attempt to ensure that abuses against workers remain within controllable limits.[8] Notice that this sector of the state employs a large number of people in activities which are not productive either in the narrow economic sense or in the sense of satisfying human needs.

The fourth sector of the state is that which provides services in the form of direct money grants to people, that is, social security in the form of pensions, unemployment relief, sickness benefits, etc. These benefits were introduced by the so-called welfare state in order to ensure that those people who could not find employment, or who could not work, or who were engaged in studies preparatory to employment, had sufficient income to survive. This is a very important factor in ensuring mass support for the state and the whole system. For if the unemployed and unemployable were forced to beg or starve, this might generate demands for replacing the economic system. Social security is, therefore, the price which the economic system pays for legitimacy and political stability. This sector also requires the employment of a large number of public servants, whose functions are to screen applicants for eligibility and to ensure that speedy payments are made to genuine applicants.

From the above it can be seen that the bulk of the labour employed in the state sector is not productive labour, in the sense of generating profit. The services provided by the last three sectors are not part of the capitalist production process, although they may indirectly benefit and support that process. These state services are not market-replacing except in the first sector. The early capitalist state was much smaller and employed fewer people—its major function was to provide and enforce laws which ensured the defence of the country, the protection of private enterprise and the prevention of personal crime. There was little by way of general services; social security was virtually unknown. The growth of the various sectors and functions of the state has, therefore, changed the general character of Western society itself.[9] This change has been a significant one for the private sector of economy. For the capitalist forces have had to come to grips with a society in which a substantial number of people (up to 50 per cent in some Western countries) are employed by state bodies of one kind or another. Their labour is, therefore, not directly exploited for the generation of profit.

Yet this growth, combined with the democratic ideology which legitimizes it, has given rise to tremendous problems for the modern state. One source of problems is the tension between different sectors within the state itself. Should more be spent on defence or more on education? Should pensions to the old be increased, or should they be cut out or reduced? Should police forces be expanded in view of the increase in crime? The governments and bureaucracies of the state have a large number of decisions to make which affect the general allocation of resources within these sectors. The way in which these resources are distributed depend on *value judgements* by the government and the central administrative sector.[10] These judgements are made in response to the contradictory demands on the state.

The state funds its services through capital which can be generated from direct taxes on workers and companies, indirect taxes on goods and private services, taxes on accumulated wealth and capital gains and profits made by state-owned market-replacing enterprises. Since, in many Western societies, the last two measures are kept to a minimum (thus Australia has no capital gains tax and few profit-making state enterprises), the bulk of state revenue is generated from the private sector of the economy.[11] Since socialization of profitable enterprises is rarely carried out, and since there are few taxes on wealth (to introduce them would threaten the structure of capitalist economy), the state can only increase its services if it intervenes either to increase direct or indirect taxes on workers, or to tax companies more heavily, or engages in more and more deficit spending. All these measures provide the basis for a crisis in the state.

In the period of growth beginning with the end of World War II until the end of the 1960s, many Australians, relying on neo-Keynesian economics, believed that there could be increasing development of the public sector (i.e., government services of all kinds) and that sufficient money to pay for this expansion could be raised without threatening the general structure of an economy based on profit. This belief could be maintained during a period of full employment and little inflation.[12] In the 1970s, when both inflation and unemployment hit hard, this was exposed as an illusion.

Yet if the state refuses to change the general character of the economy, it is severely restricted in its capacity to respond to demands from the people. On the one hand, the state cannot pay for the increased services by indefinitely increasing taxation on individuals, for it then faces two unpalatable consequences. Firstly, individuals may rebel by withdrawing mass support from the government, or even the state as a whole. An example of the rebelliousness which excessive taxation on individuals can bring is the so-called California tax revolt, where people cut back taxes by referendum. A second consequence is that individuals cut back on their spending on goods and services, since their disposable income is decreased by tax increases. This results in a drop in consumer demand, which can affect sections of the capitalist economy very severely.[13]

There is also a limit to the amount of taxation that the government can impose upon companies without undermining the general structure of capitalist economy. Thus if companies are taxed beyond a certain point, they would simply react by concluding that it is not profitable to work in Australia and invest their money elsewhere. They could also seek to sustain profit levels by rationalizing measures, which usually involve cutting back on staff—either by replacing workers with machines or by simply pressurizing the remaining workforce to produce the same goods with fewer workers. Both of these measures result in increased unemployment; which also leads to a reduction in mass support for the government or the state as a whole.[14]

Hence the modern Western state cannot indefinitely call on the economy to provide the resources to pay for its maintenance and expansion. Conversely, it cannot simply cut back all these services and dismantle the whole structure. For the society has grown accustomed to the provision of a wide variety of services by the state sector. There can be no wholesale dismantling of all or most of these services without a tremendous loss of public support for the government and the system as a whole.[15]

Habermas claims that it is very difficult for the modern state to balance these various demands on it. This is because a contradiction in values exists within the state. It can be shown thus: as the welfare state develops, the demand for government services increases considerably (see Chapter 4). There are definite demands made on the state within a democratic culture for increased *equality* in the provision of health, education and other such services. At the same time, there are demands from the economy to provide the conditions for profit and investment, that is, for an increase in economic *inequality* (see Chapter 2). This tension becomes very serious during a time of economic recession, such as that afflicting Western nations in the 1970s.

James O'Connor, in his book *The Fiscal Crisis of the State*, argues that, in order to cope with these pressures, states will be faced with increasing budget deficits. The situation is made worse when growth in state expenditures (in order to keep pace with inflation and to continue to fulfil at least some demands for state services) outstrips growth in the economy as a whole.[16] Faced with this situation, many governments make cutbacks in public expenditure, particularly in the social security and general services sector. These sectors are seen as inimical to capitalist enterprise and are constantly under attack from conservatives.

However, as Habermas points out, there is a limit to the

action which a modern state can take to reduce these sectors, for it is dependent upon wider public support or legitimation.[17] What would happen if unemployment benefits were cut out completely? The unemployed would be forced to find some means of support in a system where few jobs were available. This could lead to rebellions, mass demonstrations, violence and a resultant undermining of the legitimacy of the state. Furthermore, even if these 'disturbances' could be contained, it would require substantial strengthening of police forces (which may involve almost as much state expenditure as would be saved by cutbacks). Thus it would not be a sensible move to attempt to completely abolish various social welfare benefits. However, the rate of benefit can be fixed so that it is not adjusted to match the inflation rate, thereby cutting the benefit. Here it becomes difficult for people to live on the unemployment benefits provided, but not impossible. There could still be anti-government activity, but it would be at a lower level.

Even significant reductions in welfare and social services may not resolve the fiscal crisis of the state during economic crisis. For increased unemployment and decreased growth leads to a reduction in the gross receipts which the state can tax to fund its own services. An example of this is Mr Fraser's economic manoeuvres during 1977–79. After offering a small tax cut aimed at reviving the economy (and winning the election), the government was faced with a massive deficit. This, in turn, forced it to impose a tax surcharge in 1978, supposedly for one year. However, the deficit again grew: Fraser was thus forced to keep the tax surcharge indefinitely.[18] There were also ominous signs that further cuts would be made in education and welfare expenditure. The popular support of the Liberal government has consequently plummeted. Habermas believes this kind of situation to be general in Western capitalist societies. Under the pressure of the economic crisis, the government is apt to act in an irrational and contradictory fashion. Habermas calls this situation a *rationality* crisis in the state: there is an irrationality in the way in which a government, and/or the state, manages the different sectors within its domain and the economic and socio-cultural systems outside it. I call this a *state political crisis*—for it normally leads to loss of support for the government forces.[19]

The problem is that the state is required to steer the economy towards more growth and profitability, while at the same time sustain, or even increase, the level of state services. Yet, generally, it is restricted to actions within the existent economic framework: it usually does not challenge the general character of capitalist economy. The problem is compounded by the fact that during economic crisis, there is a dramatic increase in social problems. An army of social workers is then required to curb the occurrence of crime, drug addiction, juvenile delinquency, suicides etc., when such problems become prevalent in a culture, as will be shown in Chapter 4. These social problems demand urgent attention and also drain the finances of the public sector.[20]

Economic and rationality crises tend to reinforce each other. For when economic crises arise, the government(s) of the state tend to panic and bring in well-tried formulas to ameliorate the situation, usually, as we have seen, by cutbacks on public spending in social security and general services. However, the measures a government adopts with respect to public expenditure are theoretically subject to public approval. Thus the government is restricted by the consequences of its actions on mass support. The removal of support can take place at two levels: either a rejection of the government of the time (which may result ultimately in a change of the governing party) or the feeling that any alternative government could provide no real change to the structure. In this latter case an undermining of the legitimacy of the whole state is possible.[21] This is not to deny that with massive support from the media for the policy of the government (as occurs in Australia), the people could be persuaded that the cutbacks are necessary and not withdraw support on that account alone.

However the situation in capitalist economies is more serious. For the causes of the present economic crisis will not be eradicated simply by cutting the budget deficit of the state. Cuts in the deficit may lead to a reduction in inflation, but that, in itself, will not eradicate the other symptoms of crisis—heavy unemployment, lagging investment and stagnation.

Thus, in Australia, in the last three years there have been large reductions in the expenditure of the state in services and welfare (although little reduction in the overall budget). State moneys have been moved from services and state employment to direct handouts to companies in the form of subsidies and allowances.[22] This redistribution of wealth, employing the power of the state, involves a change in the relations between labour and capital. The profitability of many companies has consequently increased. Yet there has been little increase in investment, little growth in the economy. Reduction in government services has been accompanied by a marked increase in unemployment. The reduction in real wages has not, as some expected, led the private sector to employ more people. Hence the economic crisis continues.

Habermas believes that there is a tendency for economic crisis to become legitimation crisis—a withdrawal of support for the system as a whole. However, I believe that this is not necessarily so. For, in a party democracy, it is possible to withdraw support, not from the state as a whole, but only from the governing party within the system.[23] This is a very important safety valve within the Western state. Thus a state political crisis may force a change of government before a serious undermining of legitimacy has occurred. Sometimes, however, a government persists with an irrational policy, even to the point of undermining its own legitimacy. I shall offer two examples in later chapters to support this view: the Liberal government's persistence with the Vietnam war and the Labor government's economic strategy in 1974.

The political crises in Australia will be discussed in Part

III of this book. For the moment, we must turn to consider other aspects of the current crisis, namely those in the socio-cultural system and in legitimation processes.

II
Australian Society and the Problem of Legitimacy

4

The Socio-Cultural System and Motivation Crisis

I have already suggested that intertwined with the current economic crisis in Western society is a serious crisis in the socio-cultural system. To understand this crisis, we need first to consider the general character of the social structure of society, and in particular the extent to which these structures fashion a meaningful social identity for people in society.

A SOCIAL IDENTITY AND ITS BREAKDOWN

Normally, each person within a social system has a social identity, a set of social roles which he (or she) adopts. He might see himself as a teacher, a father, a sportsman, or as having a certain status within the community, and so forth. These different roles he adopts go to form a complex entity which constitutes his social identity.

Each social role usually involves specific rules; for example, there are specific rules that a bride in our culture must follow. But, of course, there are many cases where we adopt roles in which we do not make conscious reference to the rules; we have already accepted those rules and internalized them in our own being. The way one behaves towards one's parents, towards one's teachers, or—if one is a teacher—towards one's students, are common cases of internalized rules.

What is the significance of social identity and the social roles connected with it? Why do sociologists and social theorists talk about these as intricate parts of the social system? The reason is, I believe, because they give meaning to human activity.[1] A person's life has meaning to the extent that that person has a social identity and is able to perform various roles in a satisfactory fashion. This definition of meaningfulness is an important one for a culture.

I shall return to this point presently, but first consider this problem: what are the processes through which one acquires a certain social identity? Other persons within the culture and/or society as a whole determine the social identity that one has and the roles which one will pursue. The human being grows up with an identity fashioned by parents, teachers and peers who imbue in him/her the values and norms of the social system as a structural whole. I shall discuss here the view of Emile Durkheim,[2] because his theory of social identity seems the most illuminating and because it is the theory on which Habermas bases his concepts of motivation and legitimation crises, which I employ in my analysis.

Durkheim believes that the social identity of the individual is provided thus:

Society as a whole specifies the central social roles one is to perform and the meaning one attaches to those roles. Durkheim conceives of this dimension of social determination in terms of a continuum, whose opposite poles are egoism and altruism:

Degree of social differentiation

$$\longleftarrow \qquad\qquad\qquad\qquad \longrightarrow$$

EGOISM	ALTRUISM
Excessive individuation of self from society	Excessive identification of self with society

This allows Durkheim to speak of two different kinds of society. Firstly a society may 'produce' individuals who are essentially the same in that they are all capable of performing most of the roles which society requires of them. In such a society, there would be a minimal economic division of labour and little need for specialization. Each person (of the same sex and age) is theoretically capable of replacing any other. In this society, therefore, there is *minimal social differentiation*: the priority of the whole over the parts pervades all aspects of the society. Durkheim calls this a society with a 'mechanical solidarity'. Persons in such a situation would be in a state of altruism, that is, their individual identity is identical to that of the collective consciousness of the society.

Secondly, a society may produce individuals who have specialized roles to play as in modern industrial societies where there is considerable economic division of labour. Thus we have society creating individualism; such a society is ascribed an *'organic solidarity'*.[3] When such social differentiation reaches an extreme, we have the opposite of altruism, namely, egoism.

Durkheim also believes that society decrees the kinds of values the individual should hold, the kinds of goals to be pursued and the expectations to be held for the achievement of those goals. Again, we can conceive of two possibilities which constitute extreme ends of a continuum. The individual, on the one hand, could find every goal, value, expectation, etc., determined by society with little or no choice available to him. Individual autonomy would therefore be virtually non-existent. This is the situation of *fatalism* and again it is predominant in societies characterized by mechanical solidarity. In contrast to this, at the other pole, there is the situation of *anomie*. Here, rather than there being excessive determination of values, goals, etc., there are insufficient determinations, or conflict between those determinations, so that the extent of social integration is affected. This occurs primarily in societies with organic solidarity.

Thus Durkheim states: 'Society awakens in us the feeling of the divine. It is at the same time a Commandment which imposes itself and a reality qualitatively superior to the individuals which calls forth respect, devotion, adoration'.[4] The quality of sacredness is, however, not attached directly to its source—society as a whole—but rather to a collective and transcendent force: the god or gods of religion. Thus it is religion and religious philosophies (what Habermas calls 'traditional world views') which, until the latter part of the twentieth century, have performed the role of reinforcing the commands of society, in its attempt to give each person a sense of individual worth, while integrating him into a whole. This religion gave to man a system of practices, rites, etc., 'which is turned towards action which it demands and regulates'.[5] Thus the individual was given goals, values, ideals, etc., by which his/her life was regulated, for they were tied to the metaphysical significance of life, as conceived in that culture.[6]

This thesis on social integration is well illustrated in Durkheim's famous discussion of suicide. There are three kinds of suicide, corresponding to the three positions, egoism, anomie and fatalism. Egoistic suicide results from 'excessive individuation': the individual becomes a 'mystery to himself, unable to escape the exasperating and agonizing question: to what purpose?';[7] he no longer feels he has a meaningful place in society or the cosmos. Durkheim describes this absence of society and its laws so: 'If this dissolves, if we no longer feel it in existence and action about and above us, *whatever is social in us is deprived of all objective foundation*'.[8] Man, then, requires something which transcends him and enforces his sense of being. Under excessive egoism, he loses this and suicide can result.

A similar situation occurs in the case of anomie. Here the individual's social identity is tied to the status he has achieved within society in terms of the goals he is allowed to pursue and the expectations (also given by society) that he has of achieving those goals. When these expectations are frustrated, he feels that life/society has deceived him. This leads to melancholy, and a 'more or less irritated disgust with life'. This anomie, the feeling of the total lack of direction and purpose of life, may also result in suicide.

Both excessive egoism and anomie lead to a breakdown of

one's social identity. From the political perspective, the interesting case is not that of particular persons who are driven to suicide, but rather the case of the majority who somehow manage to cope with egoism and anomie in a society like ours with its excessive individuation. For we live in an age of extreme individualism, when private 'freedom' is pursued as a major value. Note, for example, the enormous changes in sexual mores in the last twenty years—from rules determined by society to a complete do-your-own-thing philosophy. This situation puts many individuals into a state of anxiety. On the one hand, people have greater choice: on the other hand, they have feelings of guilt, dread, not quite knowing whether what they are doing is right.[9]

In earlier times the particular roles and goals set for individuals in society were reinforced by an appeal to religion. How one should behave in one's life, the general purposes of one's life, and the very meaning of life itself were determined by religion. When used in this fashion, religion was a particularly effective tool for cementing the social order,[10] because it offered a plausible world-view, a metaphysical explanation of life. It told one, not only what the general purpose of one's life ought to be but also the meaning of death, and the meaning of suffering. It gave one 'strength' to stand up, to accept setbacks and the frustration of one's expectations.

However, as the philosopher Nietzsche foresaw, Christian religion has died in Western societies of the twentieth century.[11] By this, he means simply that the majority no longer believe in a religious world-view and therefore do not determine their life goals and values in accordance with religious principles. The physical sciences have given us many explanations of phenomena, and of the universe, in which God appears to be redundant. It seems that physical and biological science could explain everything, including human behaviour.[12]

This 'scientific' world-view has given rise to a new concept of man. However this conception that we have of ourselves is one which gives much less meaning to life than the previous religious conception. One of the major differences here concerns the problem of death. Thus when I die, the religious conception offers me heaven, whereas the non-religious conception offers 'the end'. According to existential philosophers, this latter conception changes social life dramatically.[13] Whereas we had a tight rein on the sort of general goals which people were pursuing, now we open up all possibilities. 'Everything', says Dostoevsky, 'is possible if there is no God'.[14]

As a consequence of this, it becomes more difficult for society to enforce and legitimate roles and rules—many of which can appear arbitrary. To compensate for this, society has relaxed, abandoned or changed many values, so as to reinforce one new overall general goal: the pursuit of pleasure through material goods. Meaning in people's lives now takes a new form—ethical hedonism. This however, is widely perceived as being incapable of providing sufficient social integration.

This development of a culture in which the basic value is the pursuit of pleasure for its *own* sake has been identified as a major focus of the current crisis in Western society by several analysts.[15] Yet they differ markedly as to the social and political implications of the crisis. In what follows, I shall contrast two views—those of John Carroll and Habermas. Both are concerned with the problems of how social identities are provided for individuals, and how those individuals come to perform roles which maintain the basic institutions, and hence the integration, of society.

The Australian sociologist, John Carroll, describes modern culture as remissive-hedonistic.[16] He explains:

> At the moral level, remission represents forgiveness of all sins; at the instinctual level, release from all controls . . . Objective grounds for guilt are being abolished; no one and nothing is to blame, the only responsibility borne by the individual is that he choose

his pleasures successfully. The Puritan goals of ascetic control, sensual renunciation and high sublimation, are giving way to the anti-pagan god of polymorphous perversity, of prolific, uncensored indulgence of impulse.[17]

According to Carroll, this dominant influence in modern culture is not only immoral, but creates a serious problem of integration for society. For many individuals still retain vestiges of the previous culture, that of puritanism. Carroll paints a picture of the puritan in noble terms: he was concerned with the 'spiritual intensity' of life; he had both passion and self-control; he pursued a vocation to which he was deeply committed; he took personal responsibility before God and man for his actions. Thus, the 'cardinal socio-cultural problem' of contemporary Western society becomes 'how individuals with inherently puritan character dispositions can adapt to their chosen hedonist ideology'.[18]

However, this way of posing the problem suggests that the two types of ideologies and values are the only possibilities. Indeed, as one reads Carroll's description of the two forms, one expects him to call for a return to puritanism and all it stands for. However, he rejects this 'conservative' response, and argues instead for a new, though unspecified, puritan-remissive ideology.[19] It is not clear, however, what the redeeming features of the remissive type are.

The problem is that Carroll has not placed sufficient weight on the other side of modern hedonist and materialist culture, even though he clearly recognizes it, as in the following passage:

... in the public domain, the erosion of the Protestant ethic has been paralleled by the gargantuan proliferation, to a degree unforeseen even by Marx, in individual size and overall range of practice, of bureaucratically organized institutions. The power of these institutions today is inestimable. They directly control patterns of work, leisure and consumption;

they indirectly influence all spheres of social life from the decisions of governments to the constitutions of families.[20]

Thus it is not simply that individuals have voluntarily abdicated responsibility and devotion to duty, as Carroll suggests. Rather it has been taken from them. Most are rendered powerless to make *significant* decisions with respect to their own lives. All they can do is to select between a range of pleasures offered to them. These two aspects of modern culture reinforce each other, giving rise to what Marcuse has termed a 'one-dimensional man'.[21] The problem with this is that the areas in which the individual can make decisions are not only boring, as Carroll remarks, but increasingly meaningless.

Most people recognizing the above would be likely to call for more democratic participation and more socialism. But not Carroll. He claims that these two responses to the cultural crisis are 'paranoic'.[22] The paranoid is a person who represses the recognition of the internalized presence of the old culture, and devotes himself with revolutionary zeal to living the style of the new.[23] This seems a harmless definition, until one recognizes that Carroll wishes to use it to claim that radical students and others who want to change the power structure of society are psychologically sick. He accuses them of both delusions of persecution and delusions of grandeur.[24]

This is simply a bit of nonsense based on confusion. Yet there is a lesson to be drawn from it. In analysing the evils of modern culture, with its hedonistic and materialist values, we should not lose sight of the causes of this situation, the increasing domination of life by the ruling class—with its economic, political and bureaucratic sectors. Carroll's failure to appreciate this side of the matter has led him to reject all those who seek to change this situation and create a world in which the hedonistic ideology would be tempered by a spirit of co-operative responsibility.

Habermas also believes that there are crises of social integration. These crises are due to the fact that society fails to reproduce individuals who have a meaningful social identity and who feel that they have a significant role to play in the society.[25] Habermas points out that capitalist society has always been parasitic on pre-capitalist religions and philosophies, as well as pre-capitalist social structures, to ensure this meaningful social identity. His thesis is that

> Bourgeois culture as a whole was never able to
> reproduce itself from itself. It was always dependent
> on motivationally effective supplementation by
> traditional world-views.[26]

What this means is that a capitalist society relies on a mixture of pre-capitalist and modern beliefs, values and social relations. Thus Habermas claims that a purely bourgeois ideology without reliance on earlier religious views cannot provide sufficient meaning in the lives of people for them to be satisfied with their social identities and to continue un-problematically to carry out their roles in society. For example, he claims that

> Genuinely bourgeois ideologies offer no support, in the
> face of the basic risks of existence (guilt, sickness,
> death) to interpretations that overcome contingency; in
> the face of individual needs for wholeness, they are
> disconsolate.[27]

However, as I have said, belief in religion has dropped dramatically and metaphysical world views have been gener-ally rejected. As Habermas says, 'Religion has retreated into the regions of subjective belief'.[28] It is no longer capable of imposing its authority on social life. At the same time, traditional pre-capitalist social forms and relations (such as the family) have either been dismantled or dramatically changed.[29] This has undermined the social identities of many individuals: life appears to have little basic meaning. Thus the dramatic increase in marital breakdown has shaken those who saw a meaningful identity in being a husband or a wife.

This loss of meaning must be made up. It is usually done, as noted, by increasing emphasis on physical pleasures, on possessive individualism—people believing that they can find meaning by accumulating more material goods—and on achieving promotion within sub-systems. Indeed this latter is part of the legitimating philosophy of the modern state: 'social rewards should be distributed on the basis of individual achievement'.[30]

However, as Habermas points out, in advanced capitalist societies such achievement is now measured primarily on the person's success with formal schooling. This puts pressure on the system which has pretensions to democracy to move towards more equal opportunities in education. At the same time, however, the economic system is less capable of changing to absorb people within it at the occupational levels for which the education system has formally prepared them. This disharmony between expectations of occupational role and status, and the actual jobs they can find, leads more people to work for 'extrinsic motives' only, that is, for material rewards.

Yet possessive individualism has also changed in character. Increasingly the capitalist economy, through advertising, seeks to create wants in people for goods they do not require. This is done by linking the possession of such goods to exaggerated claims of status and satisfaction. There is a dual danger in this: people make demands for more and more goods, as a basic right, and people find that the goods supplied do not provide the meaning in their lives which had been promised. The consequence of all this, as Habermas sees it, is: 'The less the cultural system is capable of producing adequate motivations for politics, the educational system, and the occupational system, the more must scarce meaning be replaced by consumable values'.[31]

A vast array of 'social problems' thus arises, concerned, in one way or another, with the loss of meaning and the consequent shattering of social identity. Dramatic rises in the rate of break-up of marriage, increases in drug addiction, crime, rape, suicide, and mental illness—these are symptoms of the general phenomenon; it pervades the whole culture.[32] Habermas calls this 'a motivation crisis'. For Habermas does not believe that the economy is a self-contained system. *Work motivations*—on which the economy relies for its continued reproduction—stem from the socio-cultural sphere. Yet these motivations are lower in a situation where social life is *not* integrated and a meaningful social identity not secured. The socio-cultural crisis thus aggravates the economic crisis as described in the last chapter. For workers no longer 'know their place' in the system of things and make more material demands in the vain search for a significant life under capitalism.

There is a further crisis that stems from this inability to reproduce a culture with sufficient social integration: the *legitimacy* of the state and the general structure of society may be thrown into question. This will be discussed in Chapter 6A. For the moment, however, I turn to examine the features of socio-cultural crisis as they manifest themselves in Australia.

B AUSTRALIAN CULTURE: MATERIALISM AND RELIGION

In the next two sections, I shall argue that Australia is undergoing a crisis of social integration, due to the way in which Australian culture and society have evolved. I shall argue that life is becoming increasingly meaningless to many people and that a large number of Australians are not experiencing sufficient recognition of their identity and worth as persons. This process is, I shall claim, giving rise to an increase in social problems such as crime and drug addiction, and also an increasing emphasis on more and more material goods.

In putting forward this view, I do not wish to imply that there is anything like an Australian national character which is essentially materialistic and selfish. For I do not believe that there is such a thing as an Australian essence or identity.[1] The Australian people cannot as a totality be identified with a particular stereotype such as the 'ocker', which substitutes a term for an explanation.[2] Australia contains its proportion of humane and well-intentioned people, as well as a number of 'bastards'. I thus reject theories which ascribe to Australians a selfish and materialistic nature or essence, as if they were born with this. Nor do I accept conservative theories that human nature is essentially selfish and acquisitive (see Chapter 5B).

Rather, I shall focus on those trends in Australian culture which any investigator needs to look at if he or she is attempting to apply the theory of cultural crisis (developed in Section A) to a specific culture. Such an analysis would need to consider the extent to which materialist and hedonist values have taken root in Australia, and the extent to which religious views determine and shape people's lives. In the next section, I shall look at the general structure of the Australian family and the extent to which it is changing or breaking down. I shall relate this to the status of women, and some views on the character of intimate relations in Australia. Finally I will consider certain symptoms of social breakdown such as crime, drug addiction and juvenile delinquency.

Materialism and hedonism
The charge of materialism has been levelled at Australian culture by a variety of commentators. Perhaps the most notorious of these is psychiatrist and sociologist, Ronald Conway. Indeed, in *The Great Australian Stupor*,[3] Conway sums up Australian culture thus: material wealth = pleasure = happiness = reason for living = notion on which the whole Australian way of life is based. This materialism has had two stages in its historical development:

> The Depression warped the psychological attitudes of a whole generation. It helped to place a widening gulf between young people born after 1940 and their

parents, for whom the worst possible disaster was the loss of material security . . . younger matrist-oriented Australians today no longer feel much sympathy with the fears and material concerns of their elders. It is not money, but the pleasures it can buy, which is the real focus of their attention.[4]

In the first stage, materialism was pursued to achieve *security* through the accumulation of goods, money and property. After the war, with economic growth, a second stage arose. It was not money itself which was important, but the use of money to purchase material goods and services which gave pleasure. This hedonism, the pursuit of pleasure for its own sake, is also Donald Horne's concept of the driving force within Australian life.[5] What of the centrality of sport in Australian culture? It is only a small minority who actually practise a sport as distinct from those who use it either as a means of gambling or to behave as aggressive spectators. Conway claims that this latter 'pleasure'—an extremely popular pastime in Australia—is simply aggression, channelled away from the struggle for worthwhile causes, into the essentially meaningless pursuit of 'barracking' for one side or the other. As he sees it:

In a country where excuses for public violence were few, the Australian passion for a day at the football or a spin at the races had been a valuable and painless way of discharging some natural aggression. But by the Second World War, attitudes to sport had become a yardstick by which most men and many women were judged. It was assumed that to be a good sportsman was to incarnate the most desirable human qualities; to be indifferent to sport was to be un-Australian or a 'bloody old woman'.[6]

Nevertheless it is clear that, though Australians are second to none in their admiration of sportsmen, the image of them as spending their time in the pursuit of healthy exercise is mostly a myth. Indeed, most Australians, particularly children, spend a large amount of time glued to the television set (the rate of TV watching is one of the highest in the world).[7]

What, then, are the hallmarks of Australian materialism? Its characteristic feature is *suburban living* and all which that implies. Indeed Donald Horne wrote that 'Australia may have been the first *suburban* nation'.[8] He links this directly with materialism: 'Australia was one of the first nations to find part of the meaning of life in the purchase of consumer goods'.[9]

Yet it might be asked: what are the elements in this suburban life style which are conducive to pleasure? Surely, as Barry Humphries has often satirically implied, suburban living is often dull, boring, without excitement or challenge.[10] This observation might throw doubt on Conway's view of the Australian as an irredeemable hedonist. Are we to believe that all those millions of Australians, separated by fences from each other in their suburban houses with their own gardens, TV sets and modern appliances, are living a life of uninterrupted pleasure? This is not the observation of social workers, psychiatrists and others who perceive this lifestyle close-up.[11]

Perhaps, then, the pleasure is experienced in the quality of family life, in the relations between husband, wife and children? Again, as we shall see in Section C, this appears an unreal representation of the Australian family. Could the source of hedonism lie in the pursuit of sexual and sensual gratification? If so, then Conway believes that it is not achieved; he describes the attitudes of Australians towards sexuality as 'mechanical', involving a search for 'frequency and variety rather than quality'.[12] His views on the majority are based on generalization from case studies:

In the consulting room, one can observe how readily sex becomes a tasteless compulsion among young people with a libido high enough to sustain it. Orgasm follows orgasm, each no more ultimately satisfying than its predecessors. In such cases as these, marriage itself is undertaken partly in boredom, partly in the wish for stability and comfort, but above all in the subconscious hope that through marriage, sex will be made somehow more meaningful, more imbued with the spirit of giving and belonging. But a wedding ceremony is no magic incantation, and the compulsive copulator before marriage tends to remain in much the same dilemma after it.[13]

I venture to suggest that the pursuit of a suburban life-style, and the accumulation of all kinds of material goods that accompany it, is not consciously pursued as a means to pleasure, but is rather pursued because of a tradition established by the socialization processes in society. Thus many young people pursuing this ideal leave their families to 'set up house' only to find themselves in an alienated and lonely environment. Indeed the problem of the isolated and lonely housewife has reached serious proportions.[14]

If this life-style is increasingly alienating and fails to provide either meaning or pleasure, why does it continue? There are two major reasons. Firstly, the suburban household is in the interests of consumer capitalism. Each nuclear family must have its *own* refrigerator, furniture, TV, washing machine, etc. This keeps the level of demand high and postpones crises in overproduction (see Chapter 3A). Secondly, the suburban life-style reinforces the privatization of life, the general tendency for people to turn inward and isolate themselves from others. Human relationships with non-intimate others become superficial. They are often based on utility, on using the other for one's own purposes, and not on any kind of respect. This privatization also means that people make a distinction between their own little world and the structures and institutions of society as a whole. They then only partici-pate in the latter to the extent that it helps them to satisfy their private desires; they do not participate because of any notion of the common good or their obligation to humanity. Donald Horne detected this tendency in Australia from the mid-1960s, although he represented it as tolerance rather than indifference:

> People don't care about what goes on unless it directly confronts or interferes with them. This is just about as high a degree of public tolerance as one can expect from a community; not to go out of one's way to interfere with others. Tell an Australian about something nasty that's happening in another suburb, or another street and he may express a harsh opinion about it and then conclude that it takes all sorts to make a world. He doesn't start a reform movement. It's no business of his.[15]

McGregor also detects the same tendency, yet believes that it is generally a good thing.

> The Australian's concentration on his home and family life represents a turning away from the wider community and the world of politics, commitment and social participation . . . There are some advantages in such a disengagement: the man who lives in a bung in Padstow is much *freer*, much less oppressed by community pressures and conformism, than Dublin terrace dwellers or Naples proletariat . . . The Australian suburbanite is probably freer of the stifling pressure of social authoritarianism than any other city dweller in history.[16]

Here McGregor is, I believe, expressing the ideology which is used to justify and support privatization and suburban living. These are said to be valuable because they give each individual freedom from social constraints. In his own suburban house, he is free to pursue whatever he wishes. His behaviour is private. It does not need to conform to any social, political or religious ideal. Yet this ideology is false—for this freedom is an illusion. The philosophy of 'mind your own business' has another side to it: 'nobody gives a damn'. The 'freedom' which negates public participation and decision-making also denies public recognition to the individual, and his role in society. If Australia is one of the most highly suburbanized societies, with very high degrees of privatization, it is also a society in which a high proportion of individuals experience a loss of personal identity and a high degree of social isolation, thus giving rise to many social problems.

Furthermore, McGregor is mistaken in supposing that this privatization means that the pressure of social authoritarianism is removed. For, while suburban living isolates the individual, it does not thereby leave all decisions to him/her. Rather, as is shown by the monotonous similarity of the suburbs of Australian cities, this life-style is itself subject to specific rules and obligations, such as respecting the privacy of the neighbours. The move to privatization, while it has dispensed some social controls, has imposed others.[17]

The picture that emerges from this is that the average Australian couple is subject to pressure to purchase their own suburban home, isolate themselves from relatives and friends, accumulate as many goods for the home as possible, while using this context to find social recognition and a meaning for life. No wonder they turn increasingly to drugs (particularly alcohol) and television.

Religion and socialization
Perhaps, then, a meaningful social identity is provided for the average Australian through religion. Thus Hans Mol, author of the book *Religion in Australia*, which was based on a survey of several thousand people carried out in 1966, states:

> We constantly hear about the churches being
> outmoded or religion having irrevocably lost its

educational, legitimating and welfare functions in modern society. Nevertheless church attendance in Australia does not differ very much from what it was 100 years ago.[18]

Indeed, an International Gallup Poll in 1970 reported that 95 per cent of Australians believe in God and that 63 per cent believe in 'life after death'.[19] Other statistics show that nearly 90 per cent identify themselves with a particular religion and are married in churches.[20] Yet this matter requires further examination.

Even in 1966, Mol found that church attendance was low—with the exception of Catholics. Of those who identified themselves as religious, 52 per cent of Anglicans, 36 per cent of Presbyterians, 34 per cent of Methodists and 19 per cent of Catholics never or hardly ever attended church. Furthermore, of the remainder, 27 per cent of Anglicans, 30 per cent of Presbyterians, 25 per cent of Methodists and 12 per cent of Catholics attended only occasionally, that is, less than once a month.[21] Only 27 per cent of the total attended church regularly and the overwhelming majority of these were Catholics (60 per cent of whom attended three or more times a month).

From this data, a peculiar phenomenon arises. Although according to the census of that year, 89 per cent identified themselves as religious (less than 1 per cent were non-Christian), only approximately a quarter of these regularly attended churches. This suggests that religion has increasingly become privatized, that is, a private matter for the individual rather than a public or communal affair. This impression is borne out by the data from Mol, on p. 149, based on a distinction between public worship and private belief.[22]

From this we can see that while 87 per cent of his survey identify themselves as religious, only 27 per cent are public believers. The remainder divide into those who firmly believe in God but do not attend church regularly (24 per cent) and a large number (36 per cent) who are vacillating in their belief

Types of Religious Commitment in Australia

	Percentage	Goes to church regularly	Prays daily	Believes in God without doubt	Percentage disapproving of pre-marital sex
Orthodox believer	17	Yes	Yes	Yes	90
Public believer	10	Yes	No	Yes	72
Private believer	8	No	Yes	Yes	82
Believing secularist	16	No	No	Yes	66
Vacillating secularist	20	No	No	?	54
Consistent secularist	16	No	No	No	27

in God, and rarely attend church. Thus 60 per cent of the population claim to be religious, yet make little public expression of their religion.

Under these circumstances, it is difficult to ascertain to what extent religion determines patterns of social life and secures a meaningful place for people. One thing is clear, however. Because of the demise of the social character of religion, it can no longer act as an external force constraining behaviour and the patterns of social interaction. The church has lost a considerable amount of its collective authority over the people as a whole. Nevertheless, it still plays a significant role in the socialization of individuals, particularly orthodox believers. Thus, while the average Australian is unlikely to refrain from some activity because an archbishop declares it to be 'sin', the consciousness that it is sin is often socialized from childhood and often creates guilt feelings. To illustrate, in the table above, I have listed the percentage of people disapproving of pre-marital sex. What is interesting about this is, as Mol says: 'Attitudes do not necessarily, however, coincide with the actual behaviour'.[23] Even in 1966, it was clear that a large proportion of young people indulged in sexual relations before marriage.

Hence, there appears to be a division in the Australian personality between harsh moral attitudes towards pre-marital sex, adultery, etc., and actual behaviour in sexual relations. This division is precisely the one which Carroll referred to (see Section A), between the puritan character and the hedonist/materialist culture. The average Australian, in 1966, appears to have thought of himself in quasi-puritan terms, as a religious person believing in conservative moral values, but nevertheless constantly lapsing into hedonism and breaching those values.

Much has changed since 1966. The latest figures show a dramatic reduction in religious commitment.[24] The reason for this is, I believe, that the privatization of religion has reduced its authority, not only in public life, but also within the family. Puritan parents have grudgingly come to accept the values of the new hedonist culture and have been less strict in enforcing the older, religious patterns.

In the 1970s, many church leaders—in attempting to escape the charge of hypocrisy—have made strong efforts to embark on social crusades for progressive political causes, such as action to help the poor, to assist the underdeveloped world and to combat racism.[25] These actions, while in the true spirit of Christianity, may be too little, too late to achieve a resurrection of church support. Nor are these radical ministers and priests necessarily supported by the majority of their congregations on these matters.[26]

Nevertheless this new radical action by the churches is welcome and a far cry from the intervention by the Catholic Church against socialism and the ALP in the bishops' statement on socialization.[27] Consider just two clauses:

(b) The philosophy and programme of strict Socialism
—the taking over and operation by the State of the

entire machinery of production, distribution and exchange—are Marxist in origin, and cannot be reconciled with Christian teaching.

(c) Where the meaning which is given to the programme of Socialisation is the same as that given above to Socialism strictly so called—Socialisation, in that sense, cannot be reconciled with Christian teaching.[28]

Statements like this support the view that Christianity is simply the religion of the ruling class and of capitalism. Yet, when Christ urged people to give up all their possessions to the poor and to follow him, or when he said that it is more difficult for a rich man to go to heaven than to pass through the eye of a needle, surely he was not defending huge inequalities of wealth nor defending enormous profit at the expense of exploiting people? In making this statement, the bishops abandoned the basic values of Christianity of equality and charity, in favour of oppression and greed.

Furthermore their action hastened the demise of religion—for in supporting capitalism rather than democratic socialism, they co-operated in the re-orientation of the values of Australians towards the god of material wealth and material growth. The economy continued the long process of legitimizing itself by converting people to a social and later on ontological commitment to a materialist view of the world and of life. Religion was thus increasingly rejected as irrelevant in providing meaning for life.

In conclusion, then, while the young may have escaped guilt feelings by rejecting religion and pursuing hedonism (and hence escaped the division between a puritan character and a hedonistic life-style), they have been left with little metaphysical foundation on which to base their social identity. Thus neither the privatized, suburban life-style nor religion provides a basis for meaningful identiy for the majority. Perhaps then this identity is secured within the family and in the distinctive roles of men and women. I turn to consider this matter now.

C   CRISIS IN AUSTRALIAN SOCIAL STRUCTURES

The changing Australian family

> The question is therefore not whether the family will
> survive, for that is like asking whether men and
> women will survive. The question is how best to help
> each other live in love and security and in a manner
> which allows each one of us to grow. The answer lies
> not in the action of individuals, but in society itself, in
> our values and the extent to which we are prepared to
> accommodate to change.[1]
>
> Royal Commission on Human
> Relationships, vol. 4, pp. 3–4.

In this part, I shall argue that the Australian family as presently structured does not allow for the parents to grow and develop as people, and further that it often aggravates the problem of finding a meaningful social identity in the context of a disintegrating culture.

The Australian family pattern is now the nuclear family, that is, the husband, wife and children constitute one functional whole, in which other relatives play a minimal role or are completely excluded. The prevalence of the nuclear family in Australia is often seen as a product of migration—people having to survive by themselves in a strange environment as a single couple. It has been intensified by materialism and suburban living.[2] Thus relationships with relatives within the extended family are fast disappearing. The supremacy of the nuclear family has the consequence that grandparents are put away in old people's homes, or are isolated from their children and grandchildren, aunts and uncles are rarely seen, cousins rarely even referred to.

The number of children and the pattern of child-bearing has been changing in Australia. Thus from 1947 to 1966 an unusual situation arose—the baby boom. In this period average family size jumped to nearly four children. What was responsible for this rise? The post-war economic boom provided a material basis for having children which had been unknown in Australia for decades. People took advantage of it. Many migrants who came over from a war-ravaged Europe had larger families to compensate for lost relatives. This situation produced a whole set of problems in education, health, and welfare services, as the state failed to plan in advance for the increase in numbers.

However, since 1966, there has been a rapid trend towards the two-child family. The pattern of bearing these children has also changed. Couples are delaying families a lot more, and having children closer together. Most women are completing their families by the age of thirty-two. Thus women are compressing the time of child-bearing to a six-year span. Many then spend the remaining years of their life in the rearing of the children they have borne, or in the pursuit of careers.[3]

It might be thought that through marriage and having children, people—particularly women—secure a social identity for themselves and a role within society. To some extent this is so. However, is this identity meaningful and coherent? Lyn Richards, in her excellent book *Having Families*, claims that in the modern Australian family, the 'roles are no longer easy to occupy because the rules are confused and contradictory'.[4] In her surveys, she shows that people do not marry and have children out of some conviction that it will make their lives happier, more fulfilling or more meaningful. Rather, it was a deeply socialized 'fact' that one would marry and have children:

> Parenthood, like marriage, was taken for granted.
> 'Why not stay single?' and 'Why not stay childless'
> had been equally non-questions. Virtually none of the
> men or women had asked either question of themselves
> or their partners.[5]

153

Yet the result of this falling into marriage and children is to create a form of identity crisis, particularly for women.

> For most women an important part of the problem was the disparity between their ideas of who they had been and who they now were. They had been competent, independent, in charge of their everyday world and its demands. They were now, they felt, manifestly incompetent, and tied down to the demands of infants who could make arbitrary demands on their attention twenty four hours a day.[6]

It appears then, on the evidence of this survey, that motherhood *by itself* is insufficient to provide many women with a meaningful identity, and may even create contradictory desires and values. Hence, many women seek to return to work or study, after the first few years of child-rearing. Even if they do not work, they usually seek 'outside interests'.

Why is this role no longer satisfying for many women? The reason is, simply, that child-rearing is no longer considered a valuable task by the community and hence no longer brings with it social recognition for the person mostly involved, the mother. Previously, as is shown in Dan Adler's 1958 survey, the mother had found her identity by taking over almost completely all the decisions in the home.[7] Adler demonstrated that whereas 90 per cent of American fathers participated in all major aspects of family life, none of the Australians in his sample did. Further, Conway points out that in Adler's survey

> the three regions most rarely entered by the Australian father were those involving overt displays of affection, demonstration of concern through shared play and help and the offering of good example by a demonstration of love and solidarity with the mother. Yet these regions of fatherly default are those in which the effective and healthy identification of the child with both parents is chiefly learned.[8]

154

Conway identifies several factors responsible for the above situation. The first, and most important, ties up with the dominance of materialist values. To prove himself, the male must spend an excessive amount of his time outside the home, accumulating as much money as possible. This is because males identify themselves in terms of success with material wealth (their ego identification comes about in this particular way). In addition, erotic and affectionate relationships between parents (to the extent that they exist) are hidden away from the children, and the Australian father 'is often unable to convey affection to his children beyond a gruff, superficial bonhomie. He relies chiefly upon rewards and punishments to maintain his position'.[9]

In contrast to this view, Tim Kupsch believes that the Australian family pattern is a mixture between matriarchy and patriarchy, the former stemming from American culture and the latter from the British.[10] Since both these cultures have a strong impact on Australian culture (particularly through television shows), they have been synthesized into what he calls a *madonna complex*. While a woman may be given little credibility as a person, a friend, a lover, a creative being with a mind of her own, she is nevertheless worshipped and placed on a pedestal in her role as mother and child-bearer. This schizoid attitude allows males to belittle and humiliate women in general, while 'respecting' their wife at home. This view is consistent with that of Conway (that Australian society is matrist). For, as he also notes, outside her context as 'mother', the Australian woman knows her place. Nor can she expect anything but rough and non-affectionate treatment by her man, when she is not seen as mother.

Both the nuclear family and the madonna complex are well suited to the interests of capitalist economy. Women become the dominant determiners of what shall be consumed in the household. Since, in this culture, they are socialized to be much more open to suggestion and advertising techniques than men, they often become compulsive consumers. This also places pressure on the man to work harder and strive for promotion in order to secure more material goods for the family. This divides the sexes further and ensures that a genuine common front by husband and wife against the manipulation and exploitation will not be achieved.

Yet, paradoxically, these same materialist pressures are a major determinant in the breakdown of marriage and family life. Since the wife often feels her role as mother to be insubstantial, she turns—as Habermas predicts[12]—to more and more material goods for meaning. As Lyn Richards notes:

> Freedom was seen most often in terms of ability to
> acquire material goods, and was therefore associated
> with selfishness—but it was still envied. Acquisition
> of material goods, in other contexts, was highly valued
> by almost all couples.[13]

Pressures on both husband and wife are increased. If the husband is unable to supply increased material goods and the wife unable to work, her feelings of frustration and identity loss will often turn on him. The result is marital tension, with its attendant symptoms of wife-bashing, child abuse and finally divorce (see below). Indeed the rate of divorce has increased dramatically in the last six years.

If the argument above is correct, this reflects the fact that the culture has created completely unrealistic expectations about the relation between marriage and personal fulfilment. These expectations were bound to be frustrated under the strain of the modern marriage. In this situation, people are faced with a conflict within themselves. Should they sacrifice themselves to the higher good of the family unit ('for the sake of the children') or should they follow liberal individualist principle and pursue their own happiness? Whichever way they resolve this dilemma, it is often accompanied by a crisis in their social identity. Since the decision to part is rarely truely mutual, one partner is often faced with a shattering of an identity she/he had come to rely on. Indeed, it is because of this fear of identity loss that many unhappy people stay married.

Personal relationships and meaning

These problems of insufficient social recognition and break-down of identity are not only prevalent in marriage and the family. They are also widespread in all personal relationships in society. To both married and unmarried people, the media and popular culture emphasize that individuals' personal happiness comes in the quality of their intimate interactions with others (lovers and friends).[14] Yet often such relationships result in disappointment—and therefore frustrate the search for identity. There are various reasons for this:

(i) During the 1960s and 1970s, continuous changes in values and expectations in, for example, sexual relations between people, have given rise to a serious instability in human relationships. This can make it very difficult for persons who seek to define their social identity by a focus on such relation-ships. The liberal ideal of 'do your own thing' can, by itself, seriously threaten people who would like there to be more rules which everyone can live by. This desire to reinforce a shaky identity may result in greater demands for a return to conservative social structures.

(ii) The stereotyped sex-roles of men and women in modern society, although they are breaking down, make it difficult to achieve genuine relations between people based on respect and affection. This is particularly so in Australia, according to certain social observers, because of the debasing of sexuality in Australian culture. I have already quoted Conway's view that Australian sexual relations lack meaning and are 'mechan-ical'. This view is also held by a considerable number of radical women writers.[15] Thus Dixson, in *The Real Matilda*, claims that these relations are 'immature' and 'ugly'. She says:

> in describing sexual intercourse as a 'naughty'
> Australian men are manifesting a retarded quality that
> is both personally backward and socially and
> historically backwards, expressing attitudes stemming
> from as far back, perhaps, as the mid-nineteenth
> century.[16]

157

(iii) Far too often people's sexual relations are based on ignorance or on a non-caring superficial attitude to intimacy. As Ann Deveson reports:

> In Australia unwanted pregnancies are occurring at the rate of 100,000 a year. Something like 60,000 abortions are performed annually. Young people are particularly vulnerable. They have a low rate of effective contraception, and a high proportion of unwanted pregnancies and abortion. Thirty per cent of abortions are performed on girls aged less than twenty. A survey of women attending the Fertility Control Clinic in Melbourne reported that at the time of conception, 74 per cent of the teenagers were using no method of contraception.[17]

The incidence of venereal and other sexually related diseases seems also to have increased; reported levels of VD rose by 20 per cent from 1971 to 1975.[18]

Even the apparent intimacy between males achieved in 'mateship' is seen by many as an escape from the awkwardness and inadequacy which Australian males have in achieving meaningful relations with women, based on respect for the latter as persons. Some observers such as Craig McGregor believe that the companionship of women is not rated highly at all. He remarks: 'Indeed the male who spends too much time with women is likely to be regarded with some suspicion —not much of a man at all, a mere sissy, or a skirt-chaser'.[19]

Conway believes that even this mateship tradition is a reflection of a deep-seated problem:

> What keeps so life-consuming and emotionally impoverishing a cult of male behaviour so alive for generations after its social and historical relevance? The answer is that the old stallion is now decked out for a different motive—to mask the fact that the men of the nation are more privately manipulated and motivated by their womenfolk than any public attitude

of theirs dare reveal. Such men compulsively seek the company of their own sex in bars and at sporting fixtures, not for the honest purging of self-exchange but to air those unrealized fantasies of manhood which the domestic rut at home has now made impossible.[20]

In his search to explain the mateship behaviour, Conway created a furore when he argued that 'one finds evidence of latent homosexuality on an astounding scale' amongst Australian males.[21] I myself reject this view, although it is an impression easily gained. As Horne says: 'There is a socially homosexual side of Australian male life (of a "butch" kind) that can involve prolonged displays of toughness in male company. Men stand around bars asserting their masculinity with such intensity that you half expect them to unzip their flies'.[22] Notice that all these authors see mateship as a negative, and far from meaningful, social relation.

Indeed, Conway suggests that this mateship behaviour is a clinging 'to the shallower rituals of comradeship, as the starving man eats grass in lieu of bread'.[23] His argument is that in attempting to escape from the domination of their wives, and from their feelings of inadequacy as males implemented by their mothers, Australian males are obsessed with 'power drives, acquisitive activity and the narcissistic chase after physical well-being'.[24]

I find this explanation unacceptable; for it suggests that wives are more mature and adjusted than men to the problems of modern society. Yet Conway has not taken sufficient account of the inferior social status accorded to women in Australian society and their treatment as second-class persons or even, in some cases, as non-persons. We must examine this matter, if we are to determine whether the roles of 'being a man' or 'being a woman' provide a sufficiently meaningful basis for social identity.

The oppression of women in Australia
The Royal Commission on Human Relationships, in its careful

and well-documented report, opens its discussion on sexual inequality thus:

> The theme of this chapter is that women in Australian society do not share equally with men in status, power or responsibility. That women suffer discrimination, injustice and inequality. That there are measures which can be taken to redress the balance, and that these should be taken up as soon as possible.[25]

The forms of this inequality are all-pervasive, extending through the economy, the political system, education and the social system.

Consider, for example, wage levels. Studies by Margaret Power, an economist specializing in the women's labour market, show that at the 1968 census the annual income of full-time women employees was 59 per cent that of male incomes, a discrepancy which tended to get larger among the professional and technical groups, and older workers.[26] The reasons suggested for this are that women have less access to overtime, receive less in over-award payments, are unemployed for longer periods and do not have equal access to higher positions in firms. The report stated that implementation of equal pay would have only a minor effect on the differential, because women as a rule do not find jobs where work is equal to that of men, but are concentrated in lower-income occupations. In addition, of course, promotion within companies is heavily biased in favour of men. Rarely do women achieve top positions in either public or private employment.[27]

One reason for these inequalities is that we have an education system which reinforces attitudes that discourage female aspirations and deny girls equal educational experience. Until very recently, girls were less likely to have tertiary or technical education. This was borne out by a report of a study group from the Schools Commission entitled 'Girls, School, Society'. Their findings were that from World War II until

1973, 50 per cent of the females left school by the age of fifteen and 80 per cent left school by form V. Since 1973, the situation has improved with as many girls as boys completing form VI. Yet although girls do better in all subjects except mathematics and physics, only 33.3 per cent of the university population and 26 per cent of the college population are females.[28]

The basic reason for this continues to be the stereotyping of males and females into sex roles. There is a fundamental dichotomy set up between femininity and achievement. The view that 'the woman's place is in the home' is still very prevalent. Various studies have indicated significant differences in the self-esteem which females have as compared to males. Furthermore, success and achievement in academic work is more central to the self-definition of males than females who are inclined to rate themselves more highly in interpersonal confidence and popularity.[29]

These differences in attitude can result in different development of competence in girls from boys, which is then used to support the thesis of the inferiority of women. Thus Edgar concludes his study of 14- to 15-year-olds in government schools so:

> there is strong evidence to suggest that girls are denied
> access to a wide range of equipment for competence
> and develop a self-image more negative than positive.
> Their future is defined for them and by them in more
> limited terms than it is for boys, and so their actual
> performance reinforces the expectations of women's
> lower status in society generally.[30]

In addition to the education system, the media strongly reinforces sex-role division. The Royal Commission reported:

> the media often popularizes unthinking attitudes
> toward women, their appearance, domestic life, their
> husbands and children. Female sexuality is exploited

by giving currency to words which belittle women and leave them as sex objects—'chick', 'bird', 'sheila' [31]

It is clear that in the modern nuclear family being a housewife is conducive to isolation, lack of stimulating company and a severe economic dependence on the man, which often results in women being forced to accept severe maltreatment within marriage—such as constant psychological and physical debasement. Indeed there is evidence that the incidence of wife-beating is widespread in Australia and extends across classes.[32]

The Royal Commission concluded that discrimination against women was a deeply ingrained aspect of Australian life. It suggested, amongst other things, that:

(1) abortion should be up to the woman (to third month of pregnancy) with counselling;

(2) women's refuges ought to be set up for women needing to leave husbands;

(3) schools ought to take up the problem of discrimination in a big way;

(4) political parties ought to encourage women to stand for election to achieve equal representation;

(5) child care should be made readily available, especially for low income families;

(6) contraception should be freely available;

(7) discrimination against women in the workplace should be strongly combated;

(8) unions should encourage more leadership by women.[33]

Three issues arise at this stage

(i) What are the causes of this oppression of women?

(ii) How can they be eradicated?

(iii) What should social relations be like if they are to admit equality and respect? These questions have been the focus of an extensive debate and an enormous literature.[34] I shall confine myself to some brief remarks only.

Firstly, as to the causes of oppression, a substantial number of feminists believe either that most men individually dominate and oppress women or that men as a group or a class collectively oppress all women. Those who hold the former view seek to identify the individual male as the culprit, to blame him for their oppression and to gain their liberation by detaching themselves from him and/or changing his chauvinist attitudes.[35] While this approach has some limited application, it suggests that each individual male is to be held responsible for his treatment of, and expectations towards, women. This, however, entirely misses the point that it is in the context of a whole culture, in which distinct sex roles have been socialized, that he acts in the way that he does.

Furthermore, this view suggests that men individually are receiving all the benefits of sex-role stereotyping at the expense of women. Against this, I would argue that just as women are forced into the role of a sex object, men are increasingly forced to become *success objects*. By this I mean that the man who becomes the most desired and attractive in Australia is the one who has succeeded in his sphere of interest, his work and/or his sport.[36] The man who is not doing well in these areas is not considered to be particularly attractive. The most desirable men are the most powerful, particularly if their career also brings with it either public esteem or material wealth. Thus, because of this prevalent attitude, men are forced to compete with each other as to who is most successful in achieving material rewards, fame, promotion, increases in status. This puts an oppressive pressure on males, which forces them to repress the co-operative and affectionate side of their nature.

Instead of accepting Conway's explanation of mateship in terms of homosexuality, one could argue that it is simply an attempt to escape from this situation, by getting together with one's mates. Here, while there is a form of friendly competition, it does not take the form of competition in the 'success object' role. Rather I believe that mateship is often a genuine attempt to create an egalitarianism which does not exist in men's relations within the work situation or in the presence of women.

The second explanation, that men as a whole form a group or class of oppressors, and that women constitute a sex class, is based on the belief that the division into sexes is socially more important and fundamental than the division into economic and social classes.[37] This is the view of Anne Summers in *Damned Whores and God's Police*. Her division of the sexes is more fundamental than 'age, class, race, religion and so on. To subsume individuals into these overriding categories is by definition sexist and, in the long run, not very elucidating'.[38] Some writers go further and argue that because women are unpaid domestic labourers, depending on the man for their income, they are clearly oppressed by men as a whole.[39]

I find this kind of analysis entirely unconvincing. While it may have been the case that nineteenth-century women had no rights to property and therefore contributed only to the accumulated property of their menfolk (those few who were in a position to accumulate property, that is), this is clearly no longer the situation. Indeed, modern divorce laws specify that the woman is entitled to 50 per cent of property, no matter what her contribution to its accumulation may have been. Furthermore, the husband is required to provide the wife with a substantial level of maintenance, even if she chooses to leave him for another man. Thus the view that the woman is simply the man's slave in accumulating *his* property is mistaken. Moreover, it cannot be the basis for a theory of the oppression of women.

Clearly, what is oppressing both men and women are the stereotyped roles which they are required to play, and the fact that most women *and* men are exploited by the capitalist process, since they belong to the working class. This is not to deny that there is also an oppressive relation between working men and their wives. It is, rather, to insist that this phenomenon needs to be explained within the context of an exploitative socio-economic system.

Let me suggest such an explanation as a hypothesis. Marx was aware that under capitalism, relationships between men and women were oppressive. Indeed there is an alienation of the female from the male. In early capitalism, the female's role is to marry and produce children; this latter is required by the system because of the need to reproduce the source of labour. The woman is therefore doubly oppressed: by the system as a whole, by her male partner. Why does the male oppress the female in this situation? One reason is his powerlessness. If as a worker within the system he feels powerless to direct his own life, he dominates the woman as an expression of his own being. At work, he is treated as a non-person, as a nonentity. So when he comes home he expects to be treated 'like a king'. The direct domination and oppression of women by men is thus a case of what I term 'the transference of alienation'. Under the terrible burden of the non-recognition given to him at work, the man attempts to achieve his worth as a person by gaining recognition from the woman: this requires that she subjugate herself to his will. This situation is a familiar one: the oppressed becomes oppressor as a reaction to his own condition.[40] Yet the subjugation of the woman cannot bring the man genuine recognition. Rather, as in the master-slave analogy, it generates resentment and eventually rebellion from the woman. When it is accepted —as it is by many women—it negates the woman as a person. She thus develops an identity which is nothing more than an appendage to her husband. She lives on her husband's image, on his social identity as a success object.

Under these circumstances, a large number of men and women in Australia are alienated—even if we define this concept in a subjective way. Thus, they feel inadequate, insecure in their social identities, isolated from the social world, constantly persecuted by their fellow persons. Hence, the social problems in society increase dramatically. The reproduction of the social structure is therefore not guaranteed. Yet change is feared, for its consequences appear even more threatening to many people than the continuation of the present insecurities.

What is required is for the majority of men and women to recognize the common source of their alienation, which lies in their domination by the ruling class, and to act in unity against it. The first step in this is the recognition that working-class men and women are *both* trapped in roles which it is in the interest of the powerful to maintain.[41] The division of roles creates a false set of identities for people to adopt and try to succeed in. Although most will eventually fail, this is a diversion from the real need to transform social and economic structures which oppress both men and women. Miriam Dixson suggests that

> Women begin from 'women are beautiful' and promote a much more substantive sharing of sexually-allocated personality characteristics and role expectations. The women's movement must lead in such a strategy, even though it benefits men just as much. It involves both; for most people, the well-being of one sex cannot be achieved without the well-being of the other . . . it would involve a new set of values, hence central change in educational institutions . . . in the economy and in the polity.[42]

In conclusion, I wish to point to some of the symptoms of social crisis which have been recorded by sociologists and the Royal Commission on Human Relations (space does not allow a full documentation). The extraordinary pressures under which people are placed during crisis may lead to, firstly, their directing their anger and frustration against themselves, thus leading to increases in suicide, drug addiction and commitment to mental institutions. This has occurred in Australia.[43] Secondly, there are increases in social evils due to tension and recklessness in relations with lovers and friends. Thus, in addition to marital breakdown (noted earlier), abortion and venereal disease have increased markedly. There have also been increases in family violence and family rape. The situation is vividly described by Deveson:

> Violence against women is not a subject society cares to acknowledge. Yet daily, and within the supposed safety of their own homes, women in Australia are

being battered, bruised, attacked with weapons, having their eyes blackened and their teeth and bones broken. Sometimes they are killed. Sometimes they die later from the injuries they have received. Their assailants are their husbands, lovers and friends.[44]

Thirdly, an alienated person may also vent his anger at other persons who are mere strangers. This results in increases in crimes against the body and the personal property of others. Statistics show that the incidence of murder, bashings and rape has grown.[45] In particular, the incidence of rape has increased alarmingly. Thus from 1964 to 1973, the number of rapes reported to police rose from 262 to 680—more than double.[46] These figures, however, are only the tip of the iceberg—for the overwhelming proportion of rapes are never reported to the police, for fear of the social stigma attached to being a rape victim. Although the majority of cases reported to police involve rape by strangers, there is evidence that many of the unreported cases involve rape by fathers, relatives, husbands and friends. Paul Wilson in his survey of rape cases, produced the following results: 30 per cent raped by father, relatives or spouse, 16 per cent raped by friend, 9 per cent raped by casual acquaintance, 37 per cent by strangers.[47] Given these facts, it is difficult to sustain the view that the rapist is simply a person who is mentally ill in any clinical sense. Rather the widespread nature of rape, and of the occupational and class positions of those engaged in it, supports the view of a deep and abiding malaise in social relations.

As Keith Windschuttle has documented, there has been an increase in crimes against property, ranging from shoplifting to armed hold-ups. He believes that these are related to the increase in unemployment. He says:

Armed hold-ups are on the increase and may also be related to unemployment. In New South Wales at the start of 1978 they were about 10 per cent higher than previous years. Professional criminals do not usually take on this sort of action. More than 73 per cent arrested for armed hold-ups are first offenders at robbery. 'Armed hold-up', police explain, 'is a cleanskin's idea on how to get some big money fast'.[48]

A further reaction of alienated people during crisis is to turn on minority groups as scapegoats, blaming them rather than the system for the social and economic ills of society. This is the most potent *modern* factor underlying the continued discrimination (and often racist attitudes) towards Aborigines and migrant Australians. This discrimination has been documented in some excellent books and several government enquiries.[49] For example, Aboriginal unemployment is estimated to be as high as 45 per cent. In some rural areas, it is more than 80 per cent.[50] Deveson writes:

Aboriginals are also over-represented in prison statistics . . . In Western Australia, where Aboriginals comprise only 2.1 per cent of the population, 30 per cent of all prisoners are Aboriginals. Anthropologist Dorothy Parker, who undertook a study of Aboriginals and criminality in Western Australia, told us that police often went beyond their duties of enforcing the law.[51]

The discrimination against, and maltreatment of, migrants occurs primarily as a consequence of their communication difficulties given an insufficient grasp of English; problems arising out of cultural differences, which may become acute for migrant children trying to cope with two cultures; the fact that migrants perform the dirtiest and physically most exhausting jobs in the community. They are thus often manipulated as 'factory fodder'.[52]

Yet the social crisis indicated by the above symptoms and by others may not necessarily erupt into open rebellion. This depends on the success of the dominant ideology in legitimizing the system.

5
Legitimating the Australian System

It might be claimed, in response to the theory of crisis developed to this stage, that there is little obvious evidence of crisis in Australian society. Everyone, of course, concedes that there are economic and social problems—such as increasing unemployment, crime and drug addiction. Nevertheless it could be argued that these are not symptoms of deep and fundamental crises. For if crisis is so basic, why has there not been open rebellion against the structures of society and the state?

The answer to this is that the ruling class not only manages to control the centres of power in western society, it also dominates the dissemination of ideas and reinforces practices which legitimize the existent power structures in the economy and the state. In this chapter I shall inquire how, and to what extent, this domination (often called a *hegemony*) is achieved. I shall examine the two major philosophies which sustain this domination—conservatism and liberalism. Thirdly I shall consider the Liberal Party in Australia, its philosophy and to what extent it contributes to ruling-class dominance. Finally, I shall examine the Australian media, and their role in promoting ideas and practices which sustain the ruling class, even in times of crisis.

A HEGEMONY: DOMINATION OF IDEAS AND PRACTICES

The notion that the working class is led to accept its oppressed position through the processes of socialization and education was first put forward by Marx.[1] In his view, the dominant ideologies of the ruling class created a *false consciousness* in the working class. Thus, even though the alienated condition of workers often prompts a raised consciousness, the system acts against them to perpetuate their false consciousness. To explain this, Marx introduces the distinction between the substructure and the superstructure of society. The former consists of the set of economic and social relations—that is, the economic relations which exist within the productive process, and those social relations involved in the reproduction of family life and hence of the source of labour; these are called concrete economic and social relations, and are the foundations of society.[2] On these is built the superstructure, a set of abstract ideas, values and beliefs. The major function of the *dominant* ideas (ideology) within the superstructure is to sustain the substructure. Thus:

> The mode of production of material life *conditions* the
> social, political and intellectual life process in general.
> It is not the consciousness of men that *determines* their
> being, but, on the contrary their social being that
> *determines* their consciousness.[3]

A crude interpretation of the above quotation is that somehow the substructure determines the content of the superstructure—that economic and social structures, particularly the division into classes, determine the content of people's consciousness.[4] Yet the power structure alone cannot explain the ideas which people generate, even though it may explain why some ideas become widely disseminated.

What then is Marx's position? As I have indicated, for Marx the substructure does not consist merely of economic relations between people. It includes all personal relations which are concrete in character. The key here is Marx's distinction between concrete and abstract levels of human thought:

> The division of labour is a true division only from the moment a division of material and mental labour occurs . . . From this moment on consciousness can emancipate itself from the world and proceed to the formation of 'pure' theory, theology, philosophy, ethics, etc. [5]

Ideas are involved in both forms of labour. We must here distinguish between the simple language and thought involved in concrete interaction, and the rationalization of it through theory. Consider an analogy. A man makes love with a woman—this is a concrete social relationship. But the next day, he feels guilty and develops a theory to justify his behaviour—he was not fully aware of the consequences of his actions, he was influenced by factors outside himself, etc. Similarly, for Marx, thought is superstructural if it seeks to explain or justify, through appeal to theoretical notions, aspects of the social world and the structures of that world. The superstructure may thus contain some theories which are true and some which are false. In an oppressive society, the *dominant* theories will be those which legitimate the existing social order. Marx calls this perpetuation of false notions 'mystification'. Just as an individual may deceive himself in seeking to explain his behaviour, a whole society may be similarly deceived by ideas which seek to justify existing power relationships.

Thus there is no necessary relationship between the substructure and the content of the superstructure (which contains many contradictory ideas). Creativity at this level of abstract ideas is, Marx believed, a basic capacity of man. However, from the fact that an idea is created, it does not follow that it will be accepted or even disseminated. This is where the substructure does influence the superstructure, in determining which ideas are going to be publicized and promoted, and which are going to be suppressed and not published. This phenomenon surrounds us daily: some ideas are promoted, others suppressed.[6] (The role of the Australian media in this will be discussed in Section D.)

Marx maintains that there is an interconnecting set of theoretical ideas which go to constitute the *dominant ideology* of the capitalist society; these ideas rationalize the existing oppressive order, by making it appear natural, reasonable, inevitable, moral, even divine. Marx does not deny that radical ideas can exist (how could he, given his own theories?), but rather recognizes that economic and political forces will act to suppress them, or to simply refuse them access to media.

This notion of domination was developed further by Antonio Gramsci. In his *Prison Notebooks*, Gramsci argues that the ruling class dominates not only the ideas and the political apparatus, but also the social practices and culture of society. This 'sturdy structure of civil society' Gramsci describes as 'a powerful system of fortresses and earthworks' which remains intact, even when the legitimacy of the state is threatened.[7]

R. W. Connell, in his book *Ruling Class, Ruling Culture*, applies Gramsci's theory to Australia.[8] He notes that Gramsci extended it 'to cover where a kind of permanent alliance existed; where a general solidarity between oppressors and oppressed had developed, with cultural processes reinforcing the political and economic domination of the ruling group'.[9] Thus, in a hegemony, the institutions of society—even though there may be differences and tensions between and within them—tend to support the same *basic* system of values and practices. Antagonistic forces and ideas are incorporated into the system so as to be made consistent with its overall goal and purposes.

Applying this to the Australian context, we may ask: to what extent is there hegemony here? Connell argues that, while hegemony is never absolute, it is very effective in maintaining and reproducing the existing power structures.[10]

There are three levels at which this is done:

(a) the level of personal politics, involving the formation of conscious ideas and attitudes;

(b) appeals to unconscious and repressed motives, such as fear of the unknown applied in justifying racist foreign policies;

(c) the inculcation of patterns of behaviour to the point where they become habitual and routine practices.

Connell's view is 'that the specific kind of affluence that countries like Australia have experienced, has meshed with much older patterns of sexual organization in ways that strongly inhibit class mobilization, both in terms of unconscious dynamics and patterns of daily activity'.[11] Connell thus believes that in their consciousness and in their practices, Australians of the working class act to reproduce the power structures which oppress them. He focuses on several factors responsible for this. I have identified six major ones, which I shall consider briefly, in order to evaluate whether the hegemony is as tight as Connell would have us believe.

(i) Socialization in childhood and adolescence

Connell's work on the socialization of children,[12] teenagers and adults produces reasonably convincing evidence on the following points. Firstly, the notion that meaning and happiness comes through the pursuit of material wealth is promoted, together with the view that inequalities in income, wealth, power and status are the natural outcome of a fair competition in which differences in people's abilities are reflected. Thus the majority of the children of manual workers, when asked to explain their failure to achieve better jobs and higher positions in society, referred to the fact that they did not believe they had enough 'brains'. This places the cause of failure not on society, but on the individual. Yet it is not an aspect of the individual which he can be held responsible for and can choose to change. The child thus can avoid feelings of guilt. Secondly, there is remarkable consistency in the reproduction of classes, *structurally defined* in terms of income and occupation, in Australia. Thus children whose parents are manual workers (Connell mistakenly identified the work-ing class with this group only: see Chapter 2D for reasons against this) will tend to produce children who also remain in this group and the same is true for his 'middle class'. This is particularly evident if one uses educational achievement and occupation as an index of class structure. Thus children of the poor will also, generally speaking, be poor.[13]

Notwithstanding this, most children of manual workers had little consciousness of their class position. Connell con-cluded from his research that

> Very few of them, very few indeed, have a firm
> consciousness of their own class position. The constant
> 'middle' self-classing among the older children and
> adolescents is much less a claim to membership of a
> middle class than it is a denial of being either wealthy
> or poor. Class is not salient as a frame of reference for
> judging the self: the children do not answer the
> question 'who am I?' in class terms. They do not have
> the shared consciousness of class membership which is
> basic to class politics.[14]

Thus, although there is an awareness of the divisions between the rich and the poor, this division is not represented as a conflict between classes.

This result is not, however, surprising. For Connell's own distinction between manual workers (his working class) and his middle class does not help in defining the conflict between classes. Most of his 'working' and 'middle' class form what I call the 'working class' and it is these, as a totality, who are in conflict with the ruling class. It is not necessary for class politics for a child to know whether he is part of Connell's middle class or not. It is only necessary that he be aware that he is exploited by a powerful ruling group, and that this exploitation takes place in the various systems of society: economy, state and social structure.

Nevertheless, the evidence presented by Connell in his

surveys of children and adolescents does show that children of manual workers are likely to have a low esteem of their own self-worth and individual capacity which ensures that they (in most cases) do not progress in society and, further, that they accept this situation as natural and even right. This phenomenon needs to be explained. Connell is surely right in identifying the education system as the culprit here.

(ii) The education system

Unfortunately, Connell does not say much about the role of the education system in achieving the above reproduction of classes. He does accept the analysis given by S. D'Urso that 'the primary function of schooling is a latent one' and 'not the cultivation of cognitive abilities' which are supposedly objectively assessed.[15] Instead,

> the hidden curriculum of the school leads the young to internalise such norms as the hierarchial disposition of power and acquiescence in one's own powerlessness, compliance with authority, job fragmentation and intrinsic job motivation, external direction and evaluation of one's work and worth.[16]

It would be interesting to study how this process operates. Connell does not believe that it is a simple matter of internalizing the values and norms of compliance to authority. Yet Connell does not explain how it is that students (and adults for that matter) with a sceptical attitude to authority come to comply with the requirements of the power structure. More research needs to be done on this. As a tentative hypothesis, however, I suggest that in the Australian process of education and socialization there is a divided attitude to authority. Firstly, when authority stems from a particular person or persons, such as the teacher, Australians tend to view it with scepticism. This is part of the 'knocking' phenomenon in Australian culture, which seeks to bring down the gifted or outstanding person. McGregor describes it as an unfortunate consequence of 'social egalitarianism'.

> There is a price to be paid for all this . . . Australians
> are so suspicious of self styled leaders that they tend to
> disparage the successful or ambitious man, and pull
> him down to their own level. Salaries and wage rates
> favour the mediocre man rather than the brilliant one.
> Cutting him down to size is a common pastime.[17]

Secondly, however, when authority is vested in societal systems, students are less inclined to be sceptical and to challenge this. For these systems are not seen as direct human creations, but as objective and natural, having a life of their own and hence difficult to change. On this view, an Australian is likely to accept a determination made by an anonymous bureaucrat within the power structure, rather than a direct order from an individual with authority.

If the above analysis is correct, the possibilities for change are limited. This is partly due to the fact that Australian teachers have generally failed to demonstrate to students that the power structures of society are *not* independent, but the creations of people and thus can be changed. Why teachers have failed in this is not clear (perhaps it has to do with their own socialization). But if the scepticism which Australians have towards individual authority is directed towards the power structures in economy and the state, their legitimacy will come into question. Since this is a strong possibility, the reproduction of these systems is not as secure as Connell claims.

(iii) Reinforcement of the suburban life-style

While Connell agrees with others (see Chapter 4B) that the move to suburban materialism was important in minimizing working-class rebelliousness, he does not believe that people simply chose this life-style. Rather there were severe economic pressures on people to move out to the suburbs. In addition,

> there was a systematic attempt to sell suburban living
> as the most desirable way of life. In the decade or so
> after the war real estate developers, builders,

consumer goods manufacturers and retailers mounted a massive campaign in the media promoting the suburbs and all the equipment of suburban living. Much of it was directed to women, playing on their sense of themselves as social managers as well as their femininity and motherhood.[18]

Connell notes that the binding factor in suburbia was not so much a new set of values and beliefs, but rather a locking into a pattern of behaviour in which people's lives are privatized. 'To buy the "little piece of earth with a house and garden" that Menzies apostrophized in a famous wartime speech, normally sent a man into debt for most of his working lifetime'.[19] Furniture and the car made this even worse.

(iv) Division of the working class through creation of an aristocracy of labour

This was done through increasing the margins between categories of workers and thereby reinforcing differences in the quantity of personal property, particularly differences in the character and status of homes. Connell notes that the division of labour which is 'a technical necessity of production' has been embedded into 'an elaborate structure of status distinctions, income differences, customary privileges and differential recruitment'.[20]

Here, however, Connell has not gone far enough in his analysis, for this division of the labour force has been carried to the point of creating two social groups—his 'middle class' office workers and his 'manual workers class'. This has had the effect of creating two life-styles and two kinds of suburb, for example, Glen Waverley (middle) versus Broadmeadows (manual) in Melbourne.[21] Though both groups are exploited in their labour, the division creates a diversion from union and solidarity as one working class. For those in the 'middle-class' group live in fear that their income will drop and that they will be unable to sustain their life-style. Conversely, the manual workers constantly seek to achieve improvements in income so that they will be able to afford houses in fashionable suburbs and thus change their life-style to that of the 'middle class'.[22]

However, while this situation creates tensions between workers, it also places increased pressures on the economic system. As some groups of workers take industrial action and achieve an improvement in their position *vis-à-vis* other groups, the latter then strike to achieve a restoration of their relative position. This puts pressure on the capitalist economic structure. Hence, income differentials which were intended to result in a reduction of worker militancy may have had the consequence of increasing pressures on the economic system.[23]

(v) Development of welfare services and the use of social workers

Connell claims that 'The state in its benign aspect, its welfare service, and general uplift departments, must be seen as an important force in the construction of hegemony'.[24] The clearest case of this is, in his view, the use of an army of social workers to give relief from poverty, family trauma and incompetence in adjusting to the requirements of Western social life. In so doing, they patch up potentially dangerous problems in the system, and make it appear benevolent. Thus Connell concludes that

> it is not hard to see the ideological effects of their
> activity in terms of legitimation, in terms of the
> definitions of poverty and suffering as aberrations, on
> the fringe of an otherwise contented community,
> rather than an integral product of our integrally
> divided social order.[25]

There are two questions which must be faced here. Firstly, would those people, had they not been given assistance by the state, blame the power structures of society and begin to rebel against them? Social problems will sustain a sense of grievance, but will people's anger be directed against the ruling class? Or will it be directed against working-class groups such as the unemployed ('dole bludgers') or the unions? This question requires a measured reply: if people have grown accustomed to receiving social welfare assistance, the state cannot completely cut this off without risking a large reduction in support.[26] As Connell notes: 'Though previously quite enterprising in denouncing the extension of bureaucracy, the Federal Liberals took over the welfare apparatus and ran it on much the same lines as before. They were not stupid'.[27] However, if this point is valid, then social welfare gains have become entrenched and cannot be drastically reduced or cut out without substantial loss in legitimacy. At the same time (as we saw in Chapters 3A and 3C), the pressure from capitalist forces is to reduce this aspect of state expenditure as far as possible. Hegemony is thus not automatically reproduced, but depends on how the state handles these contradictory pressures (more on this in Chapter 6A).

Secondly, do social workers always act to reproduce the system, or do they attempt to raise the consciousness of their clients as to the real causes of social problems? This, of course, depends on the individual social worker. Nevertheless there is evidence that, as a group, they are becoming increasingly frustrated with patching up the symptoms and more eager to tackle the structural causes of poverty and social dislocation.[28] This will inevitably lead them into a difficult position of acting within the power structure while attempting to change it. Nevertheless it seems simplistic to make the blanket claim that the army of social workers is doing nothing but reinforcing the existent structures of economic and political power.

(vi) The ruling class dominates the political process— including the 'democratic' contest between the parties. The claim here is that parties are only tolerated to the extent that they constitute no threat to the capitalist economic structure and hence no threat to the ruling class. On Gramsci's view, parties such as the ALP actually serve the interests of the dominant class, even though this may not be apparent. For, though they may have real differences with their conservative opponents about particular policies, they do not challenge the basis of class relationships (capitalist enterprise), nor do they attempt to create in the working class a consciousness which will enable that class to become a force for real social change.

While Connell accepts that this is true in Australia, he is not entirely sure of the position of the ALP. He mentions that the Labor Party is often considered by its opponents to be a threat to existing economic structures. After all, what else can explain the massive campaigns mounted to keep the ALP out of office for twenty-three years?[29] These campaigns were waged not just against the ALP but also against the unions, and other potentially rebellious groups. First there was the anti-communist campaign, orchestrated by Sir Robert Menzies and the DLP, which attempted to isolate the ALP by linking it with communist forces and thereby keep it out of power. (See Section C for a discussion of this.) Then there was a racist campaign to justify intervention in the Vietnam war, our antagonism towards China and the strengthening of our ties with the US. Thus, in the election of 1966, in which Labor was heavily defeated, there was a series of advertisements by the DLP which showed massive hordes of angry Asians followed by a picture of Asia and Australia, with an arrow showing the Asians invading us.[30]

No one would deny that the above campaigns were effective. But why did the ruling class act so concertedly to prevent the Labor Party winning office, if this party never challenges the ruling class? This matter will be taken up in Chapter 6C.

There is a further issue here: what is the political ideology by means of which the ruling class dominates the political process? When we examine this matter, we discover not one, but two major ideologies to which the ruling class (particularly its political faction) adheres, namely, conservatism and liberalism. Yet, as we shall see in the next section, there are important conflicts between these two philosophies, which are found in the Liberal Party and the media.

Of course, it can be claimed that these conflicts are exactly the sort of thing that give people the impression that there are disagreements and debates going on, while at the same time the class structure is being reproduced.[31] However, I shall argue against this view, and propose that certain aspects of liberal philosophy are radical in character, and can be used against the domination of the ruling class. Furthermore, following Habermas and Boris Frankel,[32] I shall argue that the development of more liberal social structures deepens the crisis and places more pressures on the economic structure (see Chapter 6A).

(vii) The monopoly which the ruling class has over the media and its role in legitimating the power structures of society. This very important issue will be taken up in Section E of this chapter.

We have seen the ways in which the ruling class seeks to legitimate its actions through the creation of a dominant culture, consisting of beliefs, attitudes and practices. Yet I have argued that, while there certainly is domination, the reproduction of the systems of society is not thereby guaranteed. On the contrary, there are factors conducive to breakdown, even (as we have seen) in the hegemonic processes themselves. The ruling class requires continuous vigilance and effort in order to sustain its power and property. It is not an automatic process.

Boris Frankel puts the problem thus:

> How many cuts to public sector, use-value goods and services can be tolerated? How long can bourgeois ideology cover up the class nature of budgetary priorities, given the crisis of revenue raising and the fine line between welfare cutbacks, wage cuts, consumption levels, and electoral promises? How long will it be before so-called co-option policies such as worker participation, job enrichment, human rights, anti-pollution, anti-sexist, anti-discrimination or consumer protection, either exacerbate further attacks upon capitalist social relations (because they succeed), or are revealed as mere ideological rather than substantive changes?[33]

Before we can tackle this, however, we need to consider in greater detail the political philosophies of conservatism and liberalism, the programmes and ideology of the Liberal Party, and the role of the media. I turn to these matters now.

B CONSERVATISM AND LIBERALISM

There are two general ideologies or political philosophies which are used to legitimate *most* aspects of the distribution of power and wealth in Australia, and hence the domination of the ruling class. These philosophies are very important because versions of them are embodied in the platforms of many political parties in Western states.

It is easy to get the impression that conservatives are opposed to change of any kind whatsoever. Consider for example the book entitled *Conservatism as Heresy* by John Ray, who calls himself 'a Burkian conservative'.[1] He believes

> that the Vietnam war can be justified, that conscription can be necessary, that most ecology activists are cranks, that the 20th century is the best century we have ever had, and that the 21st will be even better— that economic growth is a good thing, that scoundrels who defy the courts should be outlawed, that the White Australia policy is defensible . . . that we should have more foreign investment and continued population growth. I'm in favour of bigger cities and more home units; in favour of states' rights and against socialism. I am against government sponsored decentralisation, against government handouts to Aborigines.[2]

However, conservatism is not simply a defence of the status quo at any price; it is a much more substantial philosophical perspective. To conservatives, the economic hierarchies and social structures of society are very important for the sustenance of society as a whole. Therefore, the democratic state should seek to preserve them; it should act to sustain existing social and economic relationships and hierarchies, rather than change them either gradually or radically.

The reason for this, according to conservatives, is that these hierarchies have *proved* themselves through history. By this, they mean that just as individuals inherit property from their ancestors, we as an organized group, inherit certain social and economic structures from our ancestors and, because these structures have been part of our culture for a considerable period of time, they are in a certain sense more valuable than the lives of any group or person. For these structures have a longer history and life span than any individual.

This is the view of Edmund Burke, the 'father of conservatism'.[3] He was writing just after the French Revolution, to which he was passionately opposed; not because he was 'averse to liberty', but rather because he was opposed to 'licence'. This distinction is one which conservatives are always making: liberty to act within certain constraints is one thing: licence or permissiveness to do whatever you wish is something else. Burke considers that this is the difference between his conservative approach (the English approach, as he calls it) and the approach taken by the French revolutionaries. He says:

> it has been the uniform policy of our Constitution to claim and assert our liberties as an entailed inheritance derived to us from our forefathers; and to be transmitted to our posterity—as an estate especially belonging to the people of this kingdom, without any reference whatever to any other more general or prior right . . . Our political system is placed in a just correspondence and symmetry with the order of the world, and with the mode of existence decreed to a permanent body composed of transitory parts.[4]

Burke makes two basic claims. Firstly, these structures have an inherent value in themselves without requiring recourse to a higher principle which justifies them. Secondly, since human life, ideas, motivations are in a state of constant change—development and decay—institutions and structures which have lasted for many centuries ought not to be destroyed by revolutionary impulse, but ought to be retained. Their endurance gives them real value; they are part of the world order.

This position is based on a certain view of human nature. John Ray sums it up so:

> from my own research into people's attitudes, I've come to the Burkian conclusion that a conservative is above all someone who has a cynical or hardened view of humanity. Without condemning or disliking man he believes that man is predominately selfish and cannot be trusted always to do good. This is what does indeed make the conservative cautious about social change.[5]

The argument is that if people *are* given too much licence then, because they are selfish, they will seek the immediate gratification of their desires. This will lead to conflict and perhaps the destruction of existing social and economic structures and institutions—even though these have served them well in the past. Thus, if people are given too much power to decide too many things in one particular historical period, and to change too many structures, they will in fact destroy rather than build. This is the message of the French Revolution, as Burke sees it:

> The effect of liberty to individuals is, that they may do what they please; we ought to see what it will please them to do, before we risk congratulations, which may soon be turned into complaints . . . But liberty, when men act in bodies, is *power*. Considerate people, before they declare themselves, will observe the use which is made of *power*—and particularly of so trying a thing

184

as *new* power in *new* persons, of whose principles, tempers and dispositions they have little or no experience.[6]

Thus when persons create new movements, new demands and new social pressures, it does not follow that all these ought *ipso facto* to be satisfied; for if you satisfy them, you might undermine existing social structures which are in fact very important for the sustenance of society.

To illustrate, consider the conservative argument with respect to women's liberation. If a movement of women demands new rights and privileges, new choices, new liberties for themselves, of course, they come up against existing social structures. The conservative response is to ask: can we accommodate these demands without undermining social structures such as the family? If not, we shall oppose them. For the family has lasted for many centuries and served us well. Furthermore, women have performed these particular roles for all that time. Why then should they suddenly change? Maybe this is simply a fleeting demand that they have, or selfishness on their part. Yet the consequences of giving in to this demand may be catastrophic for society.

I do not, from the above, wish to imply that conservatives never want change. For many certainly do want to change things in the twentieth century. As I have argued in Chapter 3, our present culture is going through a period of transformation, in which some roles are breaking down or changing dramatically. The conservative, faced with this situation, wants the state or society in general to act in such a way as to stop this change and even bring back those traditional structures that have been broken down. The conservative answer to the cultural crisis is to bring back the traditional roles and structures. For example, in the family, mothers and fathers should return to their traditional functions.[7]

Secondly, a conservative might find that new irreversible circumstances have arisen to which he has to accommodate. For example, a US conservative may have supported keeping black people in their subservient position in that society. But he may find himself faced with the fact that the black people have achieved, through the constitution, certain rights and privileges which they never had before. Some conservatives would say, 'push them back to where they were before', but a thinking conservative would reject this. Rather he would accept the new black consciousness and seek to accommodate this by bringing blacks within the existing structures. Thus he would encourage the development of black capitalists, black university professors, a black upper and middle class. He thus fits them into the existing structures and any potential threat that this group posed to structures and institutions is removed.

Conservatives have no trouble reconciling democracy and inequality. For conservatives do not believe in egalitarianism. They therefore have an antipathy to real democracy, and believe that representative government in which everyone has the vote will not change the need for a ruling class. As Sir James Stephen puts it:

> Legislate how you will, establish universal suffrage, if you think proper, as a law which can never be broken. You are still as far as ever from equality. Political power has changed its shape but not its nature. The result of cutting it up into little bits is simply that the man who can sweep the greatest number of them into one heap will govern the rest. The strongest man in some form or other will always rule.[8]

The real objection to democracy is, of course, that there is a possibility that the common man may vote in governments who change the economic structures of society. The Marquis of Salisbury expressed this fear (in the House of Commons, 1864):

> They tell us that every man has a right to a share in the government of the community to which he belongs.

But they persist in forgetting that 'the suffrage' means something very much more than a share. It means an equal share. An extension of the suffrage to the working classes means that upon a question of taxation, or expenditure, or upon a measure vitally affecting commerce, two day-labourers shall outvote Baron Rothschild.[9]

Nevertheless, the extension of the vote to all persons has come about and conservatives have had to live with it. Democratic arrangements favoured by conservatives are therefore those which do *not* involve any changes to social structures and to the economic divisions between labour and capital, poor and rich. The smoothest way of doing this is when the major parties in a democracy both have policies which do not in fact interfere with existing economic and social structures. Thus in the conservatives' concept of an ideal democracy, there may be certain personality conflicts or policy differences, but not such as to threaten existing hierarchies. Such conservatives are constantly calling for 'consensus politics'. This consensus is supposedly due to the basic structures which give harmony and minimize conflict within society. Consequently, government and the state should not interfere with them, but should rather carry out few policies, run the machinery as it already exists. As Michael Oakeshott eloquently explains:

the office of government is not to impose other beliefs and activities upon its subjects, not to tutor or to educate them, not to make them better or happier in another way, not to direct them, to galvanize them into action . . . the office of government is merely to rule. This is a specific and limited activity, easily corrupted when combined with any other.[10]

It also follows from this view that political apathy is a good thing. Ray argues that 'If there's little difference between the major parties and no likelihood of other parties improving things, why worry about politics. Apathy is then the symptom of a well run and harmonious society'.[11] Here we have the rejection of the basic point which Rousseau makes: that democracy involves knowledge and active participation by the people. In the conservative perspective, democracy involves as little questioning by the people of the economic and social structures as possible, and hence as little participation in decision-making by the people as can be achieved.

What of equality of rights within democracy? For conservatives, there are no unconstrained human rights. For example, the conservative attitude to homosexuality, generally speaking, is that it undermines the family structure and the traditional roles in human relations. Consequently while people have certain rights with respect to their sexuality, this should not extend as far as homosexuality. The liberal perspective, on the other hand, maintains that the state has no right to interfere in certain areas of human life that are private, and therefore has no right to make laws prohibiting homosexuality between consenting adults.

Conservatives are therefore generally opposed to liberalism. They see it as a major factor in the breakdown of traditional structures of society. An interesting example of this conflict was the 1977 report by the Human Relations Commission.[12] Mr Fraser called it 'horrifying'; yet the report was grounded on taking seriously liberal principles about human relationships.

The other major theoretical perspective which is used to legitimate existing power structures is 'liberalism'. The major exponent is John Stuart Mill in his books *On Liberty* and *Representative Government*.[13] Mill's attitude to social structures and other hierarchies is very different from that of the conservatives. Mill maintains that these social structures, far from being conducive to human happiness and giving direction to life, limit the freedom of the individual. He says:

> Society can and does execute its own mandates and if it issues wrong mandates instead of right, or any

mandates at all in issues it ought not to meddle in, it practices a social tyranny more formidable than many kinds of political oppression since, though not usually upheld by such extreme penalties, it leaves fewer means of escape, penetrating much more deeply into the details of life and enslaving the soul itself.[14]

This problem with society as a whole is also present with the state, even when that state is democratic. This is because of the possibility of the *tyranny of the majority*. From the fact that the majority determines that something is right, or that the state should interfere with certain acts, it does not follow, for Mill, that they are right. Thus to the abstract concept of democracy, liberals wish to add that democracy involves limits to the power of the majority, because the rights of individuals and minorities must be respected. Yet, if the will of the majority is to be dominant, how are we going to protect the rights of this minority? Mill's answer was that the state must be based not only on the principle of democracy but also on the principles of liberty. These latter principles must be embedded in the very constitution of the state itself. Hence, for Mill, the ideal society was the one which gave full expression to the will of the majority in matters which concerned the society, and yet maximum freedom to the individual in matters which were the private concern of the individual. These ideas of Mill have been infused into the constitutions and governments of various states. They provide a justification for the rights of individuals laid down in the American Constitution and in the UN Charter.[15]

But what *are* the limits of interference in the affairs of the individual? How are we to determine those limits? Mill proposes the famous single principle:

that the sole end for which mankind are warranted individually or collectively in interfering with the liberty of action of any of their number is self-protection. That the only purpose for which power can be rightfully exercised over any member of a civilized community is to *prevent harm to others*.[16]

Notice that it is harm to others, not harm to oneself, which is the basic point here. Mill rejects the view that the state can act contrary to the wishes of the individual for his own benefit.

His own good, either physical or moral, is not a sufficient warrant. He cannot rightfully be compelled to do or forbear because it will make him happier or because, in the opinions of others, to do so would be wise or even right.[17]

But what constitutes causing harm to others? This can be brought out if we consider some examples. Clearly all direct physical violence is harm. But harm need not be physical. Surely some kinds of psychological ordeal constitute harm. But now, if we admit some psychological harm, where do we draw the line? What of the law prohibiting abortion? Is it preventing harm or is it limiting the freedom of the mother, forcing her to bear and care for an unwanted child? People have agonized over this question, without any agreement as to whether the state has a right to prevent abortion.[18]

There is thus a theoretical difficulty in determining just what constitutes harm. This is important, for any decision on whether the state should interfere on an issue will, to a certain extent, depend on whether it is classified as harm. As is recognized by some commentators, this difficulty gives rise to another.[19] If there is disagreement as to whether a particular activity constitutes harm to others, then who is to determine the issue? If we say it is the society, then we have the problem of the tyranny of the majority. If, on the other hand, it is the individual, then what of those individuals who consider oppression and degradation of others not to be harm?

In order to come to grips with this issue, Mill introduces the distinction between self-regarding and other-regarding acts. Self-regarding acts include a person's own thoughts and experiences as well as actions which affect him only. Other-regarding acts consist of those in which he is in interaction with other persons in the community, that is, they are essentially social acts.[20] Mill's thesis is often stated thus: 'The state has no right to interfere with self-regarding acts of any kind; it has only a limited right to interfere in social affairs involving interactions between several persons'.

However, as McCloskey argues in his commentary,[21] Mill believed that the state can justifiably interfere with self-regarding actions, in order to ensure that each person contributes his share to the society. Hence he approved of compulsory taxation. Thus Mill insists on 'each person's bearing his share (to be fixed on some equitable principle) of the labours and sacrifices incurred for defending the society or its members from injury and molestation'.[22]

With respect to other-regarding actions, Mill argued that if a person has harmed another in the process of fair competition, as in examinations, or has, in his behaviour, set a bad example for the other, the state has no right to interfere; and that 'if the harm is great enough to seriously interfere with individuality and self-development, and the interference by the state less, the latter may be justified'.[23] McCloskey believes that this was the basis of Mill's thoughts on economic harm, and the reason he seriously considered the case for socialism.

Consider this matter of economic harm further. Supposing a man does not look after his family economically. He refuses to work and, when they have some money, he spends it all on drink. Has the state the right to interfere in this man's life? Another simple form of economic harm is theft: when a man steals, he is economically harming those from whom he steals. Presumably the state is justified in preventing theft. Yet where do we draw the line here? For consider the case when the resources of the whole society are limited, then the accumulation of massive wealth, by a small number of individuals results in others—usually the large majority—having less, with many having very little indeed. In this case, are the poor being harmed by the economic structure? Should the state act to overcome the harm done to them? For example, if a man has no job, should the state tax others to provide him with a minimum allowance?

Liberals divide on this issue. Some would argue that the state should not act, because to do so is to interfere with the rights of the individual to his or her own wealth and property. This appeals to the notion that owning wealth is a self-regarding act. Yet, in capitalism, we speak not of wealth which is idle, but that used to buy means of production and the labour of workers. In this sense, wealth and capital are other-regarding, as Mill clearly recognized.[24]

Given that they acknowledge this point, liberals may still divide. The *laissez-faire* liberals maintain that the capitalist system with its market mechanisms allows for free exchange relations between buyer and seller of goods and of labour power. Hence the market will create the best arrangement for people to achieve the maximum expression of their individual desires.[25] Whatever harm may befall some people under this system is due to their failure to be industrious. The state should, thus, as far as possible, not interfere with the operations of economy and the market. It should merely set up laws to protect life and property from those who may seek to infringe these rights. The *social welfarist* liberals, on the other hand, argue that our experience of unbridled capitalism shows that many workers will be reduced to misery and that the unemployed, the sick and the old would starve (or sympathizers might rebel) if the state does not enforce minimum wage levels and humane conditions of employment for the former, and provide sufficient income and welfare services for the latter. These liberals believe that, by increasing services to workers, they will further integrate them into the system, improve their lot and avoid the harm caused by the laissez-faire approach.

These two perspectives have been blurred with the development of capitalism to monopoly forms. Those who believe in market competition often abandon a passive role for the state and argue that it should intervene to break up monopolies (see next section): thus a person can be laissez-faire about one aspect of economy while being interventionist about another. What most of these modern liberals share, however, is an antipathy to socialism.

This was not true of Mill himself, who took the arguments for socialism seriously, though he did not adopt it.[26] He wanted to limit severely the right to inheritance, for he did not believe—as John Locke had[27]—that the right to private property was natural and inalienable. Rather he believed that capitalism and socialism should compete with each other, and that we should wait and see which system was 'consistent with the greatest amount of human liberty and spontaneity'.[28]

McCloskey notes three important factors missing in Mill's analysis of socialism:

> First, there is none of the moral indignation of Marx, Engels, Laski and Tawney at the gross inequalities to be found in capitalist societies; in Mill's writings, there is no deep sense of the workers being shamelessly and unjustly exploited. Secondly, there is no evident awareness of the power of wealth, of what is true and important in Marxism, that capitalists may use democratic institutions to further their class interests and to oppose reform; that, if constitutional methods fail, resort may be made to violent, unconstitutional methods to oppose change and reform. Thirdly and most important, there is an almost complete unawareness, and certainly, at best, a dismissal without argument, of the argument for socialism from liberty ... that the shortcomings and inequalities of capitalist systems are impediments or obstacles to freedom and that socialism, by providing employment, reasonable minimum wages, and amenities such as health services, may foster and enlarge liberty. If the main test by

which we are to judge between socialism and
capitalism is in terms of liberty, this argument
concerning liberty is of vital importance.[29]

Even though he did not resolve this last problem, at least
Mill had an open attitude to socialism. Most modern liberals,
however, have not followed the founding father on this.
Instead they dogmatically claim a contradiction between
liberty and socialism. In so doing, they act together with
conservatives to reinforce the dominant power structures.

Yet, while the liberal philosophy is used in Western societies
to bolster and support oppressive power structures, this can
only be done by negating radical elements within that philosophy. Modern liberals who strongly support the capitalist
economy and the political and bureaucratic sectors of the
ruling class are either untrue to Mill's principles or caught in
paradoxes. Thus if they support the extension of the state's
services to reduce the harm caused to people by the economic
system, they will thereby increase the pressure on capitalist
forces. Further, if they support freedom of expression (which
Mill considered perhaps the most fundamental right), they
cannot rationally deny workers the right to organize and
express their demands, nor can they coherently deny working-class movements access to the media and the right of
public protest. Yet these means of discourse can, and do,
result in challenges to the legitimacy of existing power
relations and the domination of the ruling class. If as I predict,
this class becomes more repressive of the freedom of assembly
and expression, will the liberals stand up and be counted?
Or will they simply prove that they have been using the liberal
philosophy as a rationalization of an oppressive social order?

As economic and social crisis deepens, liberalism becomes
less useful to the ruling class in maintaining its hegemony
over ideas and practices. For the liberal goal of free and
rational debate on goals and policies and the liberal ideal of
individual rights are both dangerous, since they can be used
by the working class to press its demands and thereby

threaten oppressive power structures. Increasingly, liberalism will be replaced by 'radical' conservatism as the philosophy of the ruling class; this is happening already in the Australian Liberal Party (see next section). Increasingly, the working class will have to struggle to retain even liberal rights, such as those of assembly, expression and non-discrimination on the basis of political beliefs (see Chapter 6A).

C THE LIBERAL PARTY'S PHILOSOPHY

The most important political organization which ensures the domination of the ruling class is the Liberal Party of Australia. Until 1978, when two books appeared, very little had been written on the philosophy or ideology of the Liberal Party.[1] The reason for this is that most commentators see this party as having only a pragmatic philosophy, in that it changes its policies and platforms for the purpose of winning elections. This will not be my approach to the problem: I shall try to show that the Liberal Party operates within a definite philosophical framework, which seeks to justify rationally the present structures of power.

To see how this philosophy arose, consider briefly the factors leading to the formation of the Liberal Party in 1944. The party was formed after previous anti-Labor parties had failed or been wrecked by internal strife. Notwithstanding this, they had still managed to govern for most of the period since Federation by various deals.[2] However, when the Curtin Labor government gained power in 1941 (through the defection of two rebel anti-Labor members from Victoria) and when, in 1943, it won an election victory, the major anti-Labor group—the United Australia Party—received its death knell. For, as Menzies himself recognized, the UAP had increasingly been identified as a party of 'reaction' and 'negation', reduced to simply asserting that it was against socialism.[3] As John Lonie documents, major businessmen and front organizations for business increasingly saw the UAP as out of touch and irrelevant to the requirements of modern capitalism.[4] One of these organizations—the Victorian

Institute of Public Affairs—produced an outspoken document entitled *Looking Forward—A Post-war Policy for Australian Industry*, which its director C. D. Kemp described as a 'radical departure from deeply entrenched business notions and a great change in business thinking on major national issues'.[5] Its major claim was that it was possible to achieve full employment, responsible levels of social security and a harmonious relationship between labour and capital, through co-operation between capitalist forces and the state.

Menzies enthusiastically approved the ideas of *Looking Forward*[6] and incorporated them into the philosophy and platform of the new Liberal Party. The latent tension between the democratic state (which many conservatives had earlier opposed) and capitalist economy was to be done away with, and replaced by a spirit of co-operation. Thus the basic philosophy of Australian Liberalism, since the founding of the party, has been that the democratic state and capitalist economy are natural partners (notwithstanding the contradictory values on which they are based). By identifying democracy as necessarily intertwined with capitalism, the Liberal Party managed to represent all socialist forces as anti-democratic or creeping forms of totalitarian communism.[7] Indeed, anti-communism has been the most effective feature of the Liberal Party's strategy (see below).

Hence, while the new Liberal Party abandoned the view that the government should not interfere in economic matters, and recognized the importance of the development of the welfare state in reducing some of the more grossly inhumane aspects of capitalism, it did not propose any changes to the structure of capitalist relations. On the contrary, it came to believe that the welfare measures would strengthen the capitalist economic structure and improve both productivity and profits.[8]

Business support for the new party was thus enthusiastic, particularly when compared to that shown its predecessor. Soon it was able to call on support from a diversity of capitalist interests. Indeed the party now gains its support from all sectors of capital: from small competitive business interests to large monopolistic local companies and the multi-national corporations. In addition, it receives vast support from powerful bureaucrats, academics and professionals in the judicial system.[9] The Liberal Party's philosophy and organization have thus contributed substantially to the closer integration of the ruling class.

The Liberal Party does not seek to interfere with the capitalist economy in any way which will change its basic structure. It does, however, permit interference that is intended to support the system and make it more profitable; indeed, Liberal leaders are often championing the profit motive as the basis of economic growth. Consider two historical examples. Menzies, in a speech attacking the Bank Nationalization Bill, quoted Chifley's argument that 'since private banks are conducted primarily for profit and therefore follow policies which in important respects run counter to the public interest, their business should be transferred to public ownership'.[10] Menzies then commented:

> There is the whole argument, naked and unashamed. If it is a true argument, then all private business ought to be transferred to public ownership. The basis of it is that private profit must run counter to the public interest . . . The assumption, of course is that profit making is either improper or anti-social. Yet I remind the house that without the chance of profit and the search of profit . . . the whole of the industrial expansion of the English-speaking world since the beginning of the nineteenth century would never have been accomplished and that expansion was accompanied by an amazing increase of population and a great rise in living standards.[11]

A second example is provided by Malcolm Fraser. In his 1975 election campaign, he argued that the first priority of the government was to increase profitability for enterprise. He explained that the problems of inflation and unemployment could only be solved if we have more investment by companies and individuals. This investment can only come if the system operates in such a way as to ensure a substantial profit for those who are able to invest their resources.[12]

In both cases, the Liberal position begs the question against socialism. Of course profit is necessary for the continued successful operation of the present system. It does not, however, follow that increasing profits will, in itself, prevent economic crises. Furthermore, none of this shows that the profit system—with its greed and exploitation—is the only workable mode of economic organization. Yet this latter the Liberals have rarely attempted to demonstrate.[13]

The positive affirmation of the need for profitability has always been an important feature in Liberal philosophy. Yet more important, perhaps, than the emphasis on the positive aspects of capitalism is the Liberal emphasis on anti-communism. Indeed, it can be argued that Menzies sustained himself in power for seventeen years by a continuous stress on this theme.[14] The Labor Party was attacked for being socialist, and thus implicitly or explicitly connected with anti-democratic forces. Increasingly Menzies' attack followed this line: socialism is incompatible with democracy because socialism is like totalitarian communism, and this latter is clearly anti-democratic; hence the Labor Party is inherently dangerous and anti-democratic.

Menzies succeeded with this approach notwithstanding the fact that the Labor Party had (during the last years of its power, prior to the 1949 election) gone out of its way to disassociate itself from communists.[15] Thus Ben Chifley had used troops for the first time to break up a strike which had communist leaders—the coal-miners' strike.[16] In 1949, the Labor Party was so concerned about the attacks associating it with communism that it jailed the leader of the Communist Party of Australia. L. L. Sharkey, Chairman of the Party, was jailed for making the error of answering a hypothetical question. He was asked: 'If Soviet forces were to pursue aggressors and enter Australia, what would be the attitude of the Australian people?' He answered that 'Australian workers would welcome Soviet forces pursuing aggressors as the workers welcomed them throughout Europe, and the red troops liberated the people from the power of the Nazis'.[17] For this, Sharkey was jailed for three years on a charge of sedition, which was prosecuted by Dr Evatt, who later became Leader of the Opposition.[18]

The Communist Party at the time, though more powerful than it is today, was a minor force. Yet Menzies persisted with his anti-communist campaign. He realized that it would promote democratic capitalism as the only valid theoretical approach and it would lead the Labor Party into a mass of internal divisions. This indeed was the case. Upon his election in 1949, Menzies introduced the Communist Party Dissolution Bill. It was intended to ban the Communist Party, and bring on an election so that the Liberals could secure a majority in the Senate. Unlike Mr Whitlam in 1972, Menzies recognized that it was necessary to create an issue around which to have the election. Since anti-communism was, by this stage, growing rapidly throughout the Western world (due mostly to American propaganda compaigns which were given wide publicity in Australia), the issue was clearly the dissolution of communism.[19]

Menzies pushed this Bill through the House of Representatives. The Labor Party opposed it in the Senate. However, in so doing, they appeared to give credence to the view that their socialism was inherently intertwined with communism. Menzies then advised the Governor-General to order a dissolution of parliament, fought the election on this issue and won the majority in both Houses. From that time onwards it was mostly plain sailing for the Liberals.

However, Menzies did not give up his campaign against the Communist Party. On the contrary, after pushing the Bill through parliament and having it rejected by the High Court as unconstitutional, Menzies resolved to put the issue to the people in a referendum. This placed the Labor Party in a very embarassing position. On the one hand, they wanted to dissociate themselves from the Communist Party and yet, on the other, they had to publicly defend the right of the Communist Party to exist. Thus the Labor Party was forced into the position of defending the 'liberal' policy of free speech and assembly, and yet at the same time dissociating itself from the Communist Party. To his credit, the leader of the ALP, Dr Evatt, became the spearhead of the campaign against the referendum proposals which, to many people's surprise, were rejected by the Australian population.[20]

Although he lost the referendum, Menzies nevertheless tied Evatt, and the Labor Party in general, to the right of the Communist Party to exist; he thus persisted in labelling the ALP 'anti-democratic'. In 1956 the issue came to a head: the Labor Party split on the question of the relationship to the Communist Party.[21] The socialists within the party were attacked for being lackeys of communism, the Soviet Union, etc. The attacking group, after failing to exclude socialists from the Party, staged a massive walkout and formed a new party, initially called the Anti-Communist Labor Party, which then changed its name to the Democratic Labor Party.[22] Their second preference votes kept the Liberal Party in power for a prolonged period.

Thus Menzies' approach—of associating democracy and capitalism, and negating all attempts to introduce socialism as a possible democratic alternative—was very effective. Indeed, while his technique was tried in other Western countries, it normally did not have the effect of excluding the major opposition party for such a prolonged period. In Australia, it kept Labor out of office.

There are, however, different ways of uniting a defence of 'free' enterprise with the requirements of the modern democratic state. Within the Liberal Party, two perspectives became dominant: conservatism and liberalism. As the New South Wales Secretary of the Party said in 1973: 'I see the Liberal Party as a coalition between conservatives and liberals, and I believe that they can co-exist quite happily within the same party'. However, Peter Tiver has argued (convincingly in my view) that the matter is more complicated than this. As he illustrates, the 'great majority of Liberal parliamentarians are liberal on some issues and conservative on others'.[23] Indeed, I would go so far as to argue that the whole party is best represented in terms of a compromise between conservatism and liberalism. Further, I shall attempt to show that the character of this compromise has changed and is liable to change again.

In the last section, I distinguished two forms of liberalism: laissez-faire and welfarist. The difference between these—which centres around the extent of intervention by the state in the economy and social structures—is important to Liberal Party ideology. Thus, in the early part of the Menzies era, the attitude to economy was liberal 'laissez-faire', at least insofar as the internal operations of the economy itself were concerned. Menzies believed that the state should not interfere with the dynamism of the capitalist economy: the state should allow it to work according to its own processes and mechanisms. On the other hand, he did not assume that it would do this without government support to the social structure. So while advocating a liberal approach to the economy, for the social structure he proposed a combination of two things: conservatism with respect to the basic structures such as the family, and social welfarism for the most needy.[24] This combination was politically popular—for the social welfarist measures could be used to legitimate the humanitarian claims of the system, strengthen the nuclear family and lock people into a suburban life-style. This ensured the further integration of workers into the capitalist process (see Chapter 4B).

The government set out, not to organize capitalist production through planning and controls, but rather to establish the preconditions for such production:
(i) It had to act to ensure that there was a pool of available labour on which industry could draw. In Australia, this goal was achieved through the immigration programme. This was the most spectacular programme adopted by the Liberal

Party. It brought in hundreds of thousands of people from Europe. The programme had been introduced by the Chifley Labor government, under Arthur Calwell (later Leader of the Opposition). Menzies took it over and enthusiastically supported it because it was providing the preconditions for expansion in two ways: by producing a bigger market for goods and services and by providing a bigger labour force to fuel the developing manufacturing industries within Australia.[25]

(ii) It had to ensure adequate education for the labour force to enable production to continue in a technologically advanced society. In order to do this, and to cope with the increasing demands stemming from the immigration intake, the government expanded primary, secondary and tertiary education. Yet it was not a planned expansion; quite often there were critical shortages of teachers and buildings. Recently the Fraser government has attempted to re-orient educational planning away from general knowledge and more in the direction of skills.[26]

(iii) It had to ensure adequate means of transport and communication, particularly in a large country like Australia. From the start, Menzies recognized the importance of public spending on road systems, to ensure that raw materials and products could reach their destinations with as little cost as possible.

(iv) The government had to protect the home economy from 'excessive' international competition. It was thus required to introduce tariffs on goods imported from foreign countries. Not only do we have tariffs, but we also have quotas—this means, for example, that the total number of Japanese cars coming into Australia is limited by the action of the state. Tariffs and quotas have been the basis of sharp divisions within the Liberal Party—reflecting the interests of different sectors of the ruling class.[27]

In the above ways, the early Liberal Party ideology was liberal laissez-faire on the organization of economy, while being interventionist in setting down favourable preconditions for production. In social policies, it appealed to social welfarist and conservative principles. The social welfarist part was strictly limited, the Liberal concept being that each person should help himself. Social welfare was designed to help only the most needy, and any attempts to introduce universal social welfare schemes were very heavily criticized within the Liberal Party itself and were ultimately abandoned by Menzies. As Tiver explains:

> Menzies found himself pressed by 'two opposing considerations'. One was that the struggle for existence and progress brought out the best in man; the other, that a never-ending struggle on the fringe of reasonable existence was 'destructive of hope and humanity' . . . Menzies would continually warn against the dangers to individualism of too much reliance on the welfare state, while talking at the same time with pride of his government's 'humane record' in the field of social welfare. This equivocation persisted through to the modifications to Medibank made by Malcolm Fraser.[28]

With this combination of policies, the Liberal Party presided over a long period of economic growth, with low unemployment. The 'free enterprise' system was duly given the credit for all the blessings which had befallen 'the lucky country'. (The real reasons for growth are discussed in Chapter 3B.)

This situation continued until the early 1960s, when something unexpected happened. In 1961 there was an election which Labor nearly won; they lost by one seat which Menzies, paradoxically, held because of preferences from the Communist Party. Why was it that the man who was credited with leading the post-war growth of Australian capitalism nearly lost power? The reason was that his economic policies began to fail. In 1960, it was clear that inflation, as measured by the contemporary standards of the Western world, was getting out of hand. To deal with this, Menzies changed his laissez-faire approach and advocated intervention in the economy. He imposed a credit squeeze. This was the standard Keynesian manoeuvre when the inflation rate rose. Yet by imposing the credit squeeze and thereby restricting the level of demand, Menzies changed his ideology. He had previously attacked the Bank Nationalization Bill, arguing that the government should not have the right to interfere with the money flow. But in 1960, he had been converted to the view that the government *had* to interfere in order to control inflationary trends in capitalism.[29]

The credit squeeze, as expected, led to unemployment. The dramatic increase in the number of unemployed to 100 000 (the highest since the war) placed Menzies in a difficult position. There was great unrest at the time: in particular, amongst the immigrants who had been brought out to Australia with the promise of full employment. Hence the close election result.

This abandonment of laissez-faire principles with respect to economy has brought a lasting change in the ideology of the Liberal Party. Increasingly, intervention by means of fiscal measures to prop up capitalist economy has been required. Some of these have created deep conflicts of principle within the Liberal Party. This can be illustrated with reference to the increasing development of monopolies within Australian capitalism. For, although the Liberal Party has always made noises in favour of small business, it did not seriously consider the question of monopolies until 1960, when the following clause was added to the party platform: 'Protection of the community against any monopolies, combines and industrial organizations where, through the absence of competition or by restrictive practices, they operate in a manner contrary to the public interest'.[30] The rank and file eventually forced some action on these proposals. Yet the legislation presented to parliament in December 1962 was based on the compromise view that some restrictive trade practices might be in the public interest.[31] It did not become law until 1965, by which time crucial amendments to water down the Bill had been adopted—in particular, resale price maintenance was no longer illegal.

The issue divided the Liberals because it involved a reversal of positions. Previously, those who had believed in competitive capitalism always argued for less government interference. However, as capitalism had developed to a less competitive, more monopolistic phase, what should they do? Should they support this evolution as natural, or should they interfere, using state power, to force a return to a competitive phase? To plump for the former involves supporting a concentration of economic power; to introduce the latter is to increase the role of bureaucracy and state power. In either case, ruling-class domination is increased—but a change could upset the balance of forces in that class.

In the end, the Trade Practices Act was so weak that it was virtually useless. The powerful monopolies have won that struggle, and have thereby ensured their domination over the political wing of the ruling class. Thus while, even today, some Liberals believe that the government interferes too much in economic affairs and demand a more 'laissez-faire' attitude,[32] overall there is an increased recognition that advanced capitalist economy requires active state intervention in order to sustain profitability. This is a point on which Mr Fraser is quite adamant, notwithstanding his other conservative tendencies (see Chapter 9C).

While economic philosophy was changing in the early 1960s, there was also a dramatic change with respect to the social structure. Overseas trends, particularly in the United States, popularized the liberalization of sexual mores and family relationships. Many of these were superficial changes in dress and styles of behaviour, particularly amongst the young. Yet they were received by conservatives with dismay.[33] Even music such as rock and roll was seen by many as subversive of the values of Western society.

These developments put the Liberal Party in a difficult position. It was required to either defend the traditional structures or to support the new styles of life by appealing to 'liberal' principles. The result was a kind of inversion of the earlier conservatism with respect to social structure. This change was accelerated within the Liberal Party with the election of John Gorton as Prime Minister. Don Chipp, Minister for Customs and Excise under Gorton, relaxed considerably the censorship laws, using liberal principles to defend his actions. Many conservatives, including the DLP opposed this move as an attack on the 'moral fibre' of the country. However, Chipp was by this stage simply reflecting a *fait accompli*.

Nevertheless, there has been a continued tension in the Liberal Party on social issues, between conservatives, who want legislation to preserve old forms and liberals who want to adjust to the changes in social structure itself. This was one of the factors in the fall of Gorton as Prime Minister (see Chapter 6C). McMahon, who replaced him, attempted (rather foolishly, given the mood of the time) to contrast the Liberal Party to the 'permissive' ALP. Later Snedden adopted a much more liberal stance on these issues. This again has been reversed with the domination of the party by Malcolm Fraser—who has given the impression that he wants a return to traditional social structures, yet has realized the futility of attempting to impose this through legislation. As is shown in their response to the Human Relations Commission and their handling of women's issues, modern Liberals are extremely unlikely to do anything to encourage or support current trends towards liberalization of the social structure.

The overall impression of the Liberal philosophy (as given above) is that it changes from a liberal to a conservative perspective or vice versa, depending on the historical circumstances. Whether this is so in the future, however, depends on how long the domination of the party by Fraser and his ideological group continues. For Fraser clearly has no love for liberal principles. I believe that he has thrown together the strands of a new perspective for the Liberal Party, in which liberal principles are increasingly irrelevant. In what follows, I shall try to map out the philosophical elements of this perspective. The way in which it has been played out in recent Australian politics will be discussed extensively in Part III of this book.

In his philosophy, Fraser has abandoned the egalitarian pretensions of Robert Menzies and John Gorton. This is clearly shown by Fraser's commitment to the view that inequalities are natural and right. As several commentators have noted, Fraser consciously adopts the attitude of 'the natural superiority of those with talent, wealth and power'.[34] This attitude is not based on the division of society into races; it is not fascism. It is based on a conscious recognition of class division—with a twist. Whereas previous Liberals have tried to hide the fact that they act on behalf of the ruling class, Fraser virtually pronounces this aim, with a kind of inverted moral consciousness. To justify this point, Fraser has appealed to the philosophy of Ayn Rand. This novelist-philosopher proclaims selfishness a virtue and greed the life force of society.[35] In her novel *Atlas Shrugged* which Fraser is reputed to be very impressed with,[36] she speaks of the capitalists, intellectuals and professionals (who support the profit motive) as 'men of mind' and presents a story in which they go on strike, leaving the poor workers leaderless. This soon leads society into chaos, and proves the necessary role of capital, and its intellectual supporters. What is it that Fraser is impressed with in this fantasy? Clearly it is the concept of the ruling class as a superior and noble group, which has an important historical role. Rand believes that this group provides the dynamism, the life force of society.

However, there is a fundamental difference between Ayn Rand and Fraser. The Prime Minister does not believe that capitalists will achieve their goals on their own. Given the way in which capitalism has developed and given the *gains* made by the working class, it is necessary for the state to intervene to redress the difference. He is thus not a 'right-wing anarchist' as Deane Wells calls him.[37] Wells claims that:

> Right wing anarchists, or 'anarcho-capitalists' hold that the best form of society is one in which there is no government interference in people's lives, and no restrictions on the activities of private capital. This

> latter description fits Rand, and to the extent that
> Fraser adopts her line, it fits him too . . . It is noticeable
> that Fraser has moved to reduce the scope of
> government activity to a greater extent than any of his
> recent predecessors.[38]

Yet, as I have indicated in Chapter 3B and shall argue further in Chapter 9, Fraser has not reduced government expenditures. He has rather used state moneys to redistribute resources to capital and hence to boost profits. Furthermore, instead of leaving the capitalists to fight the working class, Fraser has brought in the state, with all its powers, on the side of profit.

Wells claims that Fraser's attacks on the working class are due to psychological instability.

> Why does Fraser, who has never himself had to endure
> privation, constantly insist that other people have to
> make sacrifices? Why does Fraser, who has never been
> faced with real danger, constantly insist that life is so
> full of perils, challenges and adversity? . . . A political
> theorist cannot answer such questions, but he can say
> this—that a man who feels such insecurities cannot
> safely be left in control of the country's government.[39]

This attempt to caricature the Prime Minister does not, however, add to our understanding of his new Liberal ideology. I have suggested that Fraser has an accurate understanding of the conflict between classes, even though his moral position on this conflict is repugnant. His actions show that he understands the structure of power in Australia and the way in which the state can be actively used to negate many of the gains made by the working class (see Chapter 9).

Fraser is therefore a *radical* conservative, one who seeks to change a historical trend. He seeks to force on the working class: reductions in the real value of wages; reductions in the services provided by the state; an increase in the pool of unemployed so as to reduce the demands of labour and to increase insecurities of workers; and an acceptance of the new situation by workers, and their representatives in unions and the Labor Party. The new Liberal philosophy thus aggressively supports capital and the ruling class; it seeks to discipline the working class and make them more 'responsible' and obedient in their performance of their tasks.

Are we likely to see a return to more liberal principles by the Liberal Party? While the current social and economic crisis continues, this seems unlikely. This does not mean, however, that Fraser's aggressive approach is likely to bring the Australian economy out of crisis. For there is a flaw in Fraser's analysis: his faith in the capitalist themselves. Although their profits have increased as a consequence of his labours, they have not re-invested these gains in Australia (see Chapter 3B). The hegemony of the ruling class is thus not guaranteed. It appears that, even for political leaders of the ruling class, life wasn't meant to be easy.

D   THE ROLE OF THE MASS MEDIA

Perhaps the most important factor in the sustenance of the hegemony of the ruling class is their almost total domination of the mass media. This issue has been extensively discussed by several excellent books and articles appearing in the last few years.[1] In this section, I can only sketch briefly what I consider to be the major points.

The mass media—radio, television, newspapers and magazines—are supposedly concerned to inform, entertain and, to a lesser degree, educate the huge audiences and readerships which they attract. Underlying these noble aims, however, is a more insidious one: the mass media seek to create and sustain a world view, a complex system of beliefs and values about life and society, which has the effect of justifying and legitimizing the existent power structures. Professor Henry Mayer puts the matter thus:

> Any medium is not a passive channel but an active shaper. It mobilises, depresses, reinforces, and

legitimises. It deeply influences attitudes towards the system we live under and whether that system needs changing . . . Thus we can always ask: why has this rather than that selection been made, whose interests does this rather than that selection promote or bypass or downgrade? To discuss the mass media seriously is to raise questions of this kind.[2]

Mayer poses the following questions to be answered in respect to the Australian media, both private and public:

Who are the controllers of reality-fashioning attempts? How did they become such? How do they maintain and enhance control? How easily, cheaply, quickly, are rival versions of reality available? . . . What can we discover as to the linkage of reality construction and the articulation of a given set of interests.[3]

I turn first to the question: Who controls the media? Except for the Australian Broadcasting Commission and a small number of community or access radio stations, the controllers of the mass media in Australia are four major companies, three of which are family concerns. These companies are the Herald and Weekly Times Ltd, News Ltd (the Murdoch family), John Fairfax Ltd (Fairfax family) and Consolidated Press Holdings Ltd (Packer family).[4] The first three own all seventeen of Australia's capital city dailies and many provincial ones as well; they also control many magazines, radio and TV stations. (Compare this with seventeen owners publishing twenty-one capital city dailies in 1930.) As Humphrey McQueen explains:

Monopoly is the right term for Australian newspaper ownership. Even though there is more than one major firm operating in the general field, there is little direct competition between them. In Perth, Hobart, and Brisbane, the Herald and Weekly Times group produce the only daily papers, while the *Herald* in Melbourne and the *Advertiser* in Adelaide do not have any immediate competition ... A 1971 survey of thirty-two capitalist countries showed that Australia had the capitalist world's second highest degree of press concentration, second only to the Republic of Ireland. Since that survey was made, Packer has sold out to Murdoch so that Australia may now lead the capitalist world in terms of the total daily circulation controlled by the three largest proprietors.[5]

The Packer family is, however, going strong in the areas of radio, television and magazines. Packer owns the Channel 9 television network and the highly influential *Australian Women's Weekly*.

Even when competition, rather than collusion, exists between these media controllers, it is not competition which allows for the expression of a variety of attitudes and points of view. Nor does it illuminate public issues and increase public awareness. For the character of the competition is governed, as in any capitalist enterprise, by the profit motive.

What is it which generates profit in the mass media industry? It is, of course, revenue from advertising. This revenue is dependent on firstly, the number of people who watch the advertisements on TV, listen to them on the radio and read them in the newspapers and magazines. The ratings or circulation is thus a critical factor for advertising revenue.[6] The more people watching, listening, reading, the more opportunity to sell. It also depends on the effectiveness of the advertising campaigns in selling products to men, women and children. As Henry Rosenbloom puts it:

> Commercial broadcasting is a surreptitious slave trade. It is a business in which audience varies directly with its size. Of course, little of this sordid market-place activity is transmitted to the victims. However, while stations promote themselves between commercial

breaks as fairy god-mothers, their trade advertisements in journals such as B & T Weekly are straight to the point: 'We can deliver more housewives between 2 p.m. and 4 p.m. than . . . ' is a common sales pitch.[7]

The modern mass media are an indispensable feature of modern capitalism. For they create through their campaigns desires in people for the many and varied goods generated by the economy—even, as is mostly the case, when people do not need such goods. A variety of discreditable and ultimately immoral practices are carried out in the pursuit of these goals. People are persuaded to purchase a vast array of products by the advertiser linking the possession of these products to such qualities as sexual attractiveness ('how's your love life?'), increases in esteem and status ('I'm foreman material') and the overcoming of fears and insecurities ('Don't wait to be told' you need a certain soap; a toothpaste 'adds confidence'). There are even claims to overcome the boring isolation of suburban life (a certain drink 'adds life and everybody needs a little life').[8] This is entirely different from an objective statement of the virtues of the product: indeed some of these products are dangerous to health and would not survive an objective assessment.

Because mass media advertising is an intrinsic part of the capitalist economy, without which the degree of over-production would be even more serious than it is, and because this advertising revenue provides the dynamic for the whole media industry (when the media are privately owned), it would clearly be absurd to expect these media to come out against the capitalist economy, or even to allow an objective assessment of it. In Australia, however, the monopolistic situation, combined with an uncritical acceptance by Australians, has meant that most arms of the media are extremely conservative politically. Thus, whereas in most Western countries there is at least one newspaper which supports the opposition party, in Australia no major paper or television station supports the ALP in any sustained way (although several papers did briefly change to support Whitlam in 1972: see Chapter 7B). This crude political bias of the media has led thoughtful newspaper managers, such as Ranald MacDonald of the *Age*, to deliver blunt warnings about the credibility of the press.[9]

The political perspective taken by the press is sometimes due to direct pressure on journalists from management, as in Murdoch's *Australian* during the 1975 election.[10] However, in most cases, such pressure is unnecessary. For the editors have been carefully chosen to conform to the political perspective which the paper wishes to project. Thus journalists' stories can be edited or run with misleading headlines, if the report does not fit the political values of the management.

Yet journalists are not all programmed to observe and write merely to suit the preferences of their employers. This can create tensions between different goals and ideals, as Allan Ashbolt notes:

> As a corollary to the basic contradiction in which a tight, oligopolistic ring of proprietors is set against a broad, heterogeneous complex of workers, there is constant tension between the largely profit-motivated drives of the employers and the essential creativity of much of the work being done by the employees. For these employees, of whatever status, are *theoretically* occupied in searching for truth, imparting knowledge and widening worthwhile human experience.[11]

Even where they may challenge the party preferences of their bosses, however, most journalists and editors do not challenge the power structures of society. As Max Walsh, editor of the *Financial Review*, noted, it is the overall commitment to existing institutions which the media wish to reinforce:

> The Establishment is a well-ordered, comfortable club to belong to, and reformist government, Labor or

> Liberal, threatens it. It is probably here that the worst
> bias of the press occurs. These taboo areas,
> unquestioned privileges of institutions . . . are not
> matters of proprietorial interference or brainwashing
> by the individual—rather they are the product of
> social and economic forces.[12]

The reinforcement of the existing structures of power takes several forms, the most important of which are:

(i) The emphasis on achievement and growth, particularly in the economy and within established social structures. The news is full of records of success or breakthrough, all *within* established hierarchies. Those who have been most successful are represented as heroes and idols (the fabulous millionaire, the glamorous actress, the sports star, etc.). The presence of such symbols of wealth and fame reinforces people's view that they have equal opportunity in the system.[13]

(ii) There is a focus on crime, and on disasters such as road accidents. These, however, are never seen as caused by the socio-economic system; rather accidents are due to error and incompetence or freakish circumstances, while crime is mostly due to the evil character of the criminal, and never to social need.[14] Related to this is the fact that Australians are given little awareness of the existence of poverty in Australia. The Henderson Report on poverty came as a shock to many people, because the impression had been created that, while there were some wealthy people in Australia, everyone else was doing quite well.

(iii) As Connell explains, the media focus on creating a middle-class image for people.[15] Indeed, from the media alone, one would hardly be aware that a substantial proportion of working Australians are engaged in manual labour. This, of course, supports the myth of classlessness. Connell remarks:

> It is obvious how overwhelmingly middle-class is the
> world as seen by the press. 81 per cent of people in the
> *News*, 87 per cent of people in the *Advertiser*, are from

white-collar occupations. The predominance of these groups would be even greater if we counted numbers of mentions rather than numbers of people, for some politicians, businessmen and senior civil servants reappear in successive stories and issues. It is hardly going too far to say that there are only three ways for a working class man to get into the paper: to become a jockey or horse trainer; to suffer a catastrophe, preferably bizarre; or to commit a rape. A working class woman has only the second way.[16]

(iv) The major discourse on ideas in the media is not on political or economic alternatives. To the extent that debate takes place, it tends to be between conservatives and liberals on fashionable social issues. One feature about such debates is that, generally, the socialist perspective is deliberately excluded. Thus the debate may be on the theme: 'Should the woman's place be in the home?' and it may raise considerable passions on both sides. But rarely will someone ask: 'What is the role of the woman in sustaining the present economic structure?' Other fashionable debates focus on such issues as living together without marriage, extra-marital affairs, abortion, divorce, homosexuality; to conservative and liberal spokesmen, those who in any way blame the power structures are labelled 'extremists'. Many magazines keep up readership by making supposedly daring explorations into these areas, and facing the viewer with provocative questions like: 'Would you have more than one lover?'

(v) The media focus on, and glorify, aspects of violence. Much has been written by concerned people about the influence of violent television shows and films on the minds of young children.[17] However, this has not resulted in any action by the state to regulate programmes for children. The simple fact is that violent shows are popular and increase ratings. There is much resistance to changing that.

There is some evidence that children and adults will mimic television violence in their own lives, particularly if they are suffering an identity crisis.[18] However, this is not the main point here. For, even those who do not resort to violence are socialized. They gain an increasing acceptance of the validity of the use of violent means against enemies and 'evil people'. This allows them to accept as legitimate the increasing use of violence by state bodies to impose their will and crush opposition to their power. Connell believes that this legitimate violence in support of the ruling class has been a dominant theme in Australian history:

> the genocide with which it began: the repression of convict resistance and bushranging; the resistance on the goldfields (where progress and property for once clashed with established authority); the intimidation of unions and a long series of official strike-breaking activities; and the constant undercurrent of official violence through police, courts and prisons by which the property system is upheld.[19]

Indeed, there is psychological evidence to suggest that children find it difficult to grasp violent shows in which there are no identifiable goodies and baddies and which are realistic in character. Sociologist Patricia Edgar's research supports the conclusion that people's apprehension of violence is mostly in the fantasy world of heroes and villains.[20] Yet this discovery can be effectively used by the ruling class. If workers' representatives, leaders of radical groups etc. can be portrayed in the media as 'baddies', this will justify the use of state force against them—for the ordinary person witnessing this concludes merely that 'they got what they deserve'. This point ties up with the next two factors on forming media hegemony.

(vi) Radical opponents to the power structure are represented in the media as extremists, evil persons, dangerous revolutionaries etc. This technique, in addition to creating an image of evil, effectively smears opponents of the system, thereby ridiculing whatever message they have to put across. Thus all socialists are seen as defenders of the Soviet regime, all radicals are seen as anarchists, all those who resist the domination of the state are seen as 'violent'. The message they seek to articulate rarely gets to the people. Consider, for example, the media's reporting of political demonstrations. Television, in particular, focuses on clashes with the police. Since the latter are seen as embodiments of rightful authority, those clashing with them lose their legitimacy even if the cause is worthwhile.[21] Yet how often is the cause discussed?

(vii) Perhaps the most extraordinary factor in media domination in Australia is the complete refusal to portray favourably the right of the working class to organize and to strike. Unions have been treated with open hostility by the media. Strikes have been strongly attacked. Indeed the very legitimacy of the withdrawal of labour has been severely questioned.[22] The focus has always been on the disruptive consequences of strikes. As McQueen notes,

> Even when the strikers are seen by the media to have just demands, the media still oppose the workers taking action. Perhaps the hardest thing to find in the media is even one example of them supporting even one strike in defence of people's rights and livelihood.
> Whole books can be filled with examples of anti-working class headlines, photos, interviews, cartoons and editorials.[23]

The continuous attacks on 'militant' union leaders has resulted in large numbers of people blaming unions for the economic crisis, for unemployment and for a whole host of other evils *without knowing why*. The media are continuously pressing the view that it is the unions who are powerful in the country, not the capitalists, nor the government. This ridiculous inversion, whereby the ruling class is able to represent itself as the victim of uncouth, undisciplined, extremist union leaders, has reached the stage where a leading union has had to produce a pamphlet showing major capitalists and headed: 'if unions had the power of these men, they would be running the country'![24]

At this stage, it might be objected that although the privately-owned media are heavily dominated by conservative views, there is surely a major alternative in our society—the Australian Broadcasting Commission. Indeed, to many Australians, the ABC is a haven from the ugly commercialism of the capitalist media. Because of this the ABC has an undeserved reputation for being left-wing. Yet, as McQueen notes, this is not borne out by the facts.

> Listening to Santamaria [an extreme conservative] who would suspect that an Age 'Poll' in April 1976 found that Liberal voters were happier with the ABC TV's political reporting than were Labor voters; that in October 1975, Liberal-National Country Party spokespeople got thirty-one per cent more time on ABC Current Affairs than did ALP speakers; that, between 13 November and 10 December 1975 (the election period), the L-NCP got slightly more ABC national news time than Labor?[25]

What makes the ABC appear radical is the political conservatism of the other media. Yet often this 'radicalism' is simply a defence of liberal principles and perspectives from right-wing attacks. This, in itself, is an important function in view of the fact that the Australian people are heavily bombarded with conservative political views and are only occasionally exposed to the liberal principles to which most Western democratic societies profess themselves to be dedicated.

This does not mean that the ABC supports socialist ideas. On the contrary, there is ample evidence to suggest that those journalists and producers who question the claims of legitimacy by the system are intimidated or even silenced.[26] The top management of the ABC is not sympathetic to the view that there should be favourable references to alternatives to the present system. This was the view of Sir Henry Bland, Chairman of the ABC 1975–76.

> I believe that the ABC as a national institution can't be seen to be attacking or denigrating other national institutions. After all this is a society in which all but a very few believe in the system . . . And I know that some people argue that creativity cannot coexist with what they see as self-censorship but this misunderstands the role of creators . . . to talk about artists and creators just being at liberty to just do what they would love to do is a lot of nonsense when you're working in an institutional system.[27]

Notice here how the attack on radical views soon turns into an attack on liberal principles. Journalists are not free to present what they perceive as the truth. They must exercise self-censorship.

Nor can it be supposed that the ABC as a whole never buckles under to the considerable political pressures placed on it. These pressures stem from the fact that the ABC's funds depend on the government and can be cut (as the Fraser government has done). Furthermore, its Commissioners are appointed by the government and can use their considerable powers to promote that government's perspective.[28] The independence of the ABC is thus never secured; at best, it is given a relative autonomy to explore certain areas, an autonomy which is likely to be severely circumscribed at election times. The bias of the ABC towards the Liberals in the 1975 and 1977 elections has been documented.

Nevertheless I do not agree with McQueen that the ABC is merely a subtle tool of the capitalist state. Within its limitations, it does allow for some forms of dialogue and some radical ideas are presented, even if only in a theoretical form. Furthermore, it is difficult for any government to completely dominate the ABC or to dismantle it. Its news and current affairs services are appreciated by a wide spectrum of the community—particularly those with liberal views. It has correspondents who assert a greater independence than those employed by the commercial stations.[29] Thus the ABC and the public broadcasting stations should play a critical role in keeping alive some forms of dialogue if, as I believe, the economic crisis deepens and the state is forced to adopt measures to silence its more effective and outspoken critics.

Thus, even though the domination of the media by forces which act to strengthen capital and the existent power structures is very extensive, there are still some alternative outlets where rational dialogue can take place and at least some of the legitimating ideology of the system can be thrown into question. The issue to be faced, however, is: can the ruling class shut down all outlets for alternative views, without destroying the claim that its power is based on open, democratic processes? In the next chapter, I shall argue that it cannot. When people begin to question the legitimacy of power structures, they cannot be crudely silenced—without undermining the basis of legitimacy. But if this critical questioning increases because of economic and social crises, the legitimacy of the state will be undermined. Either way, this situation can lead to legitimation crisis.

6
Legitimation Crisis and Its Consequences

A LEGITIMATION CRISIS

In Chapter 3 of this book I discussed the economic crisis in modern Western societies. We saw that, although the working class has achieved increases in real money wages since earlier phases of capitalism, this was achieved only with the creation of a culture and social system in which social integration is secured through material rewards and promotions within an occupational hierarchy. We saw in Chapter 4 that these material rewards and the life-style created by modern capitalism (suburban living, privatization of important aspects of social life) are not sufficiently meaningful to replace the earlier religious and traditional world views.[1] Following Habermas, I argued that in order to secure a meaningful social identity for themselves, people are placing increased demands on the economic system, already divided and conflict-ridden in the struggle between labour and capital. I argued in Chapter 4A that the *work motivations* of the working class as a whole can only be sustained if there are increased rewards for labour to allow workers to meet their higher material expectations and if there are sufficient opportunities for promotion in factories and offices to ensure that people see their continued participation as worthwhile.

We also saw, in Chapters 3A and 3B, that the capitalist forces, in responding to the increased demands from workers, have managed to avoid direct confrontation, but only by using their monopolistic powers to increase prices and thereby generate savage inflation. This was combined with cutbacks in investment, resulting in stagnation and dramatic increases in unemployment. The problems in the socio-cultural sphere —increasing demands for more wages and more job opportunities—have thus directly contributed to a deeper economic crisis.

These problems in the economy and the socio-cultural sphere have placed tremendous pressures on the state. For in modern Western society, it is the state which is held responsible for steering the economy. Thus, during a period of economic crisis, the people turn to the government of the state to resolve crisis. Yet the state is clearly limited in what it can do: it (generally) cannot interfere with the structure of capitalist economy, it cannot (normally) bring major sectors of industry and finance under public ownership and control.

Yet the government, if it is to sustain public support, must do something. Generally it will attempt one or both of the following short-term strategies:

(i) It can use state resources to subsidize companies and thereby directly increase profitability, hoping that this will result in increased investment; and/or it can offer various kinds of investment allowances in an attempt to secure an increase in economic activity and a decrease in unemployment. These measures would, however, increase the budget deficit to unacceptable limits and increase inflation, unless accompanied by savage cuts in the state's welfare, education and/or social security services (see Chapter 3C).

(ii) The government can intervene in wage negotiations so as to ensure an effective decrease in real money wages, and hence a boost in profits. In Australia, this is done by applying government pressure on companies to reject workers' demands and by government presentations to the Conciliation and Arbitration Commission.

Neither strategy is likely to resolve the crisis. The second approach, reductions in real money wages, may reduce inflation to some degree, but it will also reduce work motivation, and the level of effective demand for goods in the economy. This will then generally prevent new investment to produce more goods (as distinct from investment to produce existing levels more efficiently and with less labour, which exacerbates the crisis). Even if the creation of more unemployment results in short-term reduction of wage demands, this is not enough to ensure that people will be content with severe limitations on their material expectations: particularly since they have no meaning to life to replace materialism.

Furthermore, even if during economic crisis people reluctantly continue to perform their roles in the economic system, they place heavier burdens on the state. For they require it to provide greater social welfare and support services. The reason is twofold. Firstly, materialist values and expectations continue and are increasingly frustrated. Secondly, the increased social problems resulting from alienation and a reduced sense of the meaningfulness of life—sometimes to the point of breakdown—require social workers, counsellors and a variety of government supports.[2]

Now if at this time the state introduces the first strategy, which involves massive reductions in welfare and social services, this will result in a dramatic reduction in support for the state—particularly if the people have been socialized to expect these services. Thus if the state reduces unemployment relief or old age pensions or services in health and education to any great degree, its support will most likely be eroded.

However this reduction in support is conditional. It depends on what happens to people's belief in the state's capacity to steer the economy, and their belief in its legitimacy. As we saw in Chapter 3C, if the state fails to steer the economy out of crisis and people apprehend that this is so, this often gives rise to a state-political (or what Habermas calls a 'rationality') crisis. This crisis often results in an upsurge of support for the parliamentary opposition (unless that opposition is considered totally illegitimate).

When the state is perceived as failing to steer the economy and/or failing to provide welfare, educational and social security services, its legitimacy is increasingly questioned.[3] When the state seeks more power to deal with this, its own legitimating ideology (the principles of democracy) places further limits on what it can do. For it cannot flagrantly contradict democratic principles. Indeed, in order to secure its legitimacy, the state must:

(a) seek to demonstrate that it is part of a democratic society, in which free discussion takes place and in which certain egalitarian and universalistic values, norms and traditions are paramount;

(b) carry out at least some policies which are based on those principles. It must, for example, provide universal health care and free education for all—at least up to some levels. For if it failed to do so, it could no longer represent itself as acting on behalf of the common good of the whole people.

Thus, as I indicated in the Prologue, the state is faced with three contradictory imperatives. It must steer the economy so as to provide more profit and more goods; provide more social, educational and welfare services to the people as a whole; and *not* blatantly contradict democratic principles, and carry out some actions for the common good, to secure its claims to legitimacy. It follows that the state is limited in the actions it can carry out to solve economic and socio-cultural problems and crises without undermining its legitimacy. Yet if it remains within such limits, it may not be able to resolve the crises.

Consider this matter further. The most renowned theory of legitimacy is that of sociologist Max Weber.[4] He defined the state in terms of legitimacy: it is a body which has 'the monopoly of the legitimate use of physical force in a given territory'.[5] For Weber, legitimacy could be secured by a variety of means; there is no necessity for the power to be *rationally* justifiable, people might support the state and its government for the most obscure and irrational reasons. Habermas, on the other hand, claims that 'every effective belief in legitimacy is assumed to have an immanent relation to truth'.[6] By this he means that 'the grounds on which it is explicitly based contain a rational validity claim that can be tested and criticized independently'.[7]

Thus Habermas believes that legitimation is only secured when the ideology or beliefs on which state power is grounded at least appear to be *open to rational discussion and examination.* A state must, therefore, legitimate itself by reference to values, ideals, practices which it can, at least provisionally, be prepared to defend in debate and discourse. This does not mean that genuine discourse actually takes place: for it may be the case that communication between people is distorted. Indeed Habermas believes that in a capitalist society, complete rational discourse is not possible—people do not generally interact in an undistorted way.[8]

Nevertheless, democratic capitalist societies must allow for at least some forms of discussion and debate. This inevitably means that the state's legitimacy is questioned. However, in periods when there are no economic and social crises the state can normally deal with such challenges to its legitimacy, particularly if these challenges come only from intellectuals who are given limited access to media. Indeed, the methods discussed in Chapter 5A are quite effective in containing radicals and disaffected people, during periods of economic growth and social stability.

However, in economic and socio-cultural crises, the state's support decreases and people make more critical demands on its claims to legitimacy. It must justify its actions by constant appeals to democratic principles and the common good. However, in so doing, it virtually invites criticism as to whether its foundation is indeed democratic, and whether its actions are indeed for the common good.

At this stage, it might be objected, why couldn't the state simply decide what it wants people to believe and impose this view by use of the media, the education system, and other means at its disposal? Habermas, however, argues that there is a definite *limit to the state's capacity to legitimate itself.*

For 'there is no administrative production of meaning'.[9] By this, he means that the state cannot, through administrative fiat, change the values and social relations prevailing in the socio-cultural system. The state, in other words, cannot take over the subjective experience of individuals and give a new, different meaning to them, for these values, beliefs and practices have been absorbed since childhood.

This fact is important in two ways. Firstly, the state cannot by legislation or executive decrees change people's values to create new work motivations, or a new social identity; thus, it cannot impose a new religion or world view. This does not, of course, mean that the state is thereby rendered powerless to act in the socio-cultural field. For while it cannot directly create new meanings and new social identities for people, it can undermine existing ones. Indeed, in the past it has acted to discredit certain world views and to break down pre-capitalist social formations and values; for example, under pressure from liberals, it has brought in laws to make divorce easier, thereby breaking up much traditional family structure. As I explained in Chapter 4A, in so doing it has shattered many individuals' security in their identities as mothers, husbands, etc.

Secondly, the state cannot convince people that *any* action is consistent with democracy and the common good. Thus if people are accustomed to the freedom to assemble and publicly express their views, this cannot be taken away without undermining the legitimacy of the state. Nor can the state convince people to pursue entirely different goals and values by simply appealing to the common good or the good of the nation. For people will question whether this is so and subject the state's claims to scrutiny.[10]

The problem of legitimacy thus becomes more serious if people are persuaded that democracy means more participation by the people in decision-making and more responsiveness by the state to people's needs. As mentioned in Chapter 1A, there have been many attempts by the media and intellectuals to move away from this view of democracy to a safer

one which does not allow as much questioning of the foundations of state's power.[11] This 'elitist' view of democracy
requires contradictory responses from the citizen. Habermas
quotes Verba on this matter:

> If elites are to be powerful and make authoritative
> decisions, then the involvement, activity and influence
> of the ordinary man must be limited. The ordinary
> citizen must turn power over to elites and let them
> rule. The need for elite power requires that the
> ordinary citizen be relatively passive, uninvolved, and
> deferential to elites. Thus the democratic citizen is
> called on to pursue contradictory goals; he must be
> active, yet passive; involved, yet not too involved,
> influential, yet deferential.[12]

Habermas goes on to claim that the concept of participation
must be supplemented by 'a political culture that screens
participatory behavioural expectations out of bourgeois ideologies and replaces them with the authoritarian patterns
remaining from pre-bourgeois traditions'.[13] In this situation,
while the term 'democracy' is retained and frequently referred
to, the state—and in the terms of my analysis, the ruling class
generally—increases its power over the people.

At this juncture, it may be asked why can't the state simply
dispense with talk about democracy, and impose an authoritarian ideology, which would be more suitable for its purposes? Of course, a state could do this—but if it does, it is
most likely to undermine its legitimacy. There are two reasons
for this:

(i) An openly authoritarian ideology would conflict with
the prevalent morality in Western society—with its claims
about equality, justice and the rights of man. While vast
inequalities may in fact exist in these societies, social egalitarianism is accepted as basic to the value system. People
have come to believe that they have certain rights and
privileges; that, in a formal sense at least, all persons are

equal. Thus universalistic morality, which was very important for the development of liberal capitalism, becomes an embarrassment in late monopolistic capitalism. For it is not possible to eradicate the moral consciousness of people. The state cannot, therefore, adopt a morality of *open* inequality and injustice. Even when it adopts forms of inequality—as in wealth and income—it usually defends these by appeals to other universalistic principles such as equality of opportunity, plus the notion that inequalities in reward are the just deserts of inequality in effort and capacity. (However, notice that in adopting these last two principles to legitimate obvious inequalities, the state reinforces expectations that it will create more job opportunities and ensure that effort is rewarded.)

(ii) The state's legitimacy depends on the implicit claim that its ideology, and the values on which it is based, is true. But, as we have seen, for Habermas this claim to truth implies justification in public discourse—particularly within the media. Not only would open authoritarianism be attacked when exposed in such a public forum, but the *overt* and *crude* silencing of dissenters would lead to an undermining of legitimation—a reduction in mass support for the state.

Thus if the state is to become less democratic and more authoritarian, it must hide this fact. In a typically condensed paragraph, Habermas identifies three strategies which may be used:[14]

(a) 'The personalization of substantive issues'; for example, attacks on the integrity of persons presenting alternatives or criticizing the government.

(b) 'The symbolic use of hearings, expert judgments, juridical incantations'. By this process, experts to whom we ascribe knowledge of *how* to do things are mysteriously converted into experts on what we *ought* to do. The consequent loss of self-determination and power is not visible to the people. This can be a very effective method, particularly since human systems (such as economy) are often seen on the model of deterministic machines which require experts to steer them.

(c) The use of advertising techniques 'that at once confirm and exploit existing structures of prejudice and that garnish certain contents positively, others negatively, through appeals to feeling, stimulation of unconscious motives, etc'.[15] Here the legitimation process appeals to peoples' fears, insecurities, repressed desires for pleasure and so on, in securing the power of the state. (I have already discussed this in relation to Australia in Chapters 5A and 5D.)

Notice that, in all the above, the state attempts to legitimate itself by any means other than open discourse on values; for conscious reflection on the values on which economy, the state and social structures rely, will bring out the many contradictions discussed in this book.

But now a serious question arises: why could the state not legitimate itself indefinitely by the non-discursive means above? Why could it not perpetually avoid discourse on its own value foundations? Habermas gives a measured reply here. Even at this level, it is not possible to indefinitely postpone the question as to whether the systems of society are continuing to satisfy human needs. If the needs of people are not being satisfied, then they will become discontented with the pronouncements of experts and continuous appeal to unconscious desires.[16] This is particularly the case with the need for a meaningful identity.

This raises a further difficulty: How are we to discover what real human needs are and whether a socio-economic and political system is satisfying them? Habermas rejects three theories as to how we can gain knowledge of the basic human needs:

(i) that basic needs can be determined by looking at the biology and innate mechanisms of man, as in Freud's theory;[17]

(ii) that the needs people have can be determined by an analysis of the historical context in which they live, as in mechanistic Marxian theories;[18]

(iii) that human needs can be discovered within a functional analysis of the systems of society, as in Parsons' theory.[19]

While each of the above may refer to a source of human needs, Habermas suggests that we can only *know* what peoples' needs are on the basis of the following democratic principle: what kind of needs *would* people ascribe to themselves in general *were* they to collectively decide them, on the basis of open rational discourse 'with adequate knowledge of the limiting conditions and functional imperatives of their society'?[20] An individual can only speculate as to the answer to this problem. Only the people, democratically participating in an open discourse, can determine the answer at a given time in history.

Full democratic participation of the people, involving discourse on values and purposes, is a necessary condition for legitimation of society. While this ideal is not achieved in parliamentary democracies with capitalist economies, it nevertheless remains in the background: even a representative democracy must claim that its goals somehow reflect what the people need and want, that if they could be consulted under free conditions, they would choose these goals. This is what Habermas means by the 'implicit reference to truth' which underlies the legitimacy of democratic ideologies. He concludes that the state can only continue to have legitimacy if it allows some forms of discourse on its foundations, thus making it consistent with its claim to truth.

What if it is objected that the ideal of the democratic participation of the whole people in the running of society is an absurd one? Habermas takes on this problem in a section 'Complexity and Democracy'. Here he considers the views of Luhmann[21] who argues that modern states are so complex, that 'to demand an intensive engaged participation of all in them, would be to make a principle of frustration. Anyone who understands democracy in this way has, in fact, to come to the conclusion that it is incompatible with rationality'.[22] Further, Luhmann maintains that because of the diverse and complex means at its disposal 'there is no class of problems whose solution would, in principle, force the administration to confront the limits of its capacity'.[23] Indeed, the state defines and enforces its own concept of legitimacy, independently of the values and beliefs of the people. It only comes under attack when it fails to steer the economic system properly, or to run its own affairs efficiently. In support of this view, it could be claimed that the people do not blame the state when they are not integrated into the social system or feel a loss of identity: they blame themselves or other individuals around them. Using this, we can derive an alternative view of legitimacy: it is based, not on any claim to be reflecting the will of the people or satisfying their needs, but rather on the claim that the government has the expertise to run the bureaucracy and economy properly.

There are two points that can be made in reply to this. Firstly, Habermas concedes (as mentioned earlier) that the state often tries to legitimize itself by appeals to experts, efficiency and technical rationality. However, when the state claims to be efficient in running economy, this claim itself must be open to scrutiny. The state cannot sustain this claim in the face of economic crisis, without repressing those who claim the contrary. Furthermore, when it claims that the state bureaucracy is efficient, the question arises: efficient in achieving what goals? The claim to efficiency cannot be judged without first accepting the goal itself. Discourse on the state's efficiency will thus often lead to discourse on the state's goals, for example, an inquiry into efficiency in the education system will bring up important questions about the goals of that system and whether it satisfies people's needs.

Habermas makes a second point, illustrated below:

Participation of those affected	Planning Style	
	Incrementalist	Comprehensive
Not permitted	A	B
Permitted	C	D

This can be grasped if we consider his distinction between 'incrementalist' and 'comprehensive' planning styles. Using this, he derives the following scheme:[24]

He points out that, in a Western democracy, we usually have either A or C, that is, incrementalist step-by-step planning in which the people cannot participate (since it is left to an elite) or in which they are permitted to participate only within defined limits. In either case, the general structure of the systems of society is not changed, for this requires comprehensive planning. Nevertheless, if Habermas is right, a society in which participation is not permitted in incremental planning will quickly come under attack as to the validity of its democratic claims. Thus, if the state in planning health, social welfare or education services does not consult those affected, it is liable to be attacked both for its methods and the goals decided upon.

On the other hand, if it allows people to participate in incremental planning, this will often result in challenges to its comprehensive goals; for example, a study as to how to improve child-care facilities for working mothers may result in a debate on the explosive issue of whether women should be paid for housework. Similarly, consulting people on improved health care may result in demands for the socialization of the whole medical profession. The point here is that, even in incremental planning, fundamental value judgements are assumed. When the people participate in these processes, they often question these value judgements and point to the difference between the state's claims—to be treating all persons equally and ministering to their needs—and its actual achievements.

Once a substantial minority or a majority of people become aware of the contradiction between the state's actions and the ideology on which its legitimacy is based—whether this be its democratic pretensions or its claims to efficiency— there is a legitimation crisis in the society. Such a crisis is likely to arise when people recognize that the government is incapable of steering the economy out of crisis, or when they realize that it cannot provide sufficient state services to ensure a meaningful life-style for people and to administer to their welfare and educational needs. Under these circumstances, more people will conclude: that the state is really *not* acting for the common good, on behalf of the whole people, but is merely representative of minority interest groups. They will withdraw their support and thereby undermine its legitimacy.

A legitimation crisis of this kind can be contained. It need not result in revolutionary action; maybe the people will respond with privatized apathy. Yet Habermas believes that

> If this rough diagnosis is correct, a legitimation crisis
> can be avoided in the long run only if the latent class
> structures of advanced-capitalist societies are
> transformed or if the pressure for legitimation to which
> the administrative system is subject can be removed.[25]

Since the second possibility has been excluded, Habermas perceives a tendency for crisis to deepen, until the economy is transformed and socialism is established. Yet none of this is inevitable—an alternative possibility would be a new form of authoritarianism, in which compliance is achieved by force.[26]

However, I believe that it is unlikely that either of the above radical alternatives—democratic socialism or openly authoritarian capitalism—will be the options adopted as responses to economic, political and legitimation crises, at least not for a long time. For I believe that Habermas has underestimated three powerful short-term responses which the ruling class can make to restore legitimacy, without changing the economic structure—changing the government, preventing the formation of and/or dividing working-class groups, or shifting the blame from the state and the economic system to the individual himself. I turn to examine these responses now.

B SHORT-TERM RESPONSES TO CRISIS

Changing the government

A parliamentary democracy has a safety valve against crises in the state and in legitimacy. The existence of several political parties, particularly a major opposition party which can gain hold of the reins of power, is an important factor in sustaining the legitimacy of the whole system. For if severe problems arise within the state itself, or if the state fails to solve the economic and social crises, this can be blamed on the governing party or parties. In this way, the people can be led to believe that the problems of the system as a whole are really due to bad leadership and incompetence on the part of a particular government.

Under conditions of economic and social crisis, the ruling class is under pressure. People raise questions not only about the legitimacy of the state, but also about the power structure in the economic system. Indeed, as the state fails to steer the economy out of crisis, more and more people are open to the view that the problem lies with the divided and exploitative character of the economy itself.[1] In order to prevent this happening, it may be in the interest of the ruling class to represent economic failures, not as the fault of a system based on greed, but rather as the fault of an incompetent government which cannot steer the economy properly. In this kind of situation, it is possible (and indeed likely) that segments of the ruling class will remove support from a conservative government to a liberal or even mildly socialist one. The ruling class will generally do this, however, only if:

(a) the alternative party's programme and philosophy does not threaten the structure of capitalist economy (that is, the alternative party would have to be 'moderate' and not be interested in bringing industries under workers' ownership and control);

(b) the governing party has demonstrated itself to be incompetent in steering the economy and, in particular, in moderating the workers' demands. At this juncture, it may be very profitable to turn from a conservative government to a party which can keep down the demands of the working class by using its historical claim to represent workers. Thus a labour government may be supported by the ruling class when it may be seen as more effective than conservatives.[2] This, however, is subject to the qualification (a) above.

Even if the ruling class does not change its support to the opposition, the governing party is generally likely to lose support during times of economic and social crisis. For the people have been socialized to blame the governing party and not the economic or political system as a whole. Furthermore, it is the only *legitimate* avenue available to people who seek to change the power structure. Under these circumstances, with continuing crises in society, we can expect a very volatile electorate with swings from one party to the other in a bid to secure a meaningful solution.

This has been illustrated in Australia by the voters of New South Wales. In 1977, the voters of this most populous state gave the Fraser (Liberal-NCP) government resounding support. Yet in the State election of October 1978, the Labor State government won a massive majority over its Liberal Party opponents, with the Leader of the Opposition losing his seat. This volatility in the electorate can partly be ascribed to voter impatience with the continuing economic crisis and the failure of the Federal Liberal Party to steer the nation out of that morass. By focusing on these incapacities on the part of the Liberals, Premier Wran was able to take advantage of the increasing anxiety over unemployment. Furthermore, opinion polls after the August 1978 budget showed the Fraser government's standing had deterioriated dramatically and it would probably be defeated if an election were forced. Thus the Australian people have recently been very volatile—a substantial number who voted for the Liberals in 1977 were ready to abandon them only several months later.

Changing the government may bring a renewed sense of legitimacy and faith in the system. Yet this is unlikely to last very long. For the constant changing of governments does not, in itself, solve deep-seated crises in economy and the social system. Rather, one or both parties must be prepared to accept the kinds of radical policies required for a transformation of economy and a democratization of power.[3] In most Western countries no major party as a whole is ready or willing to take on this task, although there may be sections of labour and socialist parties willing to try (the ALP's position will be discussed in the next section). Hence the major parties tend to 'bog down' when in government, since they rely on orthodox solutions which may have worked in the past, but which are no longer relevant at this stage of advanced capitalism.

There are also two major dangers associated with the tactic of changing governments as a way of resolving crises. Firstly, voters may become disenchanted if they consider that none of the major parties has any constructive ways of resolving economic and other crises. They may come to question the party system itself, and other aspects of the process which, while it allows for some moderate changes, prohibits any attempts at radical transformation of economy. Such questioning can lead to a further undermining of legitimacy. Secondly, one of the major parties may attempt to achieve success by offering the people a *substantially* different alternative. If the people vote against a government which fails (almost inevitably) to deal with the protracted economic crisis, they may even turn to a radical opposition party and allow it to tackle the problems. Such a move could bring to power groups which, from a capitalist ideological view, threaten to use the state to change the general structure of the economy.[4] Such parties, which are democratic and socialist in character, threaten the dominant class from within the state system.

At this stage, it might be objected: surely there is no possibility of a radical party ever being able to govern. The ruling class would ensure that such a party was never elected and, that if it were, its programme would be frustrated. This is the view of certain orthodox Marxists, who appeal to Marx's notion that the state is a mere superstructure, arising from the concrete relations of production, that is, the structural relations between capital and labour.[5]

Marx believed that the theoretical justifications of economic exploitation come to be embodied in the morality, the laws and the constitutional arrangements of the state. (He might have added, had he been alive today, that they come to permeate the police, the army, the bureaucracy and other parts of the modern state.) Some Marxists have concluded that parliamentary democracy is, therefore, a farce, a sham.[6] Its function is to hide the real sources of power in society (the capitalists) by giving the appearance of offering choices to the people, and thus to perpetuate the rule of that class.

Evaluating Marx's thesis is, however, complicated, because it is not clear exactly what his position entails. Consider some possible interpretations:

(a) 'The state has no autonomous power. It is merely a set of formal powers, but has no real power of its own. The real power lies with the capitalists.' Marx, however, considers the state—while springing out of civil society—to be important for the continued administration of society. He says:

> The state is founded upon the contradiction between
> *public* and *private* life, between *general* and *particular*
> interests. The *administration* must, therefore, limit
> itself to a *formal* and *negative* sphere of activity,
> because its power ceases at the point where civil life
> and its work begin.[7]

Here the state is seen to have power, but of a limited kind, over economy and concrete social life. This explains why Marx conceives it as superstructure. But Marx was referring to the early states which had not yet developed large public and welfare sectors employing substantial numbers of people. The development of this public sector in the modern state has, I believe, made the state a much more substantial entity than Marx envisaged.

(b) 'The state, while having some power autonomous of economy, is a mere puppet of the capitalist class. It is directly or indirectly controlled by capitalists.' This view suggests an active determination of the decisions of the state by the will of the capitalist class, and assumes that the class is unified as to the direction which the state must take. But this is not so, particularly for the modern state. For, as we saw in Chapter 2D, the ruling class consists of various sectors and each of these often makes different demands on the state. Indeed it is the view of many modern socialists that the function of the modern state is precisely to co-ordinate and unify the conflicts between the different sectors of capital, such as the multinationals, the large farming concerns, monopolies and small competitive businesses.[8]

(c) 'The state has power of its own, but is limited in the expression of that power by the social and economic structures of society. It can choose to proclaim universal laws and principles, provided they do not interfere with the general structure of social and economic relations.' I believe that it is in this sense that the state is a superstructure for Marx, in its absolute dependence on pre-existing civil society. 'Only political superstition believes at the present time that civil life must be held together by the State, when in reality the State is upheld by civil life.'[9] Hence Marx believed that the state is unable to transform the structure of economy and the social relations which are intertwined with capitalism. Hence, when the state enacts laws, this is merely a formalization of already existing relations of property and power within society.

Yet, as we saw above, Marx also conceived the state as having a regulatory function, administering the contradictions between general and particular interests, the public and private sphere. How could the state do this without more autonomy from the economy and social relations? Indeed, Marx himself recognized that the capitalist state could not openly identify itself with the interests of capital. It must legitimate itself by an appeal to universal principles and the basic, intrinsic rights of man. According to Marx:

> The basis of the State in antiquity was slavery; the
> basis of the *modern* State is civil society and the
> *individual* of civil society, that is, the independent
> individual, whose only link with other individuals is
> private interest and *unconscious* natural necessity, the
> *slave* of wage labour, of the *selfish* needs of himself and
> others. The modern State has recognized this, its
> natural foundation, in the universal rights of man.[10]

However, as I have argued in Chapter 6A, it is a mistake to
suppose that the more the state emphasizes these rights in its
attempts to legitimate itself, the more entrenched capitalism
becomes. For the rhetoric of freedom and equality has
permeated civil society, and raise more demands for effective
universal action by the state—thus making it more autonomous.

Hence the development of the state as employer of labour,
combined with an increased emphasis on its democratic,
egalitarian functions, has given rise to a more powerful state
which has become much more autonomous, and much more
positive in its power than Marx had envisaged. (For a discussion of this point with respect to Australia, see next
section.)

This is not to deny that when the people elect such a party
to resolve the economic and social crises, the ruling class will
generally mobilize its forces against it. In so doing, they may
act to prevent the elected party gaining office. Again, if it
does gain office and presses its policy for change, moves will
be made to remove it from state power and/or to prevent it
carrying out its policies. In this struggle the ruling class is
likely to use its enormous economic strength. It will often
resort to dubious, perhaps unconstitutional, means. However,
the very fact that the ruling class has to mobilize against a
radical government supports the view that the state is not
automatically the tool of the ruling class. Furthermore, even

if, on the rare occasions that a radical government is elected, the ruling class manages to bring it down, success is not guaranteed at the outset. In a situation like this, the ruling class has to act with determination to secure its power.

Another interesting possibility arises when a government is elected on what appears to be a moderate platform and begins to carry out actions which seriously threaten the ruling class and the structure of economy. These actions may in fact not even be intended to damage the ruling class, but have the unintended consequence of doing so. The response of the ruling class to such a government is likely to be vicious: it is likely to feel betrayed. An example of this case is the Whitlam Labor government: I shall discuss it in detail in Part III of this book.

In conclusion, changing governments can be a useful tool during normal economic times, when there is a chance that one or both major parties will adopt policies which will stabilize the systems of society without changing their structure. However, during periods of economic crisis, matters are far more serious; for if the new government does not carry out radical policies the crisis will continue and people may eventually lose faith in the whole system. On the other hand, if a radical group is elected to government, it will be able to use the power of the state to threaten the domination of the ruling class. In such a case, a dramatic confrontation is likely; whichever way it goes, legitimacy will be shaken even further. These, however, are long-term developments. In the short term, the ruling class may be able to continue its domination by blaming others for its failures.

Repression of unions and radical movements

One major way of limiting a crisis in legitimacy is to ensure that workers' organizations cannot be effective in their demands on the economy and the state. Since the most powerful weapon which the working class has to press its demands is the strike, the government's attack is primarily directed towards the unions; for it is these organizations which unite workers to exercise that power effectively. Governments have generally thus acted to nullify the unions' powers through a variety of manoeuvres.

Firstly, a government can propagandize against unions which articulate workers' demands for more state services, and pressurize unions to limit their claims and actions to what are called 'purely industrial matters' (as distinct from 'political' demands). Thus, for example, it is acceptable for a union to go on strike against a particular firm or company if it wants an increase in wages; but it is not acceptable for workers to demand general economic transformations such as a redistribution of wealth, or more social services, or the protection of the environment. In Australia, the media heavily attack unions who strike on these so-called 'political issues'.[11]

This distinction is both absurd and hypocritical. It is absurd because, as we saw in Chapter 3A, the level of state services is part of the worker's social wage; when the state cuts such services, he must pay for them through his money wages, thus reducing his disposable income for other goods and services. It is hypocritical because the state is always intervening in industrial disputes on the side of capital. Thus, there is no political/industrial distinction for the state, only for unions.

This leads to the second ploy—political attacks on union leadership. It is paradoxical that in Australia the unions are told to keep out of political affairs, yet it is perfectly acceptable for politicians to attack union leadership. Perhaps the most classic way of doing this, and the one that has been very successful in Australia, is to attack unions in which there are communists on the executive. This 'kicking the communist can' has been, and continues to be, very successful in rousing the public consciousness against unions. Thus when a strike occurs, the media are very happy if they can discover that any member of the union executive is a communist, and can publicize his affiliation. By this means, a great number of strikes have had their legitimacy undermined and the issues involved have been obscured.[12]

Thirdly, the state can negate the effectiveness of unions by regulating union struggles with employers through bodies such as the Conciliation and Arbitration Commission in Australia. This system brings in the force of the law to impose judgements in industrial disputes, supposedly on both sides. It is not primarily a conciliation system in the sense of bringing parties together to negotiate. Rather it arbitrates and, in theory at least, can enforce its judgements with fines and imprisonment of workers and union leaders who defy it. [13]

Although the Arbitration Commission has some positive features, it can be argued that it has generally worked against the interests of labour and in favour of capital. This issue, together with general character of the Australian unions, will be discussed further in Chapter 6D. We should note here, however, that the introduction of wage indexation in 1975 has clearly legitimized and entrenched the existing distribution of income and wealth. The situation has reached the point where many unions now accept as their role the defence of the status quo—as long as wages keep pace with price inflation.

Even if the state succeeds in its strategy of taming the unions and ensures that they do not pursue political causes, this does not mean that it has effectively stifled demands from the working class. For working people will organize in ways other than through unions to press their demands. Thus as the unions become less 'political', various groups mushroom in the community to make demands on the government for health, education, social and legal services. While these groups are not necessarily radical or socialist in character, nevertheless the failure to satisfy their demands may undermine the state's legitimacy to a considerable degree.

One of the most effective forms of organization by the working class has been based around particular issues, such as the anti-Vietnam (see Chapter 7A), conservation and anti-uranium movements. These movements have been effective in eroding the legitimacy of the ruling class by means of demonstrations, petitions and other forms of mobilization of the people. In addition, there are three virtually permanent groupings which have had a considerable impact in Australia in the last ten years, although their power has recently been dissipated because of counter-attacks by the ruling class. These are the women's liberation movement and the women's groups generally; the various bodies pressing for migrant rights and for special services to migrants; the Aboriginal peoples' organizations, with their claims for land rights and self-determination.[14]

The methods used against these movements are similar to those used against unions. There is an attempt to discredit the movements as a whole, or their leaders, by representing them as 'extremists' 'communists' or 'student ratbags'. Another effective ploy is to divide these groups by offering some state services which will satisfy the moderates and divide the movement. Thus, by granting various concessions to women, migrants and Aborigines, the Fraser government has divided the above movements and thrown them into confusion.

Blaming the individual for the crisis

Everyone in Australia is now aware of the infamous technique of calling the unemployed 'dole bludgers'. At a time when more than half a million people were out of work and the ratio of vacancies to job seekers was over 20 to 1, this was still a widespread stereotype.[15] Promulgating the notion that if one is unemployed it is one's own fault is part of the strategy of avoiding legitimation crisis.

The tactic is simple: do not wait for the individual to blame the system for ruining his life, turn the attack on him or her. Make each individual feel guilty and responsible for his/her own plight. Indeed, if possible, make him/her feel ashamed. In so doing, you will prevent people coming together, joining up with others and realizing their concern. You will prevent them arriving, through communication, at a real recognition of the causes of the crisis in society and in their own lives.

The privatization of modern life (see Chapter 4) has been

very useful to the ruling class in these times of crisis. Most individuals, rather than uniting to voice their frustration and concern, turn their anger against themselves. Thus, they turn towards drugs and maybe criminal behaviour as an outlet for their frustrations. They constantly fall into depression and have feelings of inadequacy. In so doing they begin to live the failure syndrome which the system has created for them.[16]

If our earlier analysis and our account of events in Part III is correct, the social and economic problems of the Australian nation have reached crisis proportions. Yet the victims of this crisis are not visible. One reason is that organizations of these oppressed groups in the working class have not arisen, and the established organizations are generally unable to help them.[17] Another reason, however, is that through the media and the education system, the ruling class has managed to ensure that the consequences of crisis become a private affair for each person affected, rather than a public issue.

Where are those hundreds of thousands of unemployed, the thousands of unhappy people surviving on drugs and alcohol, the hundreds literally going crazy? The ruling class— particularly its political and bureaucratic arms—has managed to render them invisible. Yet they are there, each suffering in his own little world. The question is: will they continue to suffer in silence or will the moment come when their frustrations will be transformed into a fury which will sweep aside the false legitimacy of an economic and political system which has oppressed them? It may well depend on what the rest of the working class, and their leaders, do.

C CRISIS AND THE CONFLICTING PHILOSOPHIES OF THE AUSTRALIAN LABOR PARTY

In this section, we must consider the role of the Australian Labor Party during periods of crisis. Does it act to resolve crisis by changing the established power structures to attain a more democratic society and a more egalitarian distribution of wealth and income? Or does it act merely to sustain the ruling class at a time when its power is weakening?

Three views of the Labor Party's role

Many of the ALP's opponents seem in little doubt that the goals of the party are to achieve a 'democratic socialist' Australia.[1] Indeed this is a label attached to the Labor Party by the media and large sections of the public; many members of the party use this label themselves.[2] This can give the impression that the Labor Party's philosophy is based on a critique of capitalism and on the adoption of genuine socialist goals. There are three perspectives on this matter.

The first suggests that this is indeed the long-term goal of the ALP as a whole. This view focuses on the Labor Party's role as the major representative of the working class, and on the adoption within its history of radical socialist platforms. Thus at the 1919 Conference, the following was adopted as the objective of the ALP:

> Emancipation of human labour from all forms of exploitation, and the obtaining for all workers the full reward of their industry by the collective ownership and democratic control of the collectively used agencies of production, distribution and exchange.[3]

This socialization objective reflected the radical goals of the Victorian Labor Party as incorporated in its inaugural platform in 1890.[4] This platform specified how socialization was to be achieved. It included these clauses:

> 1 The nationalization of all sources of wealth and all means of producing and distributing wealth.
>
> 2 The conducting by the State Authority of all production and all exchange.
>
> 4 The saving by the State Authority of such proportion of the joint wealth production as may be requisite for instituting, maintaining and increasing national capital.
>
> 6 The just division among all the citizens of the State

of all wealth production, less only that part retained for public and common requirements.[5]

This socialization programme, or some modified form of it, has until recently been the primary objective of the Labor Party—in theory. It has of course, been interpreted in an entirely pragmatic way and it would be nonsense to suggest that the Labor Party has (since the 1920s at least) been committed to any form of total socialization of industry. However, the party has at times adopted various forms of socialization and even nationalized certain industries. Thus, perhaps the most successful Labor government, that of Chifley, carried out what has been described as 'the most considerable program of legislative and executive measures for nationalization and public enterprise in the Commonwealth's history'.[6] These measures included the establishment of boards of control for various industries, a Commonwealth shipping line, a Commonwealth aluminium ingot industry, a public whaling industry, public monopoly on atomic energy and raw materials, public development of television, governmental supervision of the New South Wales coal industry, the Commonwealth Snowy River hydro-electricity scheme, the nationalization of Australian sections of overseas airlines (Qantas) and finally the attempted nationalization of the private banks.

However, the view that the ALP as a whole is a genuine socialist party is difficult to maintain, in view of the attitudes and performances of both the Whitlam Federal government and the State Labor governments of Dunstan and Wran. Even sympathetic critics have pointed out that these governments seem confused about, or even opposed to, the aims and purposes of genuine socialism. (The Whitlam government will be discussed in detail in Part III.)

Furthermore, critics note that even the socialization objective has changed over the years, in both its meaning and its working. For example, the clause has been changed to 'the socialization of the means of production exchange and distribution to the extent required to end exploitation, and other anti-social features'.[8] This qualification has the net effect of making it ambiguous as to what the Labor Party intends to do about the capitalist economy. I shall argue presently that ambiguities of this kind are important in keeping together the various conflicting philosophies of the ALP.

A second view is presented by Hugh Emy in *The Politics of Australian Democracy*. He suggests that the Labor Party's socialism is entirely pragmatic and not based on fully articulated concepts of equality and justice.

> Apart from a brief contact with utopian socialism in the 1890's and with syndicalist doctrine during the 1920's, the party has rarely sought to articulate the premises of its socialist philosophy. Indeed, it has never been overfond of any theoretical self-examination of its own social or historical role. Instead, it has preferred to explain itself as either a party of change or as a party which attempts to secure 'a fair go' for the under-privileged (largely the working class) . . . Its pragmatic reformism distinguishes it from the social democratic parties of Europe, which has shown a greater preoccupation with ethical concepts of the just society.[9]

It seems to follow from this view that whatever steps the Labor Party takes towards transforming capitalism are more a result of accident than of design. Thus, for example, Chifley's action to nationalize the banks has been shown to be in 'response to their refusal to cooperate with ALP policy', and not part of an overall strategy to implement the socialization objective.[10]

Another politics professor, Graeme Duncan, supports this view of the Labor Party. He says:

> Even revisionist, with its implication of an ultimate goal of socialism, may be an over-generous term to apply to the party. What socialism—which has never

had an unambiguous popular meaning to the ALP—
meant to Labor in power was planned national
development (and 'Australia for the Australians'), a
significant degree of governmental intervention in the
economy (including investment in 'private' business), a
strengthening of the welfare state and defence of what
it understood by working class interests. The party has
never offered a substantial theoretical critique of its
society.[11]

Duncan believes that the reason why the ALP does not
commit itself to a programme of substantial reform is not due
to the betrayal of the Labor Party's goals by its leaders, for
the leaders reflect the wishes of the party as a whole. Nor is
it simply that, having gained the faith of the working class,
they consciously proceed to act contrary to the interests of
that class, as Catley and McFarlane claim (see below). Rather,
on Duncan's view the Labor Party is almost inevitably a
pragmatic reformist party, because it has to work within a
constitutional and economic system which has inbuilt 'political, cultural and economic limits and obstacles to radical
change'.[12] He explains:

To focus on those obstacles may, indeed, lead to
pessimism about the possibility of change:
developments such as the growth of corporatism, with
the different estates being bound together, the
apparent weakening of class conflict, the seeming
inability of reforming governments to substantially
alter very unequal distributive systems, the blandness
of a populace avoiding divisive and dramatic choices,
even though the legitimate claims and, more
profoundly, the human needs of different social groups
are not being satisfied, pose enormous problems for
socialist theory.[13]

Indeed, some Labor leaders have spoken of these limits as
the reason for inaction. Thus I do not want to quarrel with

Duncan here, if what is being offered is a psychological explanation of why certain ALP leaders reject the idea of radical change: they don't believe they can do it.

However, if the suggestion is that the social and economic conditions are such that the majority of the people are unlikely to be responsive to radical suggestions and, more seriously, are likely to resist radical actions by government, then I believe this to be nothing but a myth, and a powerful one put forward by the media and large sections of the education system, to inhibit action. For, as I argued in Chapter 3 and shall further document in Chapters 7–9, there are serious economic, social and political problems in modern Australia which often reach the level of crisis. If this analysis is correct, then the ready acceptance by large sections of the Labor leadership of the view that radical changes are impossible is not because they are realistic, as they claim, but because either they do not understand the character of the current crises and have accepted the false doctrine that the people are consciously opposed to changing the current power structures, or they are using this 'realistic' attitude as an excuse or justification for inaction.

The view that the people will not even listen to proposals for radical alternatives is one of the myths created by conservative political science. There is just as much plausibility in the view that, during economic and social crisis, the people will vote against the existing government's handling of things, even if the alternative is represented as radical.[14] I shall argue in the Epilogue that, given determination and a coherent strategy for dealing with the ruling class, a great deal can be achieved. This, however, requires sincerity in the pursuit of a just and egalitarian economic order; action rather than words in bringing the people into democratic processes.

On this point, Duncan— referring to the Whitlam government—accepts that

> even within the limits which the ALP government set itself, it failed badly in explaining, justifying and

debating policy and in encouraging participation in political life. It promised 'open government' but engaged in a great deal of evasion and secrecy, and greatly multiplied its expert advisers and friends, who seemed to do most of the participating—a veritable bonanza for academics . . . Even failing substantial institutional change, the Labor Party might have engaged in democratic rather than technocratic planning, and have achieved far more in the field of public education and persuasion.[15]

Thus we are left with this problem: given that there are severe limits on what they can do, how is it that Labor governments fail to pursue socialist objectives with sufficient determination, and with a coherent strategy? I shall offer an explanation of this below. For the moment, consider an objection to the way in which I have posed the problem: it could be argued that the Labor Party is *never* concerned to challenge the oppressive structure of the economy, that on the contrary, it actively supports and reinforces the capitalist system.

This is the third view of the Labor Party, promulgated in particular by Robert Catley and Bruce McFarlane.[16] In their book, *From Tweedledum to Tweedledee*, they see three stark alternatives for the ALP:
(i) it can 'co-operate with the trend towards this nightmare world of an international corporate economy';[17]
(ii) it can build up Australian enterprises and insist on Australian ownership and control;
(iii) it can 'introduce socialist measures (nationalization of corporations without compensation, under workers' class power) to counter managerial power and begin the long process of bringing the state under people's power'.[18] They go on to explain:

> Needless to say, the ALP has eschewed the third
> alternative. Never a socialist party, but a liberalist-

> capitalist one, in which its fighting platform has never
> been allowed to include socialism (this being left to the
> vagueness and vagaries of its 'objectives'), the Party
> manoeuvres only within the limits set by the objective
> existence of a modern monopolistic and capitalist
> economy.[19]

In their view, the Labor Party's economic policy is thus
reduced to moving between the first alternative—supporting
multi-national corporations—and the second—supporting
nationalist policies of ownership by local capitalists. In trying
to meet both these goals at once, the Labor Party's policies
inevitably appear confused and contradictory.

> As the ALP government turns this way and twists
> that in its attempts to meet the contradiction between
> growing nationalism of the Australian people and the
> growing world-wide energy crisis on the one hand,
> and the de facto economic and political power of
> transnational corporations on the other, compromise,
> retreat and sudden changes of policy have been the
> order of the day. An example of this was the decision
> of the government to reject multinational participation
> in resource development laid down by Connor in
> August 1973 and the subsequent reversal of this policy
> during Whitlam's visit to Japan in October.[20]

However, it is not clear exactly what thesis McFarlane and
Catley are presenting. There seem to be three possible views:
(a) The state is a mere superstructure of capitalism and hence
can never be controlled by forces which can bring in socialism.
Although they sometimes sound like it, I cannot see how the
above authors can consistently hold this view. For they cannot
attack the ALP for not pursuing nationalization and other
socialist goals if it is impossible to pursue such goals within
the parliamentary system. (I have presented my own reasons
against this view of the state in Chapters 3C and 6B.)

(b) The ALP has, throughout its history or in recent times, completely abandoned all attempts to change capitalism, except those designed to strengthen it. In support of this view, the authors point to remarks such as the following from Whitlam: 'The sins of capitalism in Australia today are ones of omission rather than commission and of not being sufficiently enterprising and independent'.[21]

The major factor involved here is the development of a philosophy termed 'technocratic laborism' within the ALP.[22] 'Their aim is to get the benefit of the technological and managerial revolution for society and a larger share of the fruits for the skilled working class and middle class'.[23] In Catley and McFarlane's view, these technocrats have wrested control of the Labor Party from union leaders, by insisting on the importance of professional and administrative skills in politics. The authors then discuss in detail the attempt by Whitlam to ensure that the running of the economy is in accordance with the more technically advanced sectors of capitalism. They show that the Whitlam ministry relied to an extraordinary degree on the reports of the Paris-based Organization for Economic Co-operation and Development (OECD), which gives advice on how to achieve the capitalist goals of greater investment, economic growth and profits. This group of 'experts' supported the strategy of increasing government spending on education and welfare services, but *only in return for agreements from workers to keep wages down.*

Yet, if Catley and McFarlane are correct, then it must be explained why it was that the Whitlam government sought, and achieved, greater increases in government services, together with increases in wages. In order to explain why this occurred, they point to two factors: the militant demands of the workers, whose expectations were increased under a Labor government and the division of the Labor Party between the 'Whitlamites' and the 'Laborities'. The latter, led by Dr Cairns, are said to have prevented more unemployment and a squeeze on wages.

This, however, is inconsistent with the view that the

Labor Party as a whole is 'anti' the workers. Why should Cairns and others have acted to ensure a large share for labour, even at a time of great inflation, when enormous pressures were placed on the government by capitalist forces? It also suggests that we need to see the Labor Party in terms of the conflicting groups within it—a view I shall discuss presently, but one which is not developed by Catley and McFarlane.

(c) The ALP leadership is consistently betraying the working class and the socialist movement generally, by appealing to lofty principles such as the following:

> Labor declares that every citizen has the right to industrial equality and freedom from outmoded master and servant attitudes—the creative pursuit of human values to ensure that the innate satisfactions and qualities of life never become secondary to productivity goals or ruthlessly sought after efficiency.[24]

How can a goal like this be pursued without a thorough-going critique of capitalism and a redistribution in wealth and income? The authors argue that the Labor Party is not interested in this. They refer to speeches by Whitlam in which he indicated

> that he believed that the main causes of inequality in Australia were not those arising out of ownership of wealth and property, but regional disparities in education standards and in the burden of land and housing costs on households.[25]

They attempt to show that for the ALP, equality means nothing more than the liberal principle of equality of opportunity. In this regard, they quote Bill Hayden, the present Leader of the Opposition:

> Democratic socialism is concerned to guarantee the rights of the individual to a free, happy and full life in

which freedom of choice and equal opportunity are the
privilege of all . . . The equality of which socialists
speak concerns the equality of equal chance for each
person to develop his natural talents and interests to
the best of his ability.[26]

Admittedly to call this position 'socialist' is to stretch
language beyond recognition. The point at issue is: what is
that that gives each an equal chance to pursue their talents
and interests to the best of their abilities? Australian Liberals
believe that it is the capitalist economic system which allows
this. If the Labor Party also believes this, then in what way
does it differ from its opponents and why does it pretend to
be more moral and humane than they are? If the Labor Party,
on the other hand, believes that it must introduce substantial
changes to the economic and social systems in order to achieve
these goals, why don't its representatives say so?

Catley and McFarlane claim that Labor leaders like Whitlam and Hayden make speeches appealing to the workers'
'humanity' and 'sense of justice' while at the same time
offering little substantial change of the workers' alienated
situation. This suggests that Labor leaders are insincere in
their humanitarian goals and/or are cynically manipulating
the working class for their own purposes—such as the pursuit
of power and glory. Such an analysis seems to me to rely too
much on the character and beliefs of individuals, rather than
on the nature of the social or political forces to which these individuals give expression. Attacking individual leaders such
as Whitlam, Hayden or Cairns for their beliefs and attitudes,
does not explain why men who hold those attitudes become
leaders of the party. Nor does it explain why they are able
to promote their views without challenge.

The conflicting sections of the party
While there is some truth in each of the three views of the
Labor Party presented above, they all suffer from the fact
that they treat the party as a united totality. Although the

party does manage to act in a united way on a large number of issues, we should not allow this to obscure the fact that it consists of a coalition of ideological groupings in constant tension with each other. These ideological groupings are extremely important: for the conflict between them can, and does, determine the direction of the Labor Party at a given moment.

This very approach to analysing the ALP was taken by R.W. Connell.[27] Writing in 1968 when there was much talk about a split within the Labor Party between left and right (the left to be led by Jim Cairns and the right by Gough Whitlam), Connell identified four groups of people within the Labor Party. These are as follows:

traditional socialists—'people who regard social evils as inherent in a capitalist economy, and see Labor as the means to a major transformation of society';

new radicals—'little interested in socialism, accept the welfare state, but think Labor should take a strong radical stand on "conscience" issues such as aid to Asia, White Australia, capital punishment and civil liberties';

traditional moderates—'influenced by Catholic social thought, against thorough-going socialism, deeply hostile to Communists, believe in moderate social-welfare reforms';

new technocrats—'limited interest in socialism or civil liberties; see government as a tool for social engineering; interested in urban planning, efficiency in government, social welfare, science policy, efficient election techniques'.[28]

> Cairns' outlook has some elements from the first and second of these groups: he draws support from both. Whitlam's outlook is distinctly of the fourth type: he draws support also from the third and some from the second.
> The conflict also involves a power-struggle—rather, a series of power-struggles—within the party organisation, which is well documented by the Press.

But it is much more than that: it involves different versions of what the Labor Party is about.

> Whitlam's deepest concern is efficiency and effectiveness ... Cairns' deepest concern is with justice: he believes the organisation of Australian society is radically unjust, and that it cannot be rectified by passing laws, but only by a deep social and economic transformation.[29]

Since Connell wrote this, some new radicals have merged with the traditional socialists, while others have joined the new technocrats, to form a centre-liberal group. His so-called traditional moderates are really conservatives who have some interest in social justice.

Thus I believe we can distinguish three major theoretical strands within the modern Labor Party:

(i) conservatives who want social justice;
(ii) technocrats and social welfarist liberals;
(iii) socialists who want a gradual transformation of capitalist economy.

These I think can be roughly labelled the 'right', the 'centre', and the 'left' of the Labor Party; indeed, within Victoria, this threefold division has been formalized into three factions within the party. I think the division applies informally at the national level.

Consider some philosophical differences between these three groupings. The first group—the conservatives—are remnants of the people who were very powerful within the party before the 1956 split. They are predominantly Catholic and believe in the retention of the basic economic and social structures of society. Yet they feel that certain modifications ought to be brought in to help the poor, the needy, etc. Hence they are social welfarists to a degree, in that they accept a small contribution by the state provided that it does not threaten the existing social structures. Some of these were people who joined the DLP, but felt that it could not go anywhere. Others are people who feel that they should be in the Labor Party to prevent it moving to a socialist perspective. This group is not generally dominant in the Labor Party except in New South Wales.[30]

The second group consists of a merging of two previously distinct viewpoints. The social welfarist liberals do not believe that capitalism is necessarily an unjust system—thus it ought not be completely changed (see Whitlam, quoted above). Rather, it ought to be amended, added to and given what might be called a 'human face'. So they believe in extraordinary amounts of social welfare, public spending on education, health, transport, etc. in order to sustain, improve and make much more humane the adverse features of capitalist economy. These people are easily pursuaded that this can be done when the right technical and administrative skills are applied to the capitalist economy. They are thus much attracted to the views of the new technocrats and with them form the centrist group.

On the other hand, the third grouping—the socialists—believe that the capitalist economy is fundamentally exploitative, and that only a fundamental transformation of it will achieve a just society. Within the Labor Party, they are concerned with actions and policies which will gradually transform the economy from a capitalist to a socialist one. They thus take seriously the socialization objective of the party and advocate the redistribution of wealth, workers' participation and the like.[31]

We can think of the different ALP governments in terms of which of these groups are dominant. Usually one group is insufficient by itself to be the majority and hence a coalition arises. Thus, in New South Wales at the moment there is a coalition of the right and centre groups which supports and sustains the Wran government. Wran has been concerned primarily with putting forth mild social welfare policies and running the State as efficiently as possible. Even if he wanted to introduce more socialistic policies, he would be strongly resisted by the State party machine, which is predominantly conservative. The other example here is the Dunstan-Corcoran government in South Australia which, as far as I can see, was based in the centre and drew support from both the socialists and the conservatives depending on what the issue was. Hence, within his cabinet, Dunstan had people who are much more conservative than he, and others who are clearly socialist, such as Duncan, the former Attorney-General.

Consider now the case of the Whitlam government. It was clearly a coalition of centrists and socialists, notwithstanding the fact that there were certain politicians within it who belonged to the conservative group. This is the reason why it was attempting to introduce a considerable amount of reform and a redistribution of wealth in favour of workers and the poor. On these matters, both social welfarists and socialists could agree on a common policy, even though they disagreed as to the final outcome. However, when the technocrats' claims about the capacity of the capitalist system to pay for state services proved false—during the economic crisis of 1975—serious tensions arose between these groups (see below).

At this stage, an important question arises: what is it about the philosophies of the ALP which, on the one hand, allow it to arrive at common policies, yet on the other, allow it to hold very different perspectives on the nature of the capitalist economy and on society generally? Let me take the most interesting case: the social welfarist centre group and the socialist group. Here we have the extraordinary situation of one group which maintains that capitalism can be sustained and simply amended here and there, working in harmony with another group which maintains that it must be transformed into a different economic structure altogether. An example is the redistribution of wealth and services to achieve more equality; this is a platform on which both the centre and left group can agree. Both feel that it is necessary for the state to intervene to redistribute wealth and services (through, for example, free education services, free health services) in favour of the poor and needy. Yet while both groups can agree on this redistribution, they disagree about its impact on the capitalist economy.

Thus the social welfarist technocrats believe that the capitalist system is extremely strong and capable of accommodating all kinds of increases in social welfare, pensions, handouts to the unemployed, the poor and other such redistributive measures. Indeed, some believe that the system will be improved by such redistributive efforts. This was clearly Whitlam's position.[32] Conversely, the socialists believe that such redistributive measures would squeeze the economy. Since these measures have to be paid for, it means that profitability would be reduced in the private, capitalist sector. If the latter view is correct, then Whitlam's protestations that he believed in capitalism would not be relevant— for his redistributive actions were hurting the capitalists.

This disagreement regarding the impact on economy does not, however, prevent the party arriving at common policies when they are in opposition; for these differences can be shelved for the sake of unity against the common enemy. They become important, however, if the party wins government during periods of economic and social crisis. It is during these periods that the tensions within the ALP are likely to become the most serious.

The Labor Party's response to crisis
During crisis periods, the chips are down. The Labor Party's reform programmes and its attempts to redistribute come under severe attack. The Labor Party is pressurized by the ruling class to end its reforms and to assist the floundering forces of capital.

'Whitlamites' are in a strong moral position when they proclaim the need for more equality and greater social services. But what do they intend to do if the capitalist system cannot cope with these reforms? What if their actions result in investment reductions, unemployment, inflation and stagnation? What strategy do the social welfarists have to deal with these problems, if their predictions as to the capacity of the capitalist economy to continue providing services are mistaken, as is the case during crisis? Under these circumstances, the centrist technocrats and social welfarists are likely to divide, the majority joining up with the conservatives and introducing measures which are designed to cut real money wages and to dramatically cut previous levels of social welfare spending.[33] Not only would a halt to the redistribution to labour be introduced, there could be a reversal; state moneys being actively used to support capital. Thinking along these lines is now an increasingly dominant feature amongst many parliamentary spokesmen of the ALP. In adopting a strategy of this kind, this group is in effect actively supporting the capitalist forces. Indeed, when this sector of the ALP becomes dominant in times of crisis, its leadership may be incorporated within the ruling class itself. Thus, certain right-wing Federal shadow ministers have moved to ensure that they are acceptable to the 'Establishment'.[34]

The socialists, and those centrists who join up with them, are very likely to oppose this strategy. As we saw, for them redistributive measures are steps towards a socialist transformation. Thus, they will strongly oppose the steps to negate the gains of the working class and to simply align the ALP with capital. Yet they do not seem to have developed a positive strategy here. They call for more redistribution and more public ownership of productive enterprise, yet they do not seem to have a strategy for countering the economic attacks, which will almost inevitably come once the capitalists see their interests threatened. It is very revealing that socialist ministers like Cairns seemed not to perceive what steps had to be taken to transform economy, so as to take the country out of the economic crisis which arose. Did they simply expect socialism to arise spontaneously, without resistance? Or were they already too cynical to try any fundamental changes? This, and related issues, will be taken up in Chapter 9 when the conflicts within the ALP during the 1975 crisis will be discussed.

In an economic crisis, the ALP is extremely susceptible to attack from those who would exploit its ambiguous foundation and its love-hate relationship to the ruling class. Opposition leader Mr Fraser was particularly effective when he concentrated his attacks not on the socialists but on the social welfarists, whom he represented as foolish idealists. He argued convincingly before the electorate that the ALP was incompetent because it did not know how to deal with the consequences of its own reforms and redistributive efforts. However, this was not a question of the lack of knowledge, but a lack of agreement as to how to handle the crisis. At first reluctant to abandon his cherished welfare programmes and his plans to bring mineral resources under government control, Whitlam finally buckled under the demands of the ruling class (which he represented as merely the demands of the economic situation). However, by this stage the mobilization against him had reached an irreversible stage: it was too little, too late as far as the ruling class was concerned (see Chapter 8D).

The 1975 dismissal of the Federal Labor government at first provided a new solidarity to the ALP—for they were united in their anger at the Liberals and the Governor-General. However, as the impact of this died down, it became clear that the ALP's divisions were now deeper. They began to congregate around two perspectives, depending on the nature of the 'lessons' learnt from the crisis.

The 'realist' perspective was adopted by the conservatives, many social welfarists and the technocrats. They argue that, during times of crisis the ALP's policies must be 'responsible'. By this some mean that the party, if it wins government, must act to reduce real wages, increase productivity and support profits. It must be very slow in introducing new social welfare programmes and new state services. It cannot even entertain the notion of nationalization or public enterprises—even though this is clearly the only way to resolve the current unemployment situation.[35] The reasons given for this view are that Australians are conservative and will not accept drastic changes, *even if these solve the crisis*. This extraordinary view is promoted by academics acting on behalf of the ruling class and by the media.[36] In accepting it, these 'realists' are either dishonest, or cynical. To many, their attitude to the ruling class appears to be 'if you can't beat them, join them'.

The 'socialist' perspective is increasingly seen as 'idealist' and 'utopian', even by those holding it. Many of these people suffered from the illusion that once the ALP had won power through the ballot box, it would be able to introduce changes in the capitalist system which the community would support, and that the ruling class would have no option but to accept these changes. This naive view meant that the socialist wing of the party had no theory of how to deal with the various crises which arise in society as a consequence of, firstly, policies adopted by the Labor Party itself, and secondly, the general structural contradictions inherent in the systems of Western society. When the strategy of the ruling class in destroying the government was successful, the socialists were as dumbfounded as were other Australians. They had no historical or theoretical understanding of what happens to reformist governments which refuse to actively support the ruling class during crisis (see Chapter 9).

As a result, many ALP socialists became disillusioned with the whole system and with the left-wing leaders who had failed to generate coherent strategies to deal with the ruling class attacks against the Labor government. The Marxian doctrine that even a moderate socialist government will be destroyed was embraced by many as an excuse for leaving the party in despair. The notion of achieving genuine change through state power now appears to many a hopeless goal.[37]

While this response may be understandable from a psychological point of view, it is clearly mistaken as political analysis. As I have shown in various parts of this book,[38] of course the ruling class will mobilize in times of economic crisis to protect capitalist profits and to ensure that the burdens of the crisis are borne by the workers. This should have been an expected response. Unfortunately the Labor leadership on the left was not ready with the radical solutions required to deal with the crisis in a way that would benefit the working class. This meant that the only alternative was that which the media, the bureaucratic experts, business leaders and the Liberal Party were urging the Labor Party to adopt—namely, redistribution against workers in favour of capital.

However, as I have argued in Chapter 3A, this strategy does not resolve the deep economic and social crises of modern Australia. Only a radical programme coming from Labor socialists could have resolved the crisis at that stage. Such a programme was not forthcoming.

After the ALP defeat in the 1977 Federal election, the 'realists' in the ALP increased their dominance over the socialists. When the shadow cabinet of the party was elected, the *Age* noted in a headline 'Labor Moves to the Right'.[39] In so doing, the parliamentary wing has ensured that a radical programme for dealing with crisis will not arise in the party in the near future. Thus, since both parties are *now* dominated by factions in favour of the ruling class, it seems almost certain that economic and social crises in Australia will continue and deepen, whichever party wins power. While Labor will offer some small increases in services to cushion the blow, certain ALP 'realist' spokesmen are already warning the people to accept high levels of unemployment as 'inevitable'.[40] It would have been more honest to add 'under the present system which we are not prepared to change'.

Whether or not this happens depends on how strongly the socialists within the party continue to press for radical policies in favour of the working class, and how effective they are in achieving this. Their success here depends on whether more socialists join the ALP and ensure that the move to the right is halted and reversed. Under conditions of continuing economic crisis, the conflict as to whether the ALP shall serve the ruling class, or live up to its socialist traditions and act in support of workers will be of enormous historic importance. As I shall explain in the Epilogue, it could well determine whether the economic and social crises are to be resolved in the next few years or whether they will plague Australian society for many years to come.

D THE ROLE OF UNIONS IN CRISIS

The most important group which can ensure that the working class is not forced to bear all the burdens of economic crisis, and which can take advantage of political and legitimation crisis to achieve radical structural changes in the distribution of power in Australia, is the trade unions. We must consider the character of Australian unions to determine whether they are likely to take advantage of this historical opportunity.

Marx predicted that, in a competitive capitalist economy, over-production and competition would result in reduction in prices. In order to survive, capitalists would be forced to reduce wages so that profit margins could be sustained. This would lead to increasing misery among the working class, a situation which was occurring around him at the time he was writing. Indeed, in early capitalism, workers were hardly paid enough to live on. One way to combat this tendency of the capitalist system was by organization of the workers into unions. 'Workers Unite' thus became the rallying call of the working class in its attempts to counter these oppressive conditions. Their major weapon in the struggle was the strike, which is simply the communal withdrawal by all the members of the union of their labour.

The early unionists conceived of their task in a twofold way. Firstly, in the short term, they sought the protection of workers against the attempt to reduce their wages and the attempt to make the conditions of employment even worse than they were; the corollary to this was to try and improve the wages and conditions of their members. Secondly, in the long term, they attempted to change and transform the exploitative system itself.[1] Most union leaders therefore accepted the socialist position that capitalism was exploitative.

This early situation led to certain very bitter struggles throughout the industrialized world, including Australia. The major early struggles here took place in the 1880s and 1890s and in these the employers were in a very strong position. Not only were they supported by the state, they also had a powerful weapon they could use: the lockout. In a lockout, the employer dismisses all the employees who are members of the union, and attempts to employ a completely new group of people. This is possible when there is a massive pool of unemployed, or when the unions are not co-operating with each other. These early struggles between labour and capital were often bitter and violent; in Australia, the unions were often defeated.[2] One reason for these defeats was the role of the state in actively supporting employers against unions. This led to the formation of the labour parties, established specifically to assist industrial labour in its attempts to change the exploitative system.[3]

In the early part of this century, the tide began to turn. Unions began to win better wages and working conditions, and to prevent reductions. As we saw in Chapter 3A, it became possible to have increases in wages and still sustain levels of profitability. This permitted a movement away from the absolute poverty of early capitalism, but it did not dramatically change the huge differences and divisions between rich and poor. Thus, while the unions were initially successful in achieving an increase in the standard of living, it appears that they have not been able to go further and achieve either the transformation of the economy or any reduction in the general pattern of the distribution of wealth.[4]

At this stage, it might be argued that unions are no longer concerned with the transformation of society so as to end the exploitation and alienation of workers—or even to improve workers' material conditions. This view can be supported by the following arguments.

Firstly, there is evidence that many union leaderships have been acting in the interests of the management rather than the workers. In other words, often the employers manage to incorporate the leadership of the union into their general structures. This was, and is, done in various ways: by bribes to union officials—thus many end up on boards of management when they retire; by providing unions with facilities which they would not otherwise have had; by employers specifically supporting certain candidates in union elections as against others.[5]

Secondly, there is the acceptance by many unions of the view perpetrated by the ruling class, through large sections of the media, that the proper role of unions is to limit their claims to 'purely industrial' matters. This view was not accepted by many union leaders during the late 1960s and early 1970s. ACTU President Bob Hawke then spoke out against the separation of political and industrial matters (see Chapter 5D).

> In the past, as I see it, there has been a tendency
> to draw a dividing line in unionism. On the one side
> have been placed things that are traditionally union
> matters—wages, working conditions—but on the
> other side are placed issues that are not touched by
> unions. My reasoning is that there should be no
> dividing line. Anything that constitutes discrimination
> or hardship—then in we go . . . We have a broad brief
> and that brief is the protection and advancement of the
> standard and quality of life of Australian workers and
> their dependents. Now if, for instance, one was to say
> that it is appropriate that the trade union movement
> should try to secure increased leisure for the workers
> (and no one would doubt that that is a legitimate trade
> union activity) isn't it manifestly our job to look at the
> environment, the conditions, within which and under
> which people will be able to enjoy it?[6]

Nevertheless, since the onset of the current economic crisis, the ACTU and many unions have been much more reluctant to take action to protect reductions in state services to workers and to insist on structural changes in economy.

Thirdly, there is the view that unions have allowed themselves to be incorporated into the structure of the capitalist process by accepting the incorporation of the union movement into the legal processes of the state. This has been done through the Arbitration Commission, which requires unions to register and to be governed by the processes of arbitration and conciliation. Thus Geoff Sorrell argues that the procedures and decisions of the Arbitration Commission are such that it almost inevitably acts to protect the capitalist economy and not change it.[7] It thus acts in favour of the interests of capital against labour. He quotes Commissioner Judge Wright who in a 1969 judgement said this:

> I apprehend that the philosophy of industrial arbitration legislation in this country was founded broadly upon the historical rights of people to conduct businesses in their own way within the law, to employ whom they like and to be employed by whom they like. Thus legislation of the Colonies and subsequently the Commonwealth, and in earlier time the States, withheld from their industrial tribunals power to adjudicate in disputes about the manner in which an employer should conduct his business.[8]

In support of this view is the fact that the wage indexation system can, at best, freeze the present relationship between labour and capital. It cannot improve labour's share. Indeed many union leaders seem content to protect the present levels from erosion by wage inflation rather than pushing for either extra wages or, more importantly, extra benefits for the working class. For example, Rob Jolly, the then industrial advocate of the ACTU, said after the September 1976 judgement (in which workers were granted an across-the-board 1.3 per cent increase) that the major aim of the unions was to sustain the existing purchasing power of wages to keep up with inflation.[9] There is no reference to any suggestion of changing either the exploitative character of the system or of redistributing incomes to a more equitable level.

I do not believe, however, that it can be concluded from the above arguments that unions have been incorporated into the system to such a degree that they no longer constitute a challenge to the capitalist economy. Consider once again the arbitration system. In all fairness I think it must be conceded that the existence of this system has eradicated or prevented some of the excesses of unbridled capitalism. One good consequence of the system, in its beginnings, was the introduction of the concept of minimum wage. Australia was one of the first countries in the world to introduce this concept, early in the 1920s.[10] The basic wage provided that each man's labour be rewarded at least to the extent of ensuring his physical survival as a human being. It was later expanded to include basic requirements for a person to survive within our culture.

Nor has the subjecting of unions under the present legal rules undermined union militancy or decreased the membership of unions. Indeed, one of the most significant features of the period at the end of the long boom and the beginning of the crisis has been the increase in levels of union membership (see below). As D.W. Rawson points out:

> Public control over union rules and their
> administration may be regarded as full of anomalies
> and productive of difficulties; it is not regarded as an
> attempt to bring unionism under the control of its
> enemies. Nor, in more concrete terms, is it regarded as
> marked by partiality or dishonesty . . . Most unionists
> do not seriously regard the laws regulating the
> government of unions as biased against them, and in
> most respects they have little reason to think so.[11]

Furthermore, as regards the role of the Arbitration Commission in achieving industrial peace, he says:

> At this vital point, the acceptance of the legitimacy of
> the system by the unions is at best very imperfect.

Whereas there is general acquiescence in the right of public authorities to regulate the internal affairs of unions, there is no corresponding acquiescence in their power to arbitrate industrial disputes and to enforce their decisions against union opposition. That is, there is no intention of abandoning the strike as an instrument of union policy. Strikes are concentrated in particular places and industries but belief in the 'right to strike' is almost universal among the unions, as is the expectation that strikes will actually occur.[12]

The Arbitration Commission is thus seen by many unions as a body which they will *conditionally* work with, provided that it does not completely inhibit their capacity to struggle on behalf of the working class. On certain occasions, the Commission has acted contrary to the advice of the Federal government, and given full indexation rises to workers—thus angering both political and economic leaders of the ruling class. Indeed, in the last three years, the Commission has generally *not* co-operated with the Fraser strategy of forcing workers to bear the burden of economic recovery.

Some people will argue that, in so doing, the Commission has prevented serious confrontations between the working class and the economic and political wings of the ruling class, that therefore it has ensured that no radical changes occur in this period of crisis. Against this, I have argued, however, that the crisis will continue unless such radical changes are introduced. Furthermore, it is plausible to suggest that the Commission's actions have moderated some of the attacks on workers by the Liberals and have thus prevented the short-term recovery which the latter were hoping to achieve.

Nevertheless, the Commission was not always so moderate. During most of the economic boom until the 1960s, it used its powers to impose penalties on unions and union leaders. This matter came to a head with the jailing of Clarrie O'Shea, the Victorian Secretary of the Tramways Union in April 1969, for refusing to pay a fine of $1200. After an intense campaign of widespread strikes and demonstrations by many unions, the government and the court backed down.[13] It has never since attempted to use these provisions in the law.

The years 1969–76 saw a remarkable upsurge in working-class militancy, even amongst white-collar and professional unions. During this period, union membership increased from 51 per cent of the workforce in 1969 to 57 per cent in 1976, the most significant rise being amongst women (36 per cent to 47 per cent). Besides the increased numbers of women, unions in the services industries (Liquor and Allied Trades) and in professional, clerical, and public service sectors increased spectacularly, often doubling their numbers.[14]

As a result of this, militancy amongst the rank and file increased. The number of working days lost in disputes rose to a high level in the early 1970s.[15] Furthermore, workers who had not previously used the strike weapon, such as the teachers, took industrial action to achieve improvements in working conditions. Substantial wage increases achieved during this period had the net effect of redistributing the proportion of the national product which went to workers, even though this could not—in itself—achieve much redistribution of wealth. These facts belie the claim that the majority of Australian unions now act hand in glove with employers. Even if some union leaders (particularly those affiliated with the National Civic Council)[16] may have preferred to collaborate with employers, pressures from the rank and file often force them to do otherwise.

However, these pressures stem primarily from the incorporation of workers deeper into the materialist culture rather than from any commitment to ending the exploitation of human beings on which that culture—with its social and economic evils—is based.[17] Thus Ross Martin in his book on this subject argues that Australian unions are dependent institutions. This

> is reflected in their tendency to react to events rather than shape them. Most unions for most of the time are

engaged in essentially defensive or protective operations stimulated by changing circumstances outside their control. This is exemplified, above all, in the ceaseless claims for pay increases based on such grounds as movements in the cost of living, disturbances in the relativities of different groups, and technological or other changes affecting the skills, responsibilities or job-difficulties of a specific occupational sector.[18]

What, then, has happened to the unions as anti-capitalist forces seeking to eradicate exploitation? Sorrell claims that

> Australian unionism at large (though many individuals must be excepted) has so far failed to develop any very relevant understanding of the directions in which Australian society and the economy are moving. There is no evidence of a theory, let alone a programme, for the control by workers of their own industrial environment. Unions have hardly started to come to grips with the problem of the multi-national corporation . . . finally, there is only minimal association between trade unions and any emergent radical groupings.[19]

Indeed the majority of unions seem to have abandoned any *positive* action, based on a long-term strategy to achieve a more equal and better share of the national wealth for workers, and to transform the general character of the economy so as to give workers more control of what is produced and of how the work situation is organized. Hence worker control and participation is very muted as a goal for Australian unions.

In not pursuing such a strategy, the unions open themselves up to a plausible attack from capitalist forces: by simply limiting their goals to more wages and better conditions, they are easily represented as aggressive, greedy, self-seeking organizations whose actions 'hold the community at ransom'.[20]

Of course, they would also be attacked if they pursued wider goals such as changes in the economy as a whole; they will then be accused of pursuing political goals and usurping the power of parliament. Yet this latter argument cannot as easily be twisted to create an image of unions as 'evil'. Indeed radical actions by some unions to achieve changes in the community as a whole, rather than benefits only to their own members, may gain considerable support. A good example of this is the Victorian Secondary Teachers Association. When it first become militant, it demanded general changes to education policy, more facilities for schools as a whole, more money spent on education, more classrooms, science facilities, etc. In these demands, at least at the beginning, it received majority support from the public. On the other hand, by 1978 the VSTA had turned to concentrate more on industrial disputes such as wages and promotion issues which concerned the narrow interests of its members. In going out on strike on these issues, it discovered that the public generally tended not to support it.

Returning then to our initial problem: how are unions likely to act in times of crisis and what is the likely consequence of their action? There seems to me to be four basic strategies and unions may adopt different ones.

(i) They may adopt a coherent set of goals to achieve more workers' control and public ownership of enterprises, together with a substantial redistribution of wealth.[21] This radical policy has already been adopted by some militant unions such as the AMWSU (Metalworkers). It may gain momentum as the economic and social crises deepen.

(ii) They may adopt a defensive strategy to sustain wage levels and working conditions and thus resist attempts to place the burden of the crisis on workers and their families. This has been the most popular strategy in the period of the Fraser government. Its success, however, is limited by the fact that the government can cut real money wages through increases in taxation—as in the 1978 budget.

(iii) They may struggle against the attempts by government

to cut working-class standards of living through reductions in state services such as health, education and social security. Unions have not generally been successful in this, mainly because of the capacity of the ruling class to divide the working class on this issue: it has offered the prospect of tax cuts for workers with good incomes, provided they accept reductions in assistance to the sick, the unemployed and the elderly. The Fraser government has been particularly effective in convincing middle-income earners that the reason they pay high taxes is because of state services to 'dole bludgers' and to the disadvantaged or old (which neglects the enormous amounts of government income dished out in handouts and concessions to capital and to wealthy individuals).

(iv) The unions may attempt to reach some kind of social contract with government, in which there are trade-offs: workers are offered a restoration of previous levels of social welfare, or a moratorium on more reductions, in return for agreements to cut wages. In this strategy, the working class is urged to distribute the burden of the crisis more evenly *amongst itself*. The usual argument is that wage increases to the employed leave the unemployed, pensioners and others in a disadvantaged position. If high profits are to be sustained to support this disadvantaged sector, and to sustain levels of state spending in education, health and other services of benefit to the people as a whole, unions must exercise 'restraint', meaning that they must accept reductions in real money wages.[22]

The second and third strategies, if *successfully* adopted by the union movement, will have the net effect of continuing the crisis, even in the short term. It will also create an atmosphere in which the union movement, together with other political and social groups, can pursue the first strategy. For only this will achieve a long-term resolution to the crisis. The quicker union leaders recognize and act on this, the greater will be the chances of achieving the substantial transformation of Australian society which is required.

However, it is more likely that the fourth strategy will be

adopted as a short-term solution. Here the union leadership is the most vulnerable. Faced with a moral choice between accepting wage reductions for their members or accepting reductions in state services and support to the unemployed and disadvantaged, union leaders are likely to choose the former and incorporate it in some contract between themselves and the government. Significantly, Opposition leader Bill Hayden proposed this very arrangement on 19 January 1979 as a strategy for a future Labor government.[23] This was in the same week in which BHP and other companies announced record profits.

Yet is this latter strategy likely to be accepted by the union movement? And is it likely to work? On the first point, one can gain contrasting impressions of the extent to which the union movement is likely to be subservient to an ALP government. Ross Martin believes that often union leaders accept that their link with the ALP requires them to act 'responsibly'—meaning that they should exercise wage restraint and prevent damaging strikes.[24] For the ALP's electoral fortunes are more likely to be affected by such union militancy than that of the Liberals. Nevertheless, the total failure of the Callaghan government's attempt to use the same strategy in Britain should serve as a warning to those Labor leaders who seek to impose such a contract on the labour movement as a whole.

It must be conceded, however, that such a strategy, if implemented by a Labor government, is likely to alleviate the crisis in the short term without changes to the power structure: provided that the government uses the money saved to create new employment opportunities in the public sector.[25] However, it is clear that a recovery based on this strategy will be short-lived. For though profits will remain high, demand will remain low or even decrease as a consequence of the wage reductions. The only major hope in these conditions would be a dramatic increase in Australian exports.[26]

Finally, we must consider which of the above strategies unions are likely to adopt.[27] Because of the materialism of

Australian culture, most unions are under rank-and-file pressure to adopt the second strategy for increased wages and productivity deals. The likelihood of their going along with the social contract idea will depend on two factors: the extent to which ACTU leaders, especially Bob Hawke, will push the idea even in the face of hostile opposition;[28] and the extent to which the militant unions, particularly those which have substantial numbers of socialists in their executives, will co-operate. Unless such a social contract results in a redistribution in favour of labour *or* is combined with some important steps towards workers' control, I cannot see the union movement as a whole accepting it. Yet capitalist forces are extremely unlikely to accept any contract—unless it ensures that the working class continue to bear the burdens of the current crisis.

In conclusion, then, the normal activities of unions make it more difficult to impose even a short-term solution to the crisis based on drastic wage reductions. The situation is thus likely to remain stalemated in crisis—unless and until the unions and other working-class organizations take a more positive approach and strive to achieve a structural transformation of the society, to a socialist economy, based on full democratic participation of the whole people. Is this a likely long-term consequence of economic and legitimation crises in Australia? I shall discuss this in the Epilogue of the book.

III
Crisis in Recent
Australian History

7

The Rise of Labor

In Parts I and II I have been concerned with providing a theoretical framework for the understanding of crisis. Although I have made some references to past events, my general emphasis has been on the crisis situation in the late 1970s. I now turn to the application of the theory of crisis in a more systematic analysis of the political events in Australia in the last twelve years.

A   THE VIETNAM WAR: LEGITIMACY UNDERMINED

In the Federal election of 1969, the Labor Party made a tremendous comeback after its savaging of 1966.[1] Yet this was a time of economic boom, of rising living standards and of general optimism throughout the community. Why then was the majority of the Liberals reduced from 39 to 7 in the House of Representatives? In this section, I shall argue that a major factor in the ALP's near-victory of 1969 and breakthrough into government of 1972 was the traumatic impact on the Australian people of the Vietnam war. From 1968 to 1972, the continuation of the war seriously undermined the legitimacy of the government—and even the Australian state itself.

Yet it was not always so. For initially, Australia's involvement in the Vietnam conflict, far from reducing support for conservatives, provided them with a great issue with which to undermine the labour movement. Australia's participation in the war was argued for on the grounds that we had been invited by the government of South Vietnam to support the anti-communist forces in their struggle. In fact, Australia sent advisers only because of a request from the United States. And when Australia decided to send ground troops, which required conscription of young people to fight in a war many did not want, this was not at the urging of the United States or of South Vietnam. It was an initiative of Menzies'.[2] Announcing the policy, he told the parliament:

> The Australian Government is now in receipt of a request from the Government of South Vietnam for further military assistance ... In case there is any misunderstanding, I think I should say, Sir, that we decided in principle some time ago—weeks and weeks ago—that we would be willing to do this if we received the necessary request from the Government of South Vietnam and the necessary collaboration with the United States.[3]

Yet, as was discovered from the Pentagon Papers years later, Menzies had in effect lied to the parliament on this. He had decided to send troops and afterward sought a request from the South Vietnamese Prime Minister to legitimize his actions. As Freudenburg shows, the government was in a panic in its attempts to secure such a 'request': for the decision had been leaked to the press, prior to any such 'request' arriving.[4] Indeed, President Johnson's letter congratulating Australia on her decision was received before any supposed request was made.

The secretive and dishonest circumstances surrounding Australia's entry into the war were later to become one factor in the undermining of state legitimacy. Yet at this stage, when the Labor Party under Arthur Calwell spoke out against it, it was completely isolated from popular opinion, which had seen the war as a simple case of resisting 'communist aggression'. Calwell's analysis of the situation was realistic and prophetic:

> The war in South Vietnam is a civil war, aided and
> abetted by the North Vietnamese Government, but
> neither created nor principally maintained by it. To
> call it simply 'foreign aggression' as the Prime
> Minister does, and as his colleagues do, is to
> misrepresent the facts and thereby, confuse the issue
> with which we must ultimately come to terms . . .
> Preoccupied with the idea of monolithic, imperialistic
> Communism, we have channelled our support to those
> military regimes which were loudest in their
> professions of anti-communism, no matter how
> reactionary, unpopular or corrupt they may have been.
> Humiliation for America could come in one of two
> ways—either by outright defeat, which is unlikely, or
> by her becoming interminably bogged down in the
> awful morass of this war, as France was for ten years.
> Australia's aim should have been to help end the war,
> not to extend it.[5]

Yet Calwell's warnings fell on deaf ears. An editorial in the Hobart *Mercury* sums up the prevalent attitude based on anti-communism and the fear of China, an attitude promoted by the Liberal Party and the media.

> Once again in its befuddled way, the Labor Party
> seems to be advocating a neutralist Australia—in
> another word, suicide . . . Nobody welcomes that
> Australians are to be directly involved in fighting in
> South-East Asia, but the decision has been dictated
> by one simple fact. The Government of South Vietnam
> asked for military aid under Seato. Apparently Mr
> Calwell feels that although Australia should accept
> American protection under that treaty she should

refuse to fulfil her obligations to contribute to the common defence.

The only alternative to meeting the treaty obligation is to become neutralist and wait for the Red juggernaut to roll over a lonely Australia.[6]

In January 1966, Menzies retired as Prime Minister and was replaced by his deputy Harold Holt. The new leader was even more committed to Australia's participation and pushed the matter strongly. When the first conscripts died in Vietnam in March, Holt defended his position by appeals to the fear of China: 'while the Chinese Communist philosophy of world domination persists, the whole free world is threatened'.[7]

At the time when several Western nations were beginning to oppose the American involvement in the war, and were refusing to become actively engaged in the fighting, Holt visited the United States and surprised President Johnson with his unqualified support for American policies. Holt's statement is worthy of analysis because it explains some of the deeper reasons for Australia's involvement:

The outcome of this struggle is critical for the hopes that you and we share for a better and more secure way of life for the free people of Asia . . .

But it does not take a war to bring Americans and Australians close together.

We have many mutually beneficial links. Our trade with each other, *the investment that you make with us with your capital* . . .

You have in us not merely an understanding friend but one staunch in the belief of the need for our presence with you in Vietnam . . .

And so, sir, in the lonelier and perhaps even more disheartening moments which come to any national leader, I hope there will be a corner of your mind and

> heart which takes cheer from the fact that you have an
> admiring friend, a staunch friend that will be *all the*
> *way with L.B.J.*[8] (my italics)

The last words became a political slogan which was used
effectively to swing support to the Liberals. The earlier
italicized part indicates that Liberals felt they had to support
the US in order to ensure the continuity of investment by
multi-nationals in Australia. This economic factor was of more
importance than ideological reasons. After all, as Calwell had
pointed out, the government was ideologically hypocritical
on the matter; it was trading with China, while at the same
time declaring her an enemy.[9]

Holt received some criticism for kowtowing to the United
States, but his approach paid off handsomely when Johnson
became the first and only US President to visit Australia. The
legitimacy of the war was sealed by linking it closely to
Australia's alliance with America. By this stage the hysteria
in favour of the war was so great that people who were
opposed—particularly those who dared support the Viet
Cong—were represented as virtual traitors. Under these circumstances, and given the Labor Party's strong stand, it is
remarkable that the ALP managed to retain 40 per cent of the
vote in the 1966 election.

With this conservative victory, the prosecution of the war
continued. Opponents at demonstrations, and conscientious
objectors, were very harshly treated—a number of them were
jailed. Meanwhile the situation on the ground was not
improving for the US and its allies. However, this was not
the impression given to the people. Throughout 1966, 1967
and early 1968, the media both in the US and Australia were
reporting that the American action in Vietnam—by this
stage involving more than half a million US troops—had been
successful in containing the Viet Cong and the North Vietnamese. Even the US President appears to have been misled
by his advisers with promises that increased manpower and

increased bombing of North Vietnam would soon bring victory. By early 1968, the American people were very divided on the issue and other Western powers believed there could be no military solution.

Thus when at the end of January 1968, the famous Tet offensive occurred, it proved to be the turning point of the war. General Giap, the Defence Minister of the North Vietnamese and Viet Cong forces (he was the general who defeated the French in 1954) produced another master stroke in military strategy. Within the space of three days every major centre in South Vietnam was attacked, including Saigon itself. To Johnson's humiliation, even the American Embassy was invaded. Although the Viet Cong suffered substantial losses from this operation, they managed to deliver a psychological blow of immense proportions against the Americans. The US President was virtually accused of lying to the nation as to the progress of the war or of having been seriously misled by his advisers.

The media in the US turned strongly against the war. Consequently, as one analyst put it in the Pentagon Papers:

> The political reality which faced President Johnson was that 'more of the same' in South Vietnam, with an increased commitment of American lives and money and its consequent impact on the country, accompanied by no guarantee of military victory in the near future, had become unacceptable to these elements of the American public. The optimistic military reports of progress in the war no longer rang true after the shock of the Tet offensive.[10]

President Johnson announced, several weeks after the offensive, that he would cut back the bombing and seek a negotiated settlement of the war. He accepted responsibility and declared that he would not stand again at the election due at the end of that year. Within days, contrary to the expectations of the warmongers, North Vietnam accepted the offer of talks—even though parts of its territory were still being bombed. These events led to dramatic developments in American politics. They also led to a big change in the Australian attitude to the war.

In this country, public opinion against the war, which had been progressively building up, suddenly surged forward. There were more active and violent anti-war activities such as the demonstrations of 4 July 1968. In addition to this, large numbers of young people actively disobeyed the law. They did this by disobeying the call-up laws, or by acts of violence against property of the US, and against companies that were supplying materials and weapons for the con-tinuation of the war.[11] To make matters worse for proponents of the war, there were revelations of atrocities carried out by the American troops. In particular the My Lai incident created a sensation. It was revealed that when a group of American troops went into this village, their idea of pacifying it was to line up the members of the village—men, women and children —and shoot every one of them, leaving them to die in a pool of blood. Even people who believed that it was right to oppose communism in South-east Asia started to wonder whether the means were not undermining the end.

By early 1969 public opinion polls indicated that more than half the Australian people were opposed to the war.[12] How-ever, the Liberals continued the war policy, although divi-sions developed within the party on the issue, because Richard Nixon, the new US President, believed he could satisfy opinion at home by withdrawing US troops and at the same time win the war, by building up the forces of South Vietnam. This strategy soon involved the resumption of bombing and the invasion of Cambodia.

Back in Australia, John Gorton (who replaced Harold Holt as Prime Minister) began to recognize that this issue might bring down the Liberal government. He made some noises about the possibility that Australian troops might be with-drawn from Vietnam. Yet he was not supported. The Liberals continued the Australian involvement. In so doing, however, they ensured the further radicalization of large sections of the Australian people. The question that kept arising was: if the majority of people are now against the war, how can the government democratically justify its continued involvement? Many withdrew their support from the Liberal Party.

The election of 1969 was a watershed. Yet the hope that Australia's participation would end with the defeat of the Liberals was not realized. The Liberals were re-elected, albeit by a reduced majority. Opinion polls indicated that more than 50 per cent of the people were opposed to the war, yet many of these clearly could not bring themselves to put Labor into power.

For the legitimacy of the state, this created a serious problem. Many people began to question whether or not policy could be changed democratically in Australia. The war was being prosecuted notwithstanding what the majority felt or believed. The Labor Party had tried reforming itself in order to win power and yet, after twenty years, it still seemed that all the odds were stacked against it. Parliament was increasingly seen by the anti-war activists as irrelevant to achieving the end of Australian participation.[13]

In a remarkable exercise of participatory democracy, the vocal section of the majority opposed to the war began to mobilize the people. This resulted in the huge anti-Vietnam war moratoriums, led by the prominent Labor Party spokesman, Dr Jim Cairns. He had been a vocal and consistent opponent of the war earlier than most Labor people.

After the 1969 election, the labour movement was determined to end Australia's involvement by direct action. Showing considerable courage, Dr Cairns agreed to head the moratorium movement. He was reported in the press as calling upon workers and students 'to occupy the streets of Melbourne'.[14] The inevitable attacks came against him:

> The Minister for Labour and National Service said 'it is an invitation to anarchy'. Later he called supporters of the Moratorium 'political pack-raping bikies'. The

Prime Minister said they were 'storm troopers'. The Melbourne *Herald* said 'Dr Cairns is on a perilous path'. The Melbourne *Age* said it was a 'dangerous protest', and decided that to believe 'that the street demonstrations will be non-violent seems naive in the extreme' . . . The pressure was on. But about 120,000 took action. It was a far larger crowd than had ever before supported any political cause.[15]

Notwithstanding the attacks, and the newspapers' urging people not to attend, the moratorium surprised everybody. An estimated 70 000 people marched in Melbourne alone, on Friday 8 May 1970. This event indicated that many people were prepared to do a very un-Australian thing—go out into the streets, in massive numbers, to voice their opposition to the war. Of course, it was recognized that for every person who was there marching, there were at least ten sympathizers in the society at large. As Cairns told the crowd: 'Nobody need feel worried or fearful about the will of the people. The will of the people is being expressed today as it never has been before'.[16]

The moratorium demonstrated the extent to which support for the state had been eroded in Australia: legitimacy had been seriously undermined. Furthermore, the size of the demonstration indicated that the number of people who were so deeply opposed to the war that they were prepared to risk breaking the law in order to express their beliefs was substantial. This was a direct challenge to the system itself. For it is one thing for a person to be opposed to the war, in the sense of saying 'I disagree with the Liberals' but another to refuse to obey the law, or to directly challenge the law.

Although some foolish Liberal leaders dismissed the demonstration, more thoughtful elements in the ruling class realized that such a popular movement could not easily be ignored. The media changed their tune overnight. The *Sun*'s headline was 'Democracy wins the Day'. The *Herald* ran a large picture of Cairns with the heading 'Mr Democracy' and an editorial saying the demonstration was an expression of the freedoms available in our community which were not available in other closed societies, etc.[17]

I have suggested in Chapter 6B that when legitimacy is undermined an important response of the system is changing the government. The Australian ruling class could see dramatic evidence of such an undermining, in the massive demonstrations against the war. It was necessary to ensure that this public anger would *not* be directed at the economic system in whose ideological interests the war had been prosecuted.

It has been argued that it was the brilliant personality and strategy of Whitlam which led Labor to office in 1972. While Whitlam's contribution was obviously crucial, it could be argued that Cairns' strategy of bringing out the will of the people on the issue of the Vietnam war was the significant catalyst: the ruling class were faced with an unpalatable alternative—either assist the election of a Labor government or face the prospect of the Labor Party becoming a mass movement and bringing in changes by use of demonstrations and strikes. The consequences of the latter for the socio-economic system would be revolutionary. Thus, after twenty-three years, the ruling class increasingly accepted the possibility of a Labor government.

Yet even with this undermining of legitimacy, the Liberals would not have lost power if Whitlam had not taken action to reassure capitalist forces that he had no intention of changing the structure of capitalist economy and if the Liberals had not proved incompetent in managing the conflict between different sectors of capital. The latter led to a political (rationality) crisis in the state. I turn to consider each of these factors.

B   WHITLAM'S LEGITIMIZING OF THE LABOR PARTY
Edward Gough Whitlam dominated Australian parliamentary politics from 1966 to 1975. Representations of Whitlam vary from the view that he was a great statesman who stumbled (or was ambushed) at the end of his prime ministership, to

the view that he was an evil man out to wreck Australian society, who was stopped just in time. Another popular view was that he was excellent at winning government because of his charismatic appeal but just did not know how to manage things once he achieved office.[1] My own view is that, at the personal level, Whitlam was one of those peculiar contradictions: a humanitarian with an authoritarian streak. The former quality was represented in his desire to improve the quality of life for all Australians by vastly increasing the level of government services particularly in health, education and urban development. He was also concerned to help the poor and the needy. Yet he passionately believed that the only way to do this was through achieving parliamentary power, and in this pursuit of power not for its own sake, but for what he felt it was his destiny to bring to the Australian people, Whitlam was a ruthless man.[2]

Within Labor's ideological spectrum, Whitlam was both a technocrat and a social welfarist (see Chapter 6C). Indeed, he played a major role in bringing together those who felt they could manage the economy better than the Liberals (without changing its character) and those who believed that the capitalist economy had to be supplemented by massive spending in state services. Yet Whitlam had an extraordinary blind spot: he did not acknowledge the existence of class conflict in Australia. He did not realize what was involved in the tension between labour and capital. He had little understanding of where *real* power lies in this country. In this sense, Whitlam differed from both socialists like Cairns and conservatives like Fraser. In a perceptive passage, Freudenberg recognizes why Whitlam was able to achieve the prime ministership without any cognizance of the inner meaning of economics:

In a parliamentary democracy within a capitalist system, economic decisions reflect political priorities and political choices. In the fifties and sixties, it was quite possible for politicians to believe that the days of the primacy of economics were past. These years were the hey-day of the idea of 'fine tuning', the belief that the only choice to be made was between a little more inflation or a little less employment. The philosopher's stone had been found at last: growth. For social democrats ... growth was the new touchstone, solving the dilemma between the need for profits and the demands of public welfare within the 'mixed economy' ... The internal dilemmas of the social democrat parties in the late seventies are very much the result of the failure of the golden promise of growth as an idea and as a reality.[3]

Though he did not understand socialism, Whitlam soon understood that powerful people in the media and in sections of business would never support the election of the Labor Party, unless the influence of the old-style socialists who were interested in such 'outmoded' techniques as nationalization was diminished. Whitlam set out to restructure the party, so that what he considered more moderate policies would be adopted and the influence of the socialists diminished.

Whitlam recognized that the strategy to use against the old socialists was to appeal to the concept of democracy: he attacked the party 'bureaucrats' claiming that they were unrepresentative of the rank and file of the ALP.[4] There were two branches which he was particularly concerned to reform: the Victorian and the West Australian. The secretary of the latter was the formidable Joe Chamberlain. Whitlam directly attacked him, because Chamberlain had made a public protest over the deputy leader Lance Barnard's remarks on Vietnam. Whitlam made clear the real motive behind his moves to restructure the party: 'It is not Mr Chamberlain's prerogative to interpret or enunciate the Federal policy of the ALP. If there is a Federal Labor government, he will neither state nor dictate its policy'.[5] The extra-parliamentary control of policy had to end, if Labor were to become an 'acceptable' party. Such a move would ensure that radical policies were rarely adopted, and even if adopted, they were to be ignored by members of parliament if they felt that it could not be 'sold' to the electorate.

To press for these reforms Whitlam showed considerable courage in directly attacking the Victorian Executive at its own conference.[6] After several confrontations, Whitlam brought the issue to a head: on 19 April 1968, he sent a telegram to all members of the party, telling them that he would resign and recontest his position as leader on the following Tuesday. The event which had brought on this dramatic gesture was the meeting of the Federal Executive of the party, at which Whitlam had been humiliated, when he attempted to defend Brian Harradine. The latter, an extreme right-winger, had publicly attacked members of the Victorian Executive, accusing them of communist links.[7] If Whitlam believed that his re-election was certain, he was mistaken. Under pressure from both old and new socialists, Jim Cairns stood against him. In his letter to MPs Cairns raised the question: 'Whose party is this—ours or his?' He accurately foresaw the consequences of a Whitlam victory:

> To permit Mr Whitlam to contest the leadership unopposed could leave the incorrect impression that the Parliamentary Party unanimously supports his stand.
>
> His resignation and conduct have endangered our party ... I am opposed to any attempt by any man to centralize power or to dominate his party colleagues. I cannot accede to the leader's demand that parliamentarians must agree with him in the various party conferences and executive ... This is intellectual arrogance and dangerous folly. Just this is what is involved in the present crisis.[8]

From this it can be seen that Whitlam's appeals for more rank-and-file participation were simply a smokescreen. He wanted more power for the parliamentary party in which he had a majority. In the end, he did not care to consult even with the parliamentary caucus. Describing Whitlam as Prime Minister in 1974, Alan Reid wrote:

> He demanded loyalty from colleagues, often received it, more rarely conferred it. He was suspicious of advice from his political peers, the parliamentary and machine barons of the ALP. He preferred to listen to those who shared with him the cachet of formal academic qualifications, provided those persons were outside the magic circle of the ALP Parliamentary Party and the ALP machine hierarchy and hence no threat to his determination to be the colossus of the ALP.[9]

Cairns had a different concept of democracy. He was opposed to the closed procedures of the Victorian Executive himself, because he believed that party members should participate in decision-making. Indeed, throughout his career Cairns had argued for more democratization and more participation by the people in factories and offices as well as in parliament. On the other hand, Whitlam saw democracy as centred entirely on parliament. This was shown by Whitlam's refusal to lead the protest movement against the war, which Chamberlain had asked him to do.[10] Whitlam's reply stated that he completely endorsed the idea of 'a constant mobilization of Australian public opinion to help bring an end to the war in Vietnam and I am also emphatically of the opinion that the Labor Party is the appropriate organization to develop and lead public opinion in this regard'.[11] His reason for refusing was that it would identify the ALP with only one issue and secondly that it would not be 'proper and prudent to sign statements or appear with persons expressing a less complete view than our Caucus or Conference or presenting a different emphasis'.[12] What would have happened if all other Labor leaders had taken this attitude? Nevertheless Whitlam won the vote—although much more narrowly than had been expected (38 to 32). After Whitlam's near-win in the 1969 elections, the members of the Victorian Executive were on notice. They made no steps to reform themselves to bring in more rank-and-file support or to form an alliance with the new radicals and socialists. In an extraordinarily stupid move, the Executive humiliated the State Parliamentary Leader, Clyde Holding, by issuing an alternative policy speech for the state election. This stated that aid to non-government schools would be phased out, which was in contradiction to Federal policy. Whitlam publicly condemned the Executive. As a result of this public division of the ALP, Bolte's Liberals increased their majority even though things were bad in Victoria. Everyone blamed the Victorian Executive. Thus the Federal Executive began moves to dissolve the Victorian branch and establish a new one.[13] There was a serious danger that the party could split over the issue. That it did not do so was due to the critical role of Bob Hawke, the ACTU President. Hawke had attempted to stave off intervention because of the danger that union representation in the party would be reduced—which later occurred. Yet once the intervention was a *fait accompli*, Hawke agreed to supervise the general task of the reorganization of the branch. This calmed the fears of many socialists, for Hawke at the time was identified with this position.[14] In the end, however, the new procedures were to lead to the undermining of not only the old socialists in the party, but also many new ones who had any systematic critique of capitalism. By refusing to reform the party in a way which would have benefited the cause of workers through genuine democratic reforms, the old socialists virtually ensured a long-term majority for Whitlam's so-called centre group.

Having secured the reconstruction of the ALP and reduced the influence of socialists within the party, Whitlam was able to present the image to the people of a legitimate reformer who was not about to change any fundamental institutions of society. Increasingly, powerful people in the ruling class saw him as an acceptable alternative.[15] Even if some members of his shadow cabinet were radical, there was plenty of evidence that he had virtually complete domination over the party and would keep socialists under control. This illusion lasted until the end of Whitlam's first year as Prime Minister.

C   LIBERAL POLITICAL CRISIS

On 17 December 1967, Harold Holt disappeared at sea while going for a swim and was presumed dead. This created some ferment within the Liberal Party, due to the fact that the traditional pattern of the deputy leader of the party being elected Prime Minister was not followed. It was blocked by the then Deputy Prime Minister and the leader of the Country Party, John McEwen. He made it quite clear to the press that William McMahon, the deputy Liberal leader, was totally unacceptable to him as Prime Minister, and threatened to pull the Country Party out of the coalition government. As I mentioned in Chapter 3B, McEwen had been the architect of an alliance between rural capital and manufacturing. This alliance of conflicting interests was achieved by giving huge state subsidies to the rural sector in return for large tariff protection for Australian manufacturing. McMahon had opposed the whole strategy: he felt that the Country Party was exercising an excessive influence on the Liberals in this key area of economic strategy.[1] Conflicting capitalist interests were thus represented in the apparent conflict of personalities.

The Liberal Party, which could not at that stage afford to ditch the Country Party, decided that it must reject McMahon as leader. We should note, however, that it is not clear that McMahon would have become leader, even had McEwen not stepped in. For the mood in the nation was changing towards more liberalism: there were greater demands for increased social services to be provided by the state and for more civil liberties, in line with developments in the socio-cultural realm (see Chapter 5C). Already a substantial section of the Liberal Party had moved to a more moderate position, one which was relatively progressive on social issues.[2]

The man that was chosen, John Gorton, leader of the Senate, changed to the Representatives by taking over Holt's seat, and thus became Prime Minister. Gorton was chosen because of his relatively progressive views. However, his attitudes led to a series of political crises for the Liberals, which resulted in Gorton's demise and eventually the election of the ALP to government. Gorton was chosen even though little was known of his economic philosophy. It was a measure of the confidence of the ruling class as to its dominant position economically that they seemed to care little that the leadership of the 'big business' party went to a man whose views on these matters had not been canvassed.[3] Gorton soon demonstrated his own highly individualist style as Prime Minister: he would decide policies and would announce them without consulting colleagues. Thus, during the Tet offensive in Vietnam, which occurred within a month of his election, Gorton declared—in an answer to a reporter's question—that there would be no more Australian troops sent to that country.[4] Without consulting his colleagues, he had asserted a stance on Vietnam independent of the US.

On economic issues, it was discovered that Gorton was a nationalist—in favour of more Australian participation and ownership of the huge mining enterprises that developed during his term of office. Although on this issue he was more talk than action, even the talk unsettled large sections of the Liberal Party, who were politically and ideologically aligned to the interests of foreign capital. When Gorton later introduced legislation to limit foreign takeovers of Australian companies, his action further divided the ruling class on an explosive issue. This conflict was more serious than the one over tariffs. For, while many multi-national companies which had roots in Australia supported tariffs, they viewed with alarm the attempts of Gorton's group to impose conditions on overseas ownership.[5]

Gorton also upset entrenched sections of the Liberal Party by his attitude to Commonwealth-State relations. In this matter, Gorton believed in the right of the central government to determine policies for all Australians in major areas. This was a popular move with the Australian people and with certain moderate sections of the press.[6] However it placed severe pressure on him from the State Liberal branches.

In 1968, journalist Max Walsh described Gorton's philosophy as 'a mixture of centralism in State-Commonwealth financial relations, isolation in defence matters, populism and nationalism in fiscal matters. Every one of the ingredients of that package is capable of dividing the ranks of the Liberal Party. In combination they provide an explosive mixture'.[7] Furthermore, Gorton was a social liberal who believed in social welfare to assist the sick, the elderly and the unemployed. Peter Tiver quotes him as asserting that Liberals were not opposed to socialism in its 'true' sense of 'social action to benefit the community as a whole' as distinct from socialism in the sense of the individual serving the state.[8]

Although Gorton's economic policies were the central bone of contention within the party, his opponents did not focus on this. Rather they concentrated on his private life. It seems the Prime Minister liked the company of women.[9] His enemies made serious attempts to link him to alleged indiscretions particularly with respect to his young private secretary, Ainsley Gotto, and his late night visit to the US embassy in the company of a female journalist. Gorton survived an attack based on these premises which came from back-bencher Edward St. John.

The Liberal Party's losses at the 1969 election were widely blamed on Gorton, even though it is possible that had McMahon been leader, they might have even lost government. Thus immediately after the election Gorton was challenged for the leadership. He was made aware that powerful elements of the ruling class were mobilizing against him. Yet, as soon as he won this vote, Gorton declared defiantly: 'I can only say that I am not of or in the Establishment'.[10]

Gorton's prime ministership was thus bringing into the open the conflict between liberals and conservatives within the Liberal Party (see Chapter 5C). Soon Gorton's conservative enemies again moved against him, this time successfully, after three major events—which affected both the Liberal Party and the ruling class. Firstly, in the half-Senate election of 1970, the Liberal vote dropped to a disastrous 37 per cent. This destroyed any credibility in the claim that Gorton was a vote-winner. Secondly, Gorton alienated the New South Wales Liberal Premier by reducing funds to that State during an election period. Thirdly, and importantly, there was a disastrous collapse of the mining boom. Several major companies, in particular Mineral Securities Limited, collapsed—with large losses to various sectors in the ruling class. The Gorton government was blamed, both for its failure to regulate the boom and for its apparent loss of control of economic policy. When Gorton tried to organize an Australian consortium to buy out Minsec, this generated resentment from the shareholders in whose interests it was to accept the higher overseas offers. As Connell records, this attempt failed, but merely generated more vehemence against Gorton.[11]

These conflicts over philosophy were obscured by the method used against Gorton. His fall was precipitated by the tough actions of the man whom Gorton had trusted and promoted to the ministry, Malcolm Fraser. Since Fraser's philosophy was completely different from Gorton's (see Chapter 5C), the Prime Minister should have been forewarned; yet he was not. In an extraordinary action, Fraser resigned from the ministry and vehemently attacked Gorton in parliament, accusing him of disloyalty to his ministers. In a personal statement, Fraser told parliament: 'I do not believe he is fit to hold the great office of Prime Minister and I cannot serve in his Government'.[12]

The next day, Gorton was deposed. In a tied 33-all vote, he cast the deciding vote against himself. The various sectors of the ruling class—including Frank Packer, the media boss —had succeeded in deposing him.[13] Freudenburg remarks:

It can be seen with hindsight that there were bad omens for the future Whitlam Government in Gorton's

fall. Beyond Gorton's manifest shortcomings, his Prime
Ministership posed daunting questions: would the
power grouping in Australia tolerate any departure
from their perceived norm; would State governments
tolerate any alteration in existing arrangements; would
businessmen tolerate anything which might in the
slightest degree make them uneasy . . . ?[14]

It seems paradoxical that the conservatives should have
won that struggle, given the mood of the Australian people at
the time, which was already strongly against them. It appears
to be one of those cases where individuals, through their
sheer will determine the events of history and then find that
the system forces are moving relentlessly against them. Thus
at the same time that huge demands for change were coming
from all kinds of pressure groups in the society, such as
Aborigines, migrants, pensioners and above all women (the
women's movement was very powerful by this stage), a
conservative person was chosen as Prime Minister. Yet
William McMahon, who finally realized his ambition to
become leader, seemed to be the wrong choice at the wrong
time, given the mood of the people.[15] In his first year as leader,
he seemed blithely unaware of the extent to which legitimacy
was being undermined, not only as a result of the stubborn
policy of continuing with the war, but also because of his
inability to respond to the rising demands, coming from the
socio-cultural sphere, for more equality for women and
minority groups, and more services and welfare for the needy
and disadvantaged.

Nor did the election of McMahon resolve the internal crisis
of the Liberal Party. For the party, in a peculiarly magnanim-
ous gesture, had chosen Gorton to be McMahon's deputy.
This ensured that the deep division would continue: thus
when McMahon finally sacked Gorton from the ministry in
August 1971, the image of disarray and disunity became
embedded in the popular consciousness.[16]

On the economic front, the McMahon government was subject to pressures from local businessmen against the wave of takeover attempts which occurred during the depression of share prices. Foreign capital was pouring into the country at an unprecedented rate, due to the rise in international liquidity, and the collapse of the monetary system (see Chapter 3B). Many local owners and directors put up resistance and gained coverage in the media for their cause.[17] McMahon was very slow to act on behalf of domestic capital on this issue. Indeed he added to the liquidity problem by agreeing to devalue the Australian dollar. Although McMahon finally agreed to freeze several of the takeovers until they were investigated by a government committee, little was done to prevent them either by him or by the incoming Labor administration.

During this period, demands for more social welfare, higher wages and more civil liberties were increasing, as reflected not only in massive anti-war demonstrations but also in increasingly militant union activities, backed up by a rising level of strikes, often of a disruptive character.

Thinking businessmen began to worry—for this reduction in system legitimacy threatened to undermine the continuity of profitable conditions of production. Increasing wage demands, compounded by political demands from unions for more general services, upset the fabric of economy—particularly since the demands were pressed with fervour.[18] Thus a conflict arose between the Liberal government and various sectors of business. Several important sections of the ruling class were distancing themselves from the McMahon government and even actively supporting Labor. Connell remarks that

> The Liberal Party found itself acutely short of funds for most of the election year; there was an obvious reluctance of businessmen to kick in . . . Only late in the day were large sums raised by the party, enabling it to out-spend the opposition. By contrast, the Labor

campaign was from the start rolling in unfamiliar wealth, estimated over $700,000 in retrospect—a great deal of it from business. And businessmen were prominent in the campaign itself, from Rupert Murdoch, the newspaper owner, and Patrick Sayers, sponsor of the dramatic 'Business Executives for a Change of Government' advertisements, to Kenneth Baillieu Myer, as establishment a figure as you can get, who signed a public appeal to elect a new government.[19]

At the beginning of 1972, McMahon realized that his government was in serious trouble and so introduced a series of changes which further strained his relations with capitalist forces. He did an about-turn on the economy. Previously he had taken a stabilizing approach: no expansion of the state sector, a small amount of growth, guided by a tight control on the money supply. But in 1972, realizing that the people's demands for much greater state services of all kinds were extremely heavy, he brought in a budget which increased the deficit, through a large expansion of government spending.

These manoeuvres were seen as cynical tricks to regain the flagging support for the government. To many company managers, these moves were evidence of the irrationality of the government in its attempts to steer economy. The media reported that McMahon appeared to be veering in all directions, that he did not know what he was doing.[20] Some of his own ministers were puzzled by his actions. Why had he suddenly expanded the public sector, after having attacked Labor for years for wanting to do this? The result of McMahon's action was inflation, although it was not felt until very close to the election.

The McMahon government was thus faced with a serious state political crisis. Firstly, the level of strike activity and wage increases indicated that it could not steer the economy to moderate the class conflicts within it. Secondly, the governing party was patently divided. Added to this was the apparent incapacity of the state to meet the needs of the people, and the continuing Australian participation in Vietnam. All these factors undermined the conservative reign which had existed for twenty-three years.

Only a change of government could eradicate this threat to legitimacy. Any other outcome would have given credence to those people—increasing in number—who were arguing that democracy in Australia was a farce. Thus the mood in the nation was that there should be more liberalization, more equality, more social services; in general, more democratic justice. This mood, which Whitlam masterfully caught and manipulated, meant that the downfall of the McMahon government was a real probability, provided that segments of the ruling class and the media supported the Labor Party.

There was only one thing that the capitalist forces needed to ensure that Whitlam would not nationalize any industries and that he would not challenge the structure of the capitalist economy. In a series of meetings which occurred between Whitlam, important newspaper proprietors and other influential capitalists, he reassured them on this point.[21] The election of a Whitlam government therefore became almost a certainty by the end of 1972. It would help to restore legitimacy to the system, it would achieve certain necessary changes on the Vietnam war and on welfare policy and yet it would not threaten the structure of capitalist economy. Whitlam himself believed all this.

In his campaign speech, he focused on the factors which had undermined legitimacy:

> Are you prepared to maintain at the head of your affairs a coalition which has lurched into crisis after crisis, embarrassment piled on embarrassment week after week? . . . Will you again entrust the nation's economy to the men who deliberately, but needlessly, created Australia's worst unemployment for ten years? . . . Can you trust the last-minute promises of men who stood against these very same proposals for twenty-

> three years? Would you trust your international affairs again to the men who gave you Vietnam? ... We want to give a new life and a new meaning in this new nation to the touchstone of modern democracy—to liberty, equality, fraternity.[22]

It could be objected that my explanation here does not take into account personal factors, such as the fact that McMahon was represented in the media as a bumbling fool; and the way in which Whitlam was increasingly represented as a statesmen, particularly after his successful visit to China in 1970, just prior to the historic visit of US President Nixon.[23] However, one should ask why was it that the media, which had opposed the Labor Party at virtually every election, suddenly in 1972, swung around and supported Whitlam? Why did McMahon, who as Treasurer in earlier governments had been represented as an efficient responsible man, suddenly appear a fool?

We have a tendency in Australian politics to explain events, not in terms of system forces, but in terms of personalities. In this account, I have tried to argue that factors such as the shift in the attitude of the ruling class, as a response to the undermining of legitimacy, were much more significant. Indeed it is not implausible to argue that had Labor not been elected in 1972, the undermining of legitimacy would have intensified, thus creating a serious crisis within society. In any event, the election of the Whitlam government had become very likely as a consequence of the coalition of forces which had developed—the undermining of legitimacy due to the Vietnam war and the crisis in the rationality of the state under the Liberals. In the end, then, it was 'It's Time'— the slogan that the Labor Party used. It became time for the state to show that in fact a change of government was possible in Australia, and to restore legitimacy.

8
Crisis and the Fall of Labor

A   LAYING THE FOUNDATIONS OF CRISIS

The election of the Labor government after twenty-three years of Liberal rule, while it had the consequences of restoring legitimacy and democratic respectability to the Australian state, nevertheless led to a new economic crisis. This new crisis in the economy gave rise to a series of state political crises and culminated in a legitimation crisis within Australian society.

Yet it did not appear that way at the beginning. Indeed, believing that he had a mandate from the people to introduce all the policies in Labor's extensive reformist platform, Whitlam took to the task with a missionary zeal.[1] Together with his deputy, Lance Barnard, he took over the executive government until the full ministry could be sworn in a fortnight after the election. He ordered the withdrawal of the remaining Australian troops in Vietnam and the end of conscription. He began to implement by executive decree those policies which did not require legislation. Once the full ministry was appointed, it moved swiftly towards the expansion of social, welfare and educational services. These had been promised to a variety of groups in the community and Whitlam considered that meeting these demands from the socio-cultural system was an overriding priority. The problem that had not been sufficiently thought out, and to which I shall return, was: how were these increases to be paid for?

Although when it came to office in December 1972, the economy was in poor shape (unemployment was at 100 000, the highest level since the 1961 credit squeeze, and inflation was running at 7 per cent, due to the desperate expansionary measures of the McMahon Liberal government), the new Labor leadership gave the appearance that they would quickly have the situation under control. This impression was reinforced by Whitlam's quick action to revalue the Australian dollar by 7.05 per cent.[2] Yet in a report to the government, Dr H. C. Coombs put forward a strong warning against rising prices and the possibility of a conflict in the government's priorities, if inflation became serious.[3] Whitlam's response was to speed up the establishment of the Prices Justification Tribunal, which was supposed to inhibit increases in prices. It did no such thing.

As we saw in Chapter 3B, an economic upturn occurred in Australia from the increased investment in 1971–72 and the expansionary budget of McMahon. The result was decreases in unemployment and some real growth in the economy. The Labor government was duly and mistakenly given credit for this. This economic upturn convinced them that they could implement as many extensions of the state sector as they had promised in their election platform, without regard to the operations of capitalist economy. It seemed to be blithely assumed that the economy could pay. The Labor ministers, including both socialists and social welfarists, appeared to be living in an economic dreamland.

Yet there were omens that the capitalist forces were quickly becoming unhappy. Indeed Freudenburg believes that many business leaders became frightened at Whitlam's apparently burning pace of change, even before the full ministry was sworn in:

> What went unnoticed in the excitement of the time
> was the first stirrings of uneasiness in business circles.
> There is no greater myth than that the Labor
> Government came to power on a tide of goodwill from

all sections of the community, and only through Labor's own folly, was this goodwill lost. Among businessmen, there was very little positive goodwill and at best a degree of tolerance. A Labor Government was to be tolerated on condition that it would make no real change. The hyperactivity of the duumvirate aroused uneasy suspicions. When Whitlam spoke of change, he might well be serious.[4]

This unhappiness of the ruling class gathered momentum as time went on. Its most important outward manifestation was the sudden reduction in overseas investment and the flow of money out of the country. Furthermore, new domestic investment was shrinking. The ruling class was engaging in the common tactic of a 'capital strike' in response to the reformist plans of what they saw as an over-zealous government.[5] The graph on p. 306 from *Australia Uprooted* clearly shows the dramatic drop in investment by overseas companies from an average of 40 per cent in 1970–72 to 8 per cent in 1973–74. At the same time, there was a dramatic rise in company profits payable overseas, from an average of 28.3 per cent in 1970–72 to 52.7 per cent in 1974–75.[6]

Furthermore, although the Labor government had found it extraordinarily difficult to win power (its period in opposition being one of the longest for a major party in the Western world) its members acted as if their legitimacy was completely secured. They assumed that because they had the majority in the House of Representatives they had control of the state and the nation. This myth was reinforced by the popularity of most of their actions (a notable exception here being Senator Murphy's 'raid' on the ASIO headquarters).[7] Thus there was the famous 'First Hundred Days of Whitlam', following which opinion polls showed that the government had a rating as high as 60 per cent approval from the electorate.

Yet it was during this period that they made their first very dramatic mistake. For the Labor Party, although it won the majority in the House of Representatives (the people's House),

Company profit and investment

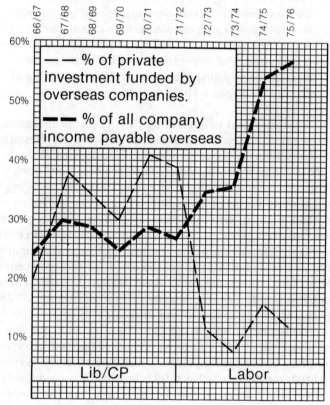

— — % of private investment funded by overseas companies.

▬ ▬ % of all company income payable overseas

Lib/CP   Labor

Reproduced with permission from the Amalgamated Metal Workers' and Shipwrights' Union

did not win the majority in the Senate. This is almost inevitable in Australia, given that only half the Senate seats are contested during a House of Representatives election. The situation was similar to that which Menzies had faced after the election of the Liberal Party in 1949. On that occasion, when the Labor Senate blocked a few bills, Menzies engineered a double dissolution of parliament, at a time when his popularity was high. He thus won his majority in the Senate.

Yet when Labor were elected to office in 1972, they had not learnt from this lesson in political tactics. For it was clear from the beginning that the strategy of the Liberals would be to use their Senate majority to block vast and essential parts of the ALP's legislative programme. Indeed, by the time the Liberals forced a double dissolution in May 1974, they had blocked more bills in the Senate than any opposition since Federation: they had twice rejected ten bills and rejected or held up more than ten others.[8] These included the bills to establish Medibank and the bill to strengthen the Australian Industry Development Corporation which was required to ensure Australian participation in major mineral and energy enterprises.

A fundamental question arises here: given that their popularity was extremely high, why did the Whitlam government not approach the Governor-General and have both Houses dissolved as soon as the Liberals blocked the first bills? Clearly, if an election had been held at that time, Labor would have gained full state power as distinct from having merely power within the one house. It is easy to say that this was gross political incompetence, or simply cowardice.[9] A better explanation, I believe, is that they did not expect that the ruling class would turn against them in the way that it did; and this merely shows that they had learnt very little from the history of the previous Labor governments.[10] Whitlam, in particular, appeared to believe that most of the capitalist forces were on his side, because some had temporarily turned towards him for the reasons that I gave in Chapter 7C. One aspect of this is Whitlam's belief that the Liberals would stick to constitutional proprieties and that, while they might block certain bills, they would not dare interfere with the major legislation of the government. In fact they went further and blocked the very capacity of the state to survive, by cutting off the money supply. Once Labor failed to take advantage of its popularity to seize control of the Senate, its political problems were inevitable.

The actions of the first Whitlam ministry reflect the division between the social welfarists and the socialists.[11] Although he had something of a reputation as a socialist, the Treasurer Frank Crean was quite conservative in his economic outlook. Whitlam himself believed that equality consisted not in a redistribution of incomes, but rather would come as a result of the expansion of state services. Two powerful people in the party disagreed with this: Clyde Cameron, the Minister for Labour, and Bob Hawke, ACTU President. The latter had felt somewhat resentful at Whitlam's failure to consult him on economic matters which affected all workers. He supported the attempts by the working class to seek and gain wage increases. Cameron also supported this wage pressure, by allowing hefty increases in the public service, which soon spread to the private sector as well. Indeed, in the years 1973–74 wage increases are estimated to have reached 35 per cent. Cameron seemed genuinely dedicated to improving labour's share in national income and supported several key union struggles, in particular the Broadmeadows strike against the Ford Motor Company.[12] To give weight to the impression that he had some understanding of class struggle, Cameron attacked the multi-national companies because of their reluctance to distribute excess profits to workers through wage increases.

It appears that several ministers believed that by allowing wage increases, they could better the lot of workers and at the same time raise more state revenue, since the wage increases automatically put workers into higher taxation brackets.[13] Thus in this first stage of Labor's economic performance, we have increased services, increased wages, increased tax revenue and a small budget deficit. This allowed for services to increase in badly needed areas—education, health, urban planning, social security, etc.

However, there was one factor that had not been taken into account sufficiently. Increases in wages mean a change in the relationship between capital and labour. In an advanced monopolistic capitalism, they immediately lead to increases in prices (see Chapter 3A). Thus from the second half of 1973, to minimize the squeeze on profits, company managers simply increased prices. Within eighteen months, a second phase arose in Labor's economic performance: a new economic crisis characterized by increases in prices, and, because the relationship between capital and labour had been temporarily upset, a kind of panic, resulting in reductions in investment and sharp rises in unemployment. I shall discuss it in the next section.

There was one more important feature in the first phase, introduced by Whitlam and the Minister for Trade, Dr Cairns. The government went on the attack against rising prices by lowering tariffs and allowing more foreign manufactured goods into the country. In July 1973, it announced an across-the-board tariff cut of 25 per cent. This lowering of tariffs resulted in the flooding of the market with foreign goods. Its eventual consequences were a further increase in unemployment, due to a reduction in domestic production, and an increased government deficit. In the short term, although the move was popular with the public, it did not stabilize prices as had been hoped.[14]

While different parts of the government were pushing in contradictory directions—some favouring the working class, others concerned not to undermine the interest of the capitalist forces—Whitlam tried to reassure an increasingly nervous business establishment that his government's intentions towards them was based on a recognition of their problems: he wanted co-operation, not confrontation.[15]

Meanwhile the political leaders of the ruling class, who had temporarily managed to regain some form of unity after the shock of the election defeat, mobilized under the guidance of Opposition Leader Snedden. At first, Snedden appeared to want to wait until the Labor Party's full term was over, so that he could develop new policies for the Liberal Party which would appeal to the middle-class electors.[16] However, under pressure from Senator Withers and the Country Party leader Anthony, he prematurely precipitated an election by rejecting the government's supply bills in April 1974. This was the wrong time for Snedden to do this, and it proved a fatal miscalculation on his part, especially since he was supposedly an expert on economic matters. For already there were signs that a serious economic crisis was about to break over the head of the Labor government. Furthermore, although the ALP had alienated some sections of business (who rejected Labor for ideological reasons), profits were still healthy at this stage, the full impact of inflation and the wage rises had not yet been felt. If Snedden had waited even a few more months, he could have been Prime Minister.

Indeed the excuse for forcing the double dissolution was too flimsy and had nothing to do with the impending economic crisis. The Labor government had tried to gain a majority in the Senate, not through the perfectly valid course of calling an election when its popularity was high (see above) but through the shifty manoeuvre of making a deal with its previous enemy, DLP Senator Vince Gair.[17] Even though Whitlam retained the majority in the House of Representatives, the Liberal-NCP were defiant. Snedden announced that 'We were not defeated. We just didn't win enough seats to form a government'.[18] Nevertheless, it was clear that he would be reluctant to force another double dissolution, unless he were assured that there was a near-certainty of victory. Indeed, after the election, Snedden showed signs of wanting to reform the party to make it more liberal and progressive in outlook.[19] Whitlam, however, was in no mood to forgive Snedden for forcing the election. Rather than recognizing the important benefits—both to the working class and to the cause of democracy—of having a liberal Opposition leader, rather than a hard-line conservative one, Whitlam was—as frequently occurred with him—obsessed with a desire to crush and humiliate Snedden. As Reid explains:

> The shrewder ALP parliamentarians were aware that Fraser was Snedden's likely successor and had already

assessed Fraser as potentially a more formidable
opponent than Snedden. They suspected that Whitlam
was pushing his tactic of denigrating Snedden too far:
that he was quite unintentionally assisting Fraser along
the road to Liberal leadership.[20]

In the months before his removal on 21 March 1975,
Snedden was under continuous pressure and was constantly
being harassed by rumours of a challenge to his own leadership. Fraser continued to profess loyalty to the leader. On
6 February, he declared that there was no likelihood of a
contest. Yet it was clear that powerful forces within the Liberal
Party establishment and within the ruling class—by this
stage dismayed at the ALP's actions—were not in the mood
to put up with a moderate like Snedden, who seemed incapable of rallying the capitalist forces, or even his own
parliamentarians, against Labor. In an extraordinary conspiracy, the deputy leader Phillip Lynch betrayed Snedden
and joined the Fraser forces.[21] Moderate Liberalism was thus
defeated for many years.

Whitlam, in directly contributing to the rise of Fraser,
ensured that the Liberal Party would achieve a leader whose
dedication to capitalist forces bordered on the messianic (see
Chapter 5C) and whose capacity to unite the ruling class
against Labor proved formidable. The rise of Fraser, coming
in the middle of the most serious economic crisis since the
war, not only ensured the destruction of the Labor government, it also made it certain that the working class would bear
extremely heavy burdens from this deep and continuing crisis.

B THE NEW ECONOMIC CRISIS

After the re-election of Labor in May 1974, Dr Cairns was
chosen by the new Caucus as Deputy Prime Minister. That
vote also demonstrated that the most popular man in Caucus
was Rex Connor, Minister for Minerals and Energy. In the
new year these two men were to both adopt the mantle of
Acting Prime Minister. Soon afterwards, both were to be
politically destroyed.

The Caucus vote indicated a move to the Left and a growing appreciation of Cairns. With the consent of Whitlam, it was Cairns who adopted the major initiatives to deal with the economic crisis, which hit the government soon after re-election. As soon as the figures for the June quarter 1974 on inflation (a massive 4.1 per cent increase) and unemployment (85 000 and rising) were available,[1] it was clear that serious economic problems lay ahead. At this stage, Cairns produced an interesting paper on the economy, arguing that the major source of the current inflation was no longer excessive demand, but rather the capacity of multi-national corporations to determine prices, irrespective of market conditions. This was similar to the theory (discussed in Chapter 3A) that increasing monopolization and capital concentration has changed the character of capitalism. Cairns correctly predicted that demand would fall off sharply. Attempts to apply a credit squeeze were mistaken: indeed it could be the case that increased inflation would be accompanied by low effective demand and increased unemployment.[2]

Cairns argued for an immediate easing of the credit squeeze imposed in September 1973. He rejected the view that there should be increases in unemployment to bring down inflation —the usual Keynesian strategy. Instead, he pressed for a mildly expansionary budget; this would allow the government to continue with its cherished programmes in education and social welfare and would ensure that the burden of the crisis did not fall on workers. Anticipating the pressure to reduce wages, Cairns adopted the proposal put forward by Clyde Cameron for indexing wages to prices.

On the other hand, the conservative economists of the Treasury submitted proposals to remedy the situation which called for sacrifices by workers, through increases in direct and indirect taxes. The Treasury also wanted cuts in government expenditure and a substantial budget surplus.[3] Lloyd and Clark report a 'curious' factor in Treasury's advice:

The Treasury projections in 1974–75 were based on the forecast of an overall domestic surplus of around

$320 million, which would provide a significant
dampener to economic activity. However, the Treasury
also recommended the raising of an extra $400 million
through tax increases and a reduction in government
spending of $600 million. These recommendations were
not taken into account in assessing the forecast surplus
of $320 million. In effect they would have added $1000
million to the surplus bringing it up to $1.3 billion. A
surplus of this order is quite unparalleled . . . Coupled
with the credit squeeze it would have produced a
massive recession in the domestic economy.[4]

Clearly, the Treasury's advice was based more on its
economic dogmatism than on any clear understanding of the
character of the crisis. As I have argued in Chapter 3B, the
new inflation was no longer due to excessive demand and to
try to counter it by recessive measures would have been disastrous. Already the credit squeeze had gone on for too long,
and had damaged private sector investment. The bureaucracy
had over-reacted to the liquidity problem of 1972. Indeed,
the volume of money decreased in 1974.[5] Freudenburg records
that Whitlam came to believe that this credit squeeze was
perhaps the worst error of the government in the economic
area.[6] I shall argue below that another error was more serious.

By the time of the framing of the budget in August 1974,
ministers were shocked by the further signs of the deepening
economic crisis. Several major companies collapsed, including
two in the finance area: Cambridge Credit Corporation and
Mainline Corporation. The government was divided on the
contradictory proposals before it. The resulting budget bore
the stamp of Cairns: it allowed for an expansion in the public
sector and in the money supply. Paul Kelly, in *The Unmaking
of Gough*, maintains that in this budget

There was virtually no restraint at all on government
outlays, which were estimated to increase by 32 per
cent with very high rises in education spending of up

to 78 per cent, health 30 per cent, social security and welfare 38 per cent, cities spending 173 per cent, culture and recreation 44 per cent—to name only the big areas of increase ... Announcing it on the evening of 17 September Crean said: 'Crucial as the fight against inflation is, it cannot be made the sole objective of government policy'.

'The government is committed to the program of social reform to improve the position of the less privileged groups in our society and to maintain employment opportunities.'[7]

The budget was a living example of the compromise within the Labor Party between the social welfarists and socialists. Cairns, Cameron and other socialists were concerned that the workers should not suffer in wage levels or in reduction of state services during the crisis. However, neither had any positive strategy to counter unemployment—which Cairns himself had predicted would rise in the private sector.[8] Admittedly, by keeping up state services, they maintained public employment at high levels. Thus it is true to argue that increases in unemployment would have been even higher, had the Treasury line been followed—as indeed was the case when Fraser cut back the state sector, after the Liberals gained power.

Nevertheless, there was only one strategy which the government could have used to make a real impact on the increasing unemployment—by expanding public ownership of productive industries, particularly those in which investment had been reduced for ideological reasons in the capital strike (see previous section). There were two ways of financing such an expansion of the productive sector of the state. Firstly, the government need not have expanded state services to such an extraordinary degree. For clearly not all of Labor's programmes in that budget were essential and the best use of state resources. Indeed, it would have been possible to retain the central programmes in education, health, welfare, etc. and still have at least $1000 million to spend on productive enterprise, since, in that particular year, the state's real income had increased as people moved into higher tax brackets. Furthermore, Labor already had plans to develop the productive sector in Rex Connor's schemes for energy and mineral development. Such rationally planned projects could have soaked up many of the unemployed. Secondly, even if Cairns had wanted to retain all of Labor's programmes in the non-productive sector, he could have raised moneys by imposing a capital gains tax or even a wealth tax, thereby ensuring that even more money was available for new productive enterprises, publicly owned.[9]

Cairns, in pursuing the socialist goal of protecting the working class from crisis, was too limited in his perspective. Admittedly, Cairns was not Treasurer at that stage, and therefore could not determine the full 1974 budget strategy. However it is unlikely that he would have proposed the taxes on capital and public enterprises suggested above, not because of any particular loyalty to the capitalist structures, such as that shown by his successor, Hayden, but because he felt powerless to introduce such changes.[10] He reveals in his book *Oil in Troubled Waters*:

> For many years before the 1972 election I was
> convinced there were severe limits upon what a Labor
> government could do . . . I was well aware when I
> became a Minister in the Labor government that I
> would be compelled to follow a policy that would help
> keep jobs and money at a satisfactory level; so
> whatever was done, it would have to be in a way that
> satisfied the private enterprise system on which jobs
> and money depended.[11]

The irony is that Cairns' failure to attempt such changes was grounded in his (false) belief of the total hegemony of the capitalist processes. Thus he says that Connor's attempts 'to build the Australian public enterprise system, and to "buy back [a little of] Australia" went beyond the capitalist hegemony,'[12] and therefore failed. Cairns had come to see the difficult as impossible. Yet, paradoxically, at that time he had a golden opportunity to push through important steps towards socialism, since he had virtual control of the party's economic policy.

Overall, then, the budget strategy, by failing to take into account the motivating forces in capitalist economy, did not achieve either a reduction in inflation, or even a significant decrease in unemployment. Since most ministers would not countenance any expansion of the state into profitable enterprises—either through nationalization or through buying out shaky companies—there was only one thing to be done: action to revive business 'confidence'. Thus it was that in November 1974, the government introduced a mini-budget which attempted to reassure the business community that the Australian Labor Party did not wish to change the structure of the economy.[13] To add spice to this, the Prices Justification Tribunal was advised by Whitlam to 'give particular attention to the problem of sustaining and stimulating an adequate level of private investment and of maintaining rates of return on capital which will induce new investment'.[14]

At this stage, the more powerful sectors of capital realized that the government was in a desperate position and sought to take advantage of it. In an extraordinarily blunt act, General Motors-Holden's threatened to sack 5000 workers unless the government met the company's demands. Whitlam, who was overseas at the time, made a rousing speech attacking multi-nationals such as GM-H who had taken millions of dollars out of Australia in profits and yet were bluntly using their power against workers and the nation.[15] After such a speech, one might have expected at least some threats to nationalize GM-H or to punish it by removing tariff protection. Nothing of the sort occurred. Instead we had the humiliating spectacle of Acting Prime Minister Cairns flying to Melbourne, visiting the GM-H directors and pleading with them to keep the workers on. If a socialist like Cairns could be made to bow so meekly before the power of the multi-nationals, what hope was there for change through the parliamentary processes? Surely it must have been events like this which persuaded Cairns to abandon the parliamentary world as irrelevant to the real sources of power in society.[16] Yet were Whitlam and Cairns bowing to inflexible system pressures or were they victims of their own beliefs in their powerlessness *vis-à-vis* the ruling class?

In an entrenched economic crisis such as the present one, there are only two courses which can bring even a short-term recovery: strong action to support profit and the capitalist forces, or action towards socialist transformation by transferring productive enterprises to public and democratic control. The Labor Party as a whole could not countenance the first alternative, although a substantial minority of ministers favoured it. A few ministers were prepared to countenance the second course in limited areas, such as minerals and energy, or government insurance. No one appeared to adopt it as a strategy for the whole economy. The result was a compromise between these two contradictory positions. The Labor government achieved an internal stalemate. Cameron and Cairns were determined that the working class would not suffer. Increasingly, Whitlam and Hayden became determined that capitalist profitability would have to be strengthened, even at the expense of workers.

In the end, the August 1974 budget's own contradictions contributed to the intensification of crisis. This was due to the fact that the budget estimate of income tax receipts was too optimistic; for the dramatic rise in unemployment meant that the state's income was also reduced. Yet there were no cutbacks in spending to accommodate this. The second Labor budget thus resulted in a massive budget deficit of $2500 million. To pay for this, Cairns—who became Treasurer—simply printed money.[17]

Even though Whitlam had tried to smooth the relations between business and the government, the depth of the crisis meant that the antipathy of capitalists became severe. Serious statements were made about the need to bring down the government.[18] For, in the 'democratic' tradition, the government was blamed for the economic crisis and its inability to restore the economy to health. As Connell records:

> an ideological campaign was launched by some sections
> of business . . . What is interesting organizationally is
> that most of it came, not from companies, but from
> groups of business ideologies organized in 'non-
> political' associations, like the Institute of Public
> Affairs in NSW . . . and in peak organizations such as
> the Melbourne Chamber of Commerce and the
> Associated Chamber of Commerce . . . One has the
> strong impression that they were intended as spoiling
> tactics, making it so hard for the government to
> achieve modest reforms that it would be intimidated
> before it moved to anything more substantial.[19]

This first stage in the mobilization of the capitalist forces soon convinced Whitlam that the stalemate must end. It would be necessary to take tough action to restore the profitability of business. In order to do this, Whitlam resolved that he would have to dismiss or move from the economic area those ministers who were strongest in supporting the claims of the working class during crisis, namely, Cairns and Cameron. Whitlam carefully prepared the ground for replacing the Treasurer and Labor Minister with Hayden and McClelland respectively. Yet in acting to destroy these men, Whitlam not only divided the party. He laid the foundation for his own destruction.

C   THE DEMISE OF THE SOCIALISTS
In the struggle between the classes, individuals are often considered dispensable. This is even more true during eco-

nomic crisis, when the fundamental issue arises as to who shall bear the biggest burdens, the capitalist forces or the workers.

By December 1974, the economic crisis had hit Australia with a vengeance: the earlier policies of tight money control, together with the fears created in various sections of capital about the 'radical' nature of the Labor government, put a dampener on investment and production. The result was a sharp rise in unemployment to 220 000.[1] The attacks on the government from the press and television achieved a new intensity. The ruling class was beginning to mobilize.

At this critical period, when the economic crisis should have engaged the full attention of all major ministers, Whitlam left Australia for a five-week overseas jaunt.[2] He placed Deputy Prime Minister Cairns in charge of the government, just three days after he had elevated him to Treasurer. As Alan Reid records, in that post, Cairns

> won plaudits for the speed and humanity with which he had reacted to the human and distressing problems of cyclone-devastated Darwin, for his promptitude in acting to save jobs for workers in the ailing motor vehicle industry and for his development of courteous and reasonably cordial relationships with the majority of State Premiers . . . ALP parliamentarians started speculating on whether Cairns would be electorally more appealing than Whitlam. But two things changed Cairns' situation rapidly and adversely. Whitlam returned to Australia. And Cairns decided to appoint Miss Junie Morosi as office manager.[3]

Whatever excuses may be made on his behalf nothing can justify the fact that Cairns permitted the so-called Morosi affair to completely overwhelm the sense of purpose which he demonstrated in his opposition to the Vietnam war and his lifelong struggle for socialism. He was in a unique historical position to promote this cause as never before. He had within his control the government's economic strategy, which he could have used to protect workers' interests during the time of crisis and perhaps even put forward proposals for more public ownership and more industrial democracy. Under these circumstances, if and when Whitlam tried to remove him from Treasurer, he would have found it very difficult. Yet he threw it all away. Cairns must surely have realized that his friendship with Morosi would be symbolized in ways completely contrary to his intentions.[4] In a remarkable interview granted to the most stridently anti-Labor newspaper, the *Daily Mirror*, Cairns proclaimed 'My love for Junie'.[5] It was to be political suicide.

What Cairns had not realized while enjoying his public notoriety was that Whitlam had already decided to move him from Treasury upon his return from overseas.[6] There are three possible explanations for this: that Whitlam had become worried about the popularity of Cairns when he was Acting Prime Minister, or that Whitlam had become convinced that the Cairns' strategy in the economy was mistaken, or both: I believe that it was both. While overseas, Whitlam had visited Paris and had gained some impressions of the actions of European countries in countering the economic crisis.[7] The strategy was simple: cutbacks in the public sector, stabilization or reductions in wages as well as massive support for capitalist forces through state funds. Cairns was opposed to all three.

Given Whitlam's ideological position, it was not surprising that during Labor's time in office socialist policies were consciously excluded by the majority in cabinet. Yet although Whitlam's brand of reform, with its strategy of paying for welfare and social services through more capitalist growth, was muddle-headed and extensively grounded in capitalist ideology, nevertheless actions by his government did rock the ruling class, especially during the economic crisis. For Whitlam had failed to realize that Australian capitalism had long relied on government supports and handouts. Labor did not need to attack that system for problems to arise—all

they had to do was to fail to actively support it. Even Freudenburg accepts that a government does not have to adopt
socialist policies to threaten capitalist forces—merely attempting to withdraw existing benefits, such as the abolition of the
superphosphate subsidy by the Whitlam government in 1974,
was seen as a threat to the accumulated privileges of the ruling
class.[8] Whitlam's strategy of vast expansion in public services
had not taken account of the response that capitalist forces
would make when state funds were redirected away from
their interests, towards those of labour, in a period when
growth had ceased.

The other minister actively supporting workers' interests
at this stage was Clyde Cameron. He had put forward the
policy of wage indexation as a means of consolidating the
gains made by workers prior to the economic crisis: Cameron
shrewdly foresaw that the pressure for wage reductions
would be extremely great and fought strongly for the indexation policy in cabinet. However, he soon demonstrated
that he would still go on supporting unions in their claims in
excess of indexation, when he backed the militant AMWU
in a pay dispute.[9] Whitlam, who had used Cameron to reform
the Labor Party, no longer needed him. His allies on the left
would not be able to stem the ruling-class attacks against
him; he turned to those on the right. It was an attempt to
create a tough new image in economic matters based on the
claim of competence in managing the economy. Yet that was
merely an appearance: the real motive was to bow to the
demands to 'revive' the private sector and re-establish business 'confidence'. What Whitlam had not realized was that it
would take more than a change of ministers and the reduction
of wages to solve the economic crisis which had deepened
and extended.

Cameron refused to leave his portfolio. Whitlam then
advised the Governor-General that he had the power to sack
ministers under the Constitution, 'on the advice of the prime
minister'. This latter qualification does not however appear
in Section 64 of the Constitution, which Kerr used.[10] As Reid

points out, in arranging the sacking of Cameron in the way that he did, 'Whitlam was sharpening the knife that would be used to cut Whitlam's own political throat six months later'.[11] According to Cairns, the purging of Cameron and himself was due to the fact that the party wanted to please the media 'without which we could not survive'. In addition to the sackings the party was 'forced' to 'resist wage and salary increases, cut budget spending significantly' and 'end all unconventional activities like overseas loan negotiations and women's liberation activities, and Rex Connor's "resources policy"'.[12]

The purging of the socialists from key economic portfolios did not, however, bring the hoped-for rise in the government's stocks. Since, in the meantime, the Liberal Party had replaced Snedden with Fraser as leader, sections of the ruling class swung behind the latter and intensified their campaign against the Labor government. The problem was that, no matter how conservative his actual policies may have been at this stage, Whitlam's style continued to appear 'radical' to many capitalists.[13] Furthermore, whatever goodwill Whitlam may have been able to establish with business interests was dissipated by the fact that he retained Rex Connor as Minister for Minerals and Energy after the 'loans affair' had blown up, even though he no longer supported Connor's programme.

The saddest thing was that, in accepting the Hayden-McClelland strategy (see below), Whitlam symbolically abandoned his cherished view that egalitarian reforms could be made in a Western society, without threatening the structure of an economy based on the accumulation of private property and large inequalities between rich and poor. He had no strategy to deal with the powerful forces, that moved against him both economically and politically, except to accede to their demands. The extent of the betrayal was proved by the Hayden budget of August 1975, which was designed to please these capitalist forces. It cut back severely on government programmes, insisted on the need to stimulate the private sector and demanded action to prevent further rises in wages.[14] The government by this stage was ready to turn against the working class and force sacrifices from it, in order to ensure the continuity of capitalist profits and the build-up of business 'confidence'.

In the end, Whitlam's strategy backfired. The government's sudden changes in economic policy—symbolized by the removal of ministers—had come to be represented as sheer incompetence in steering the economy. Labor had first carried out measures which had changed the relation between capital and labour in favour of workers. Within a year, they had completely reversed this and were focusing on the importance of sustaining and increasing the profitability of capital.[15] The result was a 'rationality crisis' in the state. The government was changing policy in its attempts to come to grips with the contradictions within the economy, but was not effectively explaining the reasons for its changes to the people. The Labor government was thus increasingly represented as in disarray and as pursuing irrational policies in economy.

Yet it was not simply the deepening economic crisis which precipitated Labor's downfall. Instead the issue which united the conservative forces in a full-scale attack was on a policy which, had it come earlier, would have allowed the Labor government to deal effectively with the crisis. For it would have increased investment and participation by the state in a productive and profitable sector of the economy, and provided both employment opportunities and money to allow the government to increase state services. I refer here to the policy which resulted in the so-called 'loans affairs', initiated by the tough Minister for Minerals and Energy, Rex Connor.

As has often been remarked, Connor was not a socialist in any fundamental sense,[16] yet his policies were the most socialist and the most serious challenge to capitalist power since World War II. The source of this challenge was Connor's nationalism. He fervently believed that Australians should own and profit from the development of their mineral and energy resources. The big problem was, how could Australian control of these resources be secured? Had Connor been able to use some of the government revenue which went into the over-hasty expansion of unproductive state services, he might have been able to secure Australian ownership, control and development which would have profited the whole people. It is here that he made his major error: he believed he could act independently of cabinet, and of the general economic strategy of the government. By doing so, however, he failed to secure funds for his productive projects, before these funds were expended in welfare programmes.

By the latter part of 1974, Connor realized that there was only one way he could secure funding to carry out his pet projects—by loan funds from overseas. As Paul Kelly points out:

> The funds could be used to satisfy Connor's grandiose development program: the completion of the natural gas pipeline . . . the petro-chemical plant at Dampier to extract natural gas liquids for conversion into motor spirit; three uranium mining and milling plants in the Northern Territory; a uranium enrichment plant; the electrification of heavy freight rail areas in NSW and Victoria; upgrading coal exporting harbours . . . research on coal conversion and solar energy; development of the north west shelf and assistance to the Cooper Basin natural gas consortium. If these projects could be funded through a massive overseas borrowing then Connor would satisfy his twin objectives of development and Australian control.
>
> The search for overseas loan funds was not an aberration. It was the natural product of Connor's policies and objectives and of the limits within which he had to operate.[17]

Connor had little difficulty convincing Whitlam that a loan should be raised. He argued that his schemes would create employment in Australia and place the major sources of energy development into the hands of the government and people. It was clear that what was proposed was a form of *nationalization* of industries; although Connor was not opposed to the idea of some private companies participating in these projects, it was obvious that the government planned to be the dominant force. But here precisely was the problem. For although socialization had been part of the Labor Party platform for many years, Whitlam had publicly given assurances that there would be no nationalization programmes.[18] Ministers realized that there would be a massive reaction if the conservative forces discovered these plans prematurely.

These considerations affected the question of how the loan could be raised. Under normal circumstances such loans go through the Loan Council, which is a body comprising representatives of the six State governments, as well as the Federal government. Both Connor and Whitlam feared that to raise money in this way would not be possible; the premiers would block it. They then embarked on a foolish campaign to raise the money through intermediaries, including a Pakistani called Tirath Khemlani.[19] A special meeting of the Executive Council on 13 December 1974 authorized Connor to borrow 'for temporary purposes' US$4000 million.

Although it raised no money in this way, and there was no loss to the Australian people, the government provided enormous ammunition for the opposition and the news media by its bungling. It was attacked for the 'amateurish' and 'underhand' way it had sought to raise the money.[20]

Yet this was not the major reason for the opposition. What alarmed the capitalist forces, especially those controlling the media, was the purpose of the loan. To them, this policy was the thin edge of the wedge, because it threatened to reintroduce the notion that the government could actually take over productive industries. (There are some nationalized industries in Australia, but most of these, with few exceptions like Telecom, are non-profit-making.) Had Connor succeeded in taking over energy resources the huge profits would have not gone to multi-national and local corporations, but into the state's budget to pay for more humane social services and for urban development.[21]

Cairns stresses another aspect of the matter:

> Trying to borrow money from Arab sources was against the interests of American and British financial houses . . . The media, which played a crucial part in this, may have chosen to attack the government on some of these grounds. But it did not. It concentrated alone on the 'overseas loans affair' . . . But if the *actual* grounds of the objection to what we were doing had been used, the issue would have appeared to be more fundamental.[22]

Indeed changes in the editorial opinions of newspapers and in the aggressiveness of their headlines are detectable from the time the existence of the loan proposal, and its real purposes, became public. Rex Connor was the major object of these attacks. As Kelly notes 'Connor became the most reviled minister in a reviled government'.[23] Yet it was not merely Connor whom the media were out to destroy—it was the whole Labor government.

In the middle of this turmoil, Whitlam made an absurd political move. In May 1975, when the government's popularity was very low, he brought on a by-election by appointing Lance Barnard to an ambassadorship. Both Hawke and ALP Federal Secretary David Combe condemned the action, but it was to no avail.[24] Whitlam had made up his mind. So had the electorate: the by-election in Bass, Tasmania was lost disastrously in a 17 per cent swing. More seriously, it gave Fraser the opportunity to test his electoral skills, and increased his support in the Liberal Party and the media.[25] Furthermore, it confirmed to observers that the economic crisis had resulted in a political crisis, with a dramatic loss of support for the government. The legitimacy of the Labor Party was virtually dissipated.

Normally, after a defeat like this, a leader would seek to

close his ranks and attempt a revival based on a show of unity. Instead, however, while evidence was accumulating of the mobilization of political, industrial and media forces against the government, Whitlam turned not against these but against his own men. On 21 July, Whitlam sacked Dr Cairns from the ministry, claiming that the latter had deliberately misled parliament. Yet it was clear that to sack the Deputy Prime Minister would traumatize the Labor Party and would simply provide further ammunition for the Opposition and the media against his government. If Whitlam had been under Opposition pressure to sack Cairns, his action may have been understandable. In fact, however, after Cairns' explanation in parliament, many Opposition members accepted it, including Malcolm Fraser who said: 'When the former Deputy Prime Minister answered that question in the Parliament, I doubt whether any member of this parliament thought he was speaking other than the truth'.[26] Whitlam's brutal action in dismissing Cairns over what was simply a thoughtless oversight (he had to use the Governor-General again: the knife was sharpened further) was seen by many Australians as a further example of his 'selfish ruthlessness'.

Whitlam said in the parliamentary debate:

> This dismissal of a Deputy Leader, from the Ministry, particularly one held in the regard—the affection—of his Party in and out of Parliament as is the honourable member for Lalor, is a tragedy for all the Party, not least its Leader. The course was taken because it had to be taken, because of standards, because of parliamentary propriety.[27]

The first sentence was prophetic. I cannot accept the second sentence as Whitlam's real motive.

With this execution, the demise of the socialists in the Labor government was virtually complete. Yet Whitlam's actions had not endeared him to the ruling class, as he had hoped. It was too little too late as far as the capitalist forces were concerned. They had already determined that the Whitlam government must fall. Whitlam himself, in destroying his socialist ministers, had ensured that whatever resistance to the mobilization of the ruling class the party could offer would be effectively neutralized.

D   LABOR'S POLITICAL CRISIS AND THE DESTRUCTION OF WHITLAM

> The question of Supply—let me deal with it this way. I generally believe if a Government is elected to power in the lower House and has the numbers and can maintain the numbers in the lower House, it is entitled to expect that it will govern for the three-year term unless quite extraordinary events intervene.
>
> Having said that . . . if we do make up our minds at some stage that the Government is so reprehensible that an opposition must use whatever power is available to it, then I'd want to find a situation in which we made that decision and Mr Whitlam woke up one morning finding the decision had been made and finding that he had been caught with his pants well and truly down.[1]

This is Malcolm Fraser, Opposition Leader speaking just after his election to the leadership of the Liberal Party. In Fraser, the ruling class gained one of the most formidable and shrewd champions of its causes. Many things have been written about Fraser which seek to denigrate his intellect and his integrity. Yet in his vigorous defence of capitalist forces and their pre-eminent need for more and better profits, Fraser has been consistent and has shown rare skill.[2] Within months of his election, Fraser was able to rally the divided sections of the Liberal Party, and to unify the different sections of the ruling class in the pursuit of one goal—the destruction of the Labor government and the return of state power firmly back into the hands of the ruling class.

The consistent and single-minded pursuit of these overriding goals has led Fraser to employ various dubious means, such as giving the assurance quoted above and yet also wanting to catch Whitlam 'with his pants down'. Fraser's use of such means in the pursuit of what he considers to be higher and greater goals, namely, the development of society through active support of capitalist forces, will be examined in Chapter 9C.

Whitlam was led into a false sense of security by Fraser—although there were clear signs of mobilization against the government within the economic and political sectors of the ruling class.[3] That Labor underestimated the tenacity of the conservatives was shown in their handling of the following key incident. In June 1975, Labor senator Milliner of Queensland died. The conservative Premier of that State, Bjelke-Petersen, saw this as an opportunity to change the balance of power in the Senate. Although there had been a long-established convention that a State government shall appoint a person from the same party to fill occasional senate vacancies, Bjelke-Petersen ignored this and appointed an anti-labour man, who declared that Whitlam 'would never get a vote from me'.[4] The ALP should have fought this tooth and nail; yet they did not. In the end, as Liberal Movement Senator Steele Hall put it: 'Let it be remembered that the Opposition succeeded only because a Labor Senator died. They did it over a dead man's corpse'.[5] The morality was dubious, but the tenacity with which they fought for their side and their vision of a capitalist Australia was admirable. The labour forces did not show such tenacity until it was too late.

Events like this should have prepared Whitlam to secure as many allies as possible for the coming showdown. Yet he did not; instead he appeared to believe that it was entirely or primarily a parliamentary battle, and that he could outwit Fraser at such tactics. In his recent book, he refers to the stacked Senate as if this were the only effective oppositional factor. Here, as he often did, Whitlam underestimated the strength of the forces ranged against him.[6] It was not just the parliamentary Liberal Party and their supporters. It was the whole corporate sector, and, by this stage, the totality of the media. Yet, while they were mobilizing themselves, Whitlam did nothing to gather support from the labour movement —from unions or the party itself. Indeed he did not mobilize them, even after the Liberals had deferred supply, so that counter pressure could be placed on Fraser.

Whitlam was also misled into believing that the media would support him after Hayden brought down his so-called 'moderate' budget, which in fact was designed to revive profitability in the private sector at the expense of labour. In his book, *The Truth of The Matter,* Whitlam remarks:

> Throughout the entire Budget crisis, our opponents
> never claimed that the budget itself was the reason for
> blocking it. Indeed it was not until May 1976 that they
> announced any economic measures of their own to
> modify the strategy of the Hayden budget. The events
> of October–November had nothing to do with the
> Hayden economic strategy of 1975.[7] (Why not? one
> might ask.)

Whitlam goes on to applaud the reception of the budget by the media, and quotes the *Financial Review*, the *Sydney Morning Herald* and the *Age* editorials on it as evidence of its quality. Yet the first paper is this country's sophisticated defender of capitalist interests; the other two played a key role in the destruction of his own government![8]

Whitlam's ambivalence towards the media and capitalist forces becomes apparent if we contrast the remarks referred to above, with the following statement made when the threat of the Senate action was imminent:

> It is because this government has attempted to make
> this parliament an instrument of reform, for long
> overdue change, for progress, for the redistribution of
> wealth, for the uplifting of the underprivileged, for the

reduction of the privileges of great wealth and deeply entrenched vested interests ... that our opponents and those vested interests have from the very beginning ... embarked on a course to destroy this government at the earliest opportunity. But what they are really doing is destroying the very basis of parliamentary democracy in our country.[9]

This very important speech showed the idealist side of Whitlam. It shows something of the humanitarian values on which his programme was grounded. However, it also shows the yawning chasm between his rhetoric—which was radical —and his actions. For what was there in the Hayden budget which involved a redistribution of wealth to the poor? What was there in it which threatened to reduce 'privilege of great wealth and deeply entrenched vested interests'? Nothing at all. The budget was in no way a threat to capitalist forces. In fact it proposed to assist them. Hayden introduced cutbacks in various important areas of government spending; he proposed fewer restrictions on multi-national corporations seeking to invest in Australia; he proposed various tax concessions designed to lift company profitability and encourage investment.[10]

If Whitlam hoped that his government—by a dramatic change of policy in favour of corporate forces—would become more acceptable to those forces and the powerful media which support them, he was deluded. Opposition leader Fraser contributed to this delusion by declaring, two days after it was presented, that Liberal Senators intended to pass the budget.[11] Yet during that month, Fraser took extensive soundings within the Liberal Party on the possibility of winning an election. What was required now was a justification for Fraser to act. As we saw, he had earlier exclaimed that he would only block Supply if certain 'reprehensible circumstances' arose. These were provided for him when certain media people, in a *conspiracy* with the leading figures of the Opposition, such as Deputy Leader Phillip Lynch, forced the 'resignation' of Rex Connor.[12] On 8 October, the Melbourne *Herald* ran a front page heavy headline 'Khemlani Tells—I've Got Connor Go Ahead', in which the Pakistani claimed that his authority to secure loan funds still continued and had not been revoked. Lynch had been informed of the substance of the article, before it appeared, and had secured a denial from the Prime Minister in the House that any minister was trying to raise funds. Though he was sick in hospital, Connor issued a statement denying that he had actively pursued the loan further—although he conceded that he had been contacted by Khemlani and an intermediary.

This provided the conservative forces with exactly what they needed. Khemlani appeared in Australia—financed by some mysterious benefactor. He issued a statutory declaration, which was published in the *Herald*, asserting that he had contacted Connor many times. Whether Khemlani's statements were true, or whether he was bribed to implicate the minister, it was the end of Rex Connor. He was forced to resign for failing to inform Treasury or the Prime Minister about his continuing contacts with Khemlani.

Why had Connor done it? To me, the reason appears to be that after his authority to raise loans was revoked on 20 May, Connor's dream for Australia collapsed. Much of resources policy was being taken out of his hands by the new Treasurer, Hayden. The idea of buying into minerals and energy enterprises had been abandoned.[13] There was only one way out for Connor: to continue to try and secure a loan, and then present the details to Whitlam with the hope that his authority would be renewed. Of course, it was an absurd proposition: but since no new strategy was offered to Connor after 20 May he was left with little alternative if he were to pursue his dream. It was Connor's desperation which led him to hide from Whitlam the fact that he was continuing loans discussions.

Yet whatever minor principle was involved in this, Whitlam should have refused the pressure to sack Connor—particularly so in view of the conspiratorial way in which the

332

Deputy Leader of the Opposition and the *Herald* had acted.[14] Indeed, the *Herald*'s articles presented to the public the view that there was something sinister or corrupt in Connor's behaviour. With this action, the conservative forces proved their tenacity and morality in the most despicable way: they destroyed the reputation of a nationalist, who refused to give up his dream for Australian ownership of resources. And Whitlam should have realized that this demise of Connor was the 'reprehensible circumstance' which the Liberals wanted.

Once Connor was gone, the collusion between the media and the Liberals intensified. As Paul Kelly explains:

> That evening Fraser spoke with senior newspaper executives from at least two out of Australia's three major newspaper chains and informed them that he had decided to force an election ... Almost without exception the press supported Fraser's decision to force an election and the *Sydney Morning Herald* and the *Age* adopted the unusual practice of running part of their editorial on page one, giving full backing to the Liberal-National Country Parties.[15]

The ferocity of the attacks was illustrated by the editorial in the *Age*. It called for the government's resignation on the basis that it no longer had the confidence of the people:

> We will say it straight and clear, and at once. The Whitlam government has run its course; it must go now, and preferably by the honourable course of resignation—a course which would dispel all arguments about constitutional proprieties, historic conventions and 'grabs' for power. It must go because it no longer has the degree of public support and acceptance that permits governments to govern effectively.[16]

Such an editorial when a non-Labor government was in power would have been unthinkable. Indeed in the many crises which have hit the Fraser Liberal government, there has not once been even a suggestion that a minister should resign.

Thus the responsible image of the Labor Party, which Whitlam had worked so hard to establish in 1967–72 (see Chapter 7B), was shattered within one year. This was not a matter of what the government was doing; it was primarily a matter of how it was represented in the media. Yet Whitlam confirmed these impressions, by disloyalty to his ministers when they were under pressure. He may have defended them in parliament as men of integrity, guilty only of small error. However, to the public, his refusal to stand by them 'demonstrated' that they were guilty of the media's much more serious accusations.[17]

The destruction of Labor's image was accompanied by a rationality (state political) crisis. To the Australian people the Whitlam government was by now represented as incompetent and irrational in its steering of economy, and underhand and corrupt in its attempts to secure overseas loans and in other matters. These matters were never actually specified: it was all a matter of suggestion and innuendo. As Freudenburg remarks:

> Fraser's performance in 1975 was one of the most concentrated single-minded and effective exercises in political destruction ever undertaken in Australian history . . . In the end, for every one who would dare say it, there were ten who believed the Labor Government was corrupt. The constant repetition of the word 'scandal' and its indiscriminate application to any controversial action of the government worked.[18]

On 18 October, Fraser announced in parliament that the 'reprehensible circumstances' had arrived and were serious enough to warrant him persuading the Liberal members of the Senate to defer supply, that is, to refuse to pass the budget, without actually rejecting it. Just exactly what these 'reprehensible circumstances' were at this stage, was not clear. After all, the major ministers under attack—Connor and Cairns—had been removed from office, the budget handed down by Bill Hayden had been a 'moderate' one—not something one could easily label as a 'reprehensible circumstance'. Nevertheless, Fraser argued that Whitlam should accept the responsibility for the dismissed ministers and that being rid of the latter did not absolve the government from complicity in the loans affair.[19]

This was the first in a series of actions which raised major constitutional questions. The issue which arose at this stage, was: did the Senate have power to defer supply? If it continued to do so, what courses were constitutionally open to the government? According to a literal reading of the constitution, the Senate does have the right to refuse to pass supply: although there is no such right specified, it is implied.[20] However, since the Senate is subject to the pleasure of the Governor-General, if we read this document literally, this course is dependent upon the Governor-General accepting this as the proper role of the Senate. This is an important consideration. For when the Senate blocked supply, Sir Richard Eggleston—an eminent constitutional lawyer and Chancellor of Monash University—was one of the few people to publicly state that such an act was contrary to the Constitution.[21] (Ironically, Sir Richard had been one of the people considered and rejected by Whitlam for the post of Governor-General.) Sir John Kerr—the Governor-General whom Whitlam *had* appointed—did not feel that the Liberals' act of blocking supply was unconstitutional.[22]

Once the budget was blocked, there was a real possibility that the government would run out of money in five to six months (by the end of November). Whitlam refused to call a general election as Fraser had insisted, resolving instead to 'tough it out' until some Liberal senators saw the folly of their ways and helped pass the budget. A similar strategy had been used successfully in Victoria last century. In this case, the State government of the day simply persevered—

they ran out of money, but continued to govern until finally the Upper House relented and passed the budget.[23]

Whitlam was determined to hold out, even after supply ran out, by arranging to borrow money from banks to continue funding the state's services. Hayden was placed in charge of these arrangements and, although he was worried about them, nevertheless managed to tie things up reasonably well. Meanwhile, however, the conservative forces were mobilizing further. There was a fear that Whitlam might call a half-Senate election as a way of escaping his fate. Hence, as Whitlam says, 'on 12 October 1975, the Liberal Party Council recommended that State Liberal governments should break the convention of seventy-five years and refuse to allow their governors to issue writs for a Senate election'.[24] He goes on to explain that his delay in recommending the half-Senate election was to protect Kerr. 'I did not wish him to be the first Governor-General to be humiliated by the refusal of the State governors to accept his request'.[25] Here an opportunity to test Kerr's loyalty was missed.

Yet at that time there were reasons for anxiety regarding the Queen's representative. The Opposition had clearly demonstrated that they were depending on him for their support. On 17 October, shadow Attorney-General Bob Ellicott released a statement outlining the Liberal view of what the Governor-General should do. It was remarkably similar to Kerr's own later justification of his actions. Ellicott argued:

> The Governor-General has at least two clear
> constitutional prerogatives which he can exercise—
> the right to dismiss his ministers and appoint others,
> and the right to refuse a dissolution of the parliament
> of either House . . . A government without supply
> cannot govern. The refusal by parliament of supply,
> whether through the House or the Senate, is a clear
> signal to the Governor-General that his chosen
> ministers may not be able to carry on. In the proper
> performance of his role, he would inevitably want to

have from the Prime Minister an explanation of how he proposed to overcome the situation. If the Prime Minister proposed and insisted on means which were unlawful or which did not solve the problems of the disagreement between the houses and left the government without funds to carry on, it would be within the Governor-General's power and his duty to dismiss his ministers and appoint others . . . [26]

The second stage of the conservative strategy was thus to pressurize the Governor-General, and to attempt to influence his decision. In the meantime, they prepared the people, through heavy propaganda. Thus the Liberals ran large advertisements in the newspapers, justifying their move against the budget and highlighting the government's 'poor economic performance'. In this, they were massively supported by a media campaign that became strident in its attacks and lost all semblance of objectivity.[27] Yet notwithstanding this propaganda, an *Age-Herald* poll published on 30 October indicated that 70 per cent of the people believed that the budget should be passed, while only 25 per cent agreed with the blocking of supply. Furthermore 54 per cent believed that Labor had a right to continue to govern, while only 44 per cent felt it should resign and call an election.[28]

Under the enormous pressure of the situation, it was not the Liberals who started to back down. Two weeks before supply had actually run out, Whitlam changed his mind and on 11 November decided to go to the Governor-General and request a half-Senate election. He believed this would clear the air as to whether the Senate had the right to block supply. However, the Governor-General had other ideas. When Whitlam arrived at Government House, Malcolm Fraser was already there sitting in another room, waiting. When Whitlam asked Kerr to agree to his request for the half-Senate election, Kerr simply asked him whether he was prepared to recommend a general election. When he innocently replied that he would not, Kerr handed him a letter containing the decision to remove him as Prime Minister.[29]

At this stage, the political crisis was transformed into a full legitimation crisis. For the Governor-General carried out two actions of extremely dubious constitutional validity, actions which placed into question the very principles of Western democracy as they applied to Australia. Firstly, he dismissed a Prime Minister who had been elected by the majority of the people, and held the confidence of the majority in the House of Representatives. Secondly, he appointed Malcolm Fraser to be Prime Minister, the first man in Australian history to hold the office without controlling the majority in the people's House. The conservative forces—in and out of parliament—had pulled off a constitutional coup. Would they succeed in resolving the consequent crisis in legitimacy? This again depended on the actions of the main participants and the dominant social forces. The conservatives, backed by united capitalist forces, won the battle and established once again the political dominance of the ruling class.

9
Repressed Crises

A   AUSTRALIA'S LEGITIMATION CRISIS

11 November 1975 was a fateful day. Not only was the majority government sacked, but the minority Opposition was given the reins of state power. The conservatives seized control of the state, without even having won an election. These two actions of Kerr were the most dramatic in a whole series of departures from existent constitutional understandings. The country was thrown into a legitimation crisis.

The responses of the various participants to the crisis provide a very important lesson in political dynamics. For, although the crisis was temporarily resolved, it was not pre-determined that legitimacy should have been restored in that particular way. Had some of the key actors and forces acted differently, the result could have been very different. Here the conservative forces had the advantage in that they were taking all the initiative and had already taken action to negate some of the impact of the legitimation crisis.[1] Whitlam and the Labor government generally were completely taken aback at the radical behaviour of the conservative forces. Notwithstanding the aggressive behaviour of the Liberal Party and of the media, the Prime Minister did not believe that they would engineer a constitutional coup. Yet Fraser had said one week before 11 November that the Governor-General would act to resolve the issue.[2] Moreover the Opposition had given a clear sign of their strategy much earlier in Ellicott's statement, referred to in the last section. Indeed, so confident were the conservatives of Kerr that, on 10 November, Ellicott asserted that the Governor-General would act in the next two days to resolve the political deadlock. Yet Whitlam paid little heed to these signs and seemed confident of the solid support of Kerr. He did not attempt to test the loyalty of the Governor-General, or find out what he was thinking and feeling.[3]

In his defence Whitlam claims that he was deliberately and callously misled by Kerr. Yet Whitlam had flippantly remarked, in the presence of Kerr and referring to the constitutional crisis: 'it all depends on who gets to the phone first, he to dismiss me or I to have him recalled'.[4] Hence Kerr was afraid that the slightest hint of adopting an independent course would have immediately led Whitlam to sack him.[5] Kerr may have been paranoid in this fear—but how irrational was it, given that Whitlam had already callously disposed of several of his own colleagues?

There is substantial evidence in support of the view that Fraser privately urged Kerr to dismiss the government and was increasingly confident that he would do so. Particularly revealing is the fact that Fraser had privately met Kerr several times during the crisis and telephoned him at least twenty-five times in four weeks.[6] And Freudenburg notes:

At his first press conference as the newly-installed Prime Minister, Fraser was asked (on the sacking) 'Why did you make such a firm and definite statement? What information did you have?' He replied: 'Only because I had a proper understanding that the Parliament of Australia is comprised of the Queen, in her case represented by the Governor-General, and the Senate and the House of Representatives.' . . . The truth is that this formula was only used by Fraser at precisely 11.50 a.m. on 11 November in his last speech in Parliament as Leader of the Opposition, made scarcely an hour before he was appointed Prime Minister.[7]

McQueen headed an article in *Politics* 1976 'None Dare Call it Conspiracy'.[8] Yet the evidence in favour of such a view seems highly plausible.

There were two important factors in ensuring that the legitimation crisis, following the dismissal, did not blow up into a serious rebellion against the state itself. Firstly, it was essential to argue that the Governor-General had no other way of resolving the deadlock, and that he had to act to resolve it. Kerr himself contributed to this by immediately publishing a statement of his reasons for his action. In it, he said:

> If a Prime Minister refuses to resign or to advise an election, and this is the case with Mr Whitlam, my constitutional authority and duty require me to do what I have done now—to withdraw his commission —and to invite the leader of the Opposition to form a caretaker government—that is one that makes no appointments or dismissals and initiates no policies, until a general election is held. It is most desirable that he should guarantee supply. Mr Fraser will be asked to give the necessary undertakings and advise whether he is prepared to recommend a double dissolution. He will also be asked to guarantee supply.
>
> The decisions I have made were made after I was satisfied that Mr Whitlam could not obtain supply. No other decision open to me would enable the Australian people to decide for themselves what should be done.[9]

In his memoirs, Sir John emphasizes over and over that he had a right and a duty to exercise his reserve powers. Let us, for argument's sake, grant him this. The question that still remains is: could Kerr have exercised his reserve powers in a fairer, more democratic way? Could he have resolved the problems in a way which was not so blatantly biased in favour of the conservative parties? Consider some alternative courses of action he could have taken.

(i) He could have dissolved both Houses of Parliament and yet allowed Whitlam to remain Prime Minister until the election. The reason given for Kerr not doing this is that Whitlam would have sacked him. But why should this be a valid *constitutional* consideration, coming from a man claiming to be doing his duty to the nation?

(ii) He could have brought Whitlam and Fraser together, told them that he would exercise his reserve powers unless a compromise was reached and hammered out a compromise with both of them. One such compromise would have been an agreement for Kerr and Whitlam to remain in their offices, the budget to be passed and a general election to be held in the new year. I believe that Whitlam should have held out for such a compromise, even after Kerr dismissed him, rather than accept Kerr's handing over power to the Liberal-National Country Party.

(iii) Even if we assume that Kerr had to dismiss Whitlam, he need not have appointed Fraser as Prime Minister. He could have used his reserve powers under Section 64 of the Constitution to appoint independent persons, acceptable to both sides, to be caretakers or administrators of the government until the election. For on a literal reading of the reserve powers, the Governor-General can appoint as ministers persons who are not members of parliament for a period of up to three months (see Chapter 1C). There are precedents for this in other Western democracies, where eminent persons such as university professors have been given the reins of government so as not to give preference to any party.[10] As it was, by appointing Fraser, Kerr was *not* neutral and gave the Liberal leader the mantle of legitimacy, which he did not deserve.

Thus, even if we concede to Kerr that he had to use the reserve powers, he could have used them more fairly and in a less partisan way. But why did he have to use these anti-democratic powers anyway? It is argued by Kerr himself that he had to use them in order to resolve a crisis. Many people have argued against this view, including the Solicitor-General Mr Byers in his opinion of 4 November 1975, which was given to Kerr.

> The point of this is that section 61 affords no ground for the conclusion that upon the Senate deferring or rejecting Supply solely to procure the resignation or dismissal of the Ministry possessing a majority in the Representatives, His Excellency is constitutionally obliged immediately to seek an explanation of the Prime Minister of how he proposes to overcome that situation.
>
> Nor do we agree with the suggestion that were the Prime Minister unable to suggest means which would solve the disagreement between the Houses and left the disagreement between the Houses and left the Government without funds to carry on, it would be His Excellency's duty to dismiss his Ministers.[11]

Two points are important here. Firstly, at the time of Kerr's actions, Supply had not yet run out. There were no visible signs of crisis, except in the newspapers. There were no signs that some state services would collapse. Even if there were signs of such a collapse of some government services, why should this particular crisis warrant action by the Governor-General, whereas others do not? Why is serious unemployment, the collapse of the Australian dollar, the declaration of war, the invasion of civil liberties—why are these things not a 'crisis' warranting action by the Governor-General, while the deferral of supply is? This question has not been adequately answered. It is not sufficient to argue that chaos is being created, for not even the Liberals would concede that the Governor-General can dismiss them, if their policies resulted in what *he* defined as economic chaos.

The implications of Kerr's actions, as many have pointed out, were serious and far-reaching for Australian democracy. The Governor-General adopted the most authoritarian interpretation of his own powers. This was shown clearly by the Governor-General's actions following the dismissal. For although he had appointed Fraser as the new Prime Minister, the Houses of Parliament had not yet been dissolved. When the news came to the Representatives that Whitlam had been dismissed, the Labor majority immediately passed a notion of no confidence in Fraser as Prime Minister.

Yet Kerr refused to pay any attention to this no confidence motion—contrary to all the traditions of Western democracy. Instead he acted unilaterally to dissolve both Houses, claiming that he was acting on advice from a Prime Minister who had never had the confidence of the House. The supreme irony was that Kerr's reasons for dissolving both Houses was the blocking of Labor's bills by the Liberals themselves. The justification was itself an absurdity and a sham.[12]

A logical consequence of the authoritarian interpretation of the constitution adopted by Kerr is as follows. A Governor-General could, by declaring that a crisis had arisen, simply dismiss the majority in parliament from government. He could then appoint any minority group in the parliament to government. According to Section 64, they could remain as ministers until such time as the Governor-General deems it necessary to have an election. Admittedly, they would be defeated in parliament on a no confidence motion. But this need not worry the Governor-General, since the precedent that the government resign immediately a no confidence motion is passed no longer holds. Thus a minority government could remain in power for many months. This could, of course, give it time to establish itself and could give it a strong advantage in any subsequent election.

I do not, however, wish to labour the point of the serious consequences for democracy, which has been discussed extensively in the literature. From my analysis of the democratic ideal in Chapter 1A and of Australia's Constitution in Chapter 1C, it can be seen that Kerr's action undermined both the principles and institutions of democracy. The very basis of the legitimacy of the state was shaken.

The implications were recognized even by conservative forces. Thus the *Age* and the *Sydney Morning Herald*, which had played key roles in precipitating the conservative actions, roundly condemned the Governor-General's act— although they supported Fraser strongly in the subsequent election. They conveyed the following message to people: although the Kerr action had not been legitimate, all that could be done was to accept it, and to allow the forthcoming general election to resolve the issues.[13] How the election was to resolve the issues, when these newspapers were strongly urging people to vote Liberal, was not explained.

There was a further serious problem which the conservative forces faced in thus undermining legitimacy. What if Whitlam refused to accept his dismissal, arguing that the Governor-General had no power to act against him in these circumstances? This raises one of the most disturbing features of the constitutional crisis, and also illustrates the lengths to which the ruling class will go in defence of its interests. For on the eve of his action, Kerr is said to have unilaterally acted, without consulting his ministers, and placed the armed forces on a grey alert.[14] Had Whitlam resisted the dismissal and attempted to continue as Prime Minister, would the conservative forces have acted to remove him by force, using the army or the police? It is my view that they would have—for there were many things at stake by this stage (see below).

What was it which propelled the Liberals to take such drastic steps and perhaps even use force? It is conceivable, after all, that the bitter division of the nation which followed the dismissal could have been much more serious and involved a direct challenge to the authority of the state. Furthermore, it was clear from opinion polls, and was the view of most commentators, that Labor would lose the next general election, even if it were to be held at the latest possible moment. So the Liberals were virtually assured of power had they waited.

I believe that the major cause was the alarm that had been created around the condition of the economy; in particular among companies which had been hard hit by inflation and were worried about the continuity of the level of profit to which they had previously been accustomed. Thus, even though Cairns and Connor had been disposed of, many businessmen were genuinely convinced that the Whitlam government had completely undermined the conditions for capitalist production in Australia.[15]

The legitimation crisis could have taken a completely different direction, had Whitlam recognized the real nature of the struggle and acted accordingly. Let us suppose that instead of accepting the removal of his commission, he simply refused to recognize the Governor-General's right to remove him from office, given that he had the majority in the House of Representatives and had not been defeated in a no confidence motion. After all, Whitlam later argued that Kerr's action was not constitutional.[16] If this is the case, why did he not refuse to accept it?

Let us consider the possible scenarios on the assumption that Whitlam had taken such a tough stand:

(a) The Liberals and the Governor-General, recognizing that they had played their cards, could have accepted that Whitlam was standing up to them and simply agreed to his compromise solution of a half-Senate election. This seems highly unlikely.

(b) Whitlam could have contacted the Queen who could have sided with the Prime Minister and decided to remove the Governor-General. This is also not a very likely outcome, notwithstanding the paranoid fears which Kerr reveals in his book.[17]

(c) The Governor-General and Whitlam could have discussed the issue and reached a compromise, agreeing at a mutually acceptable time, that there would be a general election and that, firstly, Kerr should stay in office at least until the election; secondly, that Whitlam should remain Prime Minister; thirdly, that the Liberals would pass the budget. A compromise of this kind could have been reached, had Whitlam insisted on his rights.

(d) The Governor-General could have taken an extremely tough stance—he could have reacted to Whitlam's refusal to acknowledge the withdrawal of his commission by disregarding Whitlam's claim to the office of Prime Minister. If Whitlam had then continued to act in his capacity of Prime Minister, Kerr could have ordered the police force or the armed forces to take action against him. The fact that the army had been placed on alert suggests that Kerr may have been determined to carry out this plan of action notwithstanding Kerr's later dismissal of this claim as 'nonsense'.[18] On 11 November 1978, Whitlam explained in a speech that a major reason for not resisting the sacking was because he believed that the Governor-General would have called in the armed forces or the police. He writes:

> Mr Scholes and I discussed maintaining or resuming the sittings of the House. It was in this context that I said to him that in those circumstances Sir John would call out the troops. Many people still think it incredible that Sir John could have done that. If, however, a man can interpret the Constitution, where it is silent, in a way which entitled him to perpetrate his actions of that day, how much more certain is it that he would have thought himself entitled to act when, as the Constitution expressly states, 'The command in chief of the naval and military forces of the Commonwealth is vested in the Governor-General'?[19]

Yet if the Governor-General had ordered the police to arrest the Prime Minister, would they all have acted as one unified group? Would they not have divided amongst themselves? How would the army or the public service have reacted? The possibilities are both disturbing and fascinating.

Several months after these events, Whitlam made the claim that he had saved the country from civil war. He was convinced that had he acted differently, there would have been a total collapse of legitimacy, which would have constituted a precondition for violence in the streets.[20] However, as we have learnt in recent times from such countries as India and Portugal, the struggle for democracy often requires the use of extraordinary means. Yet Whitlam was not prepared to use them. Although his opponents had resorted to the most extreme tactics, short of military take-over, he was not prepared to act outside what he considered to be the constitutional proprieties. He wanted to play the game right to the end.

> When I spoke to the Caucus and in talks with Party officials, I stressed and they all completely agreed that we should not depart from the accepted processes. We had won the 1972 and 1974 elections in accordance with the rules. We should strive to win again in accordance with the rules.[21]

However, Whitlam's refusal to stand up to actions which he considered unconstitutional nullified his subsequent attacks on those actions. In the campaign that ensued, the media and the unelected Liberal-NCP government attempted to lessen the impact of the constitutional crisis, and to make the economic crisis the central issue of the election. But would they have been successful in doing so if the country had been completely divided over the legitimate course of action to be pursued, or if the Prime Minister had been incarcerated? Thus it was ineffective for Whitlam to accept the sacking and then to condemn the ensuing situation as unconstitutional. If it were unconstitutional, then he had the right, in the first place, to refuse to accept it; and if it were constitutional then the Labor Party should not have concentrated on it alone.

This was the fundamental logical error in Whitlam's strategy. He accepted the ruling of the system, then condemned it as unconstitutional, then participated in the consequent forced election. Needless to say, this demonstrates his ideological confusion and his ambivalence towards the ruling class. He had played by the rules of the system, believing that his opponents would put the interests of democracy over and above their class interests.

Whitlam accepted the dismissal and returned to his office in a dazed state.[22] While this act may have been understandable and forgivable, the subsequent actions of the Labor Party were not. Firstly, although Labor had argued that the election had been forced by unconstitutional means, they nevertheless agreed to participate in it. This gave legitimacy to the actions of the Liberals and the Governor-General. Had the Labor Party refused to participate, the electoral process would have been exposed as the farce which it had become. For, it was clear to most people that the Labor Party would be trounced at the forced election, particularly since Fraser now had the advantage of campaigning with the mantle of Prime Minister. This tactic of refusing to participate unless new terms and conditions for a fairer election were established, has been used with some success in other countries. Yet the Labor Party did not even countenance it.

Secondly, in other countries, when the ruling class has seized power by unconstitutional or dubious means, the working people have rallied in massive demonstrations and strikes designed to bring down the government. By comparison, what happened in Australia? The major representative of the workers, ACTU President Bob Hawke, appeared on television in tears and after protesting at how unfair

Kerr had been, asked the Australian people to internalize their anger rather than to strike or to demonstrate. The people were told that by internalizing their anger, keeping things calm, the general election could be won.[23] This was political naivety of the worst kind. Keeping the lid on everything gave a further legitimacy to the action at a critical point, when the situation could have developed either way.

In any event, this tactic further divided the labour movement. While some sections of it called for internalization of anger, others demanded strikes and demonstrations. Labor supporters were caught in a bind: should they keep calm or should they demonstrate? The people were being given contradictory advice. In the end, those demonstrations which did occur were not large enough to worry the ruling class. Yet a sustained effort such as a general strike could have forced Fraser and the conservatives to compromise.

Again, the leadership of the Labor Party did not grasp the full dimensions of the struggle involved. A historic opportunity to force a showdown with the conservative forces on the principles of democracy, and on other constitutional principles, was lost. The Liberals' breach of constitutional understandings and the Governor-General's exercise of his reserve powers, both of which undermined democracy, should have been fought to the very end. Writing more than three years afterwards, Whitlam states:

> The actual events of November 1975, the conduct of Mr Fraser and his followers, the Chief Justice and State premiers, ratified by Sir John Kerr and enshrined in the Kerr interpretation of the Constitution, lead inexorably to the collapse of the system. The foundation of that system is that it has the allegiance and confidence of the overwhelming majority of the people ... A constitution riddled with such power for disruption cannot stand.[24]

Yet what did Whitlam do at the critical moment to change it?

B 'LEGITIMACY' REGAINED

> In the 19th century we Australians were in the
> vanguard of human progress. We were the pioneers of
> political democracy. But, alas, in the 20th century
> we've drifted into the camp of the last ditch defenders
> of bourgeois society. Unhappily, we remained colonials
> too long. We became hopelessly addicted to petit
> bourgeois property values . . . We must do something
> or we might be swept into the dustbin of human
> history. Four times in the 20th century we have
> deliberately chosen a conservative path. In 1916–17,
> in 1932, in December '49 and again in December '75.[1]
>
> > Manning Clark,
> > addressing Citizens for Democracy

It has been argued by cynics and pessimists that the Australian
people were not concerned with the principles of democracy
when they voted in the Liberal-National Country Party
government in 1975.[2] Yet what kind of situation did the
people of Australia find themselves confronted with? On
the one hand, there was the problem of undermined legitimacy, but on the other there was a severe economic crisis.
Thus the people were forced to make a choice here. Should
they continue to give support to the existing government as
a gesture towards the democratic processes, or should they
shift their support to the Liberals, whom the media were
representing as sound economic managers?

During 1975 the prevailing attitude towards the economy,
was that the state, and in particular the government of the
state, was primarily responsible for the economic crisis which
had arisen. Hence the major focus of the Opposition prior
to the overthrow of Whitlam was on the economy. Fraser
particularly emphasized the responsibility of the government
for the existing situation. Naturally he did not consider that
these were deep-seated problems in the character of capitalist
economy—or with the transformations which that economy

had undergone in its advanced stages (see Chapter 3A). Nor did the Labor government—caught by its own ideological ambivalence—blame the general character of capitalism, but rather emphasized that Australia was suffering because of the poor state of the international capitalist economy (see Chapter 3B). While this was partly true, it did not overcome the people's feelings that the government should have been able to protect them from the crisis.

During the campaign, the Liberals focused on the increases in unemployment and inflation. Yet Labor failed to stress the fact that it had achieved a level of redistribution of income, if not of wealth; the Whitlam period had brought substantial increases in real wages. There had been an increase in the available goods and services (for the average person). However, there was also an accompanying *decrease* in peoples' feelings of security, particularly during the period of rapid growth in unemployment which occurred in the last year of Labor rule.

Many people were of the opinion that the Australian electorate completely ignored the issue of legitimation and simply voted for the materialist goal—the pursuit of a stable economy—even though there were no guarantees that Mr Fraser would be able to provide what he had promised. To the extent that this is so, the Labor government itself had to bear much of the responsibility. Labor had not supported wage increases, on the basis of principles of social justice and redistribution. Hence people demanded more because of an acquisitive desire for material goods and not out of any claims for equality. Thus the materialist basis of social identity in Australia (see Chapter 4B) was reinforced; the people raised their expectations and the pressure on the system increased. Work motivation was increasingly geared to external reward; Labor did little to improve 'job satisfaction or even participation in decision making'.[3] As the government appeared incapable of steering the economic system to secure these material rewards, more people withdrew their support of it: their social identity and security were threatened.

Even the unions, which had previously backed the Labor government because of its generous support of wage indexation etc., had reacted against an attempt by the government to impose limits on wage increases. Labor's last year in office had been plagued by industrial unrest, reflecting the decrease in work motivation (for the theory behind this see Prologue and Chapter 4A).

It has been argued by people like Donald Horne that the Australian people, by voting Liberal, were fooled and blinded by the aggressive anti-Labor media or perhaps that they showed a callous disregard for the principles of democracy and plumped for their own material self-interest.[4] But is this so obvious? Suppose Labor had won the election, would they have been able to claim a clear mandate for the numerous constitutional changes required to ensure the continuation of democracy in an unambiguous way, that is, responsible government? The Liberals could simply have argued that the Labor win was independent of the crisis in legitimacy. They could have insisted that the economic issue was still the dominant one and that the people had preferred Hayden to Fraser as manager of the economy. Thus the election could not have resolved the constitutional issue, even if Labor had won (although it may have strengthened the argument for constitutional change). Neither Kerr's action in dismissing the government and forcing an unfair election, nor the Labor Party's strategy of participating in that election, resolved this flaw in Australian democracy.

For this reason alone, the Labor Party should have insisted that it would not participate in the election, unless and until the people had determined in an independent referendum firstly, whether or not the Senate should have the power to block, or indefinitely defer, supply to a government with the majority in the House of Representatives; and secondly, whether the Governor-General had reserve powers to dismiss a government which retained the confidence of the House of Representatives. If this strategy had been adopted, the Liberals would have been forced to compromise and there is a chance that sounder guarantees of democracy might have emerged.[5]

As it was, Labor chose to focus the constitutional issues around the personal injustice done to Gough Whitlam. 'We want Gough' become the theme of their campaign, to the delight of the Liberal strategists. For clearly, what was at stake was not the future of one man, but the principles of democratic government and, more seriously, whether the parliamentary game would continue to be so blatantly stacked against Labor. Indeed the assumption that Whitlam and his government were so unpopular that they would be voted out, regardless of the principles at stake, constituted the basis for John Kerr and the Liberals to proceed with their respective courses of action. Labor's strategists fell into this trap.

My view is that, unless compromise arrangements had been made, Labor should have refused to fight an election. There has never been an election in which the minority leader became Prime Minister prior to the election, as this is clearly unfair.[6] The consequences for the Australian people of such a refusal would have been to extend the legitimation crisis to the point of considerable disruption of the normal processes. However, the Labor Party could justifiably argue—and the majority of the people seemed to support this view—that it was the Liberals who had forced the disruption of the election process. Furthermore, it can be argued that the consequences of the Labor Party participating in the election, without at least securing the removal of Fraser as caretaker Prime Minister, were also severe: Labor gave de facto recognition and legitimacy to what had occurred, even though opposing it in rhetoric. By so doing, I believe that the Labor leaders not only set back their own party (as was shown by the result of the 1977 election), they also set back the cause of democratic change in Australia for many years.

The result of the election was a foregone conclusion. To many Australians, it appeared that there was only one way to restore social order and prevent the continuation of the constitutional upheavals, at least in the short term, and that was to vote Liberal. For if one voted Labor, what guarantee was there that the Liberals would meekly accept the result? If, as seemed likely, they remained in control of the Senate, who would prevent them blocking Supply again? The desire for political order and rational steering of the economy far outstripped the desire to vote in favour of an abstract defence of democracy. As many people argued, how could there be a threat to democracy if an election were being held?[7] This superficial view was reinforced by the Labor Party in participating in the election. The media argued that voting conservative was the only way to achieve stability and economic management.[8] The logical corollary of their argument was, of course, that there would always be trouble created for a reforming government, by a coalition of capitalist and conservative political forces. But why should one accept this state of affairs as legitimate? This was the question that remained unanswered after the events of 1975.[9]

However the restoration of 'legitimacy' was not secured simply as a result of the crushing victory of the conservative parties. For it left enormous division and bitterness in the nation amongst a substantial proportion of Labor voters. If a certain level of legitimacy had been achieved for the majority, to a substantial minority the election results merely proved the enormous power of the ruling class and their capacity to load and manipulate elections when it suited them. After the election the ruling class had state power, but the restoration of legimacy was far from complete.

Furthermore, counting against an early restoration of full legitimacy, was the creation of Whitlam as a *martyr* for the labour movement and large sections of the working class. For although he was loath to go beyond the boundaries of 'propriety' in his struggle, nevertheless Whitlam was seen by many as a man of great courage and fighting spirit in the way he sustained the election campaign which he knew he had little hope of winning.[10]

The conservative forces were aware, of course, of the

martyr image which they had created for Whitlam. Once the election was over, it became necessary not only to secure the legitimacy of the new government but to tarnish Whitlam's image. Two events were important in ensuring this: the proposed Iraqi grant to the Labor Party, and the private prosecution against Whitlam, Cairns, Connor and Murphy brought by Sydney solicitor Danny Sankey, which alleged that they had conspired to deceive the Governor-General in the loans affair. The Sankey prosecutions had considerable propaganda value and besmirched Labor's image: they were dismissed as groundless in February 1979.

The Iraqi grant (or loan) to the ALP, like the proposed loans to the Labor government, never materialized. It was an idea suggested by Bill Hartley to overcome the problem of funding for the election of 1975.[11] Laurie Oakes describes the situation at the time thus:

> By the time the December 13 election was decreed by the Governor-General the Liberal Party's campaign chest was overflowing. The party had more money than it could spend. Officials and candidates were boasting that 'we've got cash coming out of our ears'. The Liberal election budget ran to several million dollars. The Labor Party, on the other hand, was almost broke.[12]

Under these conditions and the pressure of the 'coup', Whitlam and the ALP's national secretary David Combe agreed to Hartley's suggestion that money be accepted from Arab countries, provided that there be no strings attached. At Hartley's prompting, Whitlam agreed to meet two Arab 'representatives', for breakfast at the home of an intermediary, Henry Fenscher. No discussions were made about money at this meeting. Yet Whitlam attended in the belief that half a million dollars would be forthcoming. It is unclear that any money would ever have come from Iraq. At any rate, the lengthy delay in the money coming through meant that the ALP could not pay its debts after the election. The story broke in the Melbourne *Sun* and in the Murdoch papers, the *Australian* and the *Daily Telegraph*. It soon transpired that Murdoch—whose press had carried out such a violently anti-Labor campaign during the election that his own journalists went on strike[13]—had been visited by Fenscher in London; the latter then disclosed the whole story. In the meantime, Fraser had been informed and began an investigation using the Commonwealth police.

Obviously this foolish act diminished Whitlam in people's esteem. Indeed he was fortunate to survive as ALP leader. He did so because the ALP resented being dictated to by Murdoch, and many people were outraged by Fraser's ill-considered use of the Commonwealth police. After all, as Oakes points out, early in 1975, Fraser himself had supported dubious means to raise Liberal funds from American multi-nationals.[14] Nevertheless Whitlam was severely censured by the Federal Executive of the ALP after a marathon three-day session.[15] Whitlam as martyr was besmirched, possibly forever, by this grave error. Although he survived, this humiliation put him into an introverted mood from which he hardly emerged in those final two years as ALP leader.

The most effective weapon that the conservatives had for entrenching their claim to legitimacy was, paradoxically, Sir John Kerr. Many Labor supporters felt that the constitutional 'coup' was primarily the act of one man and that he was deserving of contempt and should certainly not continue to hold the office of head of state.[16] Whitlam and his shadow cabinet contributed to this view. The result was that Kerr was subject to rowdy scenes and demonstrations wherever he went. He became a symbol of disunity and partisanship, alienated from nearly half of the Australian people.[17]

Besides any understanding that may have been made between the two men, I believe that Fraser kept Kerr on so long as Governor-General because it was in his political interest to do so. By directing the major focus of their anger at Kerr, Labor supporters lost a proper perspective on the situation. For clearly the active forces behind the 'coup', were the Liberal-NCP shadow cabinet and the capitalist interests which they represent. Kerr was merely a pawn. Yet Fraser was not satisfied with having used him in securing power, he needed him to bear the brunt of the blame. While he did so, he deflected attention from the question of the legitimacy of his government, which had grabbed power by such illegitimate means. Furthermore, Kerr became an alternative martyr figure to Whitlam. Thus, the media presented him as the poor suffering man who had done his duty and was now hounded by hoodlums and radicals.[18] The public humiliation which Kerr endured was very useful to the conservative parties. It deflected attention not only from their legitimacy, but from their policies as well. As such it meant that the incapacity of the Liberals to steer the economy did not become the major issue which the Labor Party should have made of it. The continuing presence of the constitutional crisis was assured by keeping Kerr on the scene. It provided an alternative focus for media attention. The demonstrations against Kerr—often represented by the media as violent— made it easier to obscure the constitutional violence which the conservative parties had employed in their power grab.

I shall speak in detail about Fraser's policies in the next section. One factor which was important, however, was Fraser's action to muzzle those few media outlets which were critical of him. Fraser expressed the view to confidantes that he wanted to 'take politics away from the front page'.[19] He did this in the following way:

(i) A closed government policy was adopted. Journalists were given little access to details; Fraser granted fewer interviews. Ministers were warned not to make statements on matters outside their portfolios.[20]

(ii) The public service was tightened up with respect to leaks of government documents. The conservatives had themselves used leaked documents effectively against Labor.

(iii) The access radio station 3ZZ was closed down by cutting off its funds—which were small. It had provided a useful forum for airing ideas and putting demands on the state. Its challenge to capitalist ideology was something the government would not wear.[21]

(iv) Restrictions on staff and money were imposed on the Australian Broadcasting Commission. The resulting strain finally caused some ABC workers to go on strike in 1978. (For more on the pressures on the ABC, see Chapter 5D.)

Hence, by these measures of hounding and continuously smearing Whitlam, deflecting criticism on to Sir John Kerr, and intimidating the media (on those occasions when it is critical), the ruling class managed to deflect attention from the legitimacy issue. The legitimation crisis of 1975 was thus gradually defused. However, the economic crisis, which had provided the rationale for many of the Liberals' actions, was predictably not resolved when they came into government. Indeed, as they applied the accepted remedies of cutbacks in the public sector, together with massive redistribution of state moneys to capitalists, the crisis deepened and intensified. As we shall see in the next section, the measures adopted by Fraser had little impact, except in achieving a temporary reduction in inflation. Investment, growth and employment were all down. So were real wages. The economic crisis continued and the level of unemployment reached alarming levels which would have been totally unacceptable to Australians during the 1950s and 1960s.

This raises a puzzle about the general election of 1977. If, in 1975, people had voted against Labor because of their handling of the economy, why did they not vote against the Liberals whose performance had been equally dismal, although their methods were very different? If people vote on the basis of an assessment of their economic future, how is it that they voted for the Liberals once again, since the economic situation—by all indicators except inflation—had deteriorated? Most people expected that, though Labor would not win, they would capture many of the seats which they had lost in the disastrous 1975 landslide against them. Yet Fraser virtually maintained his record majority.

Various theories were proposed to explain these events: for example, that the Australian people are conservative and although they may be concerned about the economic situation, they will not vote for a party which represents reform and change; or that the Australian people are materialistic—they support governments which promise them more goods and services. Taking these two together, the following thesis arises: the Australian people want more money to buy more goods and services, but they want to achieve this without upsetting the traditional arrangements within economy and social structure. Each wants a larger share of a cake which is to be cut up in accordance with the rules determined by the present hierarchical system. Each believes that those who strive harder will be, and ought to be, rewarded accordingly.

The best way, the argument goes, to appeal to such a set of people is to offer them a short term material benefit, within the present structure. Thus Fraser offered a reduction in income tax, specifically structured so that those who earned the most received the biggest reduction, while those who were on the minimum wage received $3 per week. This offer had a twofold appeal: it offered a material reward to everyone and yet it reaffirmed the principle that those who were in a position to earn more ought to receive a much more generous tax cut than those who earned less. It therefore reinforced Fraser's view that inequality in wealth and income is based on inequality in worth. Under the guidance of political scientist David Kemp—who claims to have established that Australians hold the above attitudes and vote accordingly[22]—Fraser consciously framed his policy to appeal to the 'middle class' using these tax cuts. Within less than one year, however, these tax cuts were removed; Fraser needed the money to prop up the profitability of inefficient Australian private enterprises. The 'middle class' was fooled again.

Fraser was helped rather than hindered by the ALP. Gough Whitlam, reduced to a pale shadow of his previous self, announced a disastrous economic policy for the election:

to take away the proposed reductions in income tax and to use the money saved to cut payroll tax (a charge carried by employers for each employee). Whitlam's argument was that, if payroll tax on employers were removed, they would increase investment and employ more people. It was economic nonsense—for what was to guarantee that the money saved by employers would be spent on investment and expansion? There was good evidence that it would simply be used to increase dividends to shareholders, or to invest overseas, or to replace workers by machines. Coming from the Labor Party it was ideologically incoherent. It placed Fraser in the absurd situation of being able to accuse Whitlam of taking money away from workers and putting it into the hands of capitalists! Of equal seriousness was the fact that the policy had been decided without consulting the Labor Party rank-and-file, or the economic committee of the party.[23]

Yet Labor could have offered a just and egalitarian policy on the tax cuts. It could have agreed to cut taxes to the same degree as the Liberals while distributing the burden more in favour of the poorer sections of the community. Thus Whitlam could have offered to cut everyone's taxes by an equal amount. This would have meant that the rich would have received proportionately less, while the poor received more. Alternatively, the increased state receipts could have been used to create more employment in government sponsored or owned productive industries. It would have been consistent with Labor's philosophy and would have permitted the party to attack Fraser for his support of vested interests and the wealthy. But it did not happen.

Was it simply Fraser's focus on materialism and conservatism which won him another huge victory? There is something wrong with this explanation. The actual campaign carried out by the Liberals employed the slogan 'Memories' —and used this to create a picture of the Whitlam years as chaos and disorder. They brought up Cairns, Connor, the Gair affair, etc.—all of which were well and truly in the past. The impression they wanted to create was that the Labor

Party was still incapable of steering the economy and, more seriously, that periods of Labor rule were bound to result in turbulence and disorder for the economic and social structures. In other words, they raised once again the question as to whether Labor had a legitimate claim to rule. The 'respectability' of the Labor Party, lost in the dying days of the Labor government, was thus difficult to regain—even with the most blatantly pro-capitalist and absurdly anti-labour policy.

The victory of the conservative forces was never so complete as in the election of 1977. They had seized state power through 'manipulation of the constitution', to use Whitlam's terms.[24] They had confronted the labour forces and these had retreated in a rout. They now called the tune as to what conditions the Labor Party must satisfy if it is to be considered a respectable alternative. In attempting to meet these conditions, the party abandoned any semblance of a radical programme—except on uranium policy. The ALP, by its inability to confront the simple fact that the struggle for power is, and must be, carried on at all levels of society and not just in parliament, has had to accept extraordinary humiliations. In its desperate attempts to appear more and more moderate, so as to be acceptable to the ruling class and their media, it has sacrificed basic principles and lost much of its soul (see next section). The conservative forces thus not only restored legitimacy, but re-established their domination —with a vengeance.

C FRASER'S STRATEGY AND THE CONTINUING ECONOMIC AND SOCIAL CRISES

While the threat to state legitimacy receded with the crushing victory of the conservatives in 1977, the economic crisis continues and has intensified—bringing a socio-cultural crisis in its wake. Fraser's own actions as Prime Minister, far from resolving this crisis, have exacerbated it. The material and spiritual sufferings of the Australian people have reached levels unknown since the days of the Great Depression. Yet

Fraser remains firmly entrenched in political power; company profits increase daily through his actions and yet the great majority of the Australian people are confused and ineffectual in opposition to those actions.

How is this remarkable feat achieved? In my discussion of Fraser's philosophy in Chapter 5C I demonstrated that he —more than any previous Liberal leader—has a commitment to the moral superiority of the ruling class, particularly the business sector. To Fraser, capitalists are generally individuals with initiative and skill who possess what they have as a reward for their own labours and capacities. Yet, as I have already indicated, Fraser also believes that these individuals and corporations are subject to unfair pressures, coming from two sources: foolish social welfarist governments which are too eager 'to meet the wishes and aspirations of their constituents' and hence expand the public sector, using heavy taxes on the private sector to pay for them (in periods of little growth, this can seriously affect company profits, resulting in cutbacks in investment and other economic ills); and power-hungry union leaders leading greedy unions who seek to grab more than their 'fair share' of the national cake by use of industrial muscle. He sees employers as relatively powerless in the face of such union forces. Hence they are often forced to concede wages and conditions which seriously impair their profitability and their capacity to compete in the local and international markets.

Fraser's belief is that capitalist forces, which normally would do very well on their own, must be protected from these pressures. There is a simple strategy for doing this: the conservatives must seize state power, they must cut back on social welfare and services as much as possible. The gains made in state moneys can then either be handed back to companies in the form of tax cuts or, more cleverly, be used to regulate investment and the structure of the economy through allowances and subsidies.[1] Thus Fraser does not believe in the 'hands off free enterprise' theory. He believes rather in regulating it to some degree, in protecting it from its enemies and in actively boosting profitability through the use of funds from general taxation.

> The total transfer of wealth from the workers to the corporations in the past 2 years approximates $4 BILLION. Therefore government spending on social services, pensions, health, schools, public transport, community services and the like, are being slashed. A large part of the savings are going on government grants, tax exemptions, investment allowances for companies. This was being carried out under the slogan 'that government expenditure causes inflation'.[2]

Of course, the tremendous human consequences of the cutbacks, which will be discussed further below, must be rationalized. Peter Tiver, writing on Fraser's philosophy, gives such an argument:

> An essential condition of . . . freedom was the possession of the material and social requisites for self-fulfilment. But welfare policy still must be seen as part of a general approach towards the creation and distribution of wealth; it must recognize the intimate connection between a healthy free enterprise and a soundly based welfare policy. Unless the policy of assistance to those in need were pursued simultaneously with policies designed to encourage achievement, the poorer members of society would suffer most.[3]

The Fraser budget of 1978 is an excellent example of this strategy. After granting temporary tax relief in 1977, the Liberals imposed a new tax burden on all workers (there were no increases in company taxes). The total Federal budget was not cut—as some have claimed—but the services in welfare and education were reduced. The health insurance scheme, Medibank, was replaced by a voluntary one. The savings to state income were then redistributed to companies in the form of allowances, which were designed to prop up profitability and encourage investment.[4] That this battery of measures was designed to benefit the capitalist forces was clearly shown when the stock market index rose dramatically immediately after the budget. The loss of support for his government, as measured by opinion polls, was nevertheless heavy as a consequence of this so-called 'horror budget'.[5] Opposition leader Hayden exclaimed that Fraser was robbing the poor to reward the rich.[6]

In the meantime, the dramatic increase in unemployment placed many members of the working class in a less powerful position *vis-a-vis* their employers and the Liberal government. Fears for job security led to a dramatic decrease in the turnover of labour—from 8.2 per cent in 1971 to 5.3 per cent in 1976 (for blue-collar workers).[7] Similarly, absenteeism has declined as people are afraid to take time off work. Keith Windschuttle concludes that

> Overall, the threat of unemployment has allowed employers to increase their discipline over labour. They have been able to impose more demanding conditions on the workforce. The results show in figures for productivity. Those who have retained their jobs have produced more per head per year, that is, productivity has increased during the recession.[8]

Furthermore, since their election, the L-NCP government has acted to cut real money wages through tough representations to the Arbitration Commission. Wage indexation has been a mixed blessing in this context. On the one hand, it has prevented the government from forcing through drastic wage cuts. The Commission Chairman, Sir John Moore, has been active in attempting to sustain workers' real purchasing power—although he has not always been successful. On the other hand, there have been three adverse consequences of wage indexation. Firstly, real wage levels have been reduced and so has labour's share of the national income.[9] As Windschuttle puts it:

> Plateau indexation began in May 1976 and by the
> December quarter of 1976 . . . had reduced real wages
> by 1.9 per cent. Between May 1976 and March 1978,
> the consumer price index rose by percentage increases
> which totalled 24.0 percentage points. For workers on
> the lowest wage levels, the indexed increases
> amounted to 21.6 percentage points gain, which
> represented a loss of 2.4 percentage points. For
> workers on average and higher wages, the losses in
> real terms were considerably more.[10]

Secondly, as we saw in Chapter 6D, there was (till the middle of 1979) a dramatic decline in the militancy of workers. This decline in the number of strikes is not primarily due to satisfaction with present functioning of the indexation system. Rather the major factor seems to be the fear of insecurity and unemployment. There is now more respect for the power of the employer. Thirdly, the introduction of six-monthly, instead of quarterly, indexation means that workers' living standards are even further reduced than is indicated in the figures. For many price rises occur in the few weeks following any indexation case and workers have to wait for six months to make up the balance. Clearly, then, wage indexation is at best a defensive policy which prevents further erosion in the standard of living of the people.

But the Fraser government's wages policies have not been restricted to working within the Arbitration Commission. Rather they have sought to attack the unions and other radical movements directly. There are several techniques that have been used here.

(i) There has been a sustained propaganda campaign to blame wage increases for the rising unemployment. Fraser's two Treasurers, Lynch and Howard, both made this claim repeatedly in radio and television interviews.[11] In 1977, when unemployment increased, front-page prominence was given to Employment Minister Tony Street's claims that 'high wages' had caused it.[12]

(ii) Fraser has taken strong action to crush militant unions when they have dared to press workers' rights. He has pressurized and even blackmailed companies and state governments to stand firm against increases. The most important case here was the October 1977 dispute in the La Trobe Valley power station between workers and the Victorian State Electricity Commission. The State and Federal Liberal governments allowed hundreds of thousands of other workers to be stood down rather than offer even a reasonable compromise to the La Trobe Valley people. In addition, Fraser attempted to prevent the workers who had been stood down being paid unemployment benefits. This callous action was an attempt to force a sizeable section of the working class to suffer for the militancy of a few of their number. The ruling class showed remarkable solidarity here. The media joined in with fulminations against the strikers. In the end, they were broken and had to return to work with few concrete gains.

(iii) The Fraser government established the controversial Industrial Relations Bureau, to regulate the affairs of unions, including the election of union officials and to penalize unions which contravene judgements of the Arbitration Commission.[13] Penalties here include de-registration of the union and fines for union leaders.

(iv) The Liberals introduced legislation enabling them to lay off public servants affected by strikes in other sectors of the state or private economy. The legislation also enables them to dismiss public servants who disobey orders, that is, who follow union directions on work bans and go-slows.[14]

Fraser has carried out these anti-labour actions to boost the capitalist forces. Unlike Whitlam, Fraser recognizes that one cannot redistribute too many resources from the private to the public sector, without endangering the structure of capitalist economy itself. However, for all its logic, Fraser's strategy has been a serious failure, except temporarily in the area of inflation control. The crisis in Australian economy and society continues unabated. For, although it has boosted profitability for large capitalist companies, it has not overcome the recession and stagnation. Unemployment has reached alarming proportions and is predicted to go even higher.[15]

I have explained the reasons for this economic failure in Chapters 3A and 3B. On the surface, Fraser claims allegiance to the monetarist solutions of Milton Friedman, that is, that cuts in government social welfare spending will defeat inflation and strengthen profitability. Yet this is not achieving new investment and growth in manufacturing and tertiary sectors. Nor is it achieving any reduction in unemployment. Except for mining, the new profits are either distributed to shareholders or are used to invest overseas. Meanwhile the suffering of large sections of the Australian people becomes more acute. The social crisis continues and is reinforced by the serious problems of the large army of unemployed.

As the crisis has continued, the remarkable unity which Fraser was able to achieve within Liberal Party ranks has begun to crack. Of course, it is easier for a Liberal leader to achieve unity within the government itself, since he appoints all ministers. They are not elected by the Liberal parliamentarians. Because they know that he can dismiss them, they are more easily disciplined and controlled by the Liberal leader. Furthermore, in appointing the cabinet, he can pick men who are philosophically of his own ilk. Thus, when Fraser was elected, his cabinet consisted mostly of MPs loyal to his conservative perspective. There were, however, several exceptions; persons who were esteemed so highly within the parliamentary party that he could not afford to exclude them. These included Jim Killen (Defence), Andrew Peacock (Foreign Affairs) and Margaret Guilfoyle (Social Security). Significantly, during 1978, Fraser held informal meetings of the cabinet from which these three were excluded. However, after signs of considerable unrest, he gave up this practice.

It is clear that whatever philosophical disagreements arise within the cabinet, these are not of a serious nature while Fraser dominates it. However, there was a serious conflict between Fraser and former minister Don Chipp, which could well have some important further repercussions. Chipp was part of the Liberal cabinet sworn in as the caretaker government. In 1975, after the December election, however, Chipp was unceremoniously dropped from the ministry. The reason was clear: Fraser had no time for Chipp's trendy liberalism and his 'concern' for the disadvantaged.[16] He had to push through a series of tough anti-welfare measures and Chipp was not the man to do it.

As Fraser moved to the right, Chipp—rather than languish on the backbenches—left the Liberal Party and established a new 'centre' party, the Australian Democrats. They are supposedly committed to true liberal principles, opposing both socialism and conservatism. Although the party gained a substantial proportion of the vote in the 1977 election (Chipp was elected to the Senate), nevertheless their impact on Fraser's policies have so far been negligible.[17] Fraser has shown a determination not to move to the so-called middle ground. So far this has paid off. However, it will be interesting to see what happens to Australian Democrat votes if, as seems likely, both the Liberal and Labor Parties adopt a more moderate image.

Another area in which some opposition has arisen to Fraser's tactics has been amongst some backbench liberal social welfarist MPs. Rumblings have developed over the savagery of the cuts, particularly where they have affected the old and the sick. Thus in February 1979, backbencher Bruce Goodluck attempted to modify the law which gave pensioners an indexed rise only once a year, instead of every six months. Fraser responded by crushing Goodluck both in the party room and the parliament. This was a considerable factor in the resignation of Finance Minister Eric Robinson who was clearly unhappy with Fraser's authoritarian tactics. Robinson was, however, persuaded to rejoin the ministry before his resignation could do any damage to Fraser.[18]

The major changes within the Fraser Liberal government have, however, been due to scandals and malpractices, rather than philosophical differences. As one would expect, the media have tried their hardest to play down these 'scandals' and only the persistent efforts of the Labor opposition have ensured that they surface. The result has been, however, that the Federal Labor Party gained an image as a 'muck-raker'. There are three such scandals worthy of mention. One is Deputy Leader Phillip Lynch's involvement in family trusts and property deals, which led Fraser to remove him as Treasurer just before the December 1977 election. The second occurred when Fraser was forced to dismiss Senator Reg Withers from the ministry after a Royal Commission suggested that he had acted improperly in the Federal electoral redistribution of a Queensland seat.[19] Both Lynch and Withers were central figures in Fraser's actions to bring down the Whitlam government. Lynch appears to have forgiven Fraser for his action, but Withers poses a potential threat—disenchanted Liberals may well organize around him. Furthermore, Ian Sinclair, deputy leader of the National Country Party, has been the focus of a New South Wales inquiry into his business affairs, and in September 1979 he resigned as Minister following serious allegations in the report on this inquiry. Significantly, Fraser supported him strongly, before and after his resignation.

Notwithstanding what some critics have said about Fraser, generally speaking he has stood by his own men. Even in the cases of Lynch and Withers, he acted because he was forced to, but not because of the pressure from the Labor Party. Unlike Whitlam, Fraser will not allow the media or the Opposition to determine whether he should act against a minister. If the minister supports his views, Fraser can show admirable solidarity with him. It would be another story, however, if a scandal should break around the head of Killen or Peacock.

In March 1979, Opposition leader Hayden made public

statements forecasting the demise of Fraser and the rise of Peacock as leader.[20] This seems to me wishful thinking; after all, Fraser still has time in which to shift from his extremist image to a more moderate one. Given that the media are very likely to co-operate in every way with such a change, I cannot see that the Liberals will drop such a tough leader, who has proved himself a winner for the party and the ruling class generally. However, even if Fraser were to persist in being so inflexible that he would lose the leadership, what is to be gained for the working class in such a change? Is Peacock as liberal and moderate as he pretends? As Tiver puts it:

> Peacock's credentials for his small 'l' liberalism are unconvincing. He would be better called a moderate, if not a liberal conservative. Peacock's view of liberalism was that liberal principles and ideals remain constant, but that their language, and application to issues, changes. Peacock's position on most issues is not different from that of most in his party, including those often thought of as 'conservatives' . . . The illusion of a 'new' liberalism is created by stating that Liberals do not disagree with many of Labor's ideals, and then putting the qualifying objection in softer tones than other Liberals and by saying that Liberals are concerned for 'people'.[21]

It is unlikely, then, that if Peacock were to become leader, he would handle the crisis very differently from Fraser. He may be more sensitive to some of the human consequences of his actions, but it is unlikely that he will be able to take any but the most cosmetic steps to relieve them.

With the conservatives firmly entrenched in state power under Fraser, yet being increasingly perceived as incapable of resolving the crisis, one might expect an enormous swing in support to the Labor Party. Although opinion polls show the ALP ahead,[22] it is not a very substantial lead, given the depth of the crisis and the clear inability of the conservatives to steer the economy out of it.

Given the above, it would be easy to argue that the Labor Party is still not accepted as a valid alternative, since it is perceived as 'too radical' by the people.[23] This, however, is a misleading representation. After all, as I mentioned in Chapter 6C, the ALP, under Bill Hayden as leader, is widely perceived as having moved to the 'right'. This perception is backed up by several pronouncements from Hayden and other shadow ministers. Thus in 1978 and early 1979, Hayden made a series of statements which indicate a substantial acceptance of the major aspects of the capitalist economy.[24] For example, Hayden had called for 'wage restraint', an exchange of 'tax cuts for wage cuts'. This seems to be a change, not only from traditional labour principles, but from Whitlam's concern for the underprivileged. More seriously, it seemed to be embracing Fraser's theory that increased profits will automatically result in increased Australian investment and soak up unemployment. In this context, it is significant that Hayden has few plans for new public enterprises to increase employment.

Why, then, have the media and the ruling class been slow to accord the Opposition full legitimacy and respectability? The reason lies with the fact that, while Hayden and most of the parliamentary party are moderates who pose little threat to the ruling class, it is becoming clear that these leaders do not reflect the views of the rank-and-file of the party and its union base. This can be shown by the results on the ALPs National Inquiry, which was held to examine all aspects of Labor policy following the 1977 election defeat.[25] Several of these policy documents, particularly that dealing with economic strategy (which argued for nationalization and more public enterprise), were much more radical than positions adopted by the parliamentary leaders.

Given this situation, there is widespread suspicion in the ruling class that the socialists are making a resurgence and that Hayden will be too weak to handle them. In its edition of 13 March 1979, the *Bulletin* ran a cover story on Hayden in which the leader is praised, except for nagging doubts about his weakness.[26] Thus, in that same edition, Alan Reid claims that Hayden 'was being pressurized by the Socialist Left and what is being described as the trendy elements within the ALP into a position that would assist the Socialist Left in its aim to capture national control of the party'.[27] Such remarks have the net effect of frightening those sections of the ruling class which are well disposed to Hayden from open support of the party. They may also act to reduce ALP support from 'centrist middle class' voters.

Yet, while clearly the present leadership is too right-wing to be representative of the ALP as a whole, this does not mean that the socialists are in control. On the contrary, several members of parliament who previously were considered 'centrists' or 'moderates' are now labelled by the media as extremists. Thus, for example, Reid claims that the Socialist Left forces are now orchestrated by former Victorian Opposition leader, Clyde Holding—previously considered a centrist. The above suggests that the media are attempting to prevent even a moderate radicalism arising within the Labor Party, never mind any ascendancy for genuine socialism. Clearly Hayden is being offered the mantle of legitimacy, if he can show that he can keep such radical elements under control and prevent their appearance in parliament.

However, there is a serious problem for the ALP and Hayden in pursuing such a strategy. What if the Liberals move to the centre prior to the next election? This would involve adopting several Keynesian-type policies on economic expansion, which Hayden is advocating.[28] Under these circumstances, Labor may suffer the same drawback as in 1977. They could be reduced to the slogan 'me too'. If such a convergence of the two parties occurs, not only will this be a further nail in the coffin of Australian democratic practice, it will also mean that the Labor Party will be defeated (unless, as seems unlikely, powerful sections of the ruling class switch to Hayden). For if the people are offered a choice between two parties with substantially the same policies, why should they vote Labor, given the nagging doubts as to where the ALP really stands?

I do not believe, however, that radical sections of the Labor Party will sit back and allow the above disastrous developments to occur unchallenged. There is already growing disquiet about this general approach. We may see a resurgence of the authority of the party's rank-and-file, and the unions, over the 'conservative' parliamentary wing. It is possible, also, that Hayden may come to recognize that only a more radical strategy allows for a way out of the economic morass. In this respect, Hayden's strong support for a capital gains tax must be considered a major progressive development. A wealth tax has also been proposed to finance social programmes for the poor and underprivileged. Hayden said in March 1979:

> If resources cannot be found through growth then they must be diverted away from those who have them in overabundance and directed to the fulfilment of urgent human needs.[29]

Significantly, this is the only major ALP policy—besides uranium mining—which the Liberals have strongly attacked. A tax on the wealthy is a step in the right direction. However it is a long way from a full-scale programme to transform the capitalist economy, and create new public enterprises and a new sense of democratic participation in the people.

Epilogue:
Long-term Responses to Crisis

I have argued up to this stage that the economic crisis inherent in advanced Western society cannot be resolved by the short term measures which have been introduced by the Liberal and Labor parties. Nor can the crisis in social structure be resolved by attempts to hide social problems away. Furthermore, the economy does not appear to be achieving any kind of sustained recovery—unemployment continues at record levels, and the prospects for change are bleak. Demand throughout 1979 has been sluggish.

Does all this mean that the reproduction of culture and hegemony of the dominant beliefs and practices are not as guaranteed as they initially appear? Can we, with Habermas, confidently predict the continuation of crisis until substantial changes in the economic and political systems are undertaken?[1] Many would reject this idea. After all, is it not the continuation of materialism, combined with a desire for stable social order and a strengthening of traditional social structures, which is used to explain the results of the 1975 and 1977 elections? Surely this conservatism and materialism are the bed-rock evidence that society has continued to reproduce itself as before?

In Chapters 4 and 5A I have given theoretical and empirical arguments against this view. I shall not repeat these here; I shall merely emphasize the main point that, when people begin to think of the system as less meaningful, they have less work motivation, or demand more goods and services in its absence. Work motivation varies in accordance with the level of meaningfulness in the social identity of people. If this is correct, the economy's performance depends not just on the steering of the state, but also on the extent to which meaningful social identity is secured.

Furthermore, I have argued (following Habermas) that the

375

state cannot by legislation or executive fiat create a new identity for people and give them a new meaning to life (see Chapter 6A). It can, of course, focus on the principles of democracy, which are the basis of legitimacy. It could thus motivate people by appealing to notions such as the common good, the general will and so forth. However, as we saw, there are inherent dangers in this. For it cannot allow unlimited democratization, in the sense of equality, participation and complete rights for all—for then challenges to the unequal and non-participatory character of the structure of both economy and the state would arise.[2]

Indeed, I argued that the democratic ideal is such an embarrassment for the modern state that it attempts to move its legitimating philosophy away from that ideal. Thus the principles of participation are quickly disappearing from even official accounts of democracy, in favour of theories of democratic elitism, supposedly based on 'realistic' concepts of man. This however raises an important problem: if the above account of democracy as given by people such as Michels, Schumpeter, Peter Bachrach and others,[3] can become the dominant ideology, can it not be used to legitimate the system during economic and social crises? Since, as we saw in Chapter 6A, under these circumstances the state is placed under greater pressure to legitimate itself, what is to prevent it moving away from democratic principles, in everything but name? Could legitimacy not be maintained under an authoritarian regime which, while formally committed to democracy, systematically denies basic rights and crushes opposition from workers and intellectuals? Habermas believes that this scenario is unlikely;[4] however I think there are good reasons for supposing this to be one of the possible long term responses to the continuing crisis.

What would a pessimistic scenario look like in Australia? We have an image of such a regime if we look at the government of Queensland under Bjelke-Petersen. This regime is characterized thus: a continuous appeal to democratic principles and the defence of the democratic system masks an attack on the basic features of democracy.[5] In practice, this regime undermines the following democratic principles:

(i) *Equality in political participation* The gerrymander in Queensland is notorious. Its impact is to ensure not only the success of the conservative parties in Queensland, but that Bjelke-Petersen's party dominates in the coalition. This latter party imposes on its coalition partners a policy of authoritarian oppression.

(ii) *Equality before the law* Although this theoretically exists in Queensland, the rough justice meted out to the Aboriginal people of that State is encouraged by the racist policies of the Premier. Rather than act to end unequal treatment of Aborigines, the State government has indirectly encouraged it.[6]

(iii) *Civil rights* The right of assembly, when that assembly is engaged in a peaceful political protest, has been removed. Throughout 1977–79 violent scenes occurred in Brisbane when the police were ordered to break up political marches.[7] The fact that this fundamental democratic right is destroyed without a popular uprising is a bad omen for the future of Australian democracy.

(iv) *Attacks on workers and their unions* The State government seeks to introduce laws to further tame the unions and make them subservient to whatever manipulation is required to ensure profits for multi-national companies. Bjelke-Petersen tries to represent unions, which in Australia are not very militant, as the cause of the nation's ills. This exercise is itself instructive—he manages to distract attention from his own authoritarian actions by making workers, and their organizations, the scapegoats.[8]

These and other anti-democratic features of the Queensland government give rise to the following question: could the whole of Australia move in this direction? What is to prevent the imposition of more authoritarian regimes who, in their anxiety to resolve the economic crisis, crack down hard on workers' demands and organizations, and increasingly reduce civil liberties? Such an authoritarian response would allow a threatened capitalist economy to redistribute resources to capital, at the expense of the people, who would increasingly bear the burdens. In order to ensure that the inevitable protests from workers, students, and intellectuals were muted, the government could probably: increase attacks on militant unions, by confiscating their finances and jailing their leaders; ban demonstrations and ensure that all 'illegal' protests are met with massive police force; move to exclude radical students and intellectuals from universities and colleges; place restrictions on the media in their presentation of alternative viewpoints (to the extent that the media would not go along with this voluntarily).

Such actions and others would, I regret to say, receive vocal support and acclamation by a substantial minority of the Australian people.[9] Many others, while not supporting them, would nevertheless accept them as actions by the 'legitimate' authority. It is far from inconceivable that one long-term consequence of the current economic crisis may be for Australia to become an illiberal, authoritarian society in which the people are repressed and the nation's resources are plundered by foreign capitalists.

Yet there are factors counting against it. Firstly, and paradoxically, there is the Federal system of government itself. Although the Federal government's powers have increased, there are still many powers which are invested in the six State governments. These powers can frustrate any attempt to impose a single authoritarian regime from Canberra. (Of course, they can also frustrate any attempt to transform the capitalist economy by use of the powers of the Federal government alone.)[10] Thus while a more authoritarian central government is a possibility (perhaps even a probability), it may find its actions frustrated by 'liberal' State governments—including moderate ALP governments.[11]

Yet a determined central government could set out to destroy such opposition in the States. It could do this by a variety of manoeuvres, including starving the State government of funds. However, there are limits as to how far this can go without requiring the use of armed force to secure obedience. While this last move cannot be entirely ruled out, it seems unlikely, since it would undermine even the formal democratic legitimacy of the state. Yet the ultimate guarantee against such an authoritarian response is a strong alliance between genuine liberals and socialists. Every invasion of the right to assemble, strike, demonstrate, express one's views, etc., must be strongly defended. Otherwise the capitalist forces which are not averse to using authoritarian means will be emboldened.

The above considerations lead me to the second possible long term response. The conservative forces are unable to impose an authoritarian order, to resolve the economic crisis. The labour forces are unable to achieve a transformation of the economy to a socialist one. A stalemate ensues—yet the economic and social crisis continues and deepens. The result is a series of political crises: governments are changed frequently, the electorate is more volatile and party loyalties much less reliable. Thus the following cycle is established: the Liberals are elected, intervene to redistribute resources to capital, but unemployment and low investment continue. Labor is then elected, intervenes to increase workers' incomes and achieve some increase in demand, but inflation soars and unemployment does not significantly increase. There is evidence that this is already happening.[12] What is to prevent this continuing indefinitely? After all, the people can became accustomed to lower expectations and greater economic insecurity.

While this is so, there are two further problems with this scenario. Firstly, Australia's mining resources—'the backbone of the country'—are being speedily exploited at the expense of its people. But they cannot last indefinitely.[13] As they become exhausted, what interest will foreign capital have in Australia? Why should it invest in manufacturing here, when it can move its capital to Third World countries in which labour is disciplined by authoritarian power? It will either remove its interests from Australia, or seek to make Australian manufacturing more 'competitive' by cutting real wages and living standards.[14] Its capacity to do the latter is, however, limited unless it imposes the authoritarian scenario discussed above.

There is a second, socio-cultural factor. It is easy to say that people will come to accept a continuing economic crisis if this persists for some time. However, if this crisis is threatening their capacity to fulfil their material expectations then a new set of values must be inculcated, based on a meaningful social identity. But the state will be unable to supply such meaning by appeal to democratic practices—for these will by then have been perceived to have failed in the resolution of crisis. Thus the state must either turn to the authoritarian response or it must encourage more liberalization and more democratization. However, if it does the latter, people's demands for a more equitable and less exploitative economic order will grow exponentially.

This leads me to the third long term response: a new form of democratic socialism, which I shall term 'participatory socialism'. Although this is an optimistic perspective, I believe it is the only rational and practicable path out of crisis available to a modern Western society. The ideal here is not unknown in Australia, indeed it has been occasionally adopted by sectors of the ALP in its radical moments, such as at its 1919 Conference.[15] The early radicals understood that a coherent strategy requires a merging of democratic principles with socialist ones. Contrary to propaganda by conservatives, this union is both rational and desirable.

What would be involved in this simultaneous democratization and socialization? Firstly, there must be the progressive transfer of more and more of the productive sector of the economy from the private sphere to the public one.[16] Secondly and simultaneously, these public enterprises must be run by democratic committees, elected by the workers in those enterprises and responsive to the needs of those workers. Thirdly, the national parliament should elect a council to co-ordinate the activities of the various public enterprises. This council would ensure that, contrary to the present system, the goods and services which people need the most are the ones provided. It would also establish new productive enterprises so as to put people back to work. Fourthly, while some differentials in income for different skills would remain, the amount of total wealth which an individual can accumulate would be limited. Each person would still have personal property (such as his house, his car, his furniture, etc.) but the gap between the rich and the poor would be narrowed. Most workers would benefit economically, although some wealthy people would lose out. Finally, there would be free social services for all who need them: health, education, recreation facilities would be vastly improved. The arts and culture would be promoted. This is not a utopian vision. A rich country like Australia can afford to provide all these basic needs and services for all its people.

It may now be inquired: by what process would such a transformation take place? Here the role of the state is crucial. I have argued that the state is not a mere superstructure and that the control of the state is extremely important to capitalist forces, for they need it to prop up the ailing economic system.[17] Thus the political struggle for the control of the state is not an irrelevancy; the class struggle has moved to the realm of the state itself.

A socialist movement must seek to extend and encourage democratic practices. It must try to ensure that the state extends and deepens its democratic foundations. Why must it do this? Because, as I have shown and as conservatives have long recognized, the democratic ideal provides the legitimation of the whole system—and it is necessary to sustain this legitimacy in the process of transition from capitalism to socialism. For if we seek to radically change society, without achieving a legitimized democratic approval from the people for such a change, we risk a massive reaction based on fear and ignorance. We create what I call a legitimation *vacuum*— and in this vacuum people will feel their whole social identity, their whole social being, threatened by the changes which are taking place.[18]

All this, it might be objected, is too naive, for all the forces of the ruling class would ensure that such a radical party would never gain government—and even if it did, that it would be swiftly overthrown. I accept that it is extremely difficult for socialists to gain formal control of the state and to exercise real power, that is, to implement policies intended to transform the capitalist system. Nevertheless I do not accept the orthodox Marxian thesis that the state, and real political power, is necessarily in the hands of the capitalists.[19] I believe that it is possible for socialists to gain and exercise real power, provided that they have a strategy whereby they can counter the attacks of the capitalists—economic, political and within the media; and provided that they have educated the working people of the nation into the view that their real interests lie with socialism, and can then turn to the people for help should attempts be made to unconstitutionally remove them from power. This is not to say that such a struggle may not eventually lead to a revolutionary upheaval. But the labour forces should not resort to such means unless and until the conservative forces try to seize power by non-democratic, illegitimate means. In Australia it is not self-evident that they would do this. Certainly, if they abandon all pretence of democratic legitimacy, it is not clear that they would succeed.

Which of the above three responses is the most likely scenario given the continuing economic and social crisis which Australia faces? It depends on the strength of democratic practice and the extent to which the Australian people will continue to tolerate an increasingly meaningless and repressive life-cycle on the one hand, and governments which offer no genuine and just solutions on the other. I leave that to the reader to estimate.

Notes

Where only an author's name and year are listed, e.g. Frankel 1978, *see* Bibliography *for further details.*

Prologue

[1] As well as Robinson 1978 and Windschuttle 1979 there have been several other works on the Australian crisis, including *The Political Process, Can It Cope?* (Australian Institute of Political Science, 1978). On Western society generally, there has been a plethora of books, including Habermas 1973 and Carroll 1977. A recent work of considerable significance is Mandel 1978.

[2] Robinson 1978, p. 3.

[3] Windschuttle 1979, p. 3.

[4] The major work of Habermas here is *Legitimation Crisis*. Other important works of his are *Knowledge and Human Interest* (Beacon, Boston, Mass., 1968) and *Towards A Rational Society* (Beacon).

1A   The democratic ideal: Rousseau

[1] See, for example, Horne 1976, ch. 9.

[2] See *Kerr and the Consequences* (Widescope, Melbourne 1977), p. 16. See also the speeches in support of these resolutions.

[3] ibid., p. 16.

[4] Quoted and discussed in Sartori 1965, pp. 26–7. For a good discussion of the philosophical justifications for democracy, see S. I. Benn & R. S. Peters, *Social Principles and the Democratic*

State (Allen & Unwin, London, 1973), especially part I.

5 For a historical account of the development of democratic thought, see Charles M. Sherover (ed.), *The Development of the Democratic Idea* (Mentor, 1968).

6 For an eloquent statement of the principle of equality, see Sydney Hook's essay in Sherover, ibid., pp. 504ff. See also Sartori 1965, ch. XIV.

7 See Immanuel Kant, *Critique of Practical Reason* (tr. T. K. Abbott, Longman, London, 1909). See R. S. Downie & E. Telfer, *Respect for Persons* (Allen & Unwin, 1969), particularly chs 4, 5 for a discussion of the inner meaning of this principle in modern philosophy.

8 Rousseau 1958, p. 54. Rousseau lived from 1712 to 1778.

9 Rousseau, *Discourse on the Origins of Inequality in Mankind*, in *The Social Contract and Discourses* (Everyman's Library, London, 1973), p. 76.

10 ibid., p. 87.

11 ibid., p. 89.

12 Rousseau 1958, p. 60.

13 ibid., p. 61.

14 ibid., p. 76.

15 ibid., p. 77.

16 ibid., p. 96.

17 ibid., p. 139.

18 This kind of argument against Rousseau can be found in the classic anti-democratic work, *Political Parties*, by Robert Michels (Collier, 1962), particularly part IA, section 2: 'Mechanical and Technical Impossibility of Direct Government by the Masses'.

19 Consider a survey carried out by the United Nations, entitled *Democracy in a World of Tensions* (UNESCO, Paris, 1951). Although all nations favoured democracy, their concepts of what it was differed markedly.

20 Sartori 1965, p. 252. For a critique of representative democracy, see C. B. Macpherson, *Democratic Theory* (Oxford University Press, 1973).

21 See G. F. Aleksandrov, *The Pattern of Soviet Democracy*, 1948.

[22] For Soviet weaknesses, see William Ebenstein, *Today's Isms* (Prentice Hall, 1970), p. 160.

[23] For an account of participatory democracy, see Pateman 1970, especially ch. II.

[24] On this kind of view of democracy, see Robert Paul Wolff, *In Defence of Anarchism* (Harper, New York, 1970), particularly part 3: 'Beyond the Legitimate State'.

[25] Sartori 1965, pp. 252–3.

[26] On the question of apathy, see Michels, op. cit., pp. 85–92.

[27] See Schumpeter 1950 and Mills 1956.

[28] The relationship between democracy and legitimacy is central to the theory of crisis. See ch. 6A.

1B Representation by parties

[1] For a further analysis of the idea of the will of the people, see John Plamenatz, *Democracy and Illusion* (Longman, 1973), especially chs 4, 6.

[2] On this point, see Plamenatz, ibid., chs 3, 4. See also H. B. Mayo, *An Introduction to Democratic Theory* (Oxford University Press, 1960), chs 4, 5.

[3] On the difference between the British and American arrangements, see Emy 1978, ch. 4.

[4] For an introduction to these institutions, see David Solomon, *Australia's Government and Parliament* (Nelson, 1973), and S. Encel, *Cabinet Government in Australia* (Melbourne University Press, 1974).

[5] Whitlam's argument can be found in Freudenburg 1978, p. 244.

[6] The socialization principle and its fate are discussed in ch. 6C.

[7] Some extremely conservative politicans, such as Premier Bjelke-Petersen of Queensland, argue that the encroachment on the States continues under Fraser.

[8] Indeed it can be argued that the majority are anti-uranium-mining, since the ALP together with the Australian Democrats received more than 50 per cent of the first preference votes. This, however, assumes that people voted primarily on the basis of this issue.

[9] For a discussion of the convergence thesis with respect to the Labor and Liberal parties, the article by A. Patience & B. Head in the book edited by them (1979).

[10] Mayo, op. cit., p. 153.

[11] ibid., p. 154.

[12] ibid., p. 87. Mayo in fact presents eight somewhat unconvincing arguments against this view.

[13] Mills 1956, chs 12, 14.

[14] I do not accept Mills' claim as having universal application to all Western democracies, for some offer substantial philosophical and policy differences between the major parties. However, the tendency he identifies is present and needs to be combated.

[15] Mayo, op. cit., p. 149.

[16] Schumpeter 1950, p. 269.

[17] For a discussion on the problems with financing political parties, see Crisp 1969, chs 8, 9.

[18] This claim has been made with respect to the Labor and Liberal parties in Australia, in Catley & McFarlane 1974. This view is criticized in ch. 6C.

1C The Australian Constitution and democracy

[1] Emy 1978, p. 8.

[2] For example, see the first edition of Hugh Emy's influential *The Politics of Australian Democracy* (Macmillan, 1974), in which the concept of democracy is given a central role in legitimizing the system (see in particular section 2).

[3] Crisp 1975, pp. 352–3.

[4] See Allan Patience in Duncan 1978, p. 98.

[5] For a full statement of the Commonwealth of Australia Constitution Act, see Howard 1978, pp. 167ff.

[6] On the powers of the Senate, see Emy 1978, ch. 5.

[7] See Allan Patience, op. cit., pp. 104ff. for some of the manoeuvres behind the formation of the Senate.

[8] Menzies, writing in the Sydney *Daily Telegraph*, 11 March 1968, quoted in Hall & Iremonger 1976, pp. 116–17.

[9] Munro, quoted in Hall & Iremonger 1976, p. 127.

[10] See Sir Richard Eggleston, in Gareth Evans (ed.), *Labor and the Constitution* (Heinemann, 1977), p. 297ff.

[11] Edmund Barton, quoted in Hall & Iremonger 1976, pp. 149–50.

[12] The importance of democratic ideology for legitimacy can scarcely be overestimated. If breaches of democratic conventions are easily secured, however, 'democracy' becomes a mere myth that is used to justify a particular group's possession of state power.

[13] See Hall and Iremonger 1976. An example is the statement by Adye Douglas, pp. 62–3.

[14] Barton, quoted in Hall & Iremonger 1976, p. 75.

[15] See ch. 8D. Ellicott produced a statement outlining the course of action (dismissal of the Labor government) that Kerr later followed.

[16] See R. J. Ellicott in Gareth Evans, op. cit., p. 293.

[17] Howard 1978, p. 70.

[18] ibid., p. 71.

[19] In Queensland the Country Party rules under a rigged system with 29 per cent of the votes giving them 43 per cent of the seats.

[20] Howard 1978, p. 45.

[21] Deakin, quoted in Hall & Iremonger 1976, pp. 64–5.

[22] See Hall & Iremonger 1976, ch. 2.

[23] ibid., p. 90.

[24] Emy 1978, pp. 13–14.

[25] In a speech on 11 November 1978, three years after his dramatic dismissal. See Melbourne *Age*, 13 November 1978, pp. 1, 9.

[26] Kerr 1978, pp. 387–8.

[27] Patience, in Duncan 1978, p. 113.

1D The formal organization of power in Australia

[1] See, for example, Crisp 1975; Claude Forell, *How We Are Governed* (Cheshire, Melbourne, 1966); Emy 1978, especially chs 7–14; and D. Solomon, *Australia's Government and Parliament* (Nelson, Melbourne, 1973).

[2] See S. Encel, *Cabinet Government in Australia* (2nd edn, Melbourne University Press, 1974).

[3] ibid., pp. 146–8.

[4] See Emy 1978, chs 13, 14. See also Jupp 1968, chs 3, 6, 7.

[5] See Emy 1978, chs 10, 11. See also J. Crawford, 'Civil Servants and Policy Making', in Mayer 1969. See also the special issue of *Publius* on Federalism, vol. 7, no. 3, 1978; includes articles by G. Sawer & R. Mathews.

[6] On the Whitlam government's experience with the public service, see Sexton 1979, chs 8, 9.

[7] See Max Weber, *The Theory of Social and Economic Organization* (Free Press, New York, 1947).

[8] See H. Jacobi, *The Bureaucratization of the World* (University of California Press, Berkeley, 1973), on the extent to which this is coming true.

[9] On the difference between Whitlam/Labor years and Fraser/ Liberal years, see Elaine Thompson, 'The Public Service', in Patience and Head 1979.

[10] See Peter Wilenski, 'Labor and the Bureaucracy', in Duncan 1978, pp. 28ff.

[11] See Sexton 1979, ch. 13, 'Limits of Power'. For suggested reforms of the public service itself, see C. Hazlehurst & J. R. Nethercote (eds), *Reforming Australian Government: the Coombs Report and Beyond* (ANU Press, Camberra, 1977).

[12] See Robert Dahl, *Polyarchy* (Yale University Press, Newhaven, 1971) and *Approaches to Democratic Theory* (Chicago University Press, 1956). For an alternative, see Kariel 1970, part 3, especially ch. 19 by Graeme Duncan & Steven Lukes, 'Democracy Restated'.

[13] Robert Presthus, 'The Pluralist Framework', in Kariel, 1970, p. 281.

[14] Emy 1974, p. 149.

[15] ibid., pp. 166–7.

[16] On the uranium conflict, see K. D. Suter, 'The Uranium Debate in Australia', *The World Today*, vol. 34, no. 6, June 1978, pp. 227ff and C. B. Down, 'The Australian Trade Union Movement and Uranium Mining', Research Paper, 1970, School of Economic and Financial Studies, Macquarie University.

[17] On the division of power between progressive and reactionary forces, see chs 1D and 2D.

[18] See P. D. Groenewegen, 'Federalism', in Patience & Head 1979, p. 68.

[19] Jean Holmes, *The Australian Federal System* (George Allen & Unwin, 1977), p. 153.

[20] For example, consider the pressure placed on Don Dunstan from capitalist forces in the motor car and other industries to abandon his policies on industrial worker democracy and other worker rights. The replacement of Dunstan by Corcoran resulted in the removal of the major socialist minister, Duncan, from the Attorney-General's portfolio.

[21] For Dunstan's own views on capitalism and socialism, see the 1976 Chifley Memorial Lecture: 'Social Democracy in the '70's: the Struggle against the Myths', (Melbourne University Australian Labor Party Club).

[22] See Holmes, op. cit., ch. 6.

[23] Groenewegen, op. cit., p. 69.

[24] Police Chief Salisbury was uncompromising in his presentation of this view. Significantly, large numbers of conservative South Australians mobilized to demand his restoration. See John Summers, 'Ministerial responsibility and the police in South Australia', *Politics*, vol. XIV, no. 1, May 1979, pp. 101ff.

[25] On the indoctrination of police in Western societies, see George E. K. Berkley, *The Democratic Policeman* (Deakin Press, Boston, 1969).

[26] This continued in the demonstrations against South African rugby teams in July 1971. Peter Hain, chairman of the Young Liberals in Britain, is quoted as saying, 'The match at Melbourne produced the most shocking police action I have seen outside South Africa'. Quoted in Playford and Kirsner 1972, p. 141.

[27] See the criticism of ASIO, and bills in Joan Coxsedge's pamphlets, published by the Committee for the Abolition of Political Police, e.g. *Top Secret*. On proposals for joint action against industrial and political rebels, see P. Bennett, 'A plan for joint military and police operations in the event of a state of emergency', in *Australian Police Journal*, vol. 32, no. 3, July 1978, pp. 131ff.

[28] See Whitlam 1979, pp. 117–18. See also my ch. 9A.

[29] Whitlam himself was aware of the possibility of such a division.

He did not resist the sacking, partly out of a desire to prevent the division of the country. (See Melbourne *Age*, 13 November 1978.) In any event, the nation *was* divided over the Kerr action.

[30] See Richard F. Hamilton, *Class and Politics in the United States* (John Wiley and Sons, 1972). On the class divisions in the USA, see also M. Irish & J. Prothro, *The Politics of American Democracy* (Prentice Hall, 1965), ch. 12, on the role of the judiciary.

[31] On the High Court's legalistic interpretation of the Constitution, see Emy 1978, pp. 22–6.

[32] See John Playford, 'Who Rules Australia?' in Playford & Kirsner 1972, pp. 142–3.

[33] A 1974 survey of 1000 prisoners by the NSW Bureau of Crime Statistics and Research showed that 66.8 per cent of prisoners were unskilled workers (their percentage in the total population was 20.4 per cent). If we add skilled manual workers to this group, the total for manual workers approximates 80 per cent. See T. Vinson, 'Crime', in A. F. Davies et al. 1977, pp. 274ff. He also shows that the upper middle class ('professional middle management') contribute only 1.8 per cent of prisoners, even though they constitute 19.1 per cent of the population at large.

[34] This situation is also serious with so-called 'legal tax avoidance schemes'. The result of the operations of these schemes is that many of the most wealthy people pay *no* tax at all, and others pay very low amounts. This exacerbates the fiscal crisis of the state: see ch. 3C.

2A Theory of capitalism

[1] For an ideological justification of this, see John Locke's theory of private property and inheritance as natural rights in his two *Treatises of Civil Government* (Dent, London, 1924), particularly the section 'Of Property' in the second treatise. For a more modern attempt, see Karl Popper, *The Open Society and Its Enemies* (Routledge & Kegan Paul, 1966, vol. 2). Popper says: 'A consistent democratic constitution should exclude only one type of change in the legal system, namely a change which would endanger its democratic character' (p. 161). Yet, clearly, changes in the character of the economy are prevented or prohibited by many 'democratic' constitutions.

[2] On the dawn of capitalism, see Giddens 1971, especially chs 2, 4, 9.

[3] For an account of the capitalist process, in favourable terms, see virtually any university text book on economics. For example, P. A. Samuelson, *Economics* (McGraw-Hill, New York, 1967).

[4] Encel 1970, pp. 332–3. The spokesman is Sir Richard Powell, speaking in 1966.

[5] The obvious fact that prices have not been reduced under conditions of so-called free competition, but have indeed increased, has been an embarrassment to pro-capitalist theorists. It raises the question: has genuine free competition ever existed in any period of capitalism?

[6] Both these tendencies were predicted by Marx. See section B.

[7] For a review of these struggles, see Robin Gollan, *Radical and Working Class Politics: A Study of Eastern Australia, 1850–1910* (Melbourne University Press, 1967).

[8] Without state intervention and union power to increase wages, capitalism would have resulted in a crisis in the reproduction of the source of labour itself, that is, workers' lives would have been threatened.

[9] See J. M. Keynes, *The General Theory of Employment, Interest and Money* (Macmillan, London, 1961).

[10] See Joan Robinson, 'Marx, Marshall and Keynes: Three Views of Capitalism', in Wheelwright and Stilwell 1976, pp. 147ff., for a comparative introduction.

[11] For an estimate of the role of Keynesian policies, see J. A. Trevithick, *Inflation* (Penguin Books, 1979). See also Holland 1975, ch. 1.

[12] Wheelwright, in Playford & Kirsner 1972, pp. 65ff.

[13] Encel 1970, p. 115.

[14] Henderson 1975, p. 14.

2B Alienated labour and classes: Marx

[1] Marx's early works can be found in L. Easton & K. Guddat, *Writings of the Young Marx on Philosophy and Society* (Anchor, New York, 1967).

2 Karl Marx, *Economic and Philosophical Manuscripts of 1844* (*EPM*), (Progress Publishers, Moscow, 1977). See, for example, pp. 68–70. For an alternative conception of the young Marx to that presented here, see Louis Althusser, *For Marx* (Penguin University Books, 1969), chs 2, 5.

3 ibid., pp. 73–4.

4 Marx criticized heavily theorists who began with man as an individual rather than as a social being, particularly John Locke (see ch. 2A, footnote 1) and Adam Smith, 'father' of classical economics.

5 The central role of inheritance had been recognized earlier by Locke, who made it one of the natural inalienable rights of man.

6 For an analysis of the doctrine of needs in Marx, see Agnes Heller, *The Theory of Need in Marx* (St Martin's Press, New York, 1976).

7 Marx, in Easton & Guddat, op. cit., p. 294.

8 ibid., p. 295.

9 See Marx's famous discussion of money, using Shakespeare, in his *EPM*, op. cit., p. 127ff.

10 For a discussion of this, see Erich Fromm, *Marx's Concept of Man* (Ungar, New York, 1961).

11 Marx was aware that certain groups of persons were difficult to classify into the two major classes. In particular, he identifies groups such as the peasants, belonging to an earlier feudal mode of production, and the administrators and managers of capital. See Giddens 1971, p. 38. See also my ch. 2D.

12 See Karl Marx, *Capital*, vol. 1 (Progress Publishers, Moscow, 1965), p. 35.

13 For a discussion of this issue, see E. J. Mishan, 'The Myth of Consumers' Sovereignty', in Wheelwright & Stilwell 1976, vol. 2.

14 Marx, *Capital*, op. cit., p. 39.

15 On the theory of money in Marx, see Bruce McFarlane, 'Inflation: Money, Gold and Marx', in *Journal of Australian Political Economy*, October 1977.

16 For a simplified discussion of capitalist dynamics, see Ernest Mandel, *An Introduction to Marxist Economic Theory* (Pathfinder, New York, 1970).

[17] For a good discussion of this, see Graeme Duncan, *Marx and Mill* (Cambridge University Press, 1973), pp. 114–26.

[18] See Agnes Heller, op. cit., pp. 40ff.

[19] See Henderson 1975, ch. 3, pp. 12–28.

[20] For a discussion of workers' control in the Australian context, see Windschuttle 1979, pp. 259–64.

[21] On the theory of workers' control, see Pateman 1970, chs III, IV.

[22] For an account of this, see Duncan 1973, especially the section 'The Life Process of Classes', pp. 120ff.

[23] For more on the problem of false consciousness, see ch. 5A on Hegemony. For a contemporary account, see Miliband 1973, chs 7, 8, on 'The Process of Legitimation'.

2C Class and inequality in Australia

[1] For an account of the relations between these three conceptions of class, see Ralf Dahrendorf, *Class and Class Conflict in Industrial Society* (Stanford University Press, 1959), part I.

[2] See Encel 1970, ch. 6.

[3] ibid., p. 88.

[4] Yet Kemp 1978 puts this forward as a surprising revelation and new discovery.

[5] For a survey of the literature on status in Australia, see Wild 1978, ch. 5.

[6] On the causes and character of the division of labour, see Emile Durkheim, *The Division of Labor in Society* (Macmillan, New York, 1933).

[7] See Encel 1970, p. 119.

[8] See Dahrendorf, op. cit., pp. 48–61.

[9] Phil Raskell, 'Who Gets What in Australia: The Distribution of Wealth', *JAPE*, May 1978, pp. 3–16.

[10] ibid., p. 7. For full details, see P. Raskell, *The Distribution of Wealth in Australia, 1967–1972* (Planning Research Centre, 1977).

[11] See P. Groenewegen, in Playford & Kirsner 1972, p. 105.

[12] See the discussion of classes in Wild 1978, ch. 4.

[13] Kemp 1978, especially chs 1, 2.

[14] ibid., especially pp. 361–7.

[15] For a critical analysis of Kemp's views, see R. W. Connell, 'The End of Class, Re-run', in *Meanjin*, no. 1, 1979.

[16] However, as Anthony Giddens points out, 'the notion of class is so fundamental to Marx's writing that, in his most important works, he takes its meaning for granted. It is an irony which has frequently been noted that the manuscripts which Marx left at his death should have broken off at the point at which he was entering upon a systematic analysis of the concept of class'. (Giddens 1971, pp. 36–7).

[17] This theory and some modern proponents are discussed in Frankel 1978, ch. 7.

[18] See Mills 1956, especially chs 1 and 12. Mills' elite consists of a large number of capitalist owners and managers. See chs 5 (The Very Rich), 6 (The Chief Executives) and 7 (The Corporate Rich).

[19] On the creation and sustenance of the ruling ethos, see ibid., chs 14, 15.

[20] See ch. 6C.

2D The ruling class: an alternative to the orthodox Marxist model

[1] See Max Weber, 'Class, Status and Party', in *Economy and Society* (New York, 1968).

[2] On the foundation of the state see Weber, 'Politics as a Vocation', in *From Max Weber*, Gerth & Mills (eds) (Oxford University Press, New York, 1958).

[3] For an account of the character of this change, see Frankel 1978, especially ch. 6. See also Harry Braverman, *Labor and Monopoly Capital* (Monthly Review Press, New York, 1974), especially parts I and III.

[4] See A. Giddens, *The Class Structure of the Advanced Societies* (Hutchinson, London, 1973), p. 51.

[5] Ted Wheelwright, 'The Concentration of Private Economic Power', in Playford & Kirsner 1972, pp. 65ff.

[6] For a more detailed account, see the AMWSU's recent booklet *Australia Ripped Off*, published in March 1979 and widely distributed.

[7] See Connell 1977, chs 3, 5.

[8] For a summary of these disparate views, see Wild 1978, ch. 6.

[9] Encel 1970, p. 4.

[10] Wild 1978, p. 114.

[11] ibid., p. 114.

[12] See ibid., pp. 112–14. However, Wild is careful not to commit himself on this issue. To me, this leaves his position obscure.

[13] Connell 1977, chs 3, 5.

[14] ibid., pp. 56, 58.

[15] The united interests of these groups in Australia have often been obscured by the media's focus on the importance of the differences between different 'levels' in the working class. See Wild 1978, chs 3, 4.

3A Theories of economic crisis

[1] From F. Engels, *Socialism, Utopian and Scientific* (International Publishers, New York, 1935), ch. III. Quoted in John Eaton *Political Economy* (International Publishers, New York, 1966), p. 145. See the whole of ch. VIII for a good discussion of these laws.

[2] See Marx, *Capital*, vol. III (Progress Publishers, Moscow, 1966).

[3] The proportion of labour power involved in the production of each item is reduced; its real value is thus reduced. This does not, however, entail that its exchange value (in terms of price) or its use value (in terms of function) will be less.

[4] See Marx, op. cit. pp. 232ff.

[5] Thus Robert Heilbroner, *The Worldly Philosophers* (Simon & Schuster, 1967), remarks: 'We hardly need document the existence of business cycles over the past hundred years ... Marx's prediction was an extraordinary bit of foresight'. p. 149.

[6] For an explanation of this tendency, see Ernest Mandel, *An Introduction to Marxist Economic Theory* (Pathfinder, New York, 1973), pp. 47ff.

[7] For a similar view, see Holland 1975, chs 2, 3. See also the appendix, 'Marx, Profits & Crises', pp. 388ff.

8 This criticism may be a little harsh on Marx, given that the development of huge multinational corporations, which often control all aspects of the production process, had not yet arisen.

9 The attempts by the Australian state to ensure competition have been minimal and have been strongly resisted. See the fate of the Trade Practices Act, (chs 5C and 7C); see also Andrew Hopkins, *Crime, Law and Business: the sociological sources of Australian monopoly Law* (Australian Institute of Criminology, Canberra, 1978).

10 For statistics on this, see Holland 1975, pp. 48–58.

11 See Chris Starrs, 'Marx's Immiserisation Thesis', in *Selected Papers from the Second Australian Political Economy Conference*, pp. 97–114.

12 From Marx, *Theories of Surplus Value*, p. 414; quoted in Starrs, ibid.

13 See Giddens 1971, pp. 55–8 for a discussion of this.

14 Employers, of course, benefited by the actions of the state in support of their cause. This role became increasingly important after the First World War. See Humphrey McQueen, 'Shoot the Bolshevik, Hang the Profiteer. Reconstructing Australian Capitalism, 1918–21', in Wheelwright & Buckley 1978.

15 On the role of the welfare state in sustaining exploitation in Australia, see Winton Higgins, 'Social Welfare and Class Warfare', in Duncan 1978, pp. 135ff.

16 On the role of wars, see Mandel, op. cit., pp. 60–2, 67–8.

17 See Brezniak & Collins, 'The Australian Crisis, from Boom to Bust', in *JAPE*, October 1977, especially part III.

18 See Ernest Mandel, *Late Capitalism* (New Left Books, London, 1975), especially chs 13, 14, 15.

19 On the increased militancy of the working class in Australia, see ch. 6D.

20 This created expectations in all people that full employment would be guaranteed. The social and psychological consequences of recent unemployment are more severe. See Windschuttle 1979, part 2.

21 See Bruce McFarlane, 'Inflation: Money, Gold and Marx', in *JAPE*, October 1977.

[22] This phenomenon is termed 'producer sovereignty' by Stuart Holland. He documents both the move to monopoly and the fixing of prices.

[23] See Milton Friedman, *Capitalism and Freedom* (University of Chicago Press, 1962); *Social Security: Universal or Selective?*, with Wilbur J. Cohen, (American Enterprise Institute for Public Policy Research, Washington, 1972), *Unemployment versus Inflation?: an evaluation of the Phillips Curve* (Institute of Economic Affairs, London, 1975).

[24] For an alternative view, see Andrew Gamble and Paul Walton, *Capitalism in Crisis: Inflation and the State* (Macmillan, London, 1976).

[25] These phenomena will be discussed with respect to Australia in chs 6B and 9C.

[26] This has been one of the factors identified by capitalist representatives as the cause of crisis. See the Trilateral Commission publication, *The Crisis of Democracy* (New York University Press, 1975).

3B The current crisis in Australian economy

[1] See the p. 1 headline of the *Australian Financial Review*, 6 December 1978, 'Fraser Hemmed In, A Stalled Economy'.

[2] Robert Hawke, reported in Melbourne *Age*, 14 February 1979, p. 11.

[3] On the nature of these cuts, see Windschuttle 1979, chs 6, 7, 10, 11.

[4] See *Rural Australia—The Other Nation* (AIPS/Hodder & Stoughton, 1979), especially the paper by Prof. Geoffrey Bolton.

[5] On the impact of the EEC policies on Australian agriculture, see the above AIPS book, especially chs 2, 3.

[6] For a detailed polemic here, see Robinson 1978, especially ch. 3.

[7] Thus Robinson 1978 concluded: 'Australia has never reached a coherent, well-organised policy towards manufacturing industry —despite two major inquiries and innumerable expressions of pious good-will', p. 95.

[8] Of course, in return for this, these companies receive huge tax concessions. Hence this is not an anti-capitalist manoeuvre.

[9] Robinson 1978, p. 45.

[10] For an analysis of the struggles between local and international

capital in the development of this industry, see Connell 1977, pp. 76ff.

[11] See Michael Brezniak & John Collins, 'The Australian Crisis, From Boom to Bust', in *JAPE*, October 1977, p. 11.

[12] On these problems, see Connell 1977, ch. 4.

[13] R. W. Connell, 'Structural Change in the Ruling Class', in Wheelwright & Buckley 1975, p. 234.

[14] See Connell 1977, ch. 5. See also his paper, 'Structure and Structural Change in the Ruling Class', in Wheelwright & Buckley 1975, pp. 227ff.

[15] Quoted by E. L. Wheelwright in *Big Business in Australia*, AIPS, 1970, p. 56.

[16] Brezniak & Collins, op. cit., p. 8. See also their discussion of the causes of the boom.

[17] The other major nation here was West Germany. Even the European Economic Community as a whole performed better than the USA.

[18] Bob Catley, 'Australia's Role in the World Crisis', in Duncan 1978, p. 227.

[19] See Joseph Camilleri, *Civilization in Crisis* (Cambridge University Press, 1976), especially ch. 6, 'Economic Transnationalism: The new Imperialism', pp. 92ff.

[20] Brezniak & Collins, op. cit., p. 10.

[21] For details of this, see G. Crough, 'A Compendium of Official Statistics of Foreign Investment Flows To and From Australia 1947–74' (Transnational Corporations Research Project).

[22] Harold Bell, 'The Large Corporation in Australia', in *Big Business in Australia* (AIPS, 1970), p. 53.

[23] After 1950, however, the union movement suffered rapid setbacks with the abandonment of quarterly cost of living allowances and the introduction of penalties against unions.

[24] D. W. Oxnan, 'The Incidence of Strikes in Australia', in J. E. Isaac & G. W. Ford (eds), *Australian Labour Relations* (Sun Books, Melbourne, 1968).

[25] See C. P. Harris, 'Income Tax and Income Distribution in Australia', in C. P. Harris (ed.), *Selected Readings on Economic Behaviour*

(McCutcheon, 1970). Harris concludes that, in fact, inequalities have worsened.

26 John Collins, 'The Political Economy of Post-War Immigration', in Wheelwright & Buckley 1975, pp. 117–18.

27 See John McEwen, 'The Role of the Country Party', in Mayer 1969, pp. 338ff.

28 Connell 1977, p. 101.

29 Catley, op. cit., p. 229.

30 On the international monetary crisis, see Kelvin Rowley, 'The End of the Long Boom', *Intervention* no. 6, June 1976.

31 Brezniak & Collins, op. cit., p. 18.

32 See Brezniak & Collins, ibid., p. 31, quote 58, where they quote several newspaper headlines such as '5000 Smaller Firms on Verge of Bankruptcy', *Australian*, 22 October 1975.

33 On the political consequences of this tariff cut, see chs 8A and 8B.

34 For an explanation of this, see the booklet, *Crisis Point in Australian Economic Policy*, by J. O. N. Perkins, 1978.

35 In particular, Minister for Labour, Clyde Cameron. His fate is recorded in ch. 8C.

36 Bruce McFarlane labelled this budget as 'arguably the most violently anti-worker budget since Menzies' (see *JAPE*, October 1977, p. 62). This seems an extreme comment, but the point is taken.

37 See headlines in Melbourne *Age*, 4 April 1979, 'Tough Line on Strikes', reporting Industrial Relations Minister Street's new campaign to keep wages down. On p. 4 of the same edition, Treasurer Howard is reported under the heading 'Workers getting too much money', urging wage cuts to achieve a proper balance. This in a year when many companies achieved record profits.

38 Robinson 1978, p. 84.

39 See ibid., chs 1, 2.

3C Political crises in the state

1 For a political economy introduction to these sectors, see Frankel 1978, especially chs 3, 6.

2 This schema can be considered an elaboration of the one given in

the Prologue, focusing on the complexities of the state system.

3 See Habermas 1973, pp. 53–4, for an outline of this and other economic functions in relation to the state.

4 On the tension between the two aims of state education systems, see Adrian Vicary's essay, 'Education and Social Relations', in Duncan 1978, pp. 184ff.

5 This is not to say that the relations of production and work motivations of those working in this state sector are not alienated. The character and causes of the alienation are, however, of a different order from that under private enterprise.

6 Although both Locke and Marx emphasized the centrality of the right to inheritance of private property, little emphasis is placed on this by either conservative or socialist ideologies.

7 Of course, governments may enforce these laws in an unequal way. Thus, in most Australian States, laws governing working conditions of employees are less stringently enforced than laws governing offences against property. This is particularly so if one considers the imbalance in police resources and personnel which goes into the detection of each of these types of crime.

8 During times of economic crisis and savage attacks on unions, conditions of employment, particularly in regard to safety, have a tendency to deteriorate. (See also ch. 6D on union power.)

9 On the development and transformation of the modern state in relation to economy, see Miliband 1973, especially chs 3, 4, 5.

10 Often there is an attempt to represent the value rationality involved in political judgements as if it were simply a matter of expertise—technical rationality. See ch. 6A.

11 Nevertheless, a substantial proportion of state income derives from taxes on the wages of public sector employees. This is one reason why it is easier to generate employment in the public sector than in private enterprise. Each public employee partly pays for his own employment.

12 Both Labor and non-Labor politicians have held this view. See ch. 5C for a discussion of Menzies, and ch. 8A for Whitlam.

13 In particular, indigenous manufacturing industry in Australia is in serious crisis. See ch. 3B and also Robinson 1978.

14 For a more detailed discussion of the causes of unemployment, see

Windschuttle 1979, especially chs 1, 2.

[15] Thus a social welfarist culture has been developed, which cannot be removed by legislation without serious challenges to state legitimacy. People label such actions 'undemocratic'. See ch. 6A.

[16] Thus, for example, if the economy grows at only 2 per cent and inflation goes ahead at 12 per cent, there will be a considerable shortfall in government revenue (of the order of 10 per cent) even to keep services at existing levels.

[17] See Habermas 1973, pp. 68–92. See also ch. 6D.

[18] This situation again changed when in 1979 Fraser introduced massive indirect taxes on petrol, beef etc., which, while temporarily alleviating the fiscal crisis, placed further burdens on workers.

[19] See Habermas 1973, pp. 61–8, 'Theorems of Rationality Crisis'.

[20] On the social problems generated by economic crisis in Australia, see ch. 4C. See also Windschuttle 1979, chs 3–7.

[21] The changing of governments may resolve crises in the short term (see ch. 5B). For illustrations in Australia, see ch. 7C and ch. 8 (Liberal and Labor crises).

[22] On the increased levels of public expenditure introduced by the Whitlam government, see R. Scotton & H. Ferber (eds), *Public Expenditure and Social Policy in Australia*, vol. 1 (Longman Cheshire, Melbourne, 1978). On Fraser's redistribution, see *Australia Ripped Off*, pp. 24–35.

[23] The latter feature is used by defenders of the elitist view of democracy (see ch. 1B and ch. 6A) to justify the existent Western system. This neglects the fact that the withdrawal of support is often a purely negative act: the people in their frustration are not expressing what they want, but merely what they do not want. See also Epilogue.

4A Social identity and its breakdown

[1] On the relationship between roles and meaning, see R. Harré & P. Secord, *The Explanation of Social Behaviour* (Basil Blackwell, Oxford, 1972).

[2] Emile Durkheim, *The Rules of the Sociological Method*, ed. E. G. Catlin (Chicago University Press, 1950).

[3] For a discussion of the distinction between mechanical and organic solidarity, see Steven Lukes, *Durkheim* (Allen Lane, 1973), pp. 147–67.

[4] Durkheim, quoted in Raymond Aron, *Main Currents in Sociological Thought 2* (Pelican, 1967), p. 61.

[5] Quoted in R. Bierstedt, *Emile Durkheim* (Weidenfeld & Nicolson, New York & London, 1966), p. 223.

[6] For an elaboration and defence of this view, see Peter Berger, *The Sacred Canopy: Elements of a Sociological Theory of Religion* (Doubleday, New York, 1969).

[7] Quoted in Bierstedt, op. cit., p. 212.

[8] E. Durkheim, *Suicide* (Routledge & Kegan Paul, London, 1952), p. 213.

[9] See Wilfred Desan, *The Tragic Finale, An Essay on the Philosophy of Jean-Paul Sartre* (Harper & Row, New York, 1960), especially ch. 4 for a discussion of 'dread' in relation to other persons.

[10] Marx, influenced by Feuerbach, considered Christianity to be a useful tool for the state to keep the masses oppressed. This is no longer unambiguously its role, as can be seen by the division between conservatives and radicals within Christianity itself.

[11] See Friedrich Nietzsche, *The Will to Power* (Vintage Books, New York, 1967), especially Book Two, parts I and II.

[12] For philosophical explanations of this 'scientistic' world-view, see J. J. C. Smart, *Philosophy and Scientific Realism* (Routledge & Kegan Paul, London, 1963), and Wilfred Sellars, *Science and Metaphysics* (Routledge & Kegan Paul, London, 1968).

[13] See, in particular, Albert Camus, *The Rebel* (Knopf, New York, 1954), and his *The Myth of Sisyphus and Other Essays* (Vintage, New York, 1960).

[14] Quoted by Jean-Paul Sartre in his famous essay, *Existentialism and Humanism* (Methuen, London, 1948).

[15] In addition to Carroll 1977 and Habermas 1973, see Herbert Marcuse, *Eros and Civilization* (Vintage Books, New York, 1955): Marcuse argues that this 'pleasure' is not genuine and free, but always based on repression.

[16] Carroll 1977, especially chs 2, 3. On Carroll's conservatism, see

his 'A conservative credo' in *Quadrant*, vol. 22, no. 6, June 1978, pp. 41–3.

[17] Carroll 1977, p. 19.

[18] ibid., p. 18.

[19] See ibid., ch. 6, especially pp. 91–4. See also statement on p. 19.

[20] ibid., p. 30.

[21] See Herbert Marcuse, *One Dimensional Man* (Beacon, Boston, 1964). According to Marcuse, Western capitalist society keeps individuals oppressed by a kind of drugging of the mind: a variety of superficial pleasures and experiences are offered to them to prevent them reflecting on the deeper problems of the meaning of their lives. I do not, however, agree with Marcuse that the system is completely successful in this.

[22] Carroll 1977, ch 5.

[23] See ibid., ch. 3, 'The Paranoid'.

[24] See ibid., p. 67 specifically, and more generally pp. 66–74.

[25] See Habermas 1973. See also Prologue.

[26] Habermas 1973, p. 77.

[27] ibid., p. 78.

[28] ibid., p. 77.

[29] On the changes in the family and the attendant problems, see ch. 3C.

[30] Habermas 1973, p. 81.

[31] ibid., p. 93.

[32] On the general increase of social problems in Western societies, see J. Camilleri, *Civilization in Crisis* (Cambridge University Press, 1976), especially chs 2, 3, 9, 12. On the Australian context, see ch. 4C.

4B Australian culture: materialism and religion

[1] For a discussion of this issue, see Tim Rowse, *Australian Liberalism and National Character* (Kibble Books, Malmsbury, Vic., 1978).

[2] To say, for example, that a person acted in a particular way because he is an 'ocker' is not an explanation, for 'ocker' refers to a person carrying out that mode of behaviour itself.

[3] Conway 1971; see cover jacket. See also his more recent work, *The Land of the Long Weekend*, (Sun Books, 1978). Conway is Senior Psychologist at St Vincent's Hospital, Melbourne.

[4] Conway 1971, p. 50.

[5] See Donald Horne, *The Lucky Country* (Penguin, 1971), especially pp. 25–9. See also D. Horne, *Money Made Us* (Penguin, 1976).

[6] Conway 1971, p. 52.

[7] Statistics on television watching show that, in 1975, women watched an average 21.5 hours per week, men 17.75, teenagers 20.33 and children 18. See *New Journalist*, no. 20, November 1975.

[8] Horne, op. cit., p. 26.

[9] ibid., p. 26.

[10] On the importance of Humphries as social critic, see Tim Rowse, op. cit., pp. 204–26.

[11] It might be claimed that the Australian is a hedonist in that he constantly wants pleasure for its own sake, even though he often fails to achieve it.

[12] Conway 1971, p. 109.

[13] ibid., pp. 118–19.

[14] See the account, 'An Australian Housewife: A disillusioning Experience', in Mercer 1975.

[15] Horne, op. cit., pp. 33–4.

[16] Craig McGregor, *Profile of Australia* (Penguin, 1968), p. 49.

[17] The new forms of imposition are, as we noted in the last section, due to the fact that more and more decisions governing the individual's life are made without his participation, e.g. decisions on economic, political and social organization. His 'social freedom' is thus increasingly trivialized.

[18] Hans Mol, *Religion in Australia* (Nelson, Melbourne, 1971). The quote is from his article, 'Family and Religion', in *The Family in Australia*, ed. J. Krupinski & A. Stoller (Pergamon, Sydney, 1974), p. 127.

[19] See esp. Norman Blaikie, 'Religious Groups and World Views', in F. J. Hunt (ed.), *Socialization in Australia* (Angus & Robertson, Sydney, 1972), p. 92.

[20] Compiled from Hans Mol, 1974, op. cit., p. 128.

20 Compiled from Hans Mol, 1974, op. cit., p. 128.

21 This meant that only 20 per cent of Anglicans, 33 per cent of Presbyterians, 31 per cent of Methodists—in contrast to a massive 70 per cent of Catholics—attended usually or nearly always.

22 See Hans Mol, 1971, op. cit., p. 44.

23 See Hans Mol, 'Religion and Sex in Australia', in Edgar 1974, pp. 189ff.

24 Although the 1976 census figures showed a continuation of formal religious adherence, this is not reflected in patterns of behaviour.

25 The World Council of Churches has received considerable criticism because of its support for the liberation movements in Southern Africa.

26 See Karel Rees-Smit, 'Goals, Values and Secular Man', in Edgar 1974, pp. 171–81.

27 Although the bishops were not opposed to all nationalization, the criterion they suggested was that citizens 'should always seek to determine whether the nationalization of a particular industry is legitimate or whether it is really only part of a more far-reaching plan'.

28 See Crowley 1973, pp. 187–8, for the full statement.

4C   Crisis in Australian social structures

1 Reported in Deveson 1978. Anne Deveson was one of the commissioners; she wrote this book to bring the Commission's major recommendations to the public.

2 The effect of this on women is discussed in Summers 1975, ch. 4, 'The Ravaged Self'.

3 Deveson 1978, p. 69.

4 Lyn Richards, *Having Families* (Penguin, Melbourne, 1978), p. 20.

5 ibid., p. 82.

6 ibid., p. 291.

7 Dan L. Adler, 'Matriduxy in the Australian Family', in *Australian Society: A Sociological Introduction*, ed. A. F. Davies & S. Encel (Cheshire, Melbourne, 1965).

8 Conway 1971, p. 88.

9 ibid., p. 92.

10 This information is based on a talk delivered by Tim Kupsch, a sociologist at Melbourne State College, to my Politics class.

11 See Conway 1971, p. 97. Conway argues that women indoctrinate their daughters to continue these roles.

12 See Habermas' theory explained in latter part of ch. 4A.

13 Lyn Richards, op. cit., p. 125.

14 See 'Women and the Australian Media', in Mercer 1975, pp. 275ff. Thus 'The young girl reading *Dolly* receives the information that dates, clothes, beauty, parties and men are not only the core of existence, but that these are the only things that should matter' (p. 282).

15 In addition to Dixson, see Summers 1975, particularly p. 185ff.

16 Miriam Dixson, *The Real Matilda, Women and Identity in Australia 1788–1975* (Penguin, 1976).

17 Deveson 1978, p. 187.

18 ibid., p. 189.

19 Craig McGregor, *Profile of Australia* (Penguin, 1968), pp. 60ff.

20 Conway 1971, p. 142.

21 ibid., p. 144.

22 Donald Horne, *The Lucky Country* (Penguin, 1974), pp. 32–3.

23 Conway 1971, p. 142.

24 ibid., p. 142.

25 Royal Commission on Human Relations, Final Report, vol. 5, (AGPS, Canberra, 1977), p. 3. On the general exploitation of women, see G. Greer, *The Female Eunuch* (Paladin, 1971) and S. Rowbotham, *Hidden from History* (Penguin, 1975).

26 See ibid. on Margaret Power's evidence, pp. 118–27. See also Deveson 1978, pp. 57–9.

27 Deveson 1978, p. 30, reports that the '1971 Census showed that women constituted 67 per cent of workers in clerical occupations, but only 11 per cent of those in executive and managerial positions'.

28 Published so: *Girls, School and Society.* Report of a Study Group of the Schools Commission, 1975. See also G. Greer, op. cit., pp. 249 ff.

[29] I am indebted to Barbara Wishart, Lecturer in Sociology, Melbourne State College, and one of the contributors to *The Other Half* (Mercer 1975), for these points.

[30] Don Edgar, in Royal Commission on Human Relations, Evidence, pp. 2769–70.

[31] Royal Commission Report, vol. 5, p. 42.

[32] See C. Gibbeson, 'Domestic Violence', Commission Research Report no. 11, 1977.

[33] Detailed recommendations are published in the Appendix to Deveson 1978, pp. 410ff.

[34] For a general discussion of the causes of women's oppression in Australia, see Summers 1975, Miriam Dixson, op. cit. See also Ruth Teale (ed.) *Colonial Eve, Sources on Women in Australia, 1788–1914* (Oxford University Press, Melbourne, 1978).

[35] Summers 1975, p. 471, says that the 'sheer enormity' of women's oppression 'has led some women into a movement of separatism, to the setting up of all women communes . . . which have intended to provide a haven where women can live and do what they like, unhampered by the interference of men'. She calls for a change in attitudes of both men and women. See pp. 467–73.

[36] This theory is developed in Warren Farrell, *The Liberated Man* (Random House, New York, 1975). See especially part I.

[37] For a critical discussion of this view, see Wild 1978, pp. 142–51. The sections are entitled 'Women as a Class' and 'Women as a Minority Group'.

[38] Summers 1975, p. 90.

[39] See Bettina Cass, 'Women's Place in the Class Structure', in Wheelwright & Buckley 1975.

[40] This transformation is best explained in Hegel's theory of the master and the slave. See G. W. F. Hegel, *The Phenomenology of Spirit*, ed. J. N. Findlay (Oxford, Clarendon Press, 1977).

[41] See especially Sheila Rowbotham, *Woman's Consciousness, Man's World* (Penguin Books, 1973).

[42] See Miriam Dixson, 'Women', in Davies et al. 1977.

[43] The dimensions of this crisis in Australia are explored in Windschuttle 1979. I do not, however, agree with his view that unemployment is the major cause of this social crisis.

[44] Deveson 1978, p. 100.

[45] See Windschuttle 1979, ch. 5, 'The Growth of Crime'. For examples, see Michael Hervey, *Violent Australian Crimes* (Cassell Australia, 1978).

[46] See Deveson 1978, pp. 160–1.

[47] Paul Wilson, Research Report for Royal Commission on Human Relations, no. 9. See table in Deveson 1978, p. 164.

[48] Windschuttle 1979, p. 97. See also David Biles (ed.) *Crime and Justice in Australia* (Sun Books, 1977), particularly ch. 2, 'Serious Crime Rates'.

[49] On the history of this exploitation, see F. Robinson & B. York, *The Black Resistance* (Widescope, Melbourne, 1977); on the plight of modern Aborigines, see C. D. Rowley, *Outcasts in White Australia* (Penguin, 1972); on modern attitudes and conflict, see Lorna Lippmann, *Words or Blows* (Penguin, 1973). See also F. Hardy, *The Unlucky Australians* (Gold Star Publications, 1972).

[50] The extent of poverty and child mortality amongst Aborigines is often worse than that of so-called underdeveloped countries. It is a measure of the insensitivity of Australian governments that this situation continues to be tolerated. Even though the Federal government has full constitutional powers on Aborigines, it has failed to use them in, for example, Queensland.

[51] Deveson 1978, p. 296. The whole of ch. 9 paints a sorry picture.

[52] See Deveson 1978, ch. 11. For some statistics on assimilation, see Charles Price, 'The Immigrants' in Davies et al. 1977, pp. 331ff. On some suggested resolutions, see Committee on Community Relations, Final Report (AGPS, 1975), and William Bostock, *Alternatives of Ethnicity* (Cat & Fiddle Press, Hobart, 1977). See also Paul R. Wilson, *Immigrants and Politics* (ANU Press, 1973).

5A Hegemony: domination of ideas and practices

[1] See Karl Marx, *The German Ideology* (Foreign Languages Publishing House, Moscow, 1964), part I. Sections reprinted in *The Marx-Engels Reader*, ed. Robert C. Tucker (Norton &·Co., New York, 1978), pp. 146ff.

[2] For discussions of the substructure-superstructure distinction, see Giddens 1971, pp. 40–5, and Henri Lefebvre, *The Sociology of Marx* (Penguin, 1972), chs 1, 2, 3.

³ Karl Marx, *Preface to A Contribution to the Critique of Political Economy* (Foreign Languages Press, Peking, 1976), p. 3.

⁴ This crude view of Marx is adopted by some supposedly eminent critics, such as Karl Popper, *The Open Society and Its Enemies*, vol. 2 (Routledge & Kegan Paul, London).

⁵ Karl Marx, in Bottomore & Rubel, 1973.

⁶ An interesting example is the suppression of Marxian ideas from Australian popular media, notwithstanding their enormous historical impact throughout the world.

⁷ See Antonio Gramsci, *Selections from the Prison Notebooks*, ed. Q. Hoare & G. Smith (International Publishers, New York), p. 238. See also comments on this in Frankel 1978, especially pp. 7–12.

⁸ Connell 1977, ch. 10. Connell was impressed by the book, Antonio Gramsci, *The Modern Prince and Other Writings* (International Publishers, New York, 1957).

⁹ Connell 1977, p. 206.

¹⁰ Thus Connell (ibid., p. 207) says: 'Hegemonic situations range from a strongly established pattern of direct controls with only marginal dissidence, through stiuations where a working class has formed an economic and social category but its mobilization is being aborted, to situations where mobilization has occurred though only within decided limits'.

¹¹ Connell 1977, p. 215.

¹² See Connell 1977, chs 7, 8.

¹³ On this point, see also P. J. Hollingworth, *The Powerless Poor, A Comprehensive Guide to Poverty in Australia* (Stockland Press, Melbourne, 1972).

¹⁴ Connell 1977, p. 150.

¹⁵ On recent attempts to gear the education system towards skills and vocations suitable to the domands of the advanced capitalist economy, see Windschuttle 1979, ch. 11, 'Education Under Attack'.

¹⁶ S. D'Urso, 'Hidden realities within schooling', *Australian Journal of Social Issues*, 1974, vol. 9, p. 144.

¹⁷ Craig McGregor, *Profile of Australia* (Hodder & Stoughton, London, 1966), p. 51.

¹⁸ Connell 1977, p. 216.

[19] ibid., p. 216.

[20] ibid., p. 217.

[21] On the differences of life-styles between the 'middle' and 'manual' classes, see Kemp 1978, especially chs 3, 4.

[22] See ibid., ch. 5.

[23] On the role of unions and the arbitration system in sustaining wage differentials, see ch. 6D.

[24] Connell 1977, p. 219.

[25] ibid., p. 219.

[26] This point is made by Habermas 1973, and is discussed in detail in ch. 5A.

[27] Connell 1977, p. 219.

[28] See Windschuttle 1979, ch. 10, 'Welfare and Social Control'.

[29] The major campaigns were the anti-communist strategy of Menzies (see ch. 5C) and the vituperative campaigns of the Democratic Labor Party. On the role of the DLP, see Paul Duffy, 'The DLP in the Seventies' in Mayer & Nelson 1973, pp. 435ff.

[30] Duffy, ibid., p. 437, says of the Liberal-Country Party coalition: 'without DLP support (in preferences) it would have lost every election since 1955'.

[31] This argument is put most forcefully in regard to Australian intellectuals by Tim Rowse, *Australian Liberalism and National Character* (Kibble Books, Malmsbury, Vic., 1978).

[32] Boris Frankel's work on this area is continuing. Glimpses of his position appear in Frankel 1978.

[33] Frankel 1978, p. 55.

5B Conservatism and liberalism

[1] See John T. Ray, *Conservatism as Heresy, An Australian Reader* (ANZ Book Co., 1974). Edmund Burke (1729–97) is the father of modern conservatism: see below.

[2] Ray, op. cit., p. xxv.

[3] Edmund Burke wrote no single great work, but rather a series of essays, the most important of which is his 'Reflections on the Revolution in France', published in his *Collected Works*, vol. III (Boston, Mass., 1901). For a discussion of other conservative

writers, see I. Gilmour, *Inside Right: A Study of Conservatism* (Hutchinson, London, 1977).

[4] Taken from an extract from Burke's 'Reflections' in *Masters of Political Thought*, vol. 2, ed. W. T. Jones (George Harrap, London, 1947), pp. 348–9.

[5] Ray, op. cit., p. xxiv.

[6] Burke, in W. T. Jones, op. cit., p. 348. For an interesting discussion of Burke, see John Plamenatz, *Man and Society*, vol. 1 (Longmans, 1963).

[7] This perspective which seeks to bring back dead social forms has been condemned by more thoughtful conservatives. For an example of more sophisticated conservatism, see Frank Knopfelmacher, 'University Crisis', in Mayer & Nelson 1973, pp. 675ff.

[8] Sir James Fitzjames Stephen, quoted in Philip W. Buck (ed.), *How Conservatives Think*, 1975, p. 88.

[9] The Marquis of Salisbury, in Buck, ibid., pp. 105–6.

[10] Michael Oakeshott, in Buck, ibid., p. 156.

[11] Ray, op. cit., p. 391.

[12] The report was also attacked by Liberal Minister D. J. Killen, an admirer of Burke who strives to be a consistent conservative. Killen took to addressing a Citizen's Rally Against Permissiveness (quoted by Deane Wells in his *Power Without Theory*, (Outback Press, 1977, p. 31)).

[13] Mill's books *On Liberty* and *Representative Government* were first published in 1859 and 1861 respectively. They are collected together in J. S. Mill, *Utilitarianism, Liberty and Representative Government*, introduced by A. D. Lindsay (Everyman's Library, 1962).

[14] Mill, ibid., p. 68.

[15] On the influence and relevance of Mill, see Duncan 1973, especially introduction and ch. 9.

[16] Mill, op. cit., pp. 72–3.

[17] ibid., p. 73.

[18] One way in which some Liberals have escaped this quandary is to allow as a ground for abortion the possibility that it may cause psychological harm to the mother.

[19] See A. D. Lindsay's introduction to Mill, op. cit. pp. xx, xxi.

20 The distinction between self-regarding and other-regarding acts has itself been attacked as untenable. See Robert Paul Wolff, *The Poverty of Liberalism* (Beacon, Boston, 1968), ch. 1.

21 See H. J. McCloskey, *John Stuart Mill: A Critical Study* (Macmillan, London, 1971), ch. 4.

22 Mill, op. cit., p. 132.

23 McCloskey, op. cit., p. 114.

24 For a discussion of Mill in relation to classes, see Isaiah Berlin, 'Two Concepts of Liberty', in *Four Essays on Liberty* (Oxford University Press, 1969).

25 This view, often called 'economic liberalism', owes much more to Adam Smith than to Mill. See Adam Smith, *The Wealth of Nations* (Penguin Books, 1970), first published 1776.

26 On Mill's view of socialism, see McCloskey, op. cit., pp. 137–41. See also Duncan 1973, pp. 272–85.

27 Locke had argued that the accumulation of property was a natural right of man, which the state could not rightfully remove: it was inalienable. See John Locke, 'An Essay Concerning Civil Government', in E. Barker (ed.) *The Social Contract* (Oxford University Press, 1971).

28 Mill, quoted in McCloskey, op. cit., p. 138.

29 McCloskey, op. cit., p. 140.

5C The Liberal Party's philosophy

1 These are Tiver 1978, and Dennis White, *The Philosophy of the Liberal Party* (Heinemann, 1978).

2 On this history, see John Lonie, 'From Liberal to Liberal: the emergence of the Liberal Party and Australian capitalism, 1900–45', in Duncan 1978.

3 See C. D. Kemp, *Big Businessmen, Four Biographical Essays* (Melbourne, 1964).

4 See Lonie, op. cit., pp. 69–75.

5 C. D. Kemp, quoted in Tiver 1978, p. 33.

6 Menzies, in a letter on 10 October 1945, said of the document: 'It is in my opinion the best piece of work of its kind done in Australia'.

[7] This was especially true of Labor's policy of nationalizing the banks. See Tiver 1978, pp. 65–71.

[8] This point is rarely referred by Liberal leaders themselves. Thus Menzies justified his health and social policies on humanitarian rather than economic grounds. See R. G. Menzies, *The Measure of the Years* (Cassell, 1970), chs 12, 13.

[9] See Tiver 1978, ch. 3, especially 'Organisation' and 'Sociology of the Liberal Party'.

[10] Chifley's aim in nationalizing the banks was to achieve greater co-ordinative powers over the whole economy. At no stage did he consider it the beginning of a campaign to bring all, or many, major companies upder public control.

[11] Menzies, speaking in parliament, 23 October 1947, quoted in Crowley 1973, p. 177.

[12] On Fraser's policies, see Tiver 1978, ch. 9. See also last part of this section.

[13] Some sophisticated defences for capitalist relations have appeared overseas, but most Australian spokesmen of the ruling class do not even bother to argue this point.

[14] On the fate of the communists, see Alistair Davidson, *The Communist Party of Australia: A Short History* (Hoover Institution Press, Stanford, 1969).

[15] Labor's actions against communists created an embittered conflict between it and the Communist Party. It is a wound which even by the 1970s had not healed.

[16] The use of troops against workers blunted the image of Labor as representatives of the working class, and alienated many Labor supporters. It is doubtful, however, whether it gained many new supporters for the Chifley government from conservatives.

[17] See Crowley 1973, pp. 212–14.

[18] *Tribune* commented, 19 October 1949: 'The leader of the Australian militant workers, who all his life has worked for world peace and for the advancement of the working class, was then led away to the Labor Government's jail'. Quoted in Crowley 1973, p. 213.

[19] Conservative academic, Frank Knopfelmacher, claimed in 1969: 'I believe that many, perhaps most of the leading Liberal politicians and publicists do not seriously believe that Communism is a serious problem for Australia, externally or internally ... For

the Liberals the Red Menace is a *sustaining myth* which keeps them in power by getting them the votes of some of their natural enemies'. Quoted in Mayer & Nelson 1973, pp. 386–7.

20 Evatt's courageous stand on this issue cost him dearly. He is said to have become obsessed with this question, to the point of psychological imbalance. This was particularly so after the Petrov spy case. See Menzies, 1970, op. cit., ch. 18.

21 See Robert Murray, *The Split, The Australian Labor Party in the Fifties*, (Cheshire, Melbourne, 1970).

22 The DLP did not, however, abandon the labour movement as a whole. Under the aegis of B. A. Santamaria, who influenced the new party through his National Civic Council, they continued to struggle for power within the unions. See B. A. Santamaria, *The Price of Freedom* (Hawthorn Press, 1966).

23 See Tiver 1978, p. 211.

24 On his views on health and social services, see Menzies, 1970, op. cit., chs 12, 13

25 On modern Liberal attitudes to immigration, see Charles Price, 'Immigration and Ethnic Affairs', in Patience and Head 1979.

26 See Windschuttle 1979, ch. 11.

27 On the divisions over tariff policy, see Connell 1977, ch. 5.

28 Tiver 1978, p. 105

29 This change was introduced by Harold Holt, who later succeeded Menzies as Prime Minister. It was imposed on 15 November 1960. See Crowley 1973, pp. 402–5.

30 See Liberal Party Platform, November 1960, clause 40.

31 For the history of this Bill, see Tiver 1978, pp. 86–91.

32 Although he is not a Liberal, the industrialist Lang Hancock has won a reputation by continuously harping on this theme.

33 At the forefront of opposition have been such extreme right-wing organizations as the Festival of Light and the National Civic Council, both perniciously pretending to represent Christianity.

34 On Fraser's own wealth, see John Edwards, *Life Wasn't Meant to be Easy* (Hale & Iremonger, Sydney, 1977), pp. 23–7. On the justification of inequality using the ideas of David Kemp, see ibid., ch. 14.

35 See Ayn Rand, *The Virtue of Selfishness* (Signet Books, 1958).

[36] Ayn Rand, *Atlas Shrugged* (Signet Books, 1957). Fraser is said to have remarked that it should be 'required reading for all politicians'. See Edwards, op. cit., p. 27.

[37] See Deane Wells, *Power Without Theory* (Outback Press, 1977), pp. 159–77. For an alternative view, see S. C. Ghosh, 'The ideological world of Malcolm Fraser', *Australian Quarterly*, vol. 50, no. 3, September 1978.

[38] ibid., p. 169.

[39] ibid., pp. 168–9.

5D The role of the mass media

[1] See in particular, Trevor Barr, *Reflections of Reality* (Rigby, 1977); Humphrey McQueen, *Australia's Media Monopolies* (Widescope, 1977); Henry Rosenbloom, *Politics and the Media* (Scribe Publications, 1978).

[2] Henry Mayer, 'What Should (and Could) We Do About the Media?' in *Mass Media in Australia* (AIPS Publications, 1976), p. 169.

[3] ibid., p. 170.

[4] For the full statistics on these four companies, plus other major ones involved in the media, see Rosenbloom, op. cit., Appendix A, pp. 152ff.

[5] McQueen, op. cit., p. 35.

[6] On the relationship between ratings and profitability in the media, see Rosenbloom, op. cit., ch. 1.

[7] ibid., p. 15.

[8] The immorality and unscrupulousness of some advertising campaigns lead to periodic outbursts from the public against them; promises are made that more control will be exercised, but little comes of it. See Rosenbloom, op. cit., ch. 5.

[9] McDonald was speaking after the incredible bias shown by the media in the 1975 crisis (see ch. 9). He said: 'Our credibility is at an all time low. In the months leading up to the last general election, the Labor Party didn't get a fair go. Media fell down in not providing enough variety in news and opinion'. Quoted in Rosenbloom, op. cit., p. 52.

[10] For good examples of this, see McQueen, op. cit., chs 3–6.

[11] See Ashbolt, in Wheelwright & Buckley 1975, p. 186.

[12] Max Walsh, quoted in Rosenbloom, op. cit., p. 23.

[13] For a further discussion of this phenomenon, see chs 4A, 5A.

[14] On the images of crime, see Connell 1977, ch. 9, 'The Media and Middle-Class Culture'.

[15] See Connell 1977, pp. 197–203.

[16] ibid., p. 198. Putting Connell's point in our terms, the myth is created that white collar occupations are the major basis of Australian life: manual work is no longer considered desirable.

[17] See P. M. Edgar & D. E. Edgar, 'Television Violence and Socialisation Theory', *Public Opinion Quarterly,* vol. xxxv, no. 4., 1971–72, pp. 608–12.

[18] See H. Himmelweit, 'Television and the Child', in B. Berelson & H. Janowitz (eds), *Public Opinion and Communication*, 2nd edn (Free Press, 1966), p. 427.

[19] Connell 1977, p. 197.

[20] In an article, 'Self-Perception and Mass Media Violence', in Edgar 1974.

[21] On police and demonstrators, see Barr, op. cit., pp. 14, 91, 92.

[22] For some case studies, see McQueen, op. cit., pp. 51–4.

[23] McQueen, op. cit., p. 51.

[24] This is not to deny that left-wing spokesmen are occasionally given prominence on the ABC—for example, Manning Clark's Boyer Lectures in 1976.

[25] McQueen, op. cit., p. 94.

[26] See Rosenbloom, op. cit., p. 36, on the case of the sacking of Terry Lane.

[27] Quoted in McQueen, op. cit., p. 113.

[28] On the consequences of this, see Rosenbloom, op. cit., chs 4, 5.

[29] On the difficulty of bringing the ABC completely under conservative control, see Patricia Edgar, 'Radio and Television', in Patience & Head 1979.

6A   Legitimation crisis

[1] The function of religious and traditional world views in securing

social integration has not been replaced by a system of meaningful allocation of roles to people. See ch. 4A.

[2] For an extensive discussion of these causes, see ch. 4A, and for the Australian context, ch. 4C.

[3] See Habermas 1973, especially part I, ch. 4 and part II, ch. 3.

[4] On Weber's theory of the state, see Julian Freund, *The Sociology of Max Weber* (Penguin University Books, 1972), ch. 4(c).

[5] See Max Weber, 'Politics as a Vocation', in *From Max Weber*, ed. Gerth & Mills (Oxford University Press, 1946), p. 78.

[6] Habermas 1973, p. 97.

[7] ibid., p. 97.

[8] The reasons for this are based on elaborate philosophical theory of the nature of human communication. See in particular, Habermas, *Knowledge and Human Interests* (Beacon Press, 1971), especially the Appendix.

[9] Habermas 1973, p. 70.

[10] It should be understood, however, that this scepticism and resistance to the state's actions will only occur in societies in which democratic rights are firmly embedded. This is not necessarily so in Australia. I shall take this up again in the Epilogue.

[11] For a discussion of this elitist view of democracy, see P. Bachrach, *The Theory of Democratic Elites* (Little Brown, 1967).

[12] From C. Almond & S. Verba, *The Civic Culture* (Boston, 1965), in Habermas 1973, p. 77.

[13] Habermas 1973, p. 76.

[14] ibid., p. 70.

[15] ibid., p. 70.

[16] See Ross Fitzgerald (ed.), *Human Needs and Politics* (Pergamon Press, Sydney, 1977).

[17] For a discussion of Freud's theory of needs in relation to modern society, see H. Marcuse, *Eros and Civilization* (Vintage Books, 1962).

[18] Modern versions of this determinism appear in Louis Althusser, *Reading Capital* (New Left Books, London, 1970).

[19] See Talcott Parsons, *The Social System* (Routledge & Kegan Paul, London, 1951).

[20] Habermas 1973, p. 113.

[21] Luhmann is a modern German social theorist whose views on the systems of society are extremely determinist: he does not take into account the subjective experience of human begins. See Habermas, ibid., part III, ch. 5, 'Complexity and Democracy'.

[22] Luhmann quoted in Habermas 1973, pp. 132–3.

[23] Habermas' view of Luhmann, in ibid., p. 135.

[24] Given in Habermas 1973, p. 133.

[25] Habermas 1973, p. 93.

[26] On the possibility of authoritarianism, see Epilogue. On some preparations for this, see A. Campbell, 'The politically motivated demonstration: implications for law enforcement', *Australian and New Zealand Journal of Criminology*, vol. II, no. 2, June 1978, pp. 95ff.

6B   Short-term responses to crisis

[1] People's attitudes to economic structure depend on the level of working class consciousness. When this is weak, the individual is prone to blame himself.

[2] Consider the substantial ruling class support for the Labour Party in Britain: it is often seen as the only party 'capable of controlling the unions'.

[3] For the argument against conservative strategies succeeding in overcoming crisis, see ch. 3B and ch. 9C.

[4] There are few examples where this has actually occurred in an advanced Western country, although it is a possibility in Italy and France. On the prospects for Australia, see the Epilogue.

[5] On the distinction between substructure and superstructure, see ch. 5A.

[6] On Marx's views on the State, see Henri Lefebvre, *The Sociology of Marx* (Penguin University Books, 1972), ch. 5.

[7] Karl Marx, in Bottomore & Rubel 1973, pp. 222–3.

[8] See Frankel 1978, especially chs 2, 3.

[9] Marx, in Bottomore & Rubel 1973, p. 226.

[10] Marx, ibid., p. 224.

[11] See Humphrey McQueen, *Australia's Media Monopolies* (Widescope, 1977), pp. 42–54.

[12] See Grant Elliott, 'The Press and the Labor Movement' in Duncan 1978, pp. 204ff.

[13] For more on the role of the Arbitration Commission, see ch. 6D.

[14] On Aborigines, see Lorna Lippmann in Patience and Head 1979, ch. 10; on womens' groups, see Anne Summers, ch. 11.

[15] For an extensive discussion, see Windschuttle 1979, ch. 8, 'Media and the Dole Bludger Myth'. Unemployment figures are constantly understated: see J. Steinke, 'Measurement of Unemployment in Australia', *Journal of Industrial Relations,* vol. 20, no. 2, June 1978, pp. 146ff.

[16] See ibid., chs 3–7. See also our prologue, footnote 2.

[17] See ibid., ch. 9, 'Political Persecution'.

6C   Crisis and the conflicting philosophies of the Australian Labor Party

[1] For example, Joh Bjelke-Petersen's constant attacks on Labor socialism. See Deane Wells, *The Deep North,* (Outback Press, 1979). For less biased accounts, see Bron Stevens and Pat Weller (eds), *The ALP and Federal Politics* (Melbourne University Press, 1976), and G. Starr, K. Richmond, G. Maddox, *Political Parties in Australia* (Heinemann Educational, 1978).

[2] See the F. E. Chamberlain Lecture by Bill Hayden, Leader of the Opposition, in *Commonwealth Record,* 26 Feb.–4 March 1979, pp. 245ff. On the changing relationship between the Labor Party and the working class, see Aitkin 1977, chs 7, 8.

[3] Quoted in Crisp 1955, p. 277.

[4] On the history of the early Labor Party, see Crisp, ibid., chs II, III. See also Robin Gollan, *Radical and Working Class Politics* (Melbourne University Press, 1966), chs 8–11.

[5] Quoted in Crisp, ibid., p. 270.

[6] ibid., p. 289.

[7] For an analysis of the Dunstan government, see N. Blewett & D. Jaensch, *Playford to Dunstan: The Politics of Transition* (Cheshire, Melbourne, 1971).

[8] At its 1979 Federal Conference the party voted to initiate a two-year debate over its socialist objective.

[9] Emy 1974, p. 374.

[10] ibid., p. 376.

[11] Graeme Duncan, 'The ALP: Socialism in A Bourgeois Society?', in Duncan 1978, p. 86.

[12] ibid., p. 94.

[13] ibid., p. 94.

[14] This of course depends on the capacity of the Labor movement to mobilize opinion away from conservative and fascist solutions and towards more progressive ones.

[15] Duncan, op. cit., pp. 193–4.

[16] See Catley & McFarlane 1974, and their 'Technocratic Laborism —The Whitlam Government', in Wheelwright & Buckley 1975.

[17] ibid., p. 3.

[18] ibid., pp. 3–4.

[18] ibid., p. 4.

[20] ibid., p. 5.

[21] From a speech by Whitlam, quoted in ibid., p. 86.

[22] This view was first proposed by Humphrey McQueen in 'Technocratic Laborism', Arena, no. 25, 1971.

[23] Catley & McFarlane 1974, p. 10. Notice here that a structural, rather than a dynamic, division of classes is given. See ch. 2C for arguments against this.

[24] Quoted in Catley & McFarlane, 'Technocratic Laborism—The Whitlam Government', in Wheelwright & Buckley 1975, p. 251.

[25] ibid., p. 256.

[26] ibid., p. 256. This appears in a Fabian Society pamphlet by Hayden entitled Implications of Democratic Socialism (1967).

[27] See R. W. Connell, 'Whitlam Versus Cairns', in Mayer 1969, pp. 369–70.

[28] ibid., p. 370.

[29] ibid., p. 370.

[30] The dominance of the NSW Labor Party by the right wing is due to the undemocratic domination of the party by a group formerly led by John Ducker. This group is gaining strength in Queensland, but not in other states.

31 See, for example, the pamphlet by Cairns entitled *Socialism and the ALP* (Fabian Society pamphlet 1963).

32 See Grant Elliott and Adam Graycar, 'Social Welfare', in Patience & Head 1979, pp. 93–7. See also our chs 8A, 8B.

33 See, for example, the proposals on prices and incomes put by R. J. Hawke to the 1979 Federal ALP Conference. The rejection of these proposals by Bill Hayden led to a public split between the two Labor leaders.

34 These include Paul Keating, mineral spokesman, Dick Klugman, health spokesman, and Senator John Button, economic spokesman. Chris Hurford and Ralph Willis have been careful not to suggest any socialist measures in the pronouncements. See, for example, Labor Statements, press releases by Labor spokesmen, nos. 15, 16, 20 (1979).

35 See, for example, Bill Hayden on nationalization and public ownership. In the Adelaide *Advertiser*, 14 January 1978, he said: 'I'm totally opposed to nationalisation, I think it's a clumsy, unnecessarily provocative tool'.

36 See, for example, the views of David Kemp, 'Political Parties and Australian Culture', *Quadrant*, December 1977, pp. 3–13.

37 Even reformists have adopted this view. See Sexton 1979, ch. 13, who argues that even a reform government is unlikely to succeed.

38 See our chs 8C, 8D; also ch 3C.

39 Substantial opposition to this rightist strategy has, however, developed in the union movement and the rank and file of the party. This is reflected in the contents of Labor Party journals during 1979.

40 For example, Hawke has argued that we must accept unemployment as here to stay in the foreseeable future and that we should help those seeking alternative life styles outside of 'the conventional employed society'. The question of how the state is to pay for increased payments to the unemployed is not raised. See Melbourne *Age*, 14 February 1979, p. 11.

6D The role of unions in crisis

1 For a comprehensive discussion of the early unionists, see J. Child, *Unionism and the Labor Movement* (Macmillan, Melbourne, 1971).

[2] On these union struggles in Australia, see ibid., ch. 7. See also Robin Gollan, *Radical and Working Class Politics: A Study of Eastern Australia 1850–1910* (Melbourne University Press, 1966), especially chs 3–6.

[3] On the relation of the early Australian Labor Party to the union movement, see Crisp 1955, chs II, III, VII. See also Gollan, ibid., ch. 8.

[4] See, for example, Encel 1970, quoted in ch. 2A.

[5] For some ways of overcoming state and employer pressures on union leaders which lead to these phenomena, see K. Coates and T. Topham, *The New Unionism* (Penguin 1974), ch. 5, 'Preconditions for Advance'.

[6] R. J. Hawke, quoted in Rawson 1978, pp. 98–9.

[7] See Geoff Sorrell, 'The Arbitration System', in Playford & Kirsner 1972, pp. 248–64. For some other views see J. Niland & J. Isaac (eds), *Australian Labor Economics: Readings* (Sun Books, Melbourne, 1975), part I.

[8] Quoted in Sorrell, ibid., p. 254.

[9] If anything, the militancy of unions during 1979, and the increase in strike activity illustrates the converse. Union actions are still the biggest challenge to ruling class domination.

[10] Its genesis was in the famous Harvester judgement by Mr Justice Higgins in 1907. He said: 'I could not certify that any wages less than 42 shillings per week for an unskilled labourer would be fair and reasonable'.

[11] Rawson 1978, p. 66.

[12] ibid., p. 67.

[13] On the O'Shea affair, see G. H. Sorrell & G. W. Ford, 'Penalties for Striking', *Outlook*, August 1969.

[14] For details, see Rawson 1978, pp. 31–8.

[15] See Rawson 1978, p. 126. See also David Plowman, *Australian Trade Union Statistics* (Dept of Industrial Relations, University of NSW, research paper no. 31, 1978).

[16] On the role of the NCC in unions, see B. A. Santamaria, *The Price of Freedom* (Hawthorn Press, Melbourne, 1966), pp. 37–47. Santamaria justifies these views in the name of Christianity and anti-communism.

[17] This is the view of many communist union leaders. See N. F. Duffy 'Unions in Action: aims and method', in Matthews & Ford 1968, pp. 42ff.

[18] Ross Martin, *Trade Unions in Australia* (Penguin, 1976), p. 134.

[19] Sorrell, op. cit., p. 263.

[20] On this view of unions, see Martin, op. cit., pp. 128–32. He also discusses the contrary view, pp. 133ff. For a left critique of this, see Ed Davis, 'Trade Unions, Myth and Reality', *JAPE*, no. 2, June 1978, pp. 17–24.

[21] For one such suggested strategy, see *Australia Ripped Off* (AMWSU Publication, 1979). See also our Epilogue, and Coates & Topham, *The New Unionism*, op. cit., parts II, IV.

[22] This strategy has been proposed in Australia by R. J. Hawke in his concept of a social contract. It clearly involves one section of the working class making sacrifices for another section without any burdens on capital.

[23] On the ABC radio program *PM*.

[24] See Ross Martin, pp. 130–1. See also D. W. Rawson, 'Unions and Politics', in Matthews & Ford 1968, especially pp. 177ff.

[25] If the savings are used merely to boost capital's profits, the crisis with tend to deepen (see ch. 3B).

[26] Both major parties are engaged in large-scale drives to increase exports in order to alleviate the economic crisis and the balance of payments problem. It is entitled 'Export Now' and directed towards Australian companies which have previously relied on the domestic market.

[27] The strong anti-union actions of the Fraser government have forced even 'moderate' union leaders to adopt a more militant strategy; for example, the legislation against government employees has resulted in several public service unions moving to the left.

[28] The ACTU Congress of September 1979 should prove critical in this regard. The policy was earlier defeated at the Federal ALP Conference in July 1979.

7A The Vietnam War: legitimacy undermined

[1] This comeback was paradoxical, given that the economy was booming. See Freudenburg 1977, pp. 158–65.

[2] See ibid., pp. 46–51.

[3] Menzies, quoted in Crowley 1973, p. 479

[4] Freudenburg 1977, pp. 48–9.

[5] Calwell, quoted in Crowley 1973, pp. 481–3.

[6] Quoted in Crowley 1973, p. 483.

[7] ibid., p. 506.

[8] ibid., p. 513.

[9] See his parliamentary speech, 15 March 1966, quoted in Crowley 1973, p. 507.

[10] Quoted in New York Times, The Pentagon Papers, (Bantam Books, New York, 1971), pp. 611–12.

[11] On the extent of civil disobedience during the war, see John Berry, 'The Vietnam Marches', in Mayer 1969, p. 205: see also 'Apathy and Riots', pp. 208ff, and 'Assorted Brickbats', p. 215ff, for a variety of views on the dissenters.

[12] See J. F. Cairns, The Eagle and the Lotus (Lansdowne Press, 1969). For a survey of the war's history through the eyes of the Australian Broadcasting Commission, see Vietnam: A Reporter's War (ABC Publications, 1975).

[13] See 'What's Wrong with Australia', by five Monash University students, in Mayer 1969, pp. 87ff. See also Humphrey McQueen, 'Bourgeois Democracy a Sham', in Mayer & Nelson 1973, pp. 176ff.

[14] See J. F. Cairns, Silence Kills (Vietnam Moratorium Committee, 1970), p. 9.

[15] ibid., p. 9.

[16] ibid., p. 37.

[17] See Melbourne Herald, 9 May 1970.

7B Whitlam's legitimizing of the Labor Party

[1] See Reid 1976, pp. 50–64, 69–74.

[2] ibid., pp. 1–2.

[3] Freudenburg 1977, pp. 77–8.

[4] For an account of Whitlam's strategy here, see Freudenburg 1977, ch. 5.

[5] Quoted in Freudenburg 1977, p. 93.

[6] Whitlam said, among other things, 'Are we as socialists to permit that power to rest, or rather sleep, indefinitely in the hands of parties whose philosophy is not quality and equality, but philistinism and favouritism? Is this what being "true to our principles" really means?' (Freudenburg 1977, p. 95).

[7] Reid 1971, pp. 101–5.

[8] Cairns, quoted in Freudenburg 1977, pp. 134–5.

[9] Reid 1976, p. 2.

[10] Whitlam's firm belief in parliamentary power lasted to the end. At the time when the conservative parties were mobilizing against him, he still saw the major fight as taking place in Parliament. Contrast this with Fraser's skilful use of the media against the Labor government (see ch. 8D).

[11] Quoted in Freudenburg 1977, p. 167.

[12] ibid., p. 168.

[13] See Oakes & Solomon 1973, pp. 18–26.

[14] Hawke had been elected as ACTU President by a combination of left Labor and Communist unions, and was considered a militant union leader.

[15] These included Rupert Murdoch, publisher of the powerful *Australian*, and Kenneth Myer of the Myer Emporium. On the moderate policies proposed, see McLaren 1972, especially ch. 4 on economic policy, chs 11 and 12 on health and education.

7C Liberal political crisis

[1] On the McMahon-McEwen conflict, see Reid 1971, pp. 40–1.

[2] See Tiver 1978, ch. 5, 'Social Policy', and pp. 180–5.

[3] Gorton was selected primarily because he was seen to be an electoral match for Whitlam. On Gorton's philosophy, see Tiver 1978, pp. 235–42.

[4] See Freudenburg 1977, pp. 124–5.

[5] For a documentation of this conflict, see Connell 1977, ch. 5.

[6] On Gorton's early relations with the press, see Reid 1971, p. 62, and contrast with later developments, pp. 337–8.

[7] Max Walsh, 'You Ain't Seen Nothing Yet', *Quadrant*, 22, no. 6, (Nov.–Dec. 1968), 16–23, at p. 21.

[8] See Tiver 1978, p. 238.

[9] See Reid 1971, especially ch. 1.

[10] See Tiver 1978, p. 240.

[11] See Connell 1977, pp. 92–101.

[12] Quoted in Tiver 1978, p. 241.

[13] On Packer's role in the downfall of Gorton, see Reid 1971, pp. 426, 438.

[14] Freudenburg 1977, p. 187.

[15] Bruce Grant remarked of him that 'He does not appear to be engaged in the issues of his time . . . He has no vision, no sense of history, no "gravitas". His responses are apparently entirely political or they are only believed when they are obviously political'. Quoted in Tiver 1978, p. 247.

[16] The reason given for Gorton's dismissal was obstensibly the publication of a series of newspaper articles entitled 'I Did It My Way', which were critical of McMahon.

[17] However a majority of companies soon came to accept the multi-nationals as an inevitable and even healthy development. See Neil McInness, 'The Challenge to Australia of the Multi-national Corporation', in Big Business in Australia (AIPS publication), ch. 3. See also the responses of several company managers, as given in the same chapter.

[18] On union militancy during this period, see ch. 6D.

[19] Connell 1977, p. 103.

[20] See Oakes and Solomon 1973, ch. 13, 'Ordeal By Television', and ch. 14, 'The Comedian'.

[21] See, for example, the report by Max Hollingsworth in the Australian, 23 August 1969, where he says 'Gough Whitlam strode into the grand ballroom of one of Austrália's finest hotels yesterday, and greeted members of the Company Directors' Association of Australia like brothers'.

[22] Quoted in Freudenburg 1977, pp. 229–30.

[23] See ibid., pp. 200–14. See also C. Lloyd & G. Reid, Out of the Wilderness (Cassell, Sydney, 1974). See also P. B. Westerway, 'Labor's 1972 Campaign Strategy', in Henry Mayer (ed.), Australia's Political Pattern (Cheshire, 1973).

8A Laying the foundations of crisis

[1] On Whitlam's view of the mandate, see Freudenburg 1977, p. 244. On the actions of the duumvirate, see ch. 16.

[2] On Whitlam's economic policies, see Barry Hughes, 'The Economy', in Patience & Head 1979.

[3] See H. C. Coombs, quoted in Lloyd & Clark 1976, p. 87. He warned that 'the Government must avoid creating conditions in which, to avoid serious loss of confidence in the value of money, it will be forced to impose restrictive policies damaging to both employment and business expectations generally'.

[4] Freudenburg 1977, pp. 249–50.

[5] I do not wish to imply that the sole cause of this outflow was a distrust of the Labor government and an intention to harness it, only that this was the major factor. Others included the deteriorating situation in the home countries of investors.

[6] *Australia Uprooted*, p. 9.

[7] On Murphy's raid, see Reid 1976, pp. 72–88, and Freudenburg 1977, pp. 262–5.

[8] On the strategy used by the Liberals, see Freudenburg 1977, ch. 19, pp. 288ff.

[9] Significantly, Freudenburg does not even consider this question in his book.

[10] The banks and other major business forces mobilized in 1947 to 1949 to undermine and destroy the Chifley Labor government.

[11] As the economic crisis deepened, most social welfarist ministers sided with the tough measures proposed by Treasury against Cairns. See next section. See also Ainslie Tolley, *Macro-Economic Policy in Australia 1972–1976* (Croom Helm, London, 1978).

[12] This strike was a significant struggle which resulted in violence by a group of workers who had been virtually locked-out. See Connell 1977, pp. 1–3.

[13] See Barry Hughes, 'The Economy', in Patience & Head 1979, pp. 13–23, for a conventional view of these wage increases.

[14] Cairns wrote in 1972: 'No "across the board" changes are acceptable. We want to know the facts and we will judge every industry on its merits.' Jim Cairns, 'Labor and Tariffs', in McLaren 1972, p. 91.

[15] Whitlam spent a great deal of time in 1974 addressing business-men's functions. Was it simply a desire to reassure or did he also crave recognition from the Establishment? See Bob Catley in Wheelwright & Buckley 1978, pp. 40–1.

[16] On Snedden's policy initiatives, see John Edwards, 'Billy Mackie Snedden—The Everest Syndrome', *Australian Financial Review*, 4 May 1972.

[17] It seems extraordinary that the socialists accepted Whitlam's actions here. Indeed, Senator Murphy was one of the main participants. See Oakes & Solomon, *Grab for Power: Election 1974* (Melbourne, 1974).

[18] Quoted in Freudenburg 1977, p. 302. On the fall of Snedden, see Kelly 1976, chs 6, 9, 10.

[19] See Tiver 1978, p. 250.

[20] See Reid 1976, p. 141.

[21] See Reid 1976, ch. 14. See also Oakes 1976, ch. 3.

8B   The new economic crisis

[1] See Freudenburg 1977, pp. 304–7.

[2] The new phenomenon of stagflation was hitting Australia with a vengeance. See chs 3A, 3B.

[3] See also the analysis by Kelly 1976, ch. 7. See also Sexton 1979, ch. 3, especially the treasury note quoted in pp. 58–9.

[4] Lloyd & Clark 1976, pp. 99–100.

[5] See ibid., p. 101. In 1974, money supply fell by 10 per cent in June and 7 per cent in September.

[6] Freudenburg 1977, p. 282.

[7] Kelly 1976, p. 70.

[8] See Cairns 1976, pp. 18–19 where he defends his policies, arguing that if Labor had adopted a policy of austerity 'unemployment would have been a million, inflation just as bad as it has been'.

[9] The ALP under Hayden seems to have recognized at least part of this and is currently proposing a capital gains tax. However, it may be too little too late to prevent a serious fiscal crisis in the state. See ch. 3C.

[10] On Hayden's action to strengthen the capitalistic structures, see ch. 8C.

[11] Cairns 1976, pp. 74–5.

[12] ibid., p. 10.

[13] See Alan Hughes, 'The Economy', in Patience & Head 1979.

[14] See Kelly 1976, p. 76.

[15] See Connell 1977, pp. 121–2.

[16] See J. F. Cairns, *Growth to Freedom* (Down to Earth Foundation, Canberra, 1979).

[17] See Oakes, 1976, ch. 6, 'Dr. Yes'.

[18] On this ideological campaign see Bob Catley, 'Socialism and Reform in Contemporary Australia', in Wheelwright & Buckley 1978, especially pp. 36–48.

[19] Connell 1977, pp. 129–30.

8C The demise of the socialists

[1] See the discussion in Lloyd & Clark 1976, ch. 12.

[2] Although the purpose of Whitlam's trip was not evident at the time, some writers believe that his consultations with the OECD resulted in the transformation of his economic ideas in favour of the Hayden strategy adopted later in 1975. See Bob Catley, in Wheelwright & Buckley 1978, pp. 42–3.

[3] Reid 1976, pp. 240–1.

[4] On the Morosi affair, see Cairns 1976, postscript pp. 1–5.

[5] See Freudenburg 1977, pp. 319–22.

[6] Reid 1976, pp. 224–7.

[7] See Bob Catley, in Wheelwright & Buckley 1978, pp. 42–3. Catley believes that this was the major reason behind the sacking of Cairns.

[8] Freudenburg 1977, p. 281.

[9] See Catley, op. cit., p. 47.

[10] The Constitution says: 'The Governor-General may appoint officers to administer such departments of State of the Commonwealth as the Governor-General in Council may establish. Such officers shall hold office during the pleasure of the Governor-General'.

[11] Reid 1976, p. 314.

[12] Cairns 1976, p. 125.

[13] This was partly due to the fact that influential sections of business had changed their attitude to public spending since they saw it as a major factor contributing to inflation and to reductions in profitability. See Catley, in Wheelwright & Buckley 1978, pp. 44–5.

[14] McFarlane described the Hayden budget as 'arguably the most violently anti-worker budget since Menzies'. Bruce McFarlane, 'Inflation, Money, Gold and Marx', *JAPE*, no. 1, October 1977, p. 62.

[15] On the details of this reversal, see Catley, in Wheelwright & Buckley 1978, pp. 48–57.

[16] On Connor's personality, see Kelly 1976, pp. 155–7.

[17] Kelly, ibid., p. 158.

[18] See Catley, op. cit., p. 41. Whitlam said 'During the period of the Labor Government there has been no initiative to nationalize industry. There will not be'.

[19] For details see Kelly 1976, ch. 12.

[20] See Freudenberg 1977, ch. 23, 'Loans'. See also Kelly 1976, chs 12, 13.

[21] For an outline of a rational programme along these lines, see the AMWSU publication, *Australia Ripped Off*.

[22] Cairns 1976, p. 9.

[23] Kelly 1976, p. 155.

[24] Hawke described the resignation as 'an act of lunacy'. David Combe called it 'preposterous'. See Kelly 1976, p. 193.

[25] On the Bass campaign, see Kelly, ibid., ch. 15.

[26] Quoted in Cairns 1976, p. 109.

[27] Quoted in ibid., p. 103.

8D Labor's political crisis and the destruction of Whitlam

[1] Freudenburg 1977, p. 314.

[2] See ch. 5C for Fraser's philosophy, and ch. 9C for his strategy.

Notes

[3] See Sexton 1979, ch. 7, 'State of Siege'.

[4] See Kelly 1976, p. 253.

[5] Hall, on 15 October 1975, quoted in Whitlam 1979, p. 60.

[6] See ibid., p. 72. 'The crisis of October–November 1975 was in truth a political crisis, fully capable of resolution by political means'. For a similar view, see Geoffrey Sawer, *Federation Under Strain: Australia 1972–1975* (Melbourne University Press, 1977).

[7] ibid., p. 63.

[8] On the role of the *Age* and the *Sydney Morning Herald*, see Kelly 1976, p. 267. On the role of the media generally, see Cairns 1976, pp. 111ff.

[9] Whitlam, quoted in his book (1979), p. 76.

[10] On the philosophy behind the Hayden budget, see Barry Hughes, 'The Economy', in Patience & Head 1979, pp. 29–32.

[11] Kelly 1976, p. 242. See the following pages for an account of Fraser's thinking over this period.

[12] For the full account, see Kelly 1976, ch. 20; Freudenburg 1977, ch. 23; Sexton 1979, ch. 10.

[13] See Lloyd & Clark 1976, chs 15, 18, for details.

[14] See Kelly 1976, pp. 260–6.

[15] ibid., p. 267. For analysis of the press actions during this period, see G. Hasler, 'The Press and Labor 1972–1974'; Roy Forward, 'Editorial Opinion and the Whitlam Government'; John May, 'The Mal-practice of Australian Journalism'; in *Politics*, vol. XII, no. 1, May 1977.

[16] See Melbourne *Age* editorial, quoted in Kelly 1976, p. 267.

[17] The Liberals used this against Whitlam in the 'Memories' commercials for the 1977 election.

[18] Freudenburg 1977, p. 318.

[19] See Kelly 1976, pp. 268–9.

[20] See Howard 1978, pp. 39, 40, 91–5.

[21] Reported in Kelly 1976.

[22] See Kerr 1978, p. 312.

[23] For the details of these struggles and the role of the governor, see R. Gollan, *Radical and Working Class Politics* (Melbourne University Press, 1966), ch. 3, 'The Struggle for Power, 1860–1880'.

[24] Whitlam 1979, p. 66.

[25] ibid., p. 67.

[26] Quoted in Hall & Iremonger 1976, pp. 187–8.

[27] Prominent amongst these were Rupert Murdoch's *Australian*, whose attacks and bias became so pronounced that it led to a strike by several of his journalists. Others who refused to comply were dismissed.

[28] See Sexton 1979, p. 221.

[29] There is some disagreement as to the actual sequence of events between Kerr and Whitlam. Much has been made of this, but I cannot see that it substantially affects the constitutional and democratic propriety of the dismissal. It is discussed in Kelly 1976, Freudenburg 1977, Lloyd & Clark 1976 and Sexton 1979, among others.

9A Australia's legitimation crisis

[1] This included their prior booking of television and newspaper space so that they heavily outdistanced Labor in the propaganda war. See Sexton 1979, ch. 12.

[2] See Kelly 1976, pp. 289–90. On Fraser's earlier dealings with the governor-general, see pp. 279–83.

[3] See Whitlam 1979, ch. 7, in which he explains the opportunities Kerr had to discuss the matter with him, but does not state that he ever considered confronting Kerr on the matter.

[4] Whitlam, ibid., p. 94. Whitlam remarks: 'If Sir John had regarded the remark as so sinister, why did he not take it up with me afterwards?'

[5] See Kerr 1978, p. 333.

[6] Reported in Whitlam 1979, p. 98.

[7] Freudenburg 1977, p. 399.

[8] See *Politics*, vol. 11, no. 1, May 1976, pp. 23ff. Contrast the articles by R. S. Parker and Joel Litvin in the same issue.

[9] Quoted in Kelly 1976, p. 359.

[10] Thus for example, in a similar situation that arose in Greece following the dismissal of the Prime Minister, George Papandreou,

a government was formed under the chairman of the Reserve Bank to prepare for elections. See C. Tsoucakis, *The Greek Tragedy* (Penguin, 1969), ch. 14.

11 Quoted in Hall & Iremonger 1976, p. 197, They provide the full statement.

12 For a list of these Labor bills, blocked by the Liberals, and now used to justify the conservative attack, see Sexton 1979, pp. 244–5.

13 See Horne 1976, ch. 7, 'Vendetta Journalism'.

14 On the security aspects underlying this, see Kelly 1976, ch. 5.

15 This and other factors are discussed in Bob Catley, 'Socialism and Reform in Contemporary Australia', in Wheelwright & Buckley 1978, pp. 52–7.

16 Whitlam 1979, ch. 9, 'Verdict on the Viceroy'.

17 See Kerr's statements in his book (1978), pp. 331–2.

18 ibid., pp. 387–8.

19 Whitlam 1979, pp. 117–18.

20 See also ibid., p. 119, where he says: 'Given the mood that the crowd was in, I dare say I could have stirred them up a lot more than I did; it was a delightful Canberra late spring evening, just the night for a pleasant walk to Yarralumla'.

21 ibid., p. 118.

22 As Freudenburg (1977, p. 395) recalls: 'In each case there was the same reaction—puzzlement followed by disbelief, outrage quickly subsiding into shocked silence ... With his colleagues in this catatonic state (better described by Daly as "stunned mullets"), Whitlam tried to work out a plan of action'.

23 Sexton (1979, p. 253) comments: 'It did not occur to him [Hawke] that Labor's vote might be so low at the election in a month's time—that it is unlikely that anything could have worsened the result for the Party'.

24 Whitlam 1979, pp. 178–9.

9B 'Legitimacy' regained

1 M. Gollan (ed.), *Kerr and the Consequences* (Widescope, Melbourne, 1977), p. 27.

2 For two alternative views on the likely fate of Labor, see 'Labor:

destined to fall?' by Peter McCawley, and 'Labor: a bubble pricked' by Robert Murray, in *Politics*, vol. XI, 7 May 1976. For a more rational view see Bob Catley, in Wheelwright & Buckley 1978, p. 56.

[3] See Graeme Duncan, 'The ALP: socialism in a bourgeois society', in Duncan 1978, especially p. 93.

[4] See Horne 1976, pp. 9–11, pp. 64ff.

[5] Significantly, Kerr uses this participation by the Labor Party as a vindication of his actions: 'In the same speech he [Whitlam] remarked on the highly proper manner in which the Labor Party had fought the ensuing election and accepted its result. This comment, which clearly shows the dismissal and dissolution as leading in an orderly manner to the routine unfolding of the democratic process, underlines the incongruity, to my mind, of suggesting there was any element of the coup or putsch in my recourse on 11 November to the reserve powers of the Crown'. See Kerr 1978, p. 388.

[6] Fraser used his caretaker powers not only to gain legitimacy, but also to allow legal proceedings to be initiated against Whitlam. See Whitlam 1979, ch. 10, 'Break of Faith'.

[7] R. S. Parker, 'Political projections and partisan perspectives', in *Politics*, vol. XI, no. 1., May 1976, pp. 12ff.

[8] On the behaviour of the media, see Sexton 1979, pp. 263–6.

[9] See Emy 1978, pp. 177ff.

[10] See the views of Clyde Cameron reported in Freudenburg 1977, p. 381. On 16 October he said in the parliament that Whitlam 'stands out like a giant against the intellectual pygmies that sit next to him'.

[11] See Kelly 1976, ch. 24, for a full account.

[12] Oakes 1976, p. 271.

[13] In a letter to Murdoch, the staff said: 'We cannot be loyal to those traditions, or to ourselves, if we accept the deliberate or careless slanting of headlines, seemingly blatant imbalance in news presentation, political censorship and on occasion, distortion of copy from senior, specialist journalists, the political management of news and features, the stifling of dissident and even unpalatably impartial opinion in the paper's columns'. See Sexton 1979, p. 265.

[14] See Oakes 1976, pp. 270–1.

[15] Whitlam's actions were described as 'grave errors of judgement', and condemned 'in the strongest terms'. For the full statement, see Kelly 1976, pp. 342–3.

[16] See Horne 1976, ch. 5. See also M. Gollan (ed.), op. cit.

[17] On this alienation, see Whitlam 1979, pp. 152–65. Sexton (1979, p. 250) remarks: 'Kerr misjudged the future. He did not envisage the possibility that he, not Malcolm Fraser, would be chief target for Labor and its supporters; that he would receive no real support from those he had brought to power once they had made good use of him'.

[18] Some sections of the media, however, called for his resignation. See Claude Forell, Melbourne *Age*, 1 April 1976.

[19] The *Financial Review*'s Max Walsh noted: 'Prime Minister Fraser and his permanent head, Mr Alan Carmody, are quite obsessed, almost to the point of paranoia, with containing the spread of information'. See Rosenbloom, *Politics and the Media* (Scribe publication, 1978).

[20] See J. M. Fraser, 'Responsibility in government', *Australian Journal of Public Administration*, vol. 37, no. 1, March 1978.

[21] See Patricia Edgar, 'Radio and Television', in Patience & Head 1979, pp. 226–7.

[22] Kemp 1978; see also our discussion of his views in ch. 2C.

[23] Although the economic policy decided at the Federal Conference of that year had been quite progressive, the campaign platform barely reflected it. This later created considerable anger in the party.

[24] See Whitlam 1979, pp. 178–9 on the outstanding constitutional dangers following the 1975 dismissal.

9C Fraser's strategy and the continuing economic and social crises

[1] See *Australia Ripped Off* (AMWSU publication, 1979).

[2] See *Australia Uprooted* (AMWSU publication), pp. 12–13.

[3] Tiver 1978, pp. 256–7.

[4] See *Australia Ripped Off*, pp. 33–9.

[5] For a report and criticism of the budget, see *Australian Financial*

Review, 16 August 1978, with the headline 'Smash Grab Budget'.

6 For a full analysis of Fraser's strategy by Hayden, see *Commonwealth Record*, 12–18 March 1979, pp. 316–18.

7 See Windschuttle 1979, p. 252.

8 ibid., p. 253.

9 *Australia Ripped Off*, pp. 22–3.

10 Windschuttle 1979, p. 255.

11 See ibid., p. 257. See also Catley, in Wheelwright & Buckley 1978, pp. 57–61.

12 See *Sydney Morning Herald*, 4 June 1977, front page.

13 On the IRB, and other aspects of Fraser's anti-Labor strategies, see Windschuttle 1979, pp. 256ff.

14 This legislation was proclaimed in July 1977 and created further confrontations with the public service unions.

15 On the employment consequences of the Liberal strategy, see Barry Hughes, 'The Economy', in Patience & Head 1979, especially pp. 40–7. From June 1976 to June 1978, unemployment rose by 133 000, an increase of 50 per cent.

16 See Tiver 1978, pp. 264–5.

17 See Tim Hewat and David Wilson, *Don Chipp* (Widescope, Melbourne, 1978).

18 On Robinson's resignation, see David Adams, 'Political Review', in *Australian Quarterly*, vol. 51, no. 2, June 1979, pp. 104–7.

19 Following the Withers and Robinson affairs, Michelle Grattan wrote in the *Age* (26 February 1979), 'But the leopard finds spot-changing difficult and Ministers still complain about the way the Prime Minister operates and arbitrarily interferes in details of their portfolios.'

20 See 'Opposition Statements', *Commonwealth Record*, March 1979.

21 Tiver 1978, p. 266.

22 See Age Polls and Morgan Polls, 1979. The failure of the media to focus on the economic crisis, and its attempts to shift blame to other groups, have been a significant factor preventing a reduction in conservative support.

23 This was the view of the Victorian ALP before the State election

of 3 May 1979. See A. Theophanous, 'The Labor Campaign', in J. Warhurst & I. Ward (eds), *Anatomy of an Election* (Hill of Content, 1979).

24 See Opposition Statements in the *Commonwealth Record* of those years. Hayden does not believe that there is a capitalist crisis. Rather he believes that an economic recovery would have occurred had it not been for the economic mismanagement by the Fraser government. See *Commonwealth Record*, 25 June–1 July 1979, pp. 869, 871–2.

25 See APSA, *Report of the National Inquiry of the Labor Party, 1979*, and compare with the recommendations of the party executive, which were much more moderate.

26 See *Bulletin*, 13 March 1979, pp. 52–6.

27 ibid., p. 20.

28 See *Commonwealth Record*, 5 March 1979, pp. 277–9 for Hayden's speech to a business seminar in which he argues for economic recovery by extended government spending in the social services sector.

29 See *Commonwealth Record*, 26 February–4 March 1979, p. 247.

Epilogue

1 Habermas himself believes that such crises may be accommodated in the short term by political actions which serve to restore a shaky legitimacy to an endangered order. See Frankel 1978.

2 It may, of course, use the rhetoric of equality to secure an unequal and non-democratic order. See chs 1 and 2 on this inequality. See also ch. 6A.

3 See Schumpeter 1950. On Michels, see ch. 1A, note 18. Bachrach's views are given in *The Theory of Democratic Elitism: A Critique* (Little, Brown and Co., Boston, 1967).

4 See Habermas 1973, part III, chs 2, 3, 4.

5 See, for example, Deane Wells, *The Deep North* (Outback Press, 1979). I do not agree with Wells' theoretical analysis. The empirical data on Bjelke-Petersen is nevertheless useful in illustrating the points made here.

6 On Bjelke-Petersen's racist legislation and his attitude to Abori-

gines, see Hugh Lunn, *Joh* (University of Queensland Press, 1978), pp. 83, 149–51.

[7] These marches were led by Labor left-wingers Senator George Georges and Tom Uren. The Queensland ALP, however, failed to support the marchers. Georges was suspended when he publicly criticized the State Labor leaders over their cowardly stand.

[8] New draconian laws have been introduced in Queensland making strikes illegal in any industry which the government declares 'essential'. The very right to withdraw one's labour is thus under severe attack. The legislation is being strongly resisted.

[9] The beliefs and actions of this authoritarian minority are given extensive publicity by the media. I believe this is the basis of the commonly held view that the Australian people are, as a whole, conservative.

[10] The federal system thus frustrates change towards socialism: see chs 1C, 1D. Nevertheless it may become a useful defence mechanism in the struggle against increasing authoritarianism and may prevent the further undermining of the rights to speak and to strike.

[11] This, however, depends on the fortitude of such 'moderate' Labor governments. Disturbingly, in 1979, Labor Premier Wran agreed with Fraser's proposal that all industrial relations powers be transferred to the Federal government.

[12] In 1979, the South Australian Labor government was (surprisingly to some) defeated at an election held 18 months early. The Liberal opposition and business forces combined in a clever campaign to blame the Corcoran government for the economic crisis, especially unemployment. Corcoran lost because he had no policies to offer the people to alleviate the situation. This is one of several examples which support our thesis.

[13] On the exploitation and the extent of overseas ownership of mining resources, see Jim Roulston and Kevin Hardiman, 'Towards an Alternative ALP Economic Policy', in *Labour Star*, August 1979.

[14] Reductions in living standards and in real wages have not, however, resulted in increased investment. See ch. 3B. See also ch. 9C.

[15] In 1979, sixty years later, the ALP was engaged in a serious

internal struggle of historic consequence: there was widespread evidence of a move to a more socialist perspective by many rank and file members, especially in Victoria.

[16] On the division between the different sectors of the state, see ch. 3C. The socialization of productive enterprises allows for their profits to be redirected to other sectors of the state, such as health, education, welfare and urban development. This would also allow for the creation of much more employment.

[17] The state is thus a necessary evil for modern conservatives: they need it to support and ensure the accumulation of wealth in the hands of the few, yet it could be used against them to establish an egalitarian order.

[18] The forces ranged against a radical government in Australia would be able to create fear and insecurity about the objectives of such a government. This can only be combated by a general strategy to counter actions by the ruling class, including the mobilization of the people in support of those objectives.

[19] See chs 2D, 3C, 5A, 6B.

Bibliography

AITKIN, D. *Stability and change in Australian politics.* ANU Press, Canberra, 1977.

BOTTOMORE, T. & RUBEL, M. (eds) *Marx: Selected writings in sociology and philosophy.* Penguin, 1973.

CAIRNS, J. F. *Oil in troubled waters.* Widescope, Melbourne, 1976.

CARROLL, J. *Puritan, paranoid, remissive.* Routledge & Kegan Paul, London, 1977.

CATLEY, R. & MCFARLANE, B. *From Tweedledum to Tweedledee: the new Labor government in Australia.* ANZ Book Co., Sydney, 1974.

CONNELL, R. W. *Ruling class, ruling culture.* Cambridge University Press, Melbourne, 1977.

CONWAY, R. *The great Australian stupor.* Sun Books, Melbourne, 1971.

CRISP, L. F. *The Australian Federal Labor Party.* Longmans, London, 1955.

CRISP, L. F. *Australian national government.* Longman Cheshire, Melbourne, 1975.

CROWLEY, F. K. *Modern Australia in documents, vol. 2: 1939–1970.* Wren, Melbourne, 1973.

DAVIES, A. F., ENCEL, S. & BERRY, M. J. *Australian society: a sociological introduction.* 3rd edn. Longman Cheshire, Melbourne, 1977.

DEVESON, A. *Australians at risk.* Cassell, Sydney, 1978.

DUNCAN, G. *Marx and Mill.* Cambridge University Press, 1973.

DUNCAN, G. (ed.) *Critical essays in Australian politics.* Edward Arnold, Melbourne, 1978.

EDGAR, D. (ed.) *Social change in Australia.* Longman Cheshire, Melbourne, 1974.

EMY, H. *The politics of Australian democracy.* Macmillan, Melbourne, 1974.

EMY, H. *The politics of Australian democracy.* 2nd edn. Macmillan, Melbourne, 1978.

ENCEL, S. *Equality and authority.* Cheshire, Melbourne, 1970.

FRANKEL, B. *Marxian theories of the state: a critique of orthodoxy.* Monograph no. 3. Arena Publications, Melbourne, 1978.

FREUDENBERG, G. *A certain grandeur: Gough Whitlam in politics.* Macmillan, Melbourne, 1977.

GIDDENS, A. *Capitalism and modern social theory.* Cambridge University Press, 1971.

HABERMAS, J. *Legitimation crisis.* Beacon Press, Boston, Mass., 1973.

HALL, R. & IREMONGER, J. *The makers and the breakers.* Wellington Lane Press, Sydney, 1976.

HENDERSON, R. *First main report of the Commission of Inquiry into Poverty.* Australian Government Publishing Service, Canberra, 1975.

HOLLAND, S. *The socialist challenge.* Quartet, London, 1975.

HORNE, D. *Death of the lucky country.* Penguin, Melbourne, 1976.

HOWARD, C. *Australia's Constitution.* Penguin, Melbourne, 1978.

JUPP, J. *Australian party politics.* 2nd edn. Melbourne University Press, 1968.

KARIEL, H. (ed.) *Frontiers of democratic politics.* Random House, New York, 1970.

KELLY, P. *The unmaking of Gough.* Angus & Robertson, Sydney, 1976.

KEMP, D. A. *Society and electoral behaviour in Australia.* University of Queensland Press, Brisbane, 1978.

KERR, SIR JOHN *Matters for judgment.* Macmillan, Melbourne, 1978.

LLOYD, C. & CLARK, A. *Kerr's king hit.* Cassell, Sydney, 1976.

MANDEL, E. *The second slump.* New Left Books, London, 1978.

MATTHEWS, P. W. D. & FORD, G. W. *Australian trade unions.* Sun Books, Melbourne, 1968.

MAYER, H. (ed.) *Australian politics: a second reader.* Cheshire, Melbourne, 1969.

MAYER, H. & NELSON, H. (eds.) *Australian politics: a third reader.* Cheshire, Melbourne, 1973.

MCLAREN, J. (ed.) *Towards a new Australia.* Cheshire, Melbourne, 1972.

441

MERCER, J. (ed.) *The other half: women in Australian society*. Penguin, Melbourne, 1975.

MILIBAND, R. *The state in capitalist society*. Quartet, London, 1973.

MILLS, C. WRIGHT *The power elite*. Oxford University Press, New York, 1956.

OAKES, L. *Crash through or crash*. Drummond, Melbourne, 1976.

OAKES, L. & SOLOMON, D. *The making of an Australian prime minister*. Cheshire, Melbourne, 1973.

PATEMAN, C. *Participation and democratic theory*. Cambridge University Press, 1970.

PATIENCE, A. & HEAD, B. (eds) *From Whitlam to Fraser*. Oxford University Press, Melbourne, 1979.

PLAYFORD, J. & KIRSNER, D. (eds) *Australian capitalism*. Penguin, Melbourne, 1972.

RAWSON, D. W. *Unions and unionists in Australia*. George Allen & Unwin, Sydney, 1978.

REID, A. *The Gorton experiment*. Shakespeare Head, Sydney, 1971.

REID, A. *The Whitlam venture*. Hill of Content, Melbourne, 1976.

ROBINSON, P. *The crisis in Australian capitalism*. VCTA, Melbourne, 1978.

ROUSSEAU, J. J. *The social contract*. Penguin, 1958.

SARTORI, G. *Democratic theory*. Praeger, New York, 1965.

SCHUMPETER, J. A. *Capitalism, socialism and democracy*. George Allen & Unwin, London, 1950.

SEXTON, M. *Illusions of power*. George Allen & Unwin, Sydney, 1979.

SUMMERS, A. *Damned whores and God's police*. Penguin, Melbourne, 1975.

TIVER, P. G. *The Liberal Party*. Jacaranda, Brisbane, 1978.

WHEELWRIGHT, E. L. & BUCKLEY, K. (eds) *Essays in the political economy of Australian capitalism, vol. 1*. ANZ Book Co., Sydney, 1975.

WHEELWRIGHT, E. L. & BUCKLEY, K. (eds) *Essays in the political economy of Australian capitalism, vol. 2*. ANZ Book Co., Sydney, 1978.

WHEELWRIGHT, E. L. & STILWELL, F. J. B. (eds) *Readings in political economy, vol. 1*. ANZ Book Co., Sydney, 1976.

WHITLAM, E. G. *The truth of the matter*. Penguin, Melbourne, 1979.

WILD, R. A. *Social stratification in Australia*. George Allen & Unwin, Sydney, 1978.

WINDSCHUTTLE, K. *Unemployment*. Penguin, Melbourne, 1979.

Names Index

Note: 'f' indicates footnote reference. The number of the footnote follows the 'f' symbol.

Names Index

Subject Index